sweetness &lightning

6

Gido Amagakure

contents

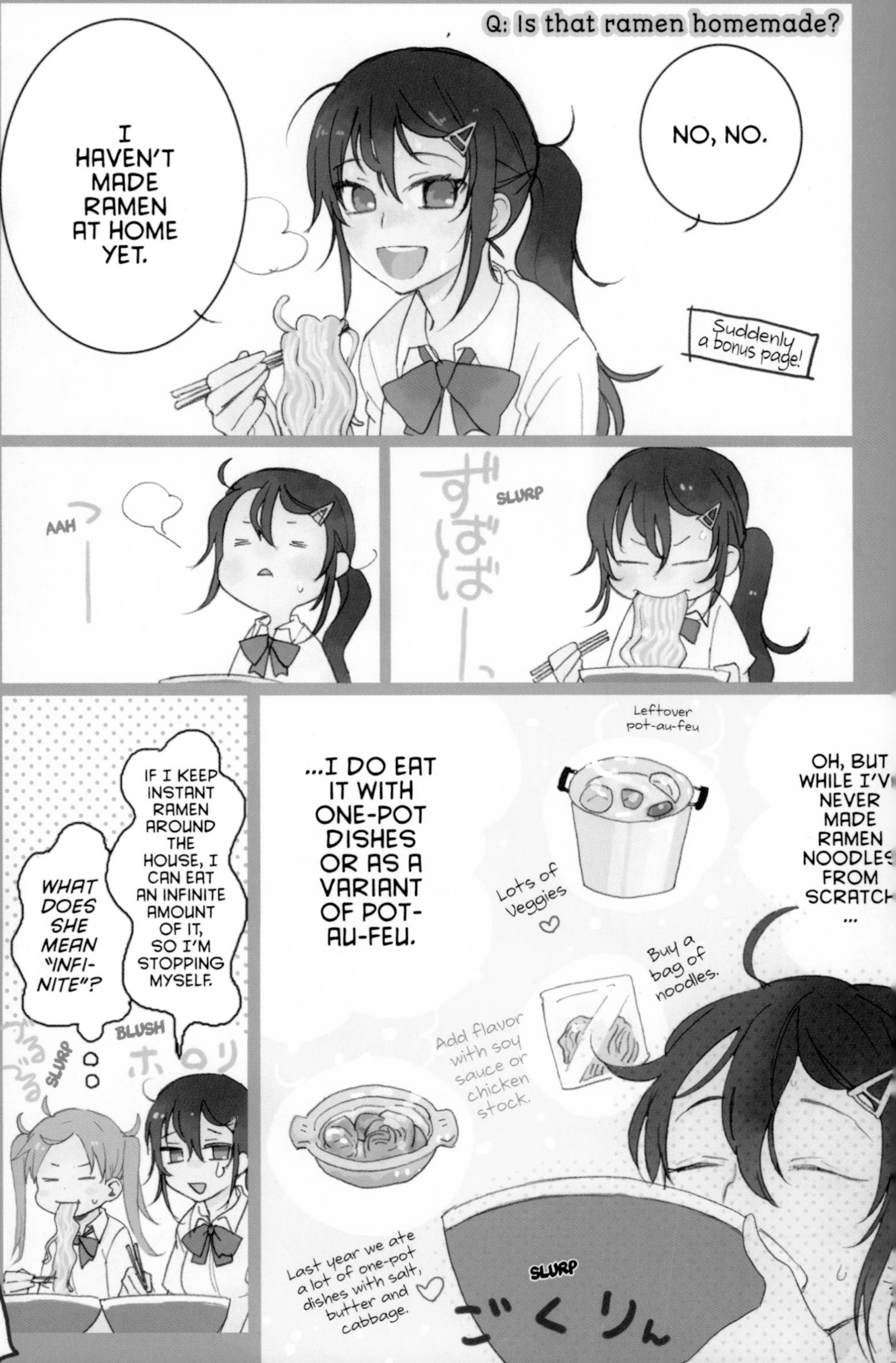
Q: Is that ramen homemade?
NO, NO.
I HAVEN'T MADE RAMEN AT HOME YET.
Suddenly a bonus page!
ずばばー
SLURP
AAH
OH, BUT WHILE I'V NEVER MADE RAMEN NOODLES FROM SCRATCH ...
...I DO EAT IT WITH ONE-POT DISHES OR AS A VARIANT OF POT-AU-FEU.
Leftover pot-au-feu
Lots of Veggies
Buy a bag of noodles.
Add flavor with soy sauce or chicken stock.
Last year we ate a lot of one-pot dishes with salt, butter and cabbage.
SLURP
ごくりん
IF I KEEP INSTANT RAMEN AROUND THE HOUSE, I CAN EAT AN INFINITE AMOUNT OF IT, SO I'M STOPPING MYSELF.
WHAT DOES SHE MEAN "INFI-NITE"?
BLUSH
ホロリ
ずるずる
SLURP
The End!

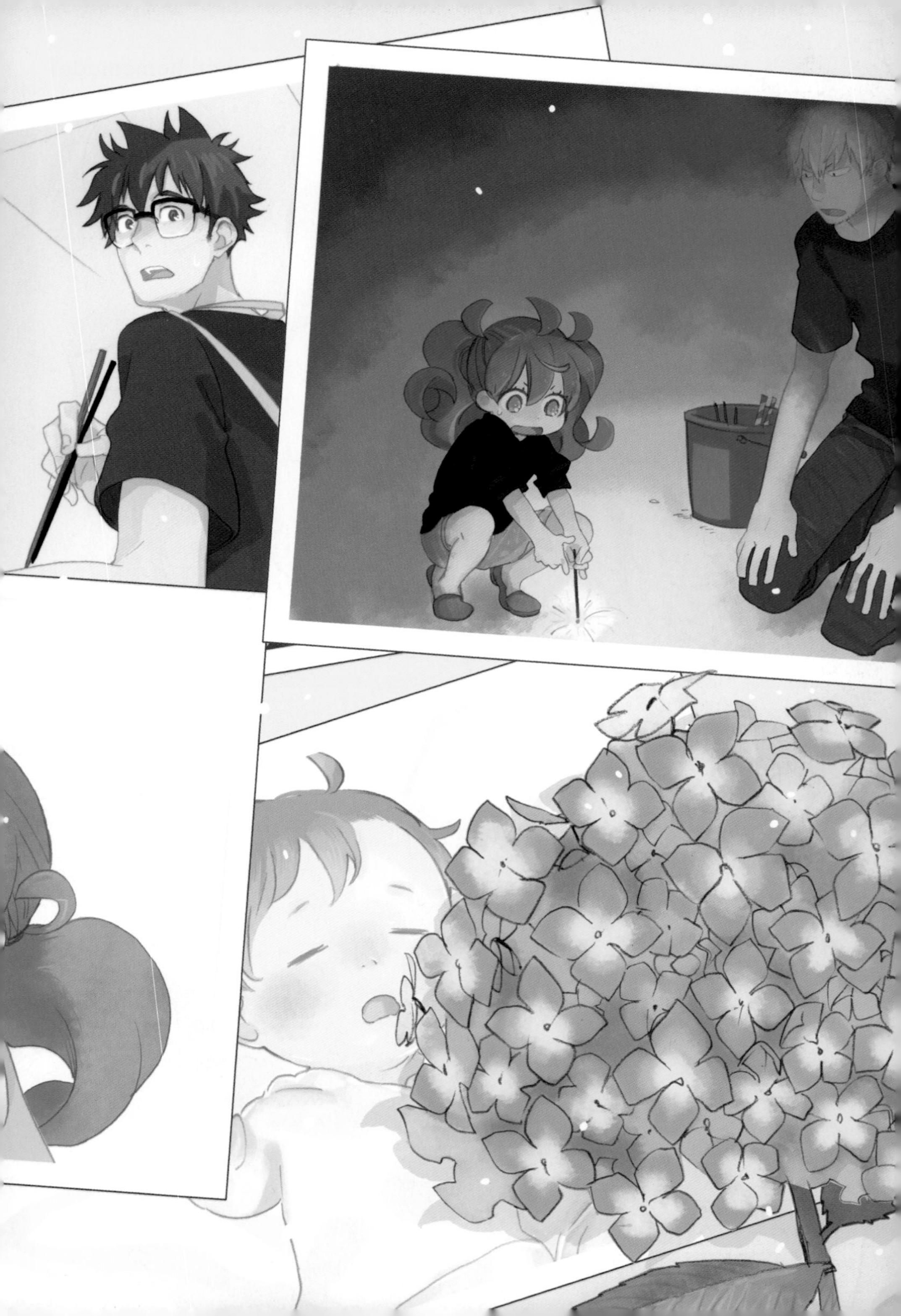

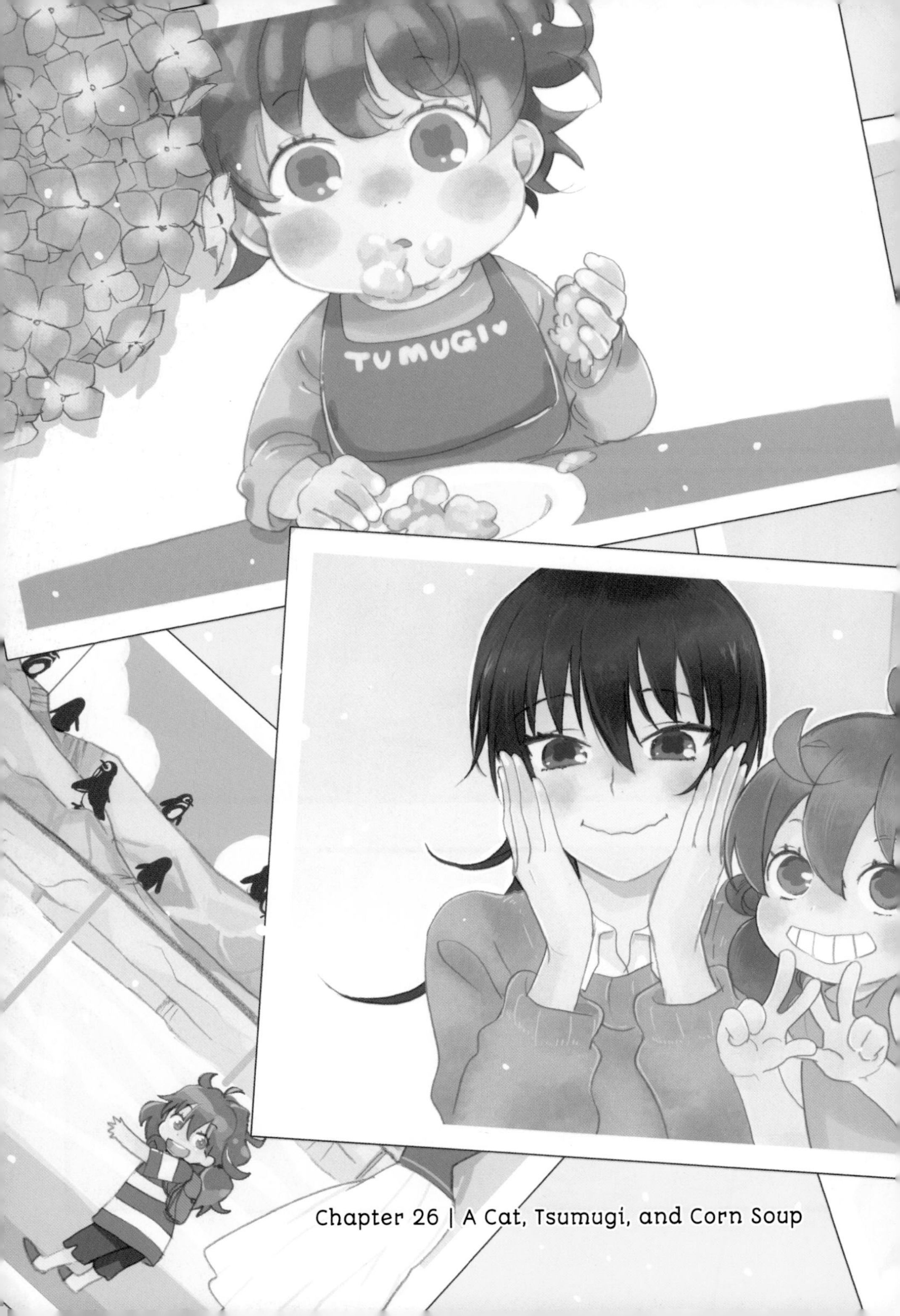
TUMUGI♥

Chapter 26 | A Cat, Tsumugi, and Corn Soup

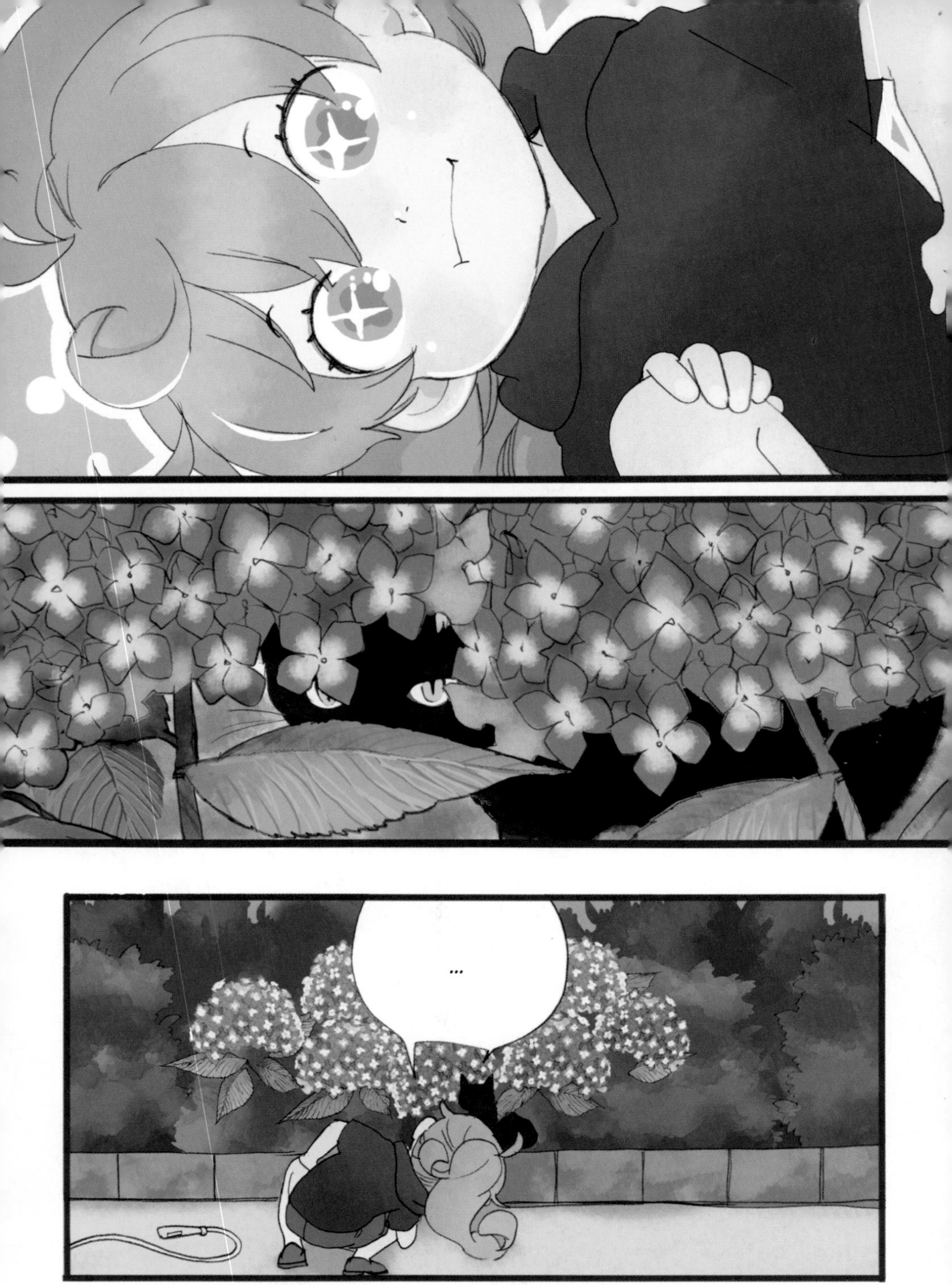
...

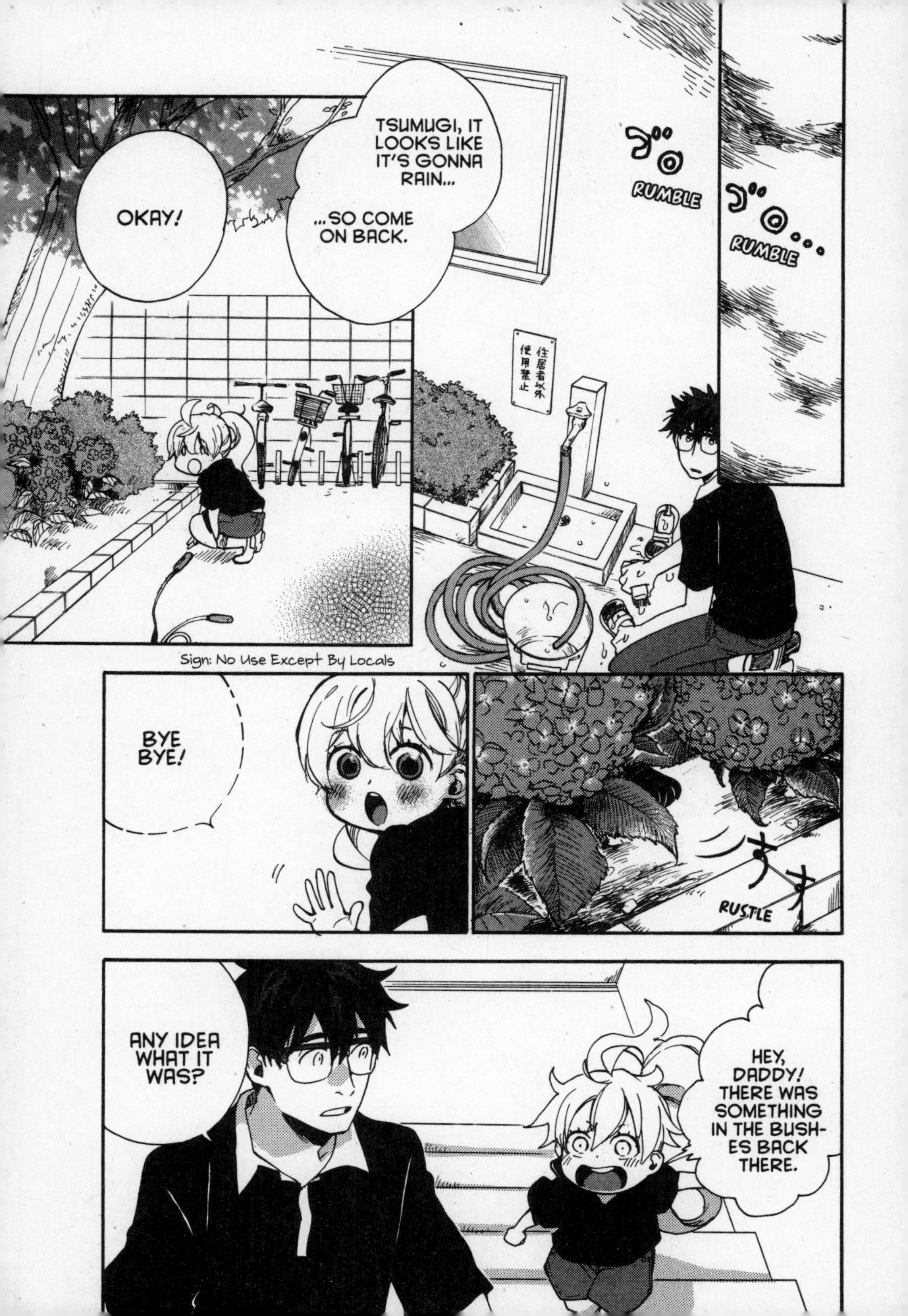
RUMBLE
RUMBLE
住居者以外使用禁止
TSUMUGI, IT LOOKS LIKE IT'S GONNA RAIN...
...SO COME ON BACK.
OKAY!
Sign: No Use Except By Locals
RUSTLE
BYE BYE!
HEY, DADDY! THERE WAS SOMETHING IN THE BUSH-ES BACK THERE.
ANY IDEA WHAT IT WAS?

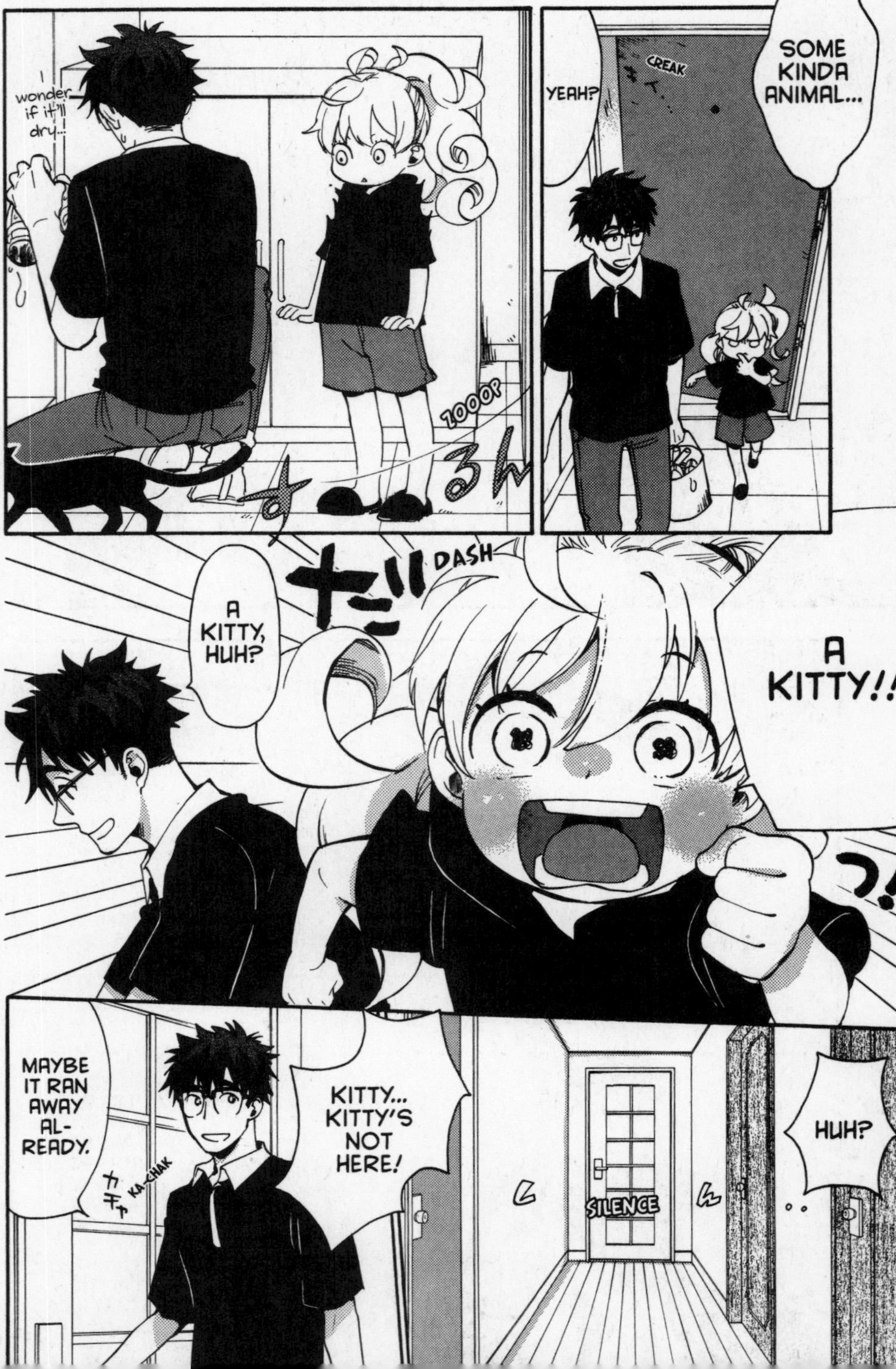
SOME KINDA ANIMAL...
CREAK
YEAH?
I wonder if it'll dry...
ZOOOP
するん
A KITTY!!
つ!
A KITTY, HUH?
DASH
HUH?
SILENCE
KITTY... KITTY'S NOT HERE!
MAYBE IT RAN AWAY AL-READY.
カチャ
KA-CHAK

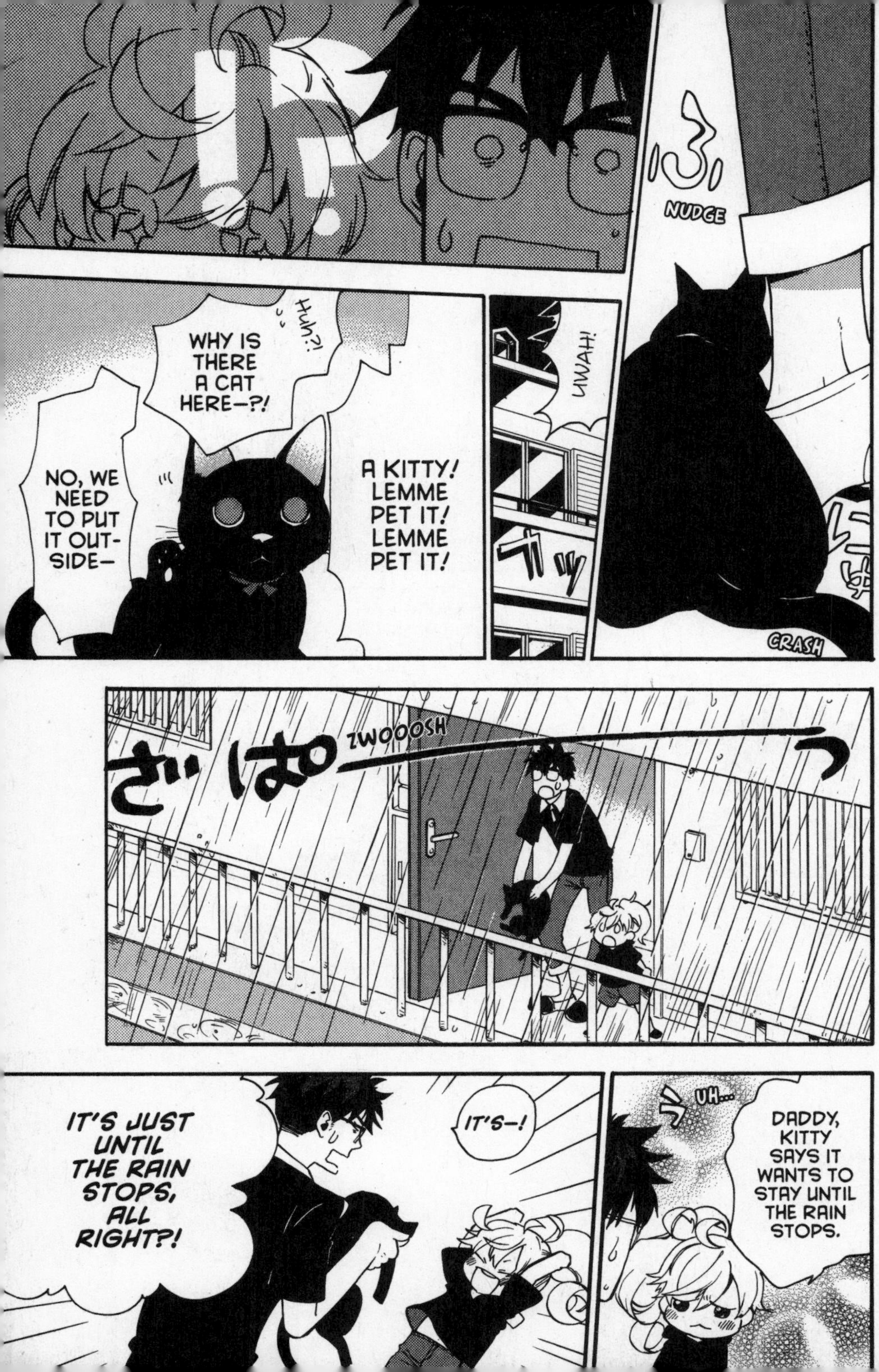
NUDGE
CRASH
UWAH!
Huh?!
WHY IS THERE A CAT HERE—?!
A KITTY! LEMME PET IT! LEMME PET IT!
NO, WE NEED TO PUT IT OUT-SIDE—
ZWOOOSH
UH...
DADDY, KITTY SAYS IT WANTS TO STAY UNTIL THE RAIN STOPS.
IT'S—!
IT'S JUST UNTIL THE RAIN STOPS, ALL RIGHT?!

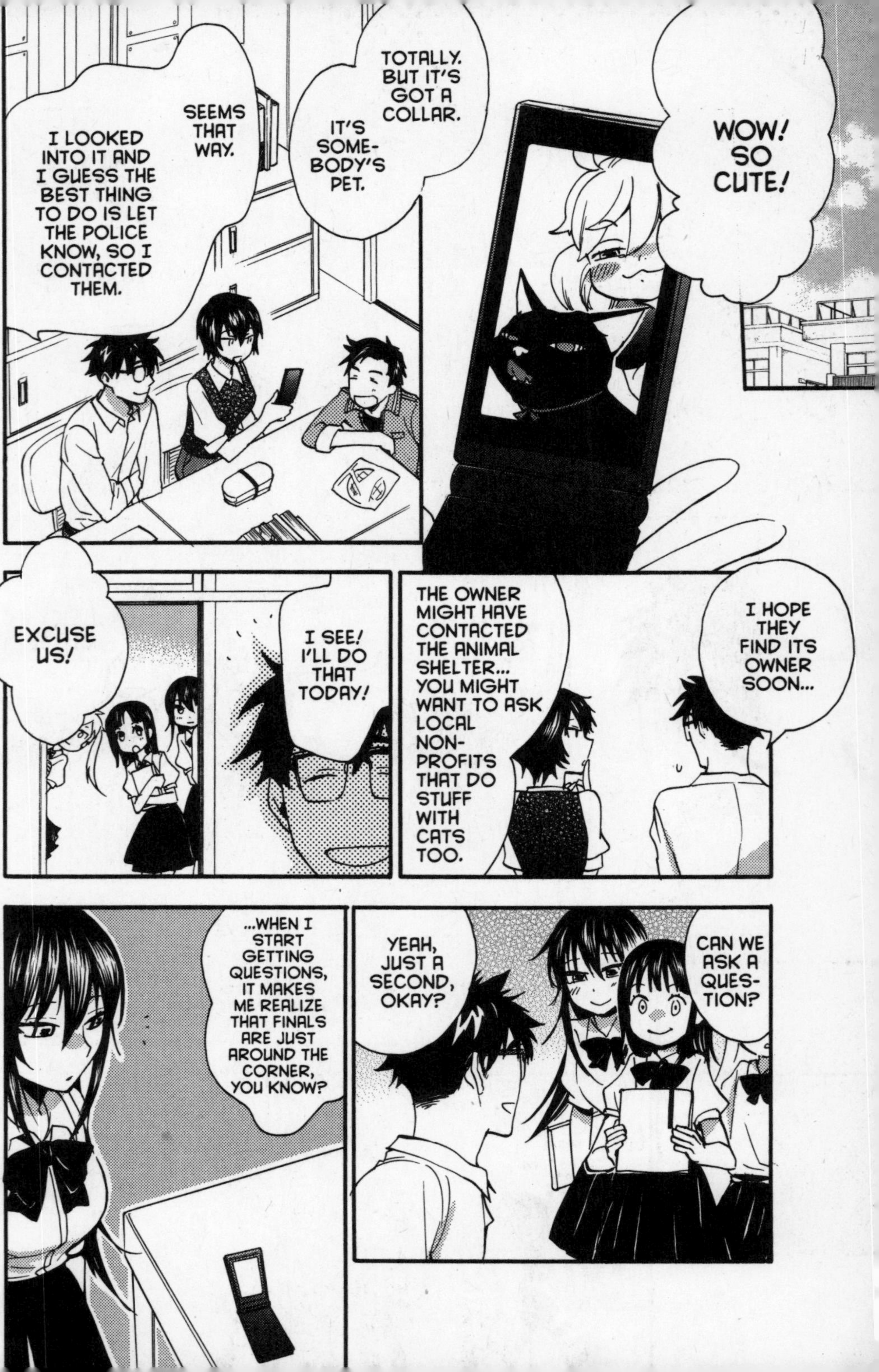
WOW! SO CUTE!
TOTALLY. BUT IT'S GOT A COLLAR.
IT'S SOME-BODY'S PET.
SEEMS THAT WAY.
I LOOKED INTO IT AND I GUESS THE BEST THING TO DO IS LET THE POLICE KNOW, SO I CONTACTED THEM.
I HOPE THEY FIND ITS OWNER SOON...
THE OWNER MIGHT HAVE CONTACTED THE ANIMAL SHELTER... YOU MIGHT WANT TO ASK LOCAL NON-PROFITS THAT DO STUFF WITH CATS TOO.
I SEE! I'LL DO THAT TODAY!
EXCUSE US!
CAN WE ASK A QUES-TION?
YEAH, JUST A SECOND, OKAY?
...WHEN I START GETTING QUESTIONS, IT MAKES ME REALIZE THAT FINALS ARE JUST AROUND THE CORNER, YOU KNOW?

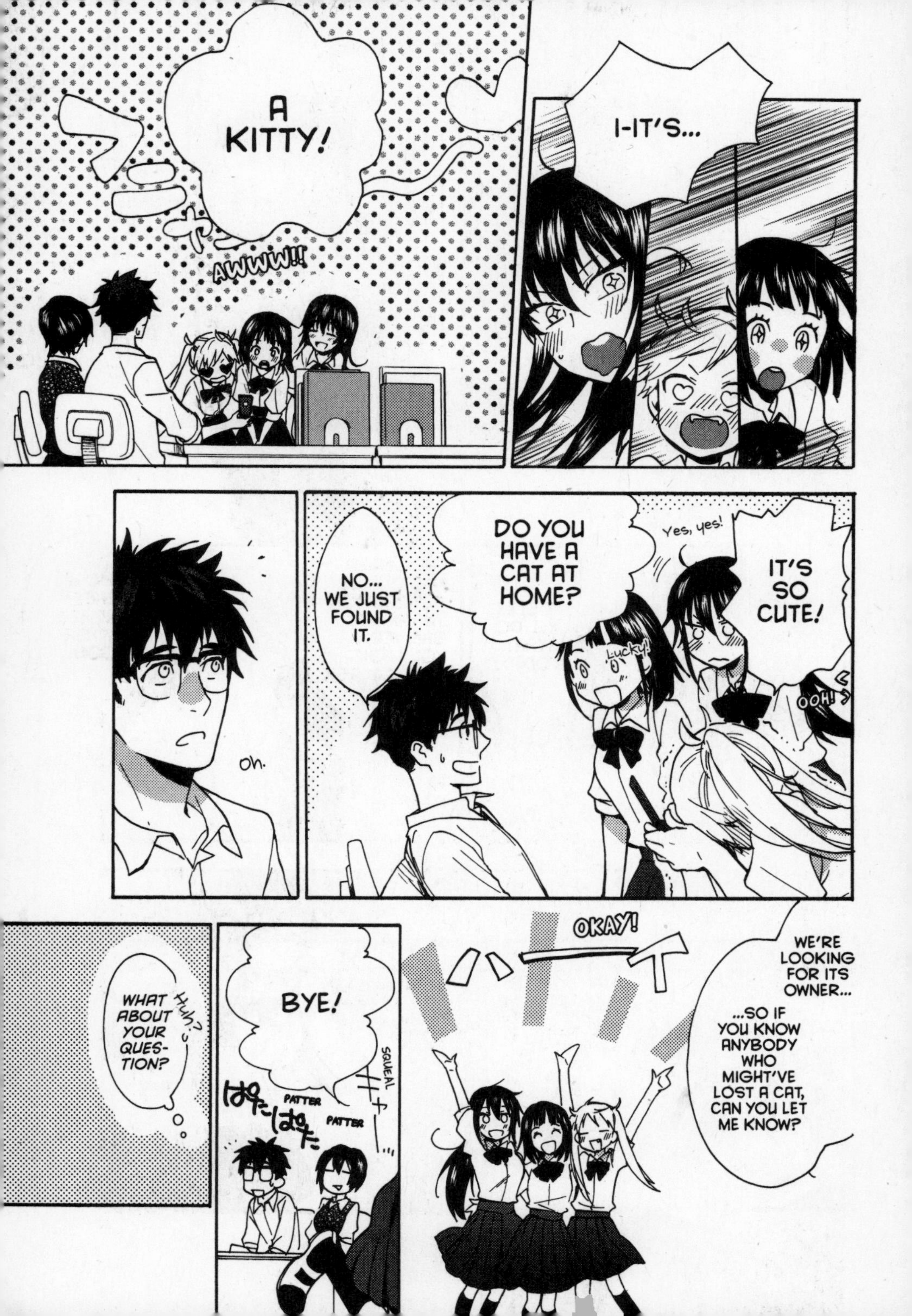
I-IT'S...
A KITTY!
AWWW!!
Yes, yes!
IT'S SO CUTE!
OOH!
Lucky!
DO YOU HAVE A CAT AT HOME?
NO... WE JUST FOUND IT.
Oh.
WE'RE LOOKING FOR ITS OWNER...
...SO IF YOU KNOW ANYBODY WHO MIGHT'VE LOST A CAT, CAN YOU LET ME KNOW?
OKAY!
BYE!
SQUEAL
PATTER
PATTER
Huh?
WHAT ABOUT YOUR QUES-TION?

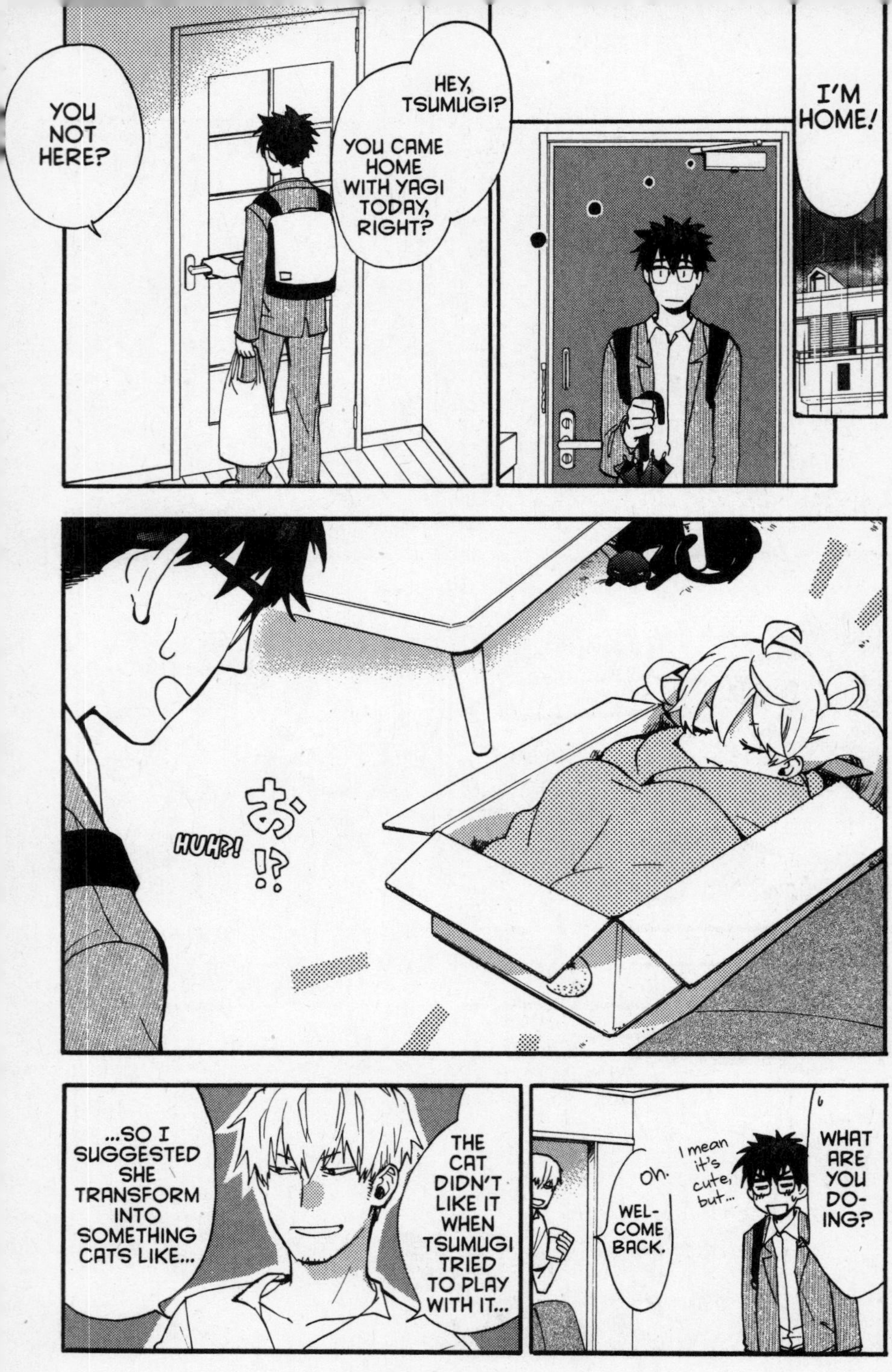
I'M HOME!
HEY, TSUMUGI?
YOU CAME HOME WITH YAGI TODAY, RIGHT?
YOU NOT HERE?
お!?
HUH?!
WHAT ARE YOU DO-ING?
I mean it's cute, but...
Oh.
WEL-COME BACK.
THE CAT DIDN'T LIKE IT WHEN TSUMUGI TRIED TO PLAY WITH IT...
...SO I SUGGESTED SHE TRANSFORM INTO SOMETHING CATS LIKE...

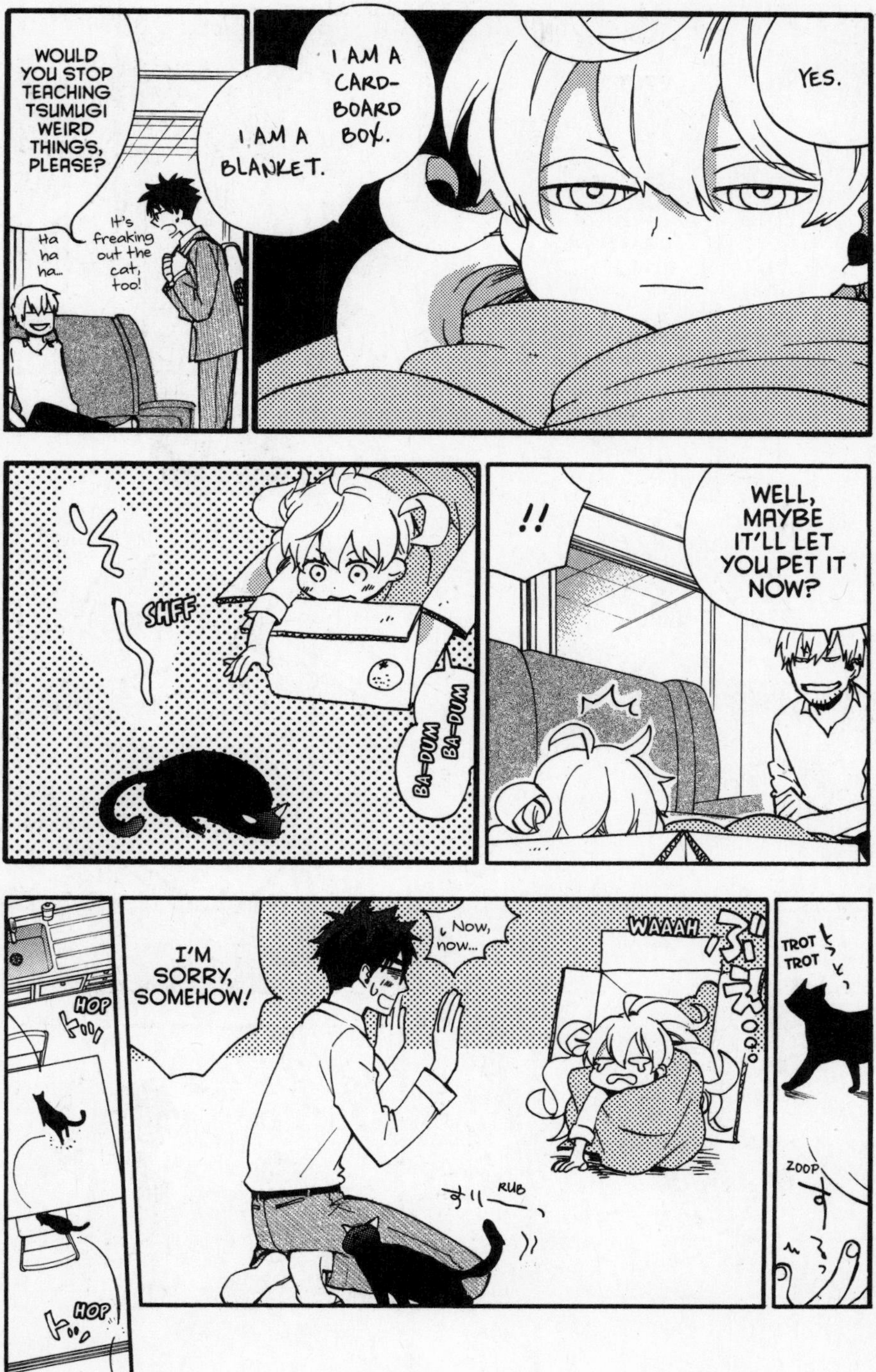
YES.
I AM A CARD-BOARD BOX.
I AM A BLANKET.
WOULD YOU STOP TEACHING TSUMUGI WEIRD THINGS, PLEASE?
It's freaking out the cat, too!
Ha ha ha...
WELL, MAYBE IT'LL LET YOU PET IT NOW?
!!
SHFF
BA-DUM BA-DUM
TROT TROT
ZOOP
WAAAH
Now, now...
I'M SORRY, SOMEHOW!
RUB
HOP
HOP

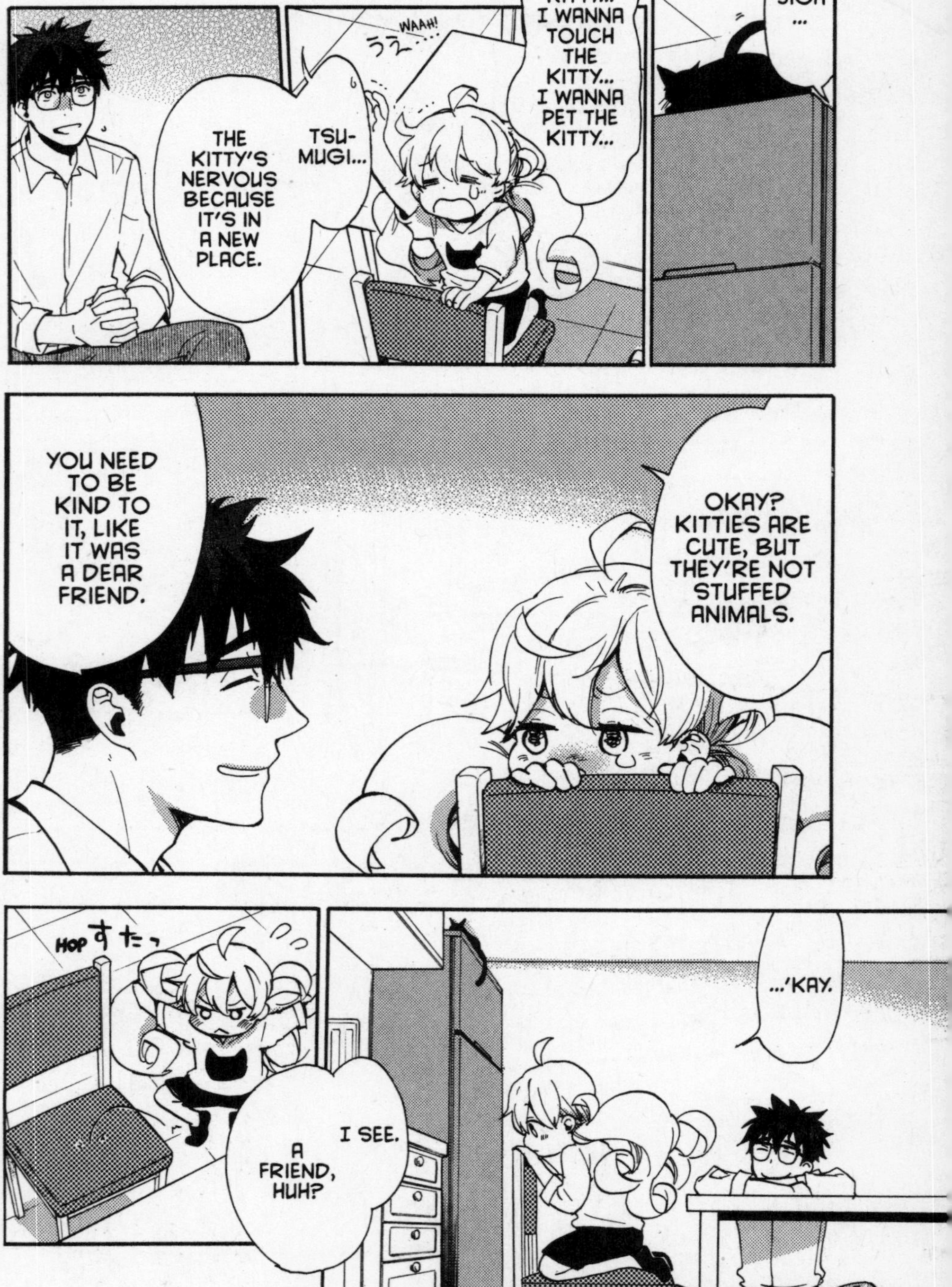
SIGH ...
KITTY... I WANNA TOUCH THE KITTY... I WANNA PET THE KITTY...
WAAH! うぇ……
TSU-MUGI...
THE KITTY'S NERVOUS BECAUSE IT'S IN A NEW PLACE.
OKAY? KITTIES ARE CUTE, BUT THEY'RE NOT STUFFED ANIMALS.
YOU NEED TO BE KIND TO IT, LIKE IT WAS A DEAR FRIEND.
...'KAY.
HOP すたっ
I SEE. A FRIEND, HUH?

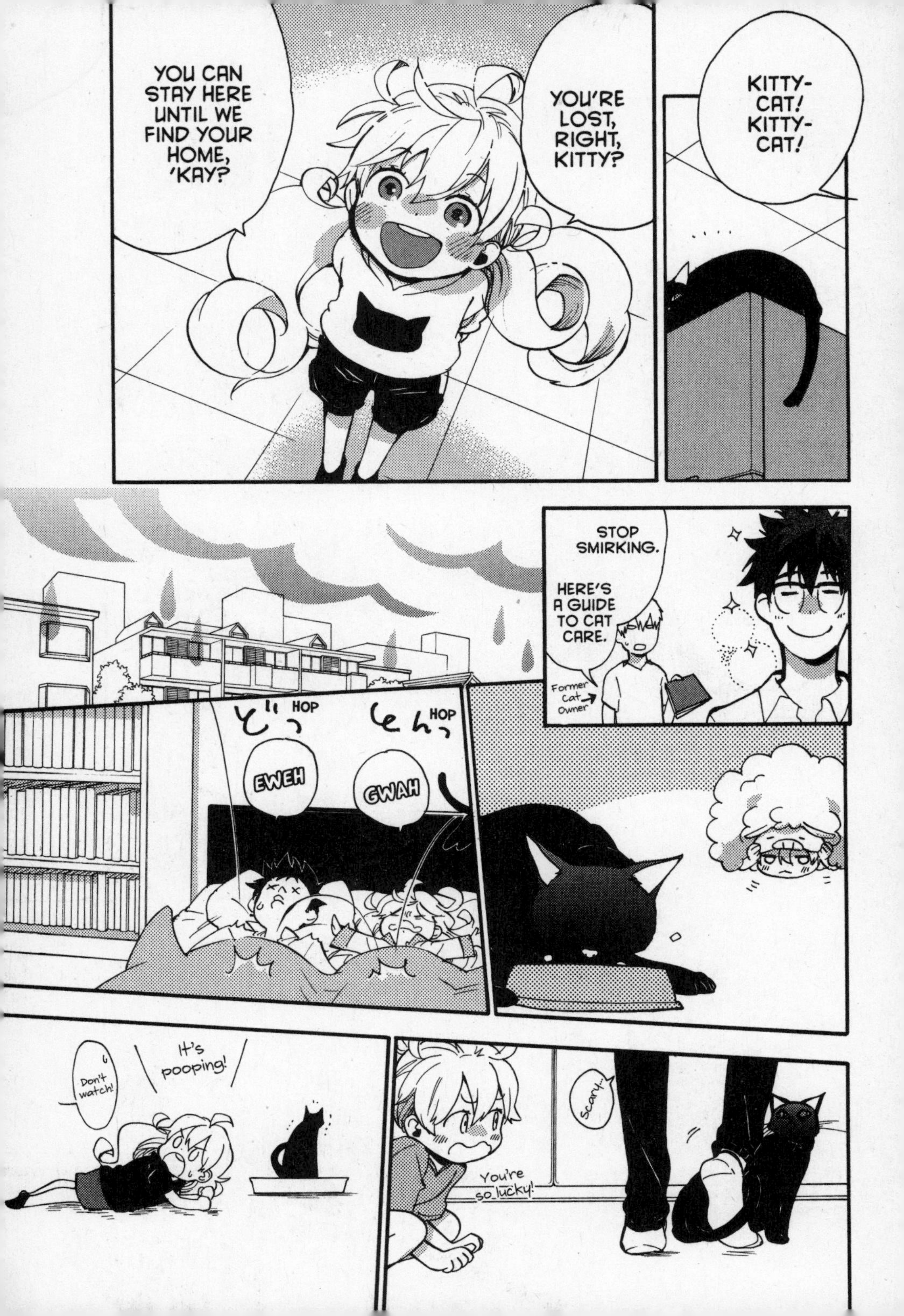
KITTY-CAT! KITTY-CAT!
YOU'RE LOST, RIGHT, KITTY?
YOU CAN STAY HERE UNTIL WE FIND YOUR HOME, 'KAY?
STOP SMIRKING.
HERE'S A GUIDE TO CAT CARE.
Former Cat Owner
HOP
GWAH
HOP
EWEH
Scary...
You're so lucky!
It's pooping!
Don't watch!

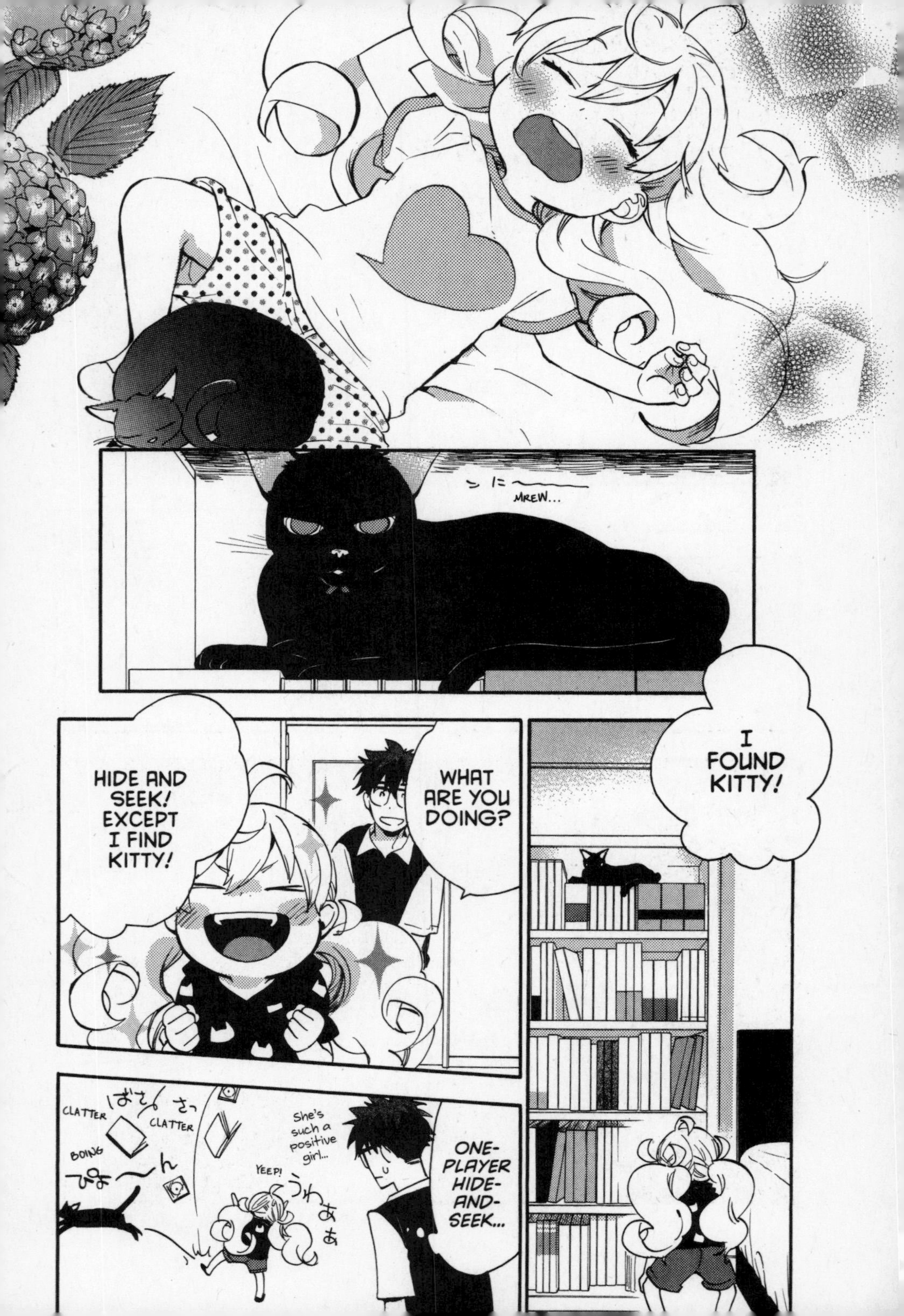
ンに〜〜
MREW...
I FOUND KITTY!
WHAT ARE YOU DOING?
HIDE AND SEEK! EXCEPT I FIND KITTY!
ONE-PLAYER HIDE-AND-SEEK...
She's such a positive girl...
うわぁぁ
YEEP!
ばさっ
CLATTER
さっ
CLATTER
ぴょ〜ん
BOING

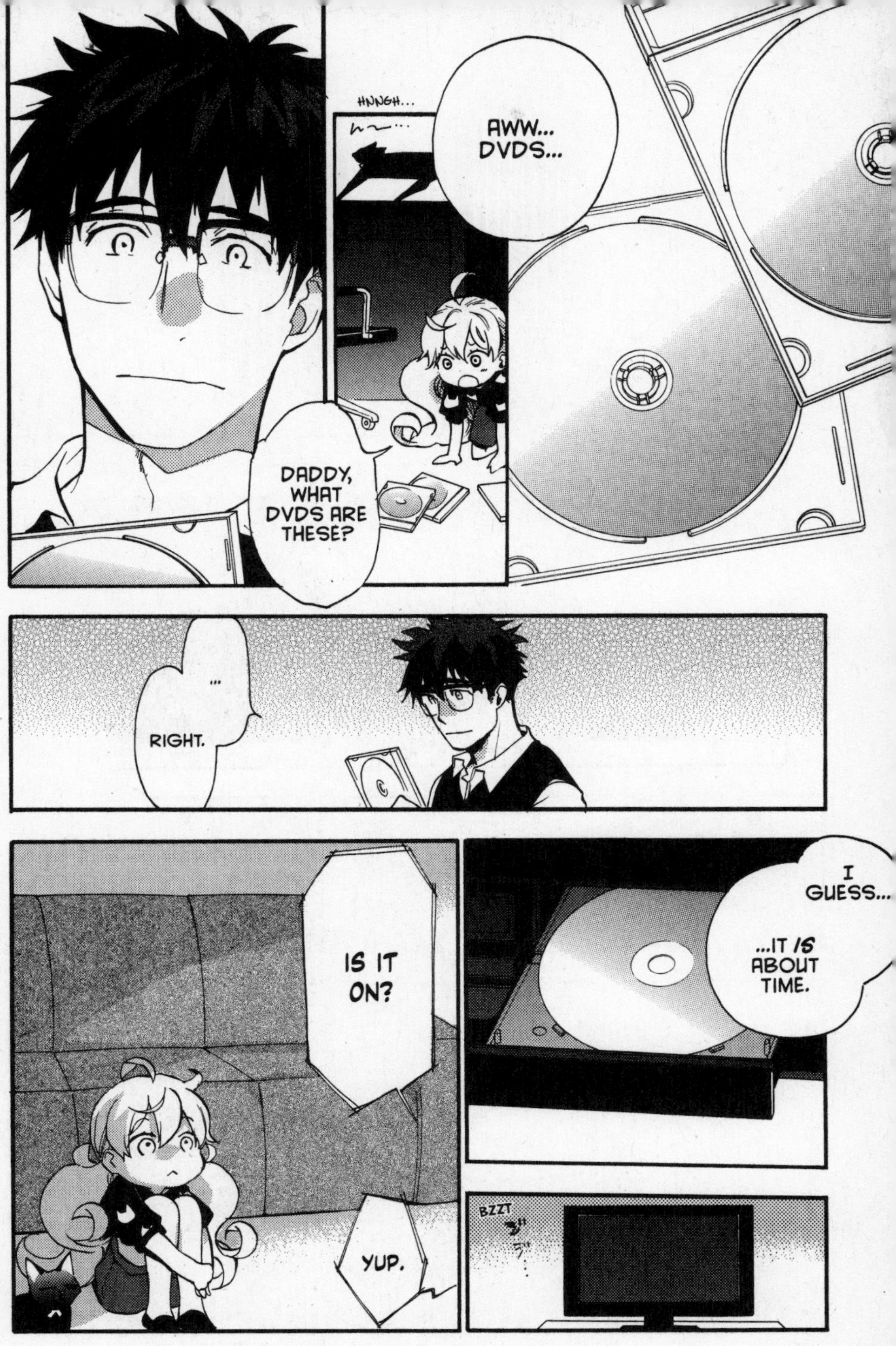
AWW... DVDS...
HNNGH...
ん〜…
DADDY, WHAT DVDS ARE THESE?
...
RIGHT.
I GUESS...
...IT IS ABOUT TIME.
BZZT
IS IT ON?
YUP.

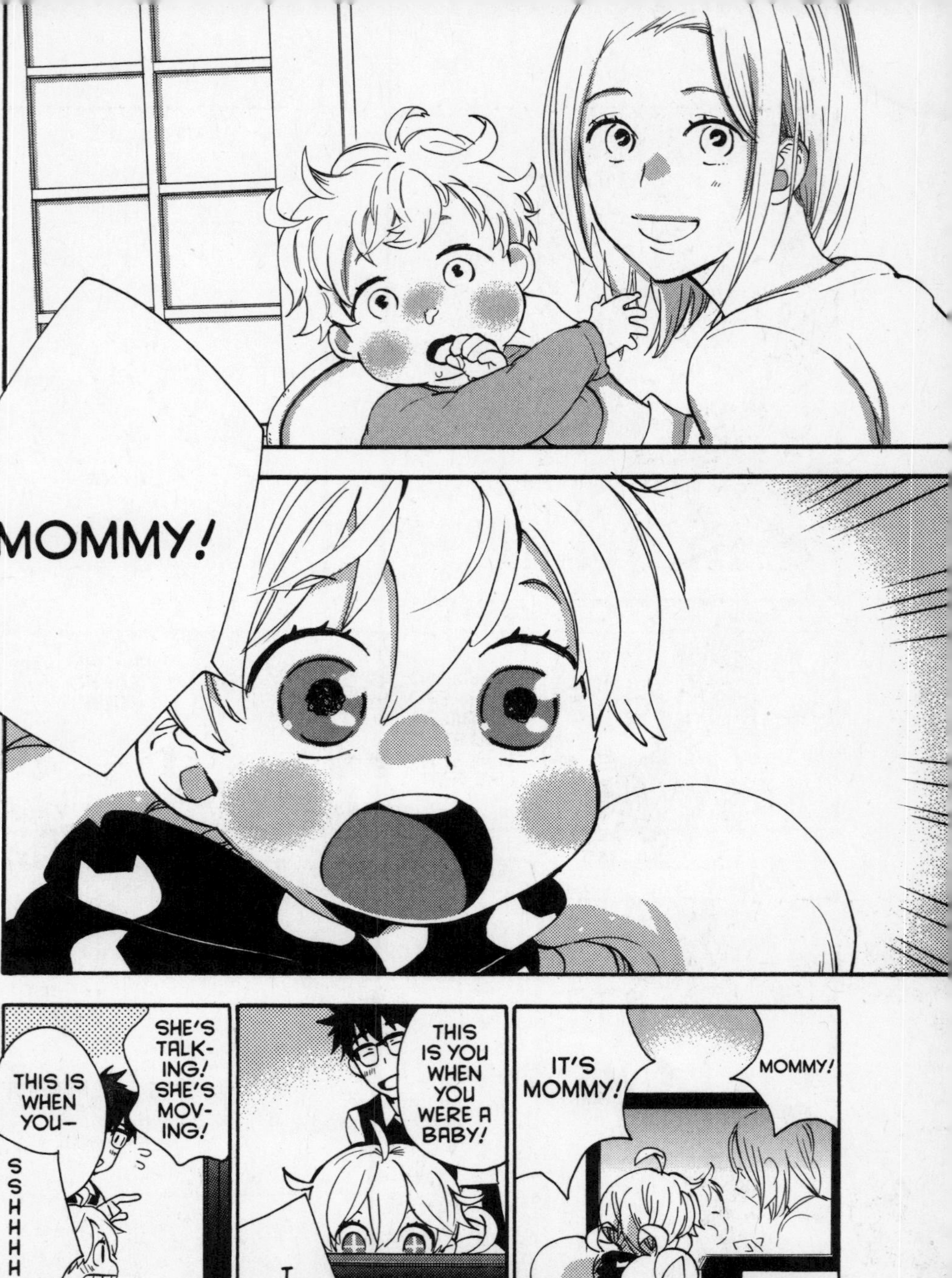
MOMMY!
MOMMY!
IT'S MOMMY!
THIS IS YOU WHEN YOU WERE A BABY!
I KNOW!
SHE'S TALKING! SHE'S MOVING!
THIS IS WHEN YOU—
SSHHHH!

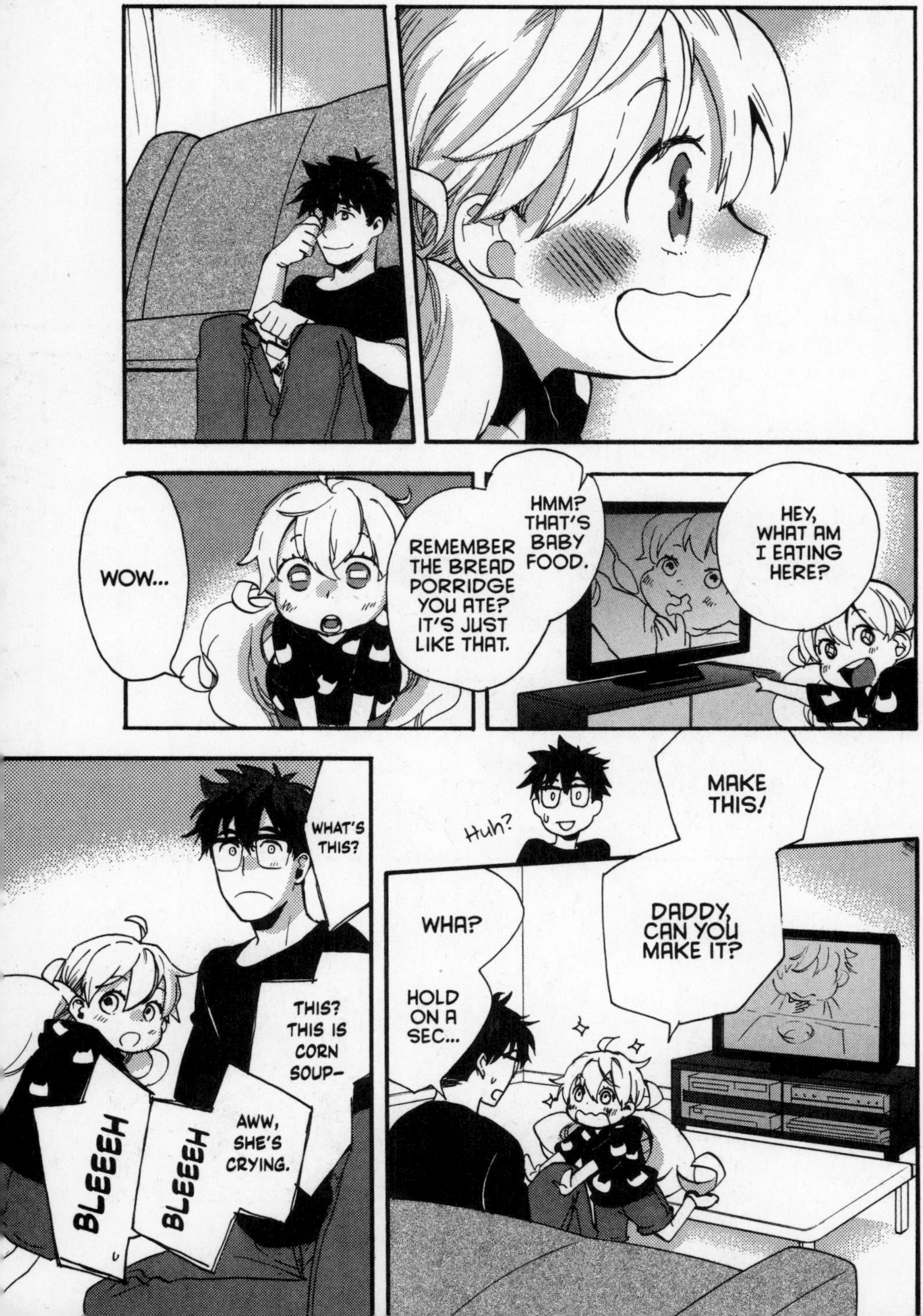
HEY, WHAT AM I EATING HERE?
HMM? THAT'S BABY FOOD.
REMEMBER THE BREAD PORRIDGE YOU ATE? IT'S JUST LIKE THAT.
WOW...
MAKE THIS!
Huh?
DADDY, CAN YOU MAKE IT?
WHA?
HOLD ON A SEC...
WHAT'S THIS?
THIS? THIS IS CORN SOUP-
AWW, SHE'S CRYING.
BLEEEH
BLEEEH

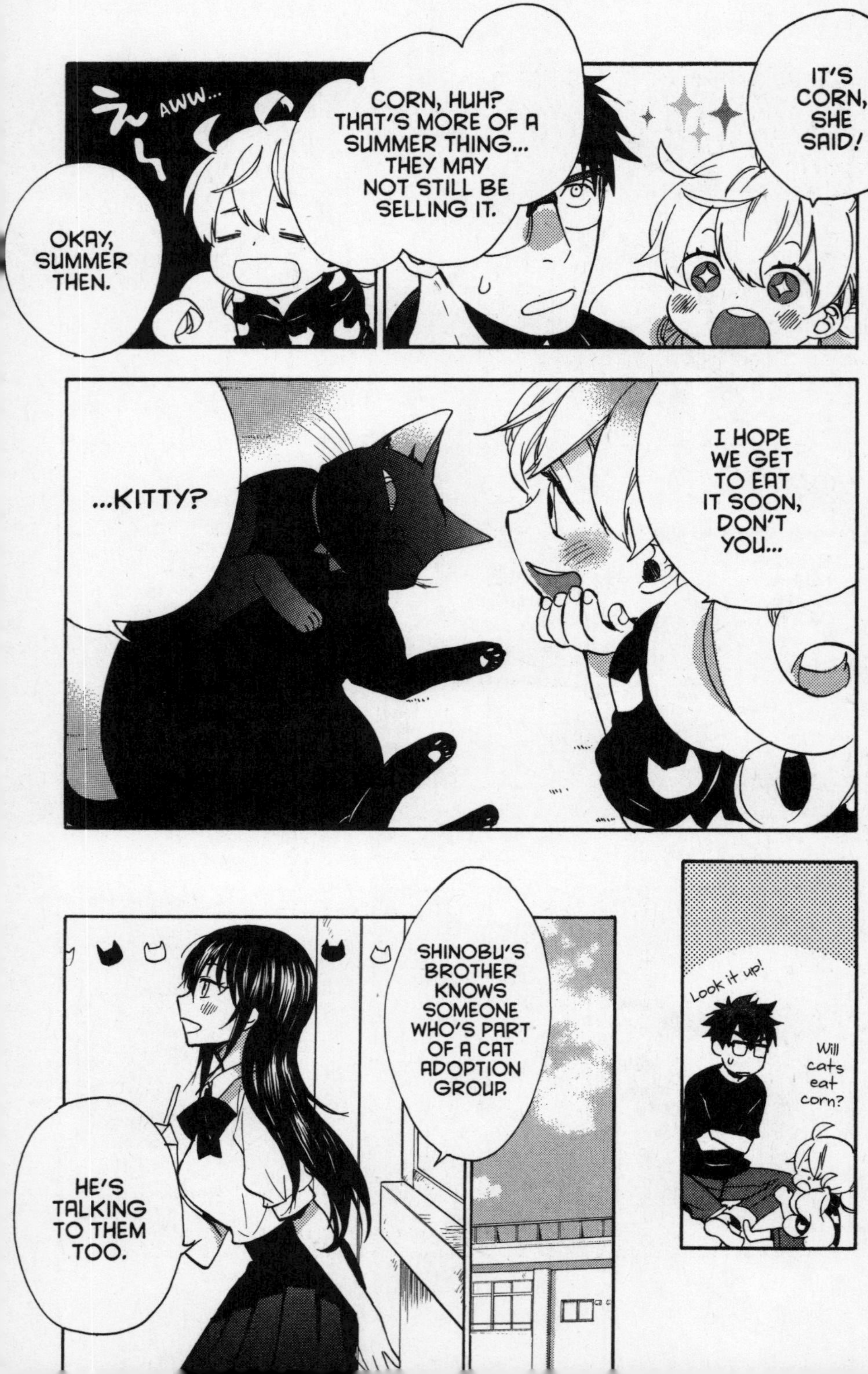
IT'S CORN, SHE SAID!
CORN, HUH? THAT'S MORE OF A SUMMER THING... THEY MAY NOT STILL BE SELLING IT.
AWW...
OKAY, SUMMER THEN.
I HOPE WE GET TO EAT IT SOON, DON'T YOU...
...KITTY?
Look it up!
Will cats eat corn?
SHINOBU'S BROTHER KNOWS SOMEONE WHO'S PART OF A CAT ADOPTION GROUP.
HE'S TALKING TO THEM TOO.

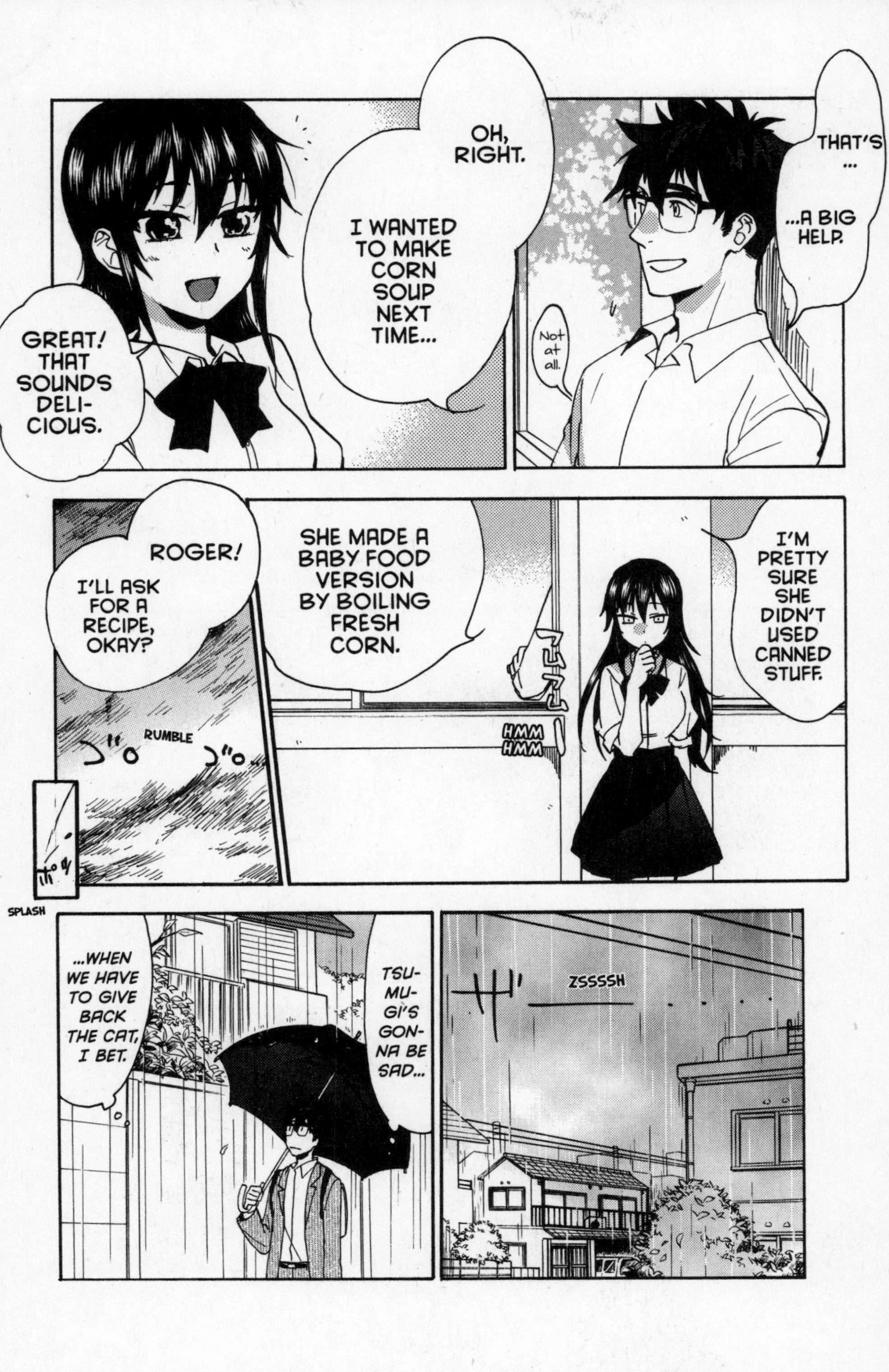
THAT'S ...
...A BIG HELP.
Not at all.
OH, RIGHT.
I WANTED TO MAKE CORN SOUP NEXT TIME...
GREAT! THAT SOUNDS DELI-CIOUS.
I'M PRETTY SURE SHE DIDN'T USED CANNED STUFF.
HMM HMM
SHE MADE A BABY FOOD VERSION BY BOILING FRESH CORN.
ROGER!
I'LL ASK FOR A RECIPE, OKAY?
RUMBLE
SPLASH
ZSSSSH
TSU-MU-GI'S GON-NA BE SAD...
...WHEN WE HAVE TO GIVE BACK THE CAT, I BET.

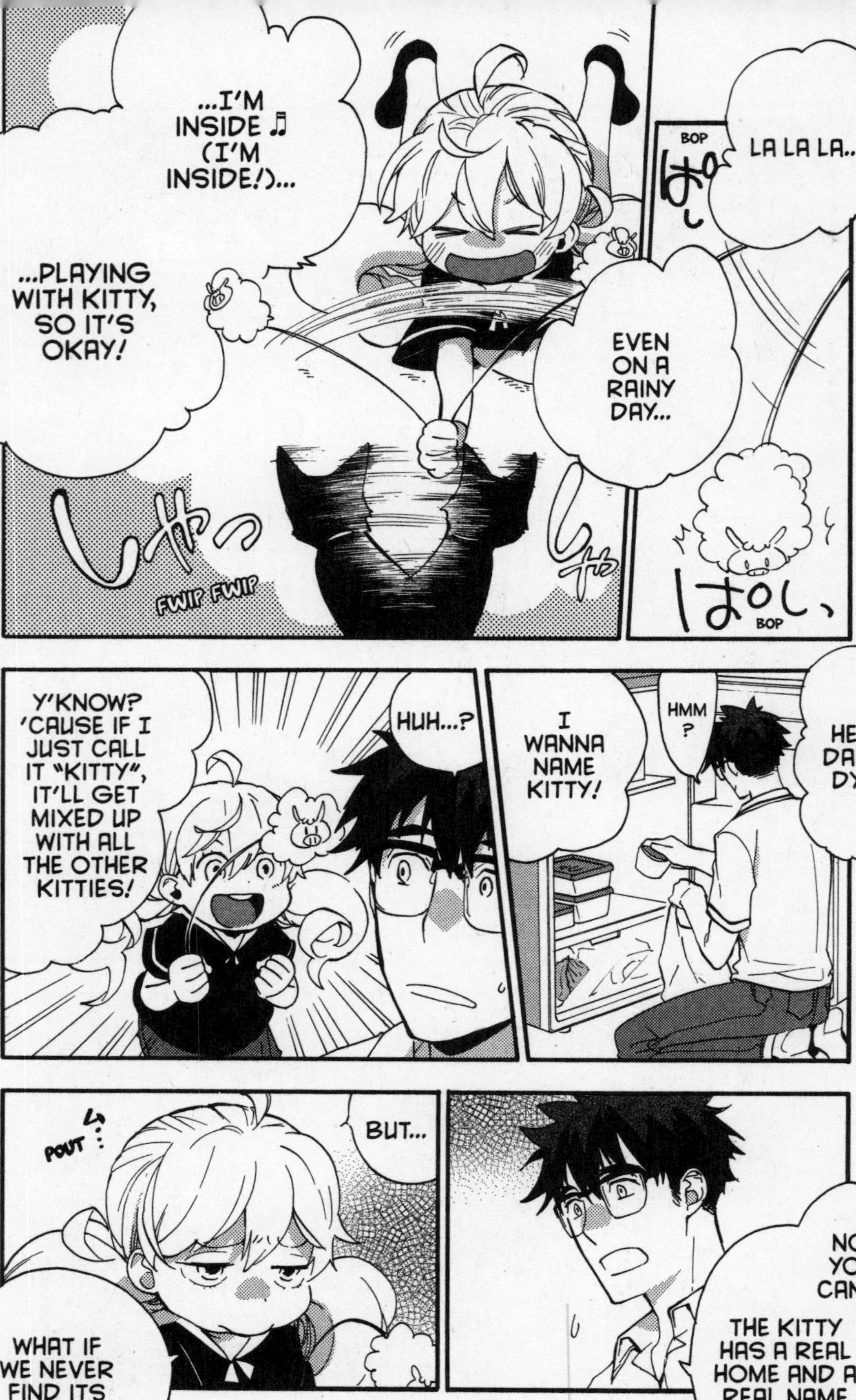
LA LA LA...
BOP
ぱし
EVEN ON A RAINY DAY...
ぱし、
BOP
...I'M INSIDE ♫ (I'M INSIDE!)...
...PLAYING WITH KITTY, SO IT'S OKAY!
しゃっ
しゃ
FWIP FWIP
HEY, DADDY!
HMM?
I WANNA NAME KITTY!
HUH...?
Y'KNOW? 'CAUSE IF I JUST CALL IT "KITTY", IT'LL GET MIXED UP WITH ALL THE OTHER KITTIES!
NO, YOU CAN'T.
THE KITTY HAS A REAL HOME AND A REAL NAME ALREADY.
BUT...
む…
POUT
WHAT IF WE NEVER FIND ITS HOME?

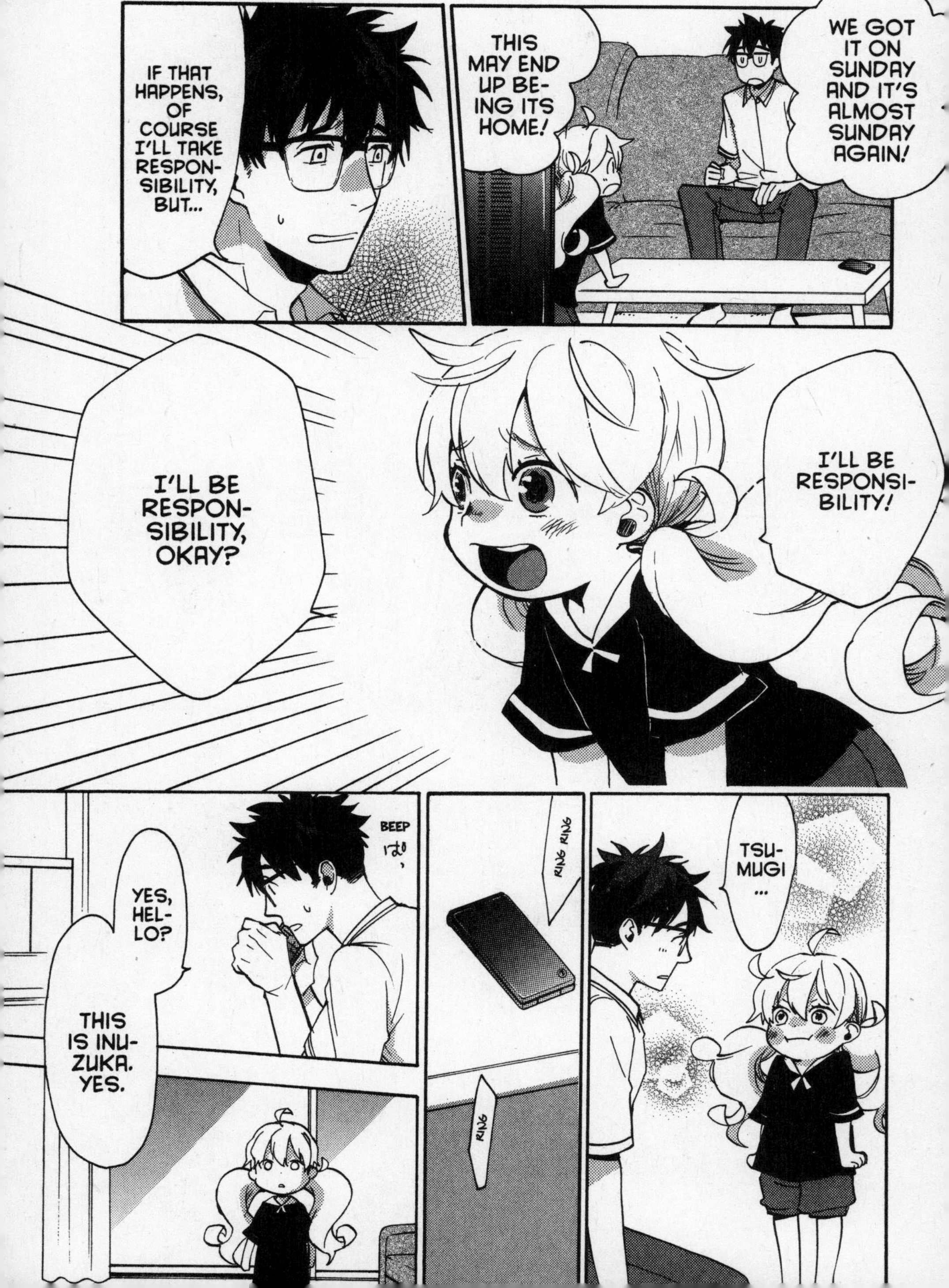
WE GOT IT ON SUNDAY AND IT'S ALMOST SUNDAY AGAIN!
THIS MAY END UP BE-ING ITS HOME!
IF THAT HAPPENS, OF COURSE I'LL TAKE RESPON-SIBILITY, BUT...
I'LL BE RESPONSI-BILITY!
I'LL BE RESPON-SIBILITY, OKAY?
TSU-MUGI ...
RING RING
RING
BEEP
YES, HEL-LO?
THIS IS INU-ZUKA. YES.

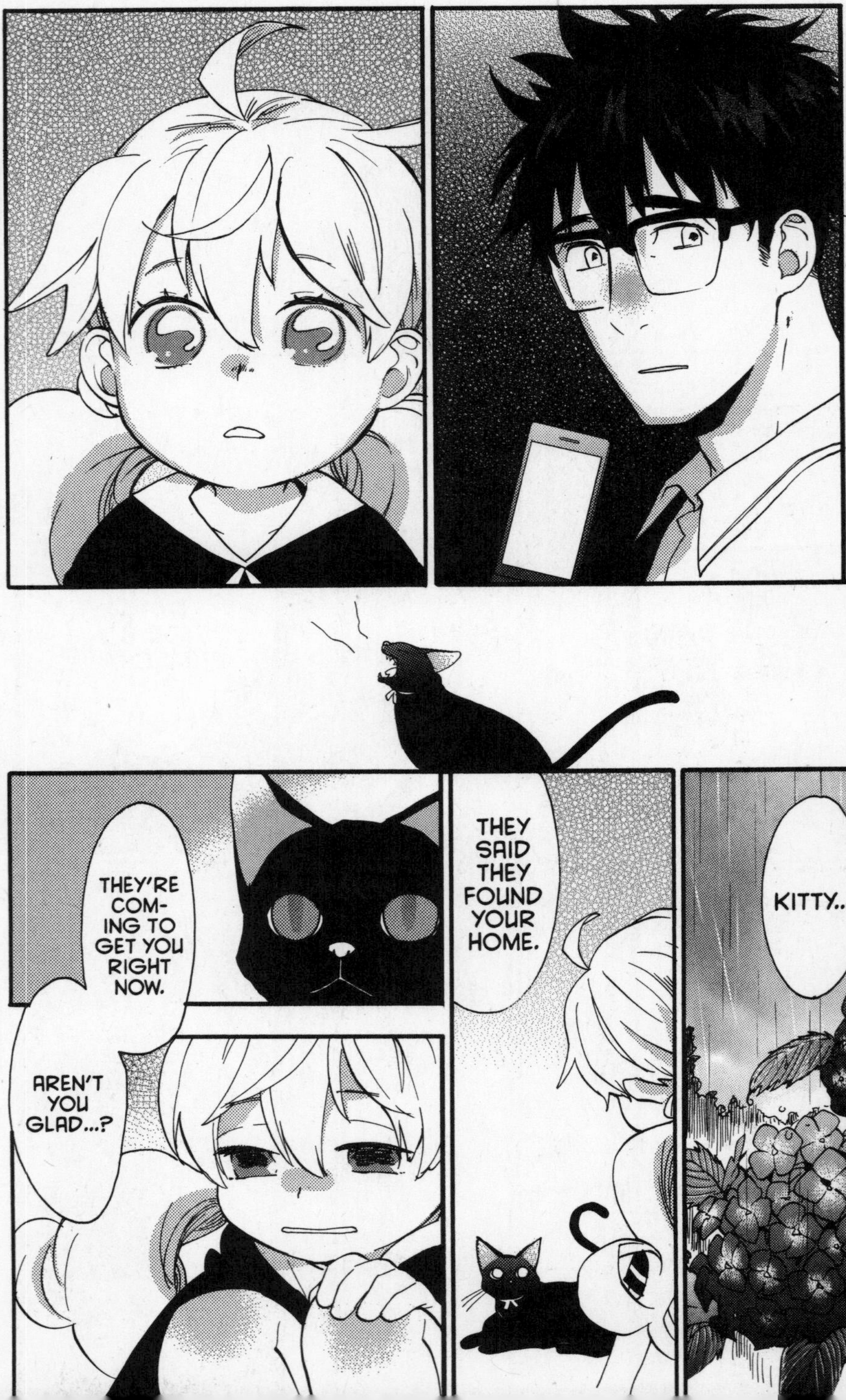
KITTY...
THEY SAID THEY FOUND YOUR HOME.
THEY'RE COMING TO GET YOU RIGHT NOW.
AREN'T YOU GLAD...?

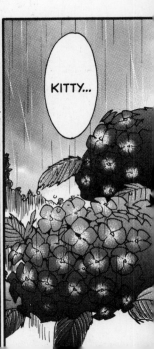

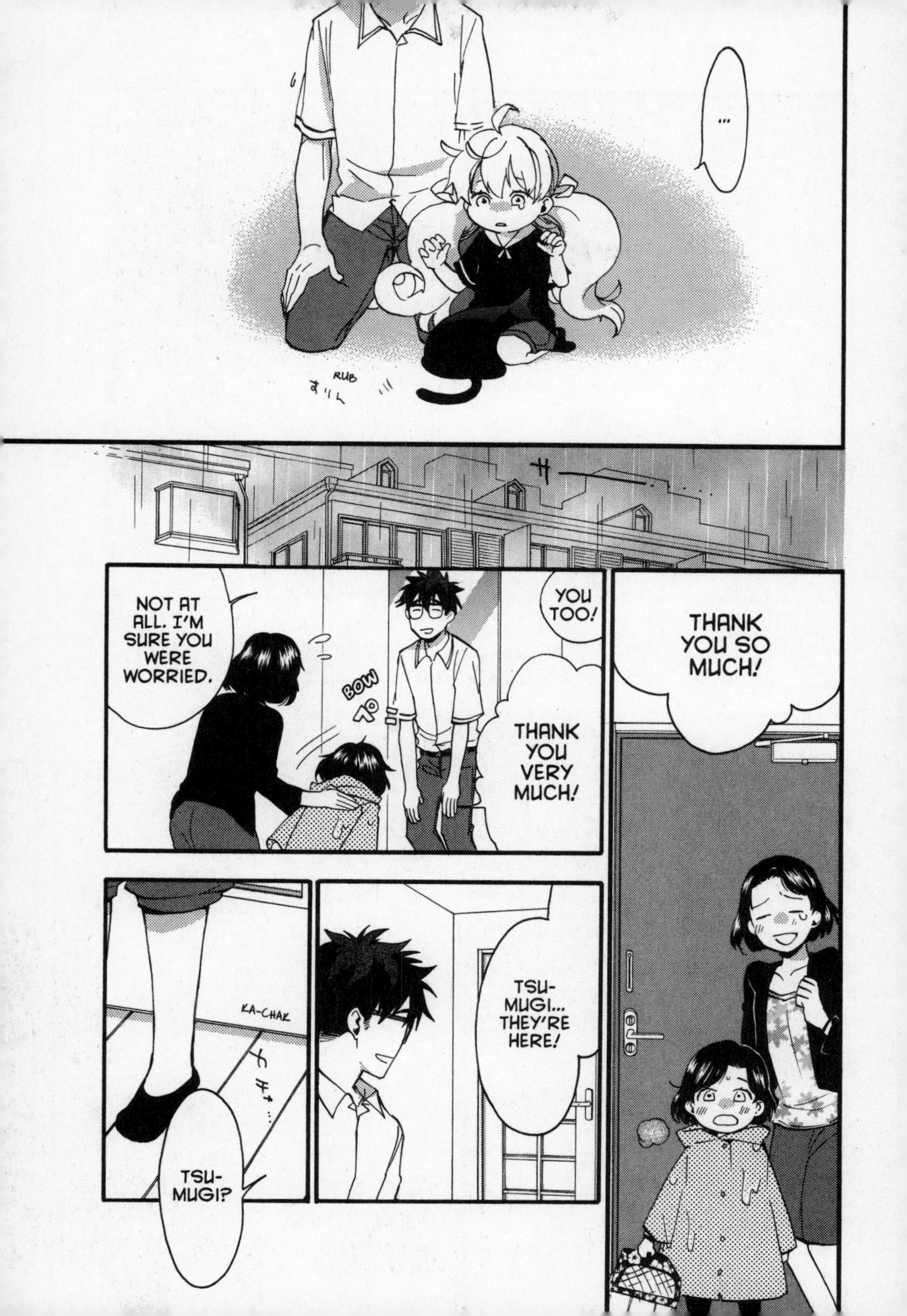
...
RUB
すりん
THANK YOU SO MUCH!
YOU TOO!
THANK YOU VERY MUCH!
NOT AT ALL. I'M SURE YOU WERE WORRIED.
BOW
TSU-MUGI... THEY'RE HERE!
KA-CHAK
TSU-MUGI?

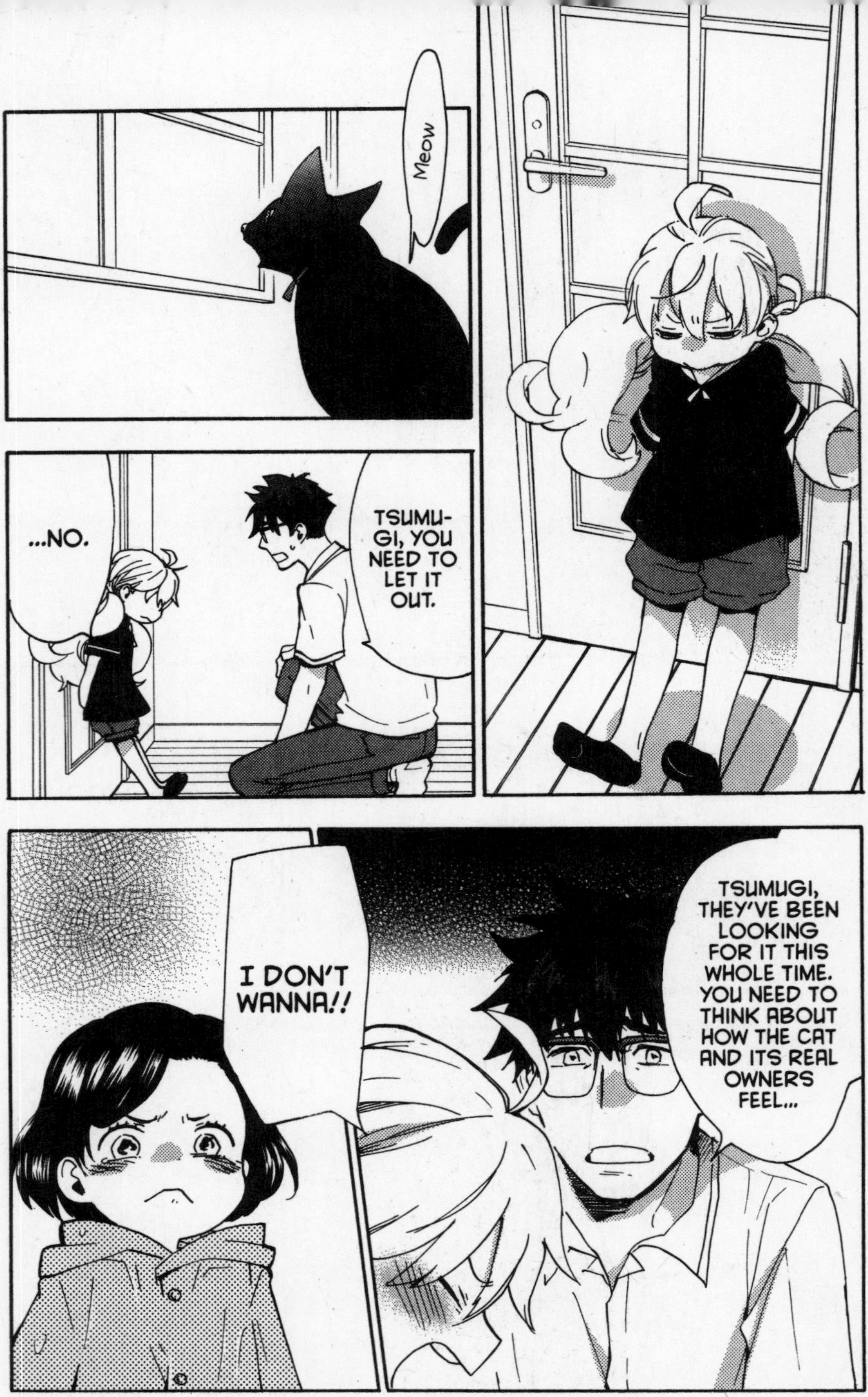
Meow
TSUMUGI, YOU NEED TO LET IT OUT.
...NO.
TSUMUGI, THEY'VE BEEN LOOKING FOR IT THIS WHOLE TIME. YOU NEED TO THINK ABOUT HOW THE CAT AND ITS REAL OWNERS FEEL...
I DON'T WANNA!!

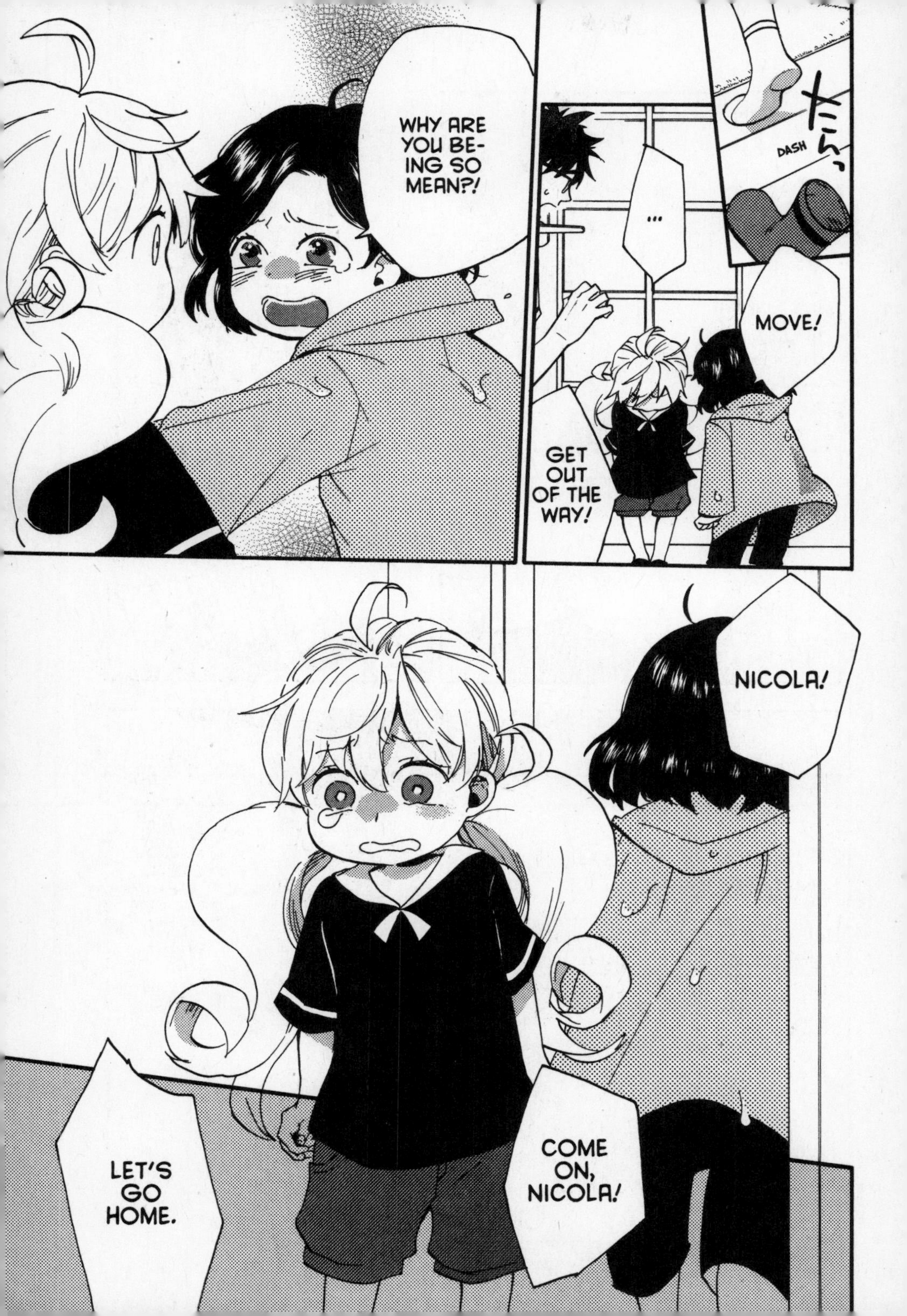
たん、
DASH
...
MOVE!
GET OUT OF THE WAY!
WHY ARE YOU BE-ING SO MEAN?!
NICOLA!
COME ON, NICOLA!
LET'S GO HOME.

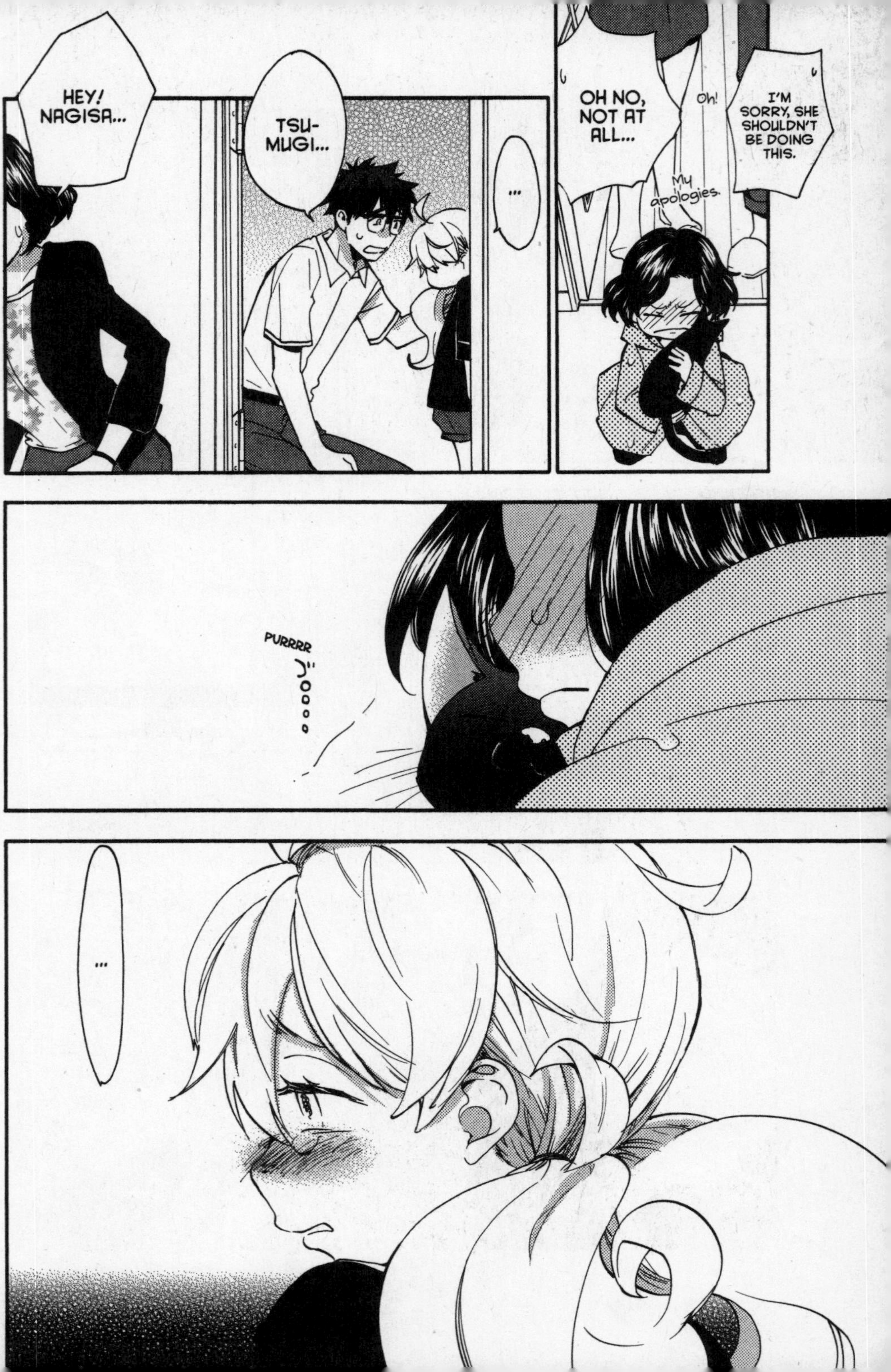
I'M SORRY, SHE SHOULDN'T BE DOING THIS.
Oh!
OH NO, NOT AT ALL...
My apologies.
...
TSU-MUGI...
HEY! NAGISA...
PURRRR
ゴロロロ
...

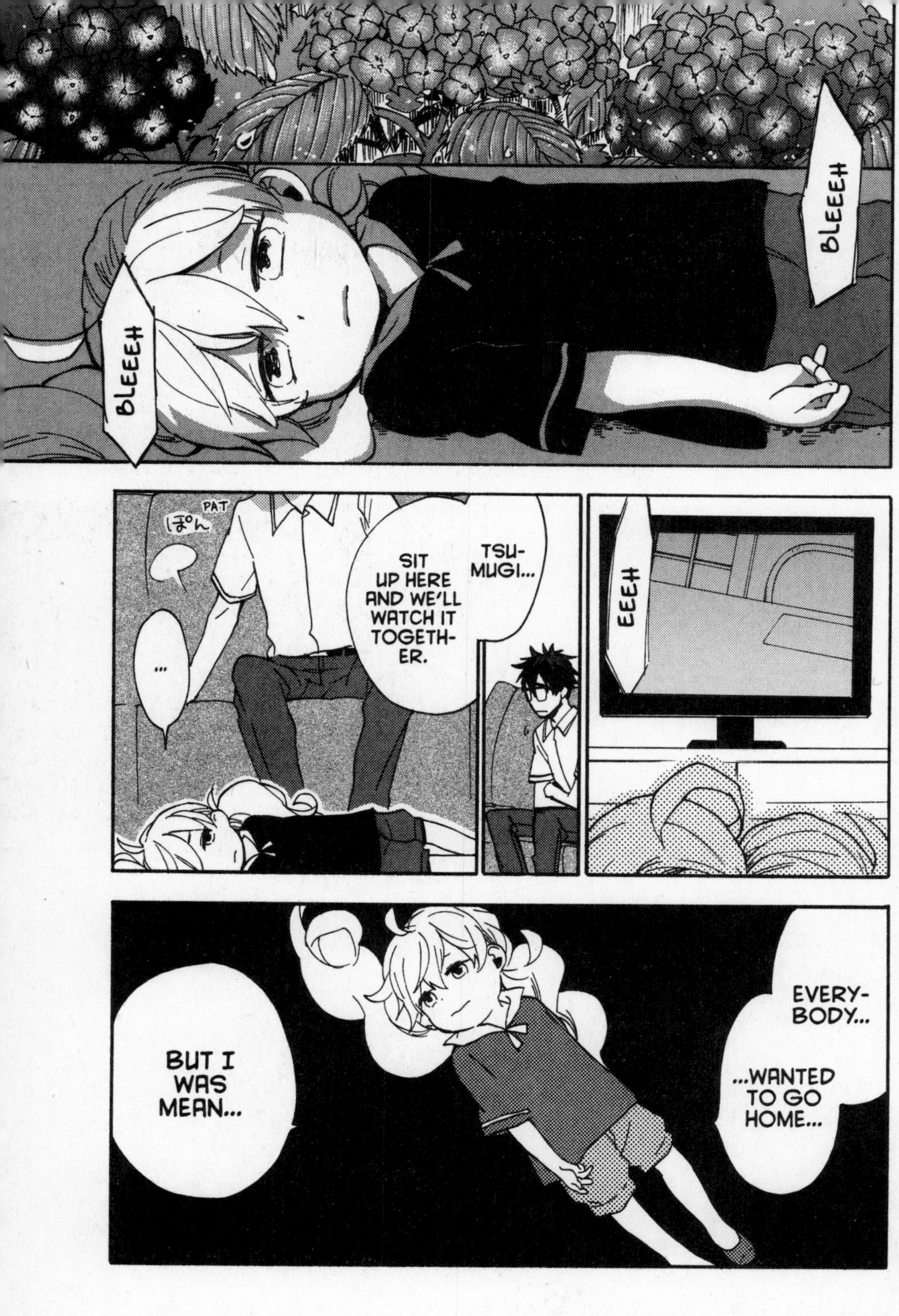
BLEEEH
BLEEEH
EEEH
TSU-MUGI...
SIT UP HERE AND WE'LL WATCH IT TOGETH-ER.
PAT
ぽん
...
EVERY-BODY...
...WANTED TO GO HOME...
BUT I WAS MEAN...

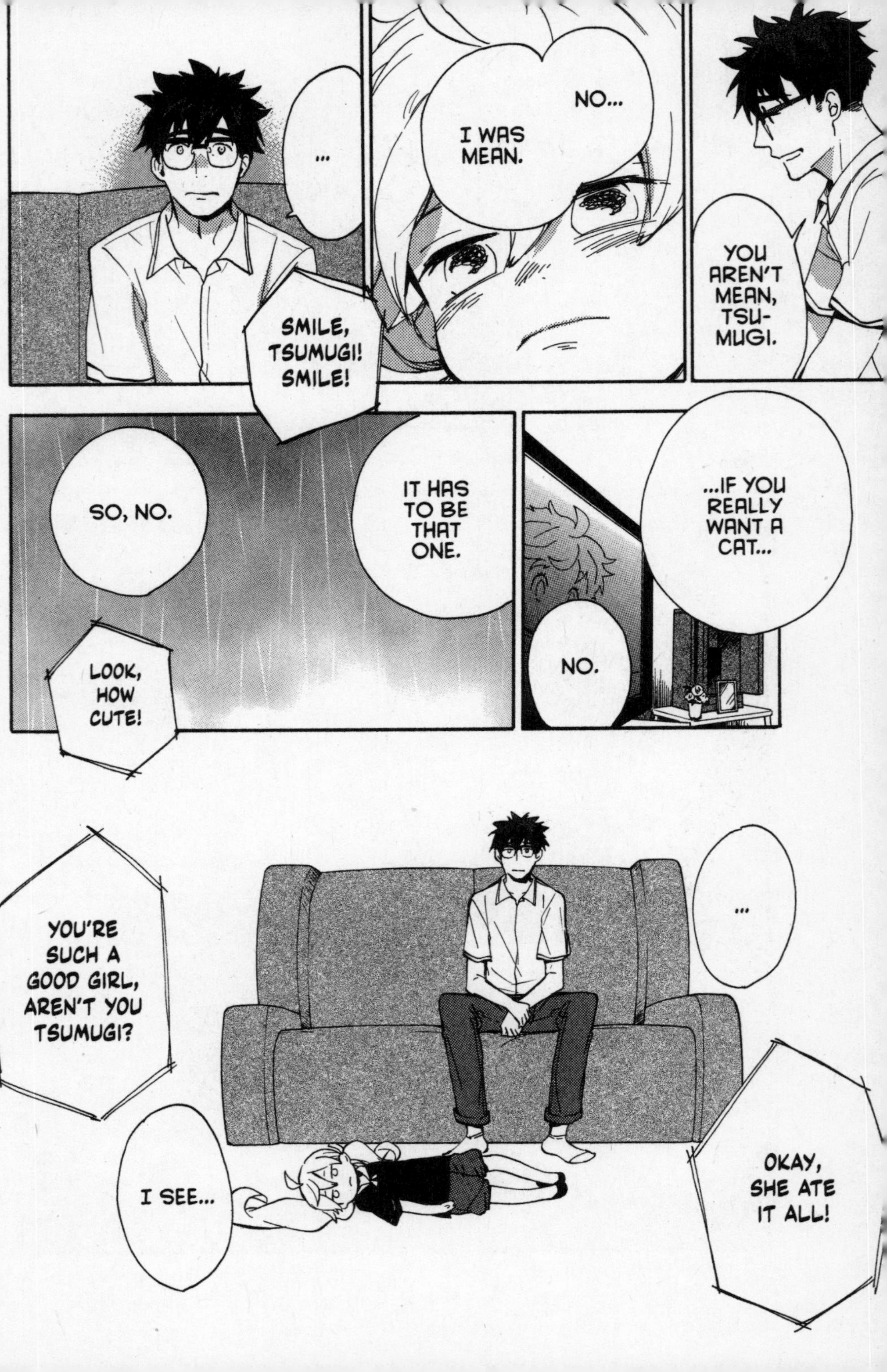
YOU AREN'T MEAN, TSUMUGI.
NO... I WAS MEAN.
...
SMILE, TSUMUGI! SMILE!
...IF YOU REALLY WANT A CAT...
NO.
IT HAS TO BE THAT ONE.
SO, NO.
LOOK, HOW CUTE!
...
OKAY, SHE ATE IT ALL!
YOU'RE SUCH A GOOD GIRL, AREN'T YOU TSUMUGI?
I SEE...

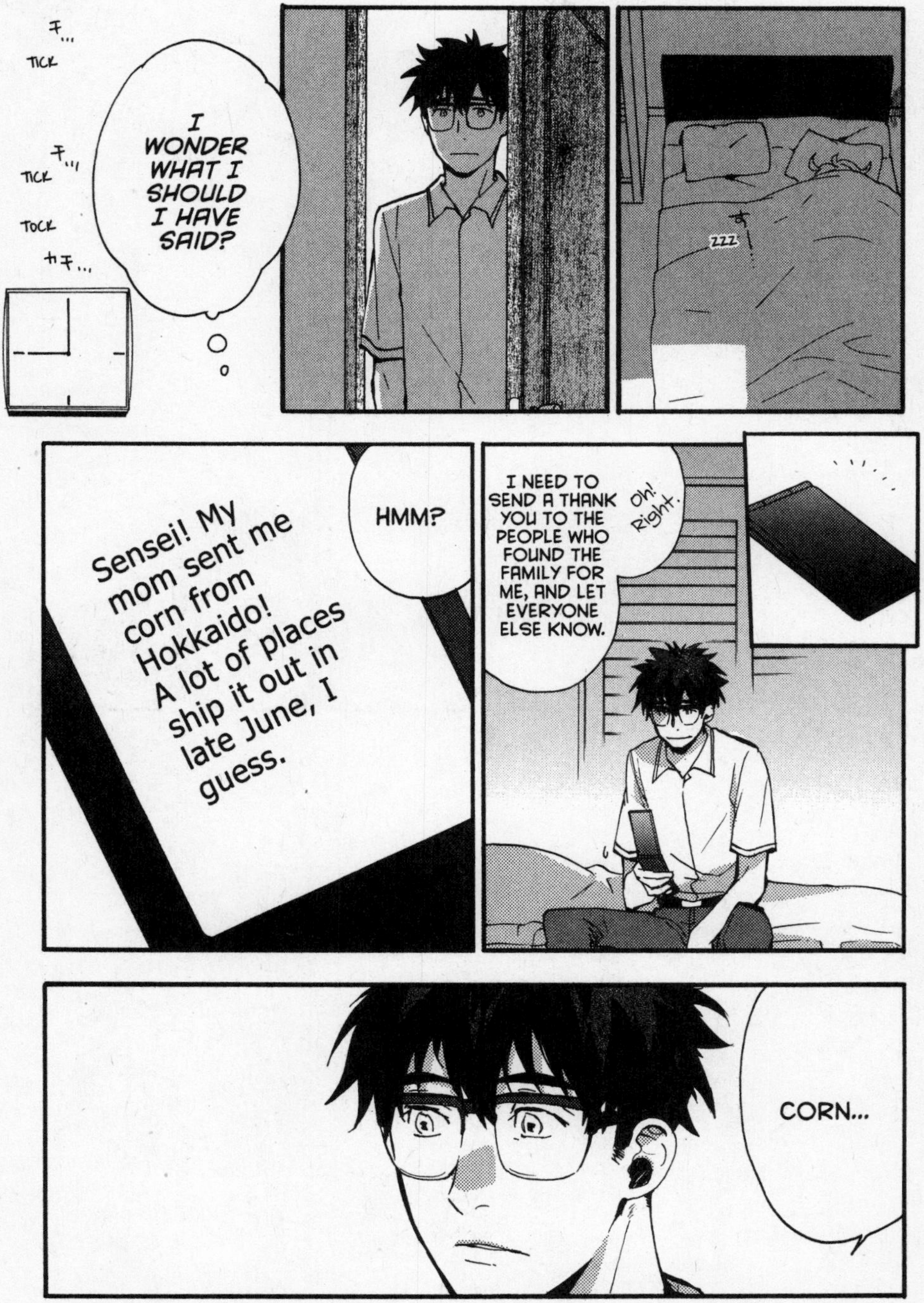
す
ZZZ
I WONDER WHAT I SHOULD I HAVE SAID?
チ...
TICK
チ...
TICK
TOCK
カチ...
Oh! Right.
I NEED TO SEND A THANK YOU TO THE PEOPLE WHO FOUND THE FAMILY FOR ME, AND LET EVERYONE ELSE KNOW.
HMM?
Sensei! My mom sent me corn from Hokkaido! A lot of places ship it out in late June, I guess.
CORN...

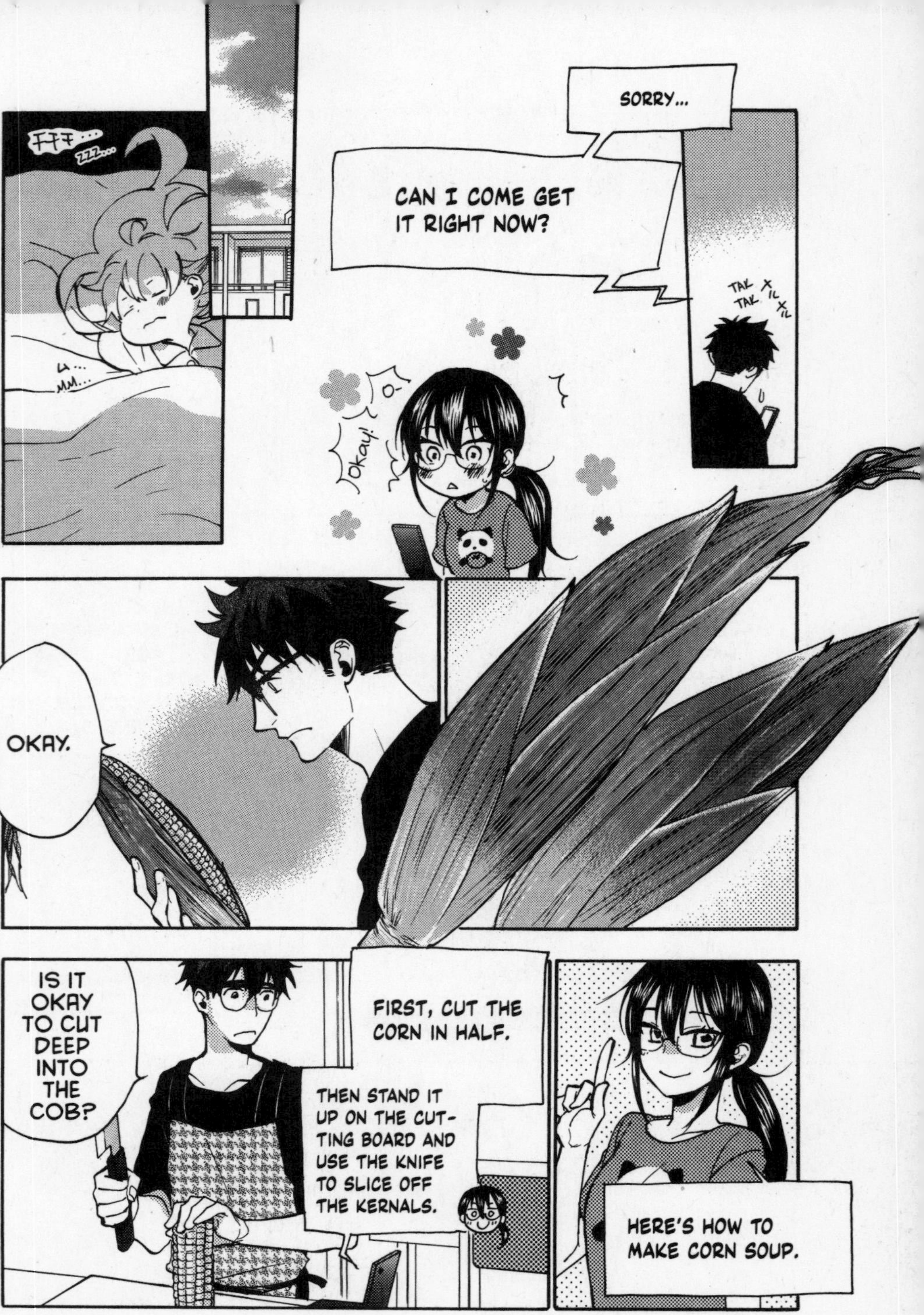
SORRY...
CAN I COME GET IT RIGHT NOW?
TAK TAK
O-
Okay!
zzz...
u... mm...
OKAY.
HERE'S HOW TO MAKE CORN SOUP.
FIRST, CUT THE CORN IN HALF.
THEN STAND IT UP ON THE CUTTING BOARD AND USE THE KNIFE TO SLICE OFF THE KERNALS.
IS IT OKAY TO CUT DEEP INTO THE COB?

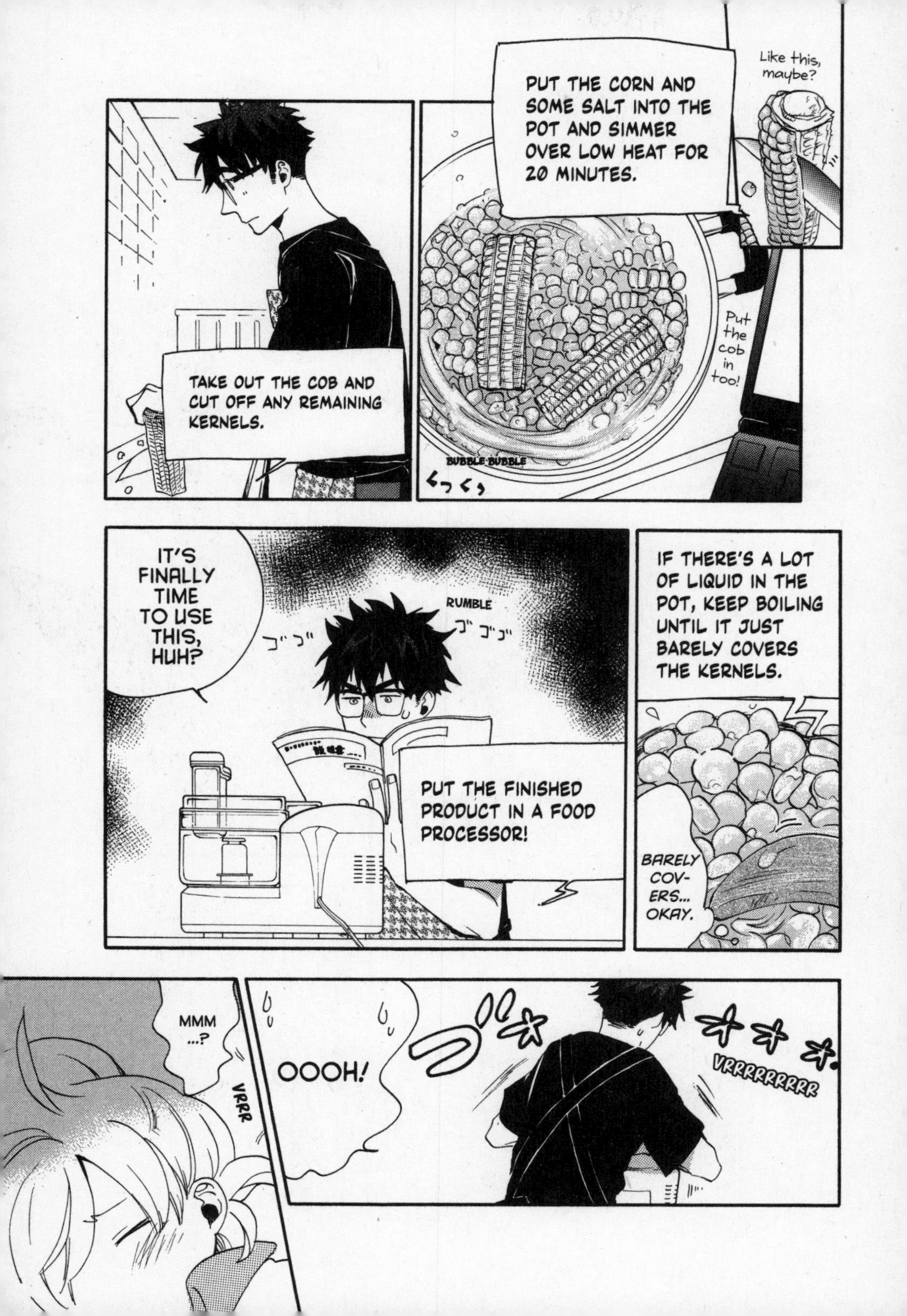
Like this, maybe?
PUT THE CORN AND SOME SALT INTO THE POT AND SIMMER OVER LOW HEAT FOR 20 MINUTES.
Put the cob in too!
BUBBLE BUBBLE
TAKE OUT THE COB AND CUT OFF ANY REMAINING KERNELS.
IF THERE'S A LOT OF LIQUID IN THE POT, KEEP BOILING UNTIL IT JUST BARELY COVERS THE KERNELS.
BARELY COV-ERS... OKAY.
IT'S FINALLY TIME TO USE THIS, HUH?
RUMBLE
PUT THE FINISHED PRODUCT IN A FOOD PROCESSOR!
OOOH!
VRRRRRRRRR
MMM ...?
VRRR

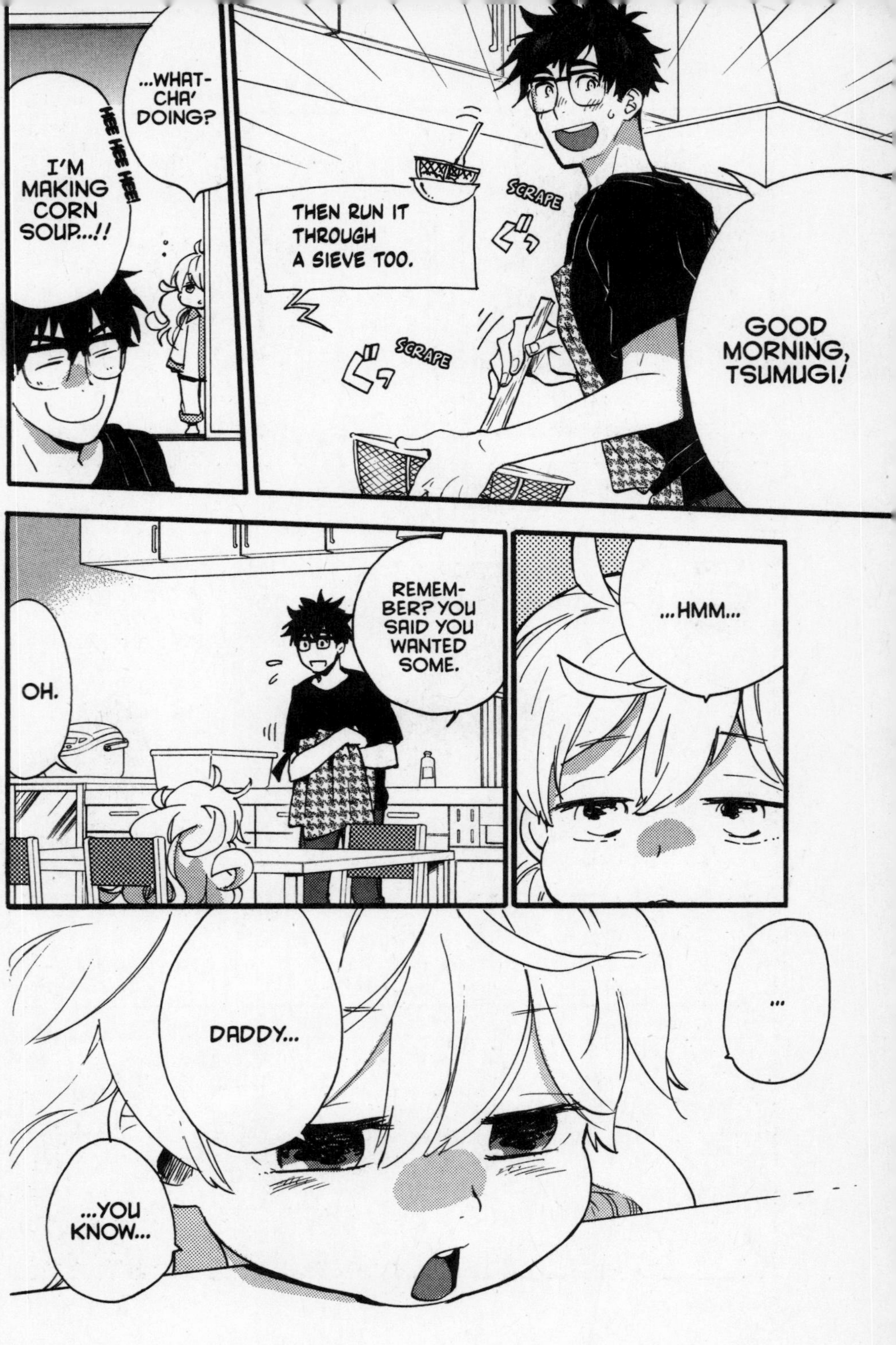
GOOD MORNING, TSUMUGI!
SCRAPE
THEN RUN IT THROUGH A SIEVE TOO.
SCRAPE
...WHAT-CHA' DOING?
HEE HEE HEE!
I'M MAKING CORN SOUP...!!
...HMM...
REMEM-BER? YOU SAID YOU WANTED SOME.
OH.
...
DADDY...
...YOU KNOW...

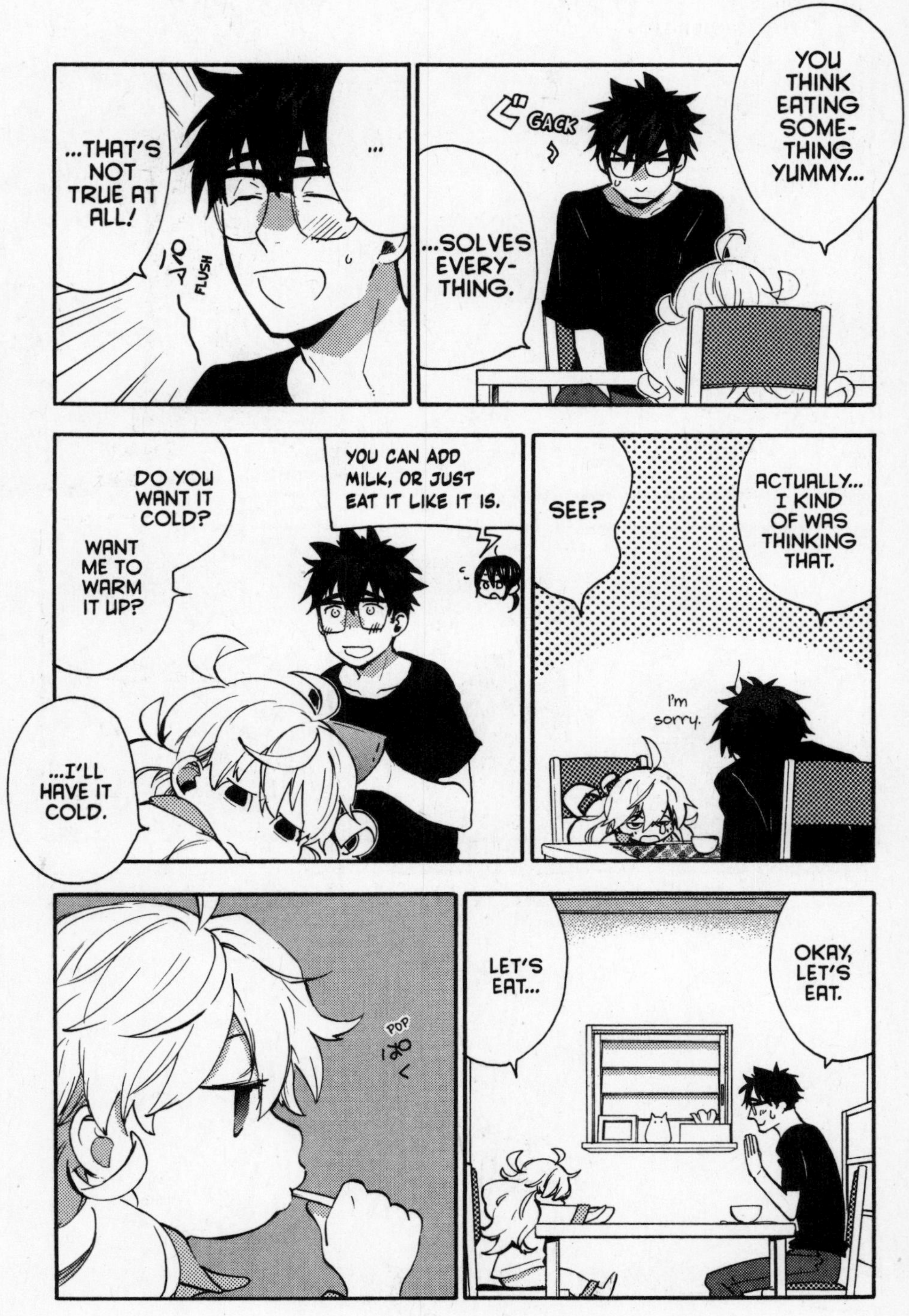
YOU THINK EATING SOME-THING YUMMY...
GACK
...SOLVES EVERY-THING.
...
...THAT'S NOT TRUE AT ALL!
FLUSH
ACTUALLY... I KIND OF WAS THINKING THAT.
SEE?
I'm sorry.
YOU CAN ADD MILK, OR JUST EAT IT LIKE IT IS.
DO YOU WANT IT COLD?
WANT ME TO WARM IT UP?
...I'LL HAVE IT COLD.
OKAY, LET'S EAT.
LET'S EAT...
POP

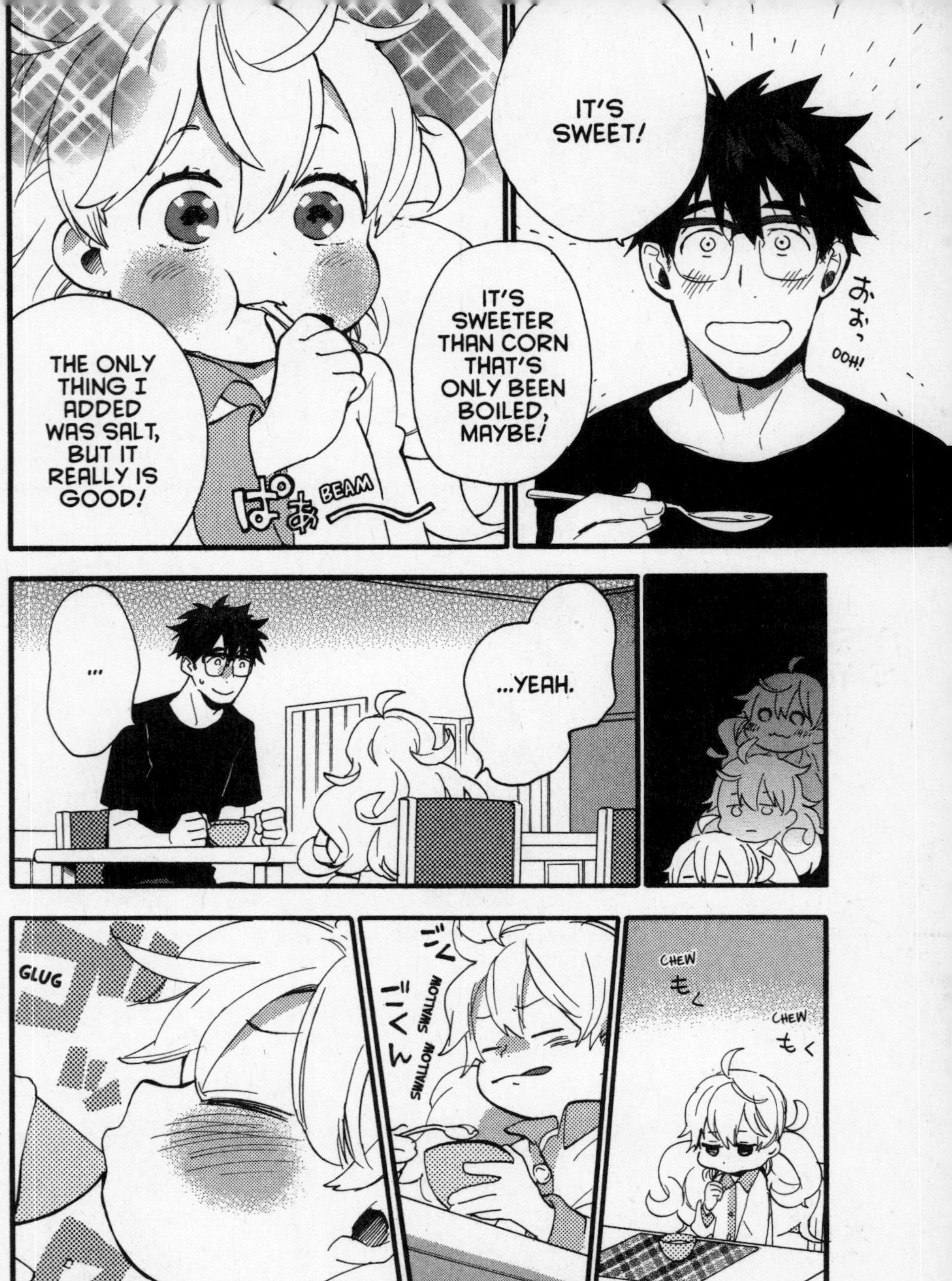
IT'S SWEET!
おぉ、
OOH!
IT'S SWEETER THAN CORN THAT'S ONLY BEEN BOILED, MAYBE!
THE ONLY THING I ADDED WAS SALT, BUT IT REALLY IS GOOD!
ぱぁ
BEAM
...YEAH.
...
CHEW
もく
CHEW
もく
ごく
SWALLOW
ごくん
SWALLOW
GLUG
GLUG

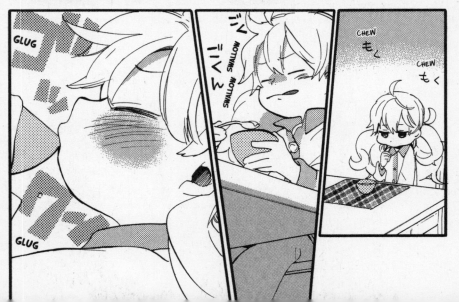

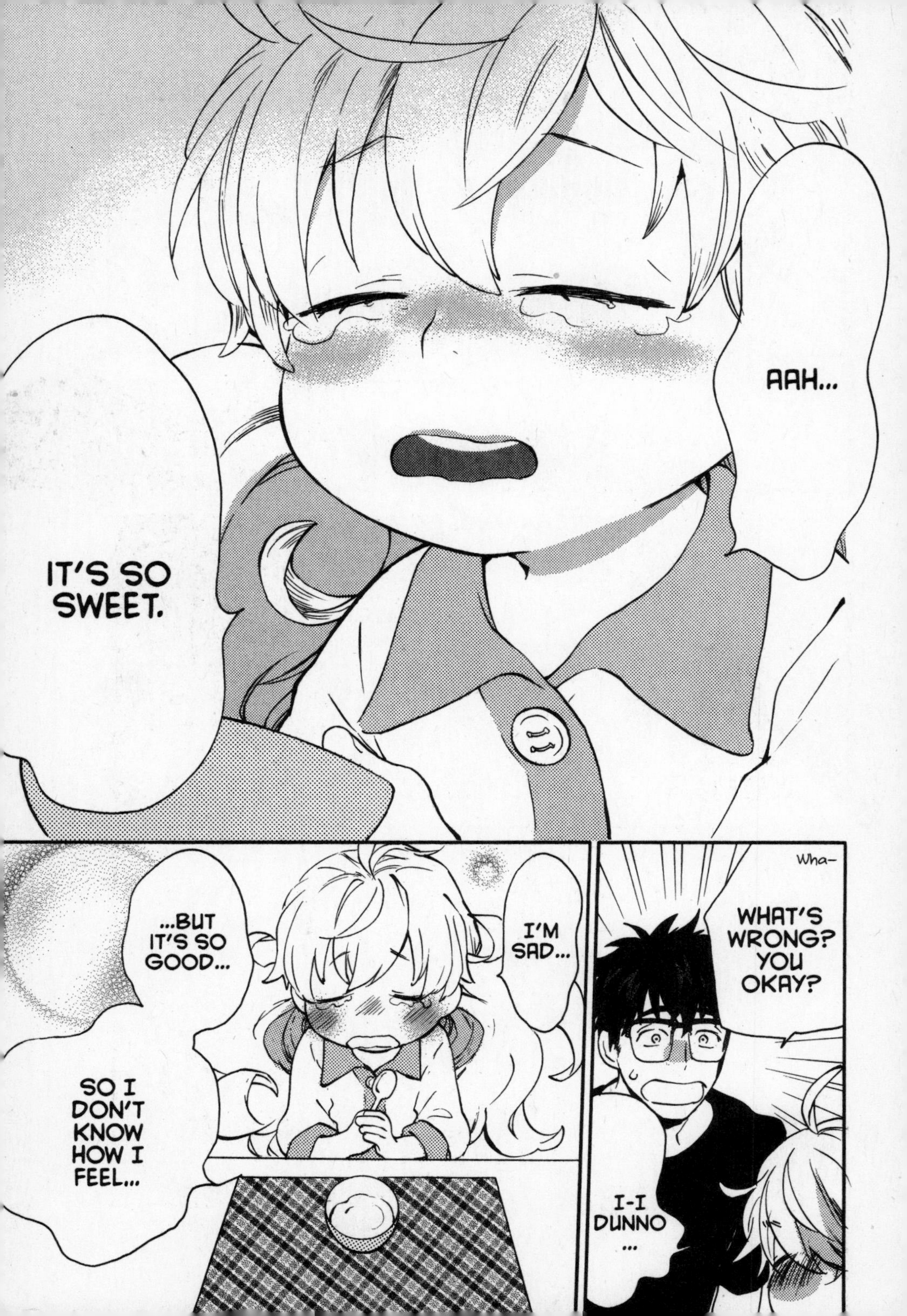
AAH...
IT'S SO SWEET.
Wha-
WHAT'S WRONG? YOU OKAY?
I-I DUNNO ...
I'M SAD...
...BUT IT'S SO GOOD...
SO I DON'T KNOW HOW I FEEL...

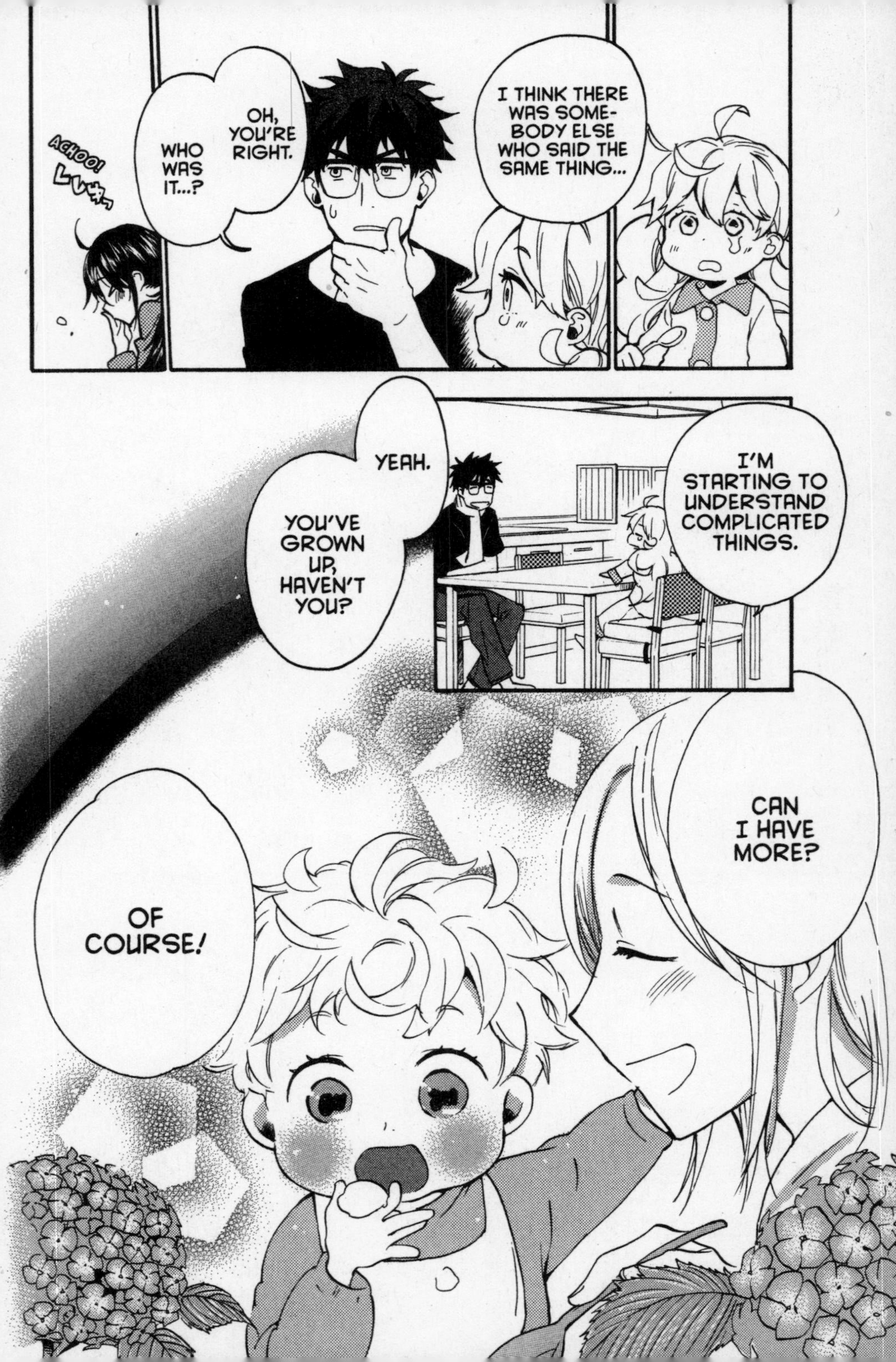
I THINK THERE WAS SOME-BODY ELSE WHO SAID THE SAME THING...
OH, YOU'RE RIGHT.
WHO WAS IT...?
ACHOO!
I'M STARTING TO UNDERSTAND COMPLICATED THINGS.
YEAH.
YOU'VE GROWN UP, HAVEN'T YOU?
CAN I HAVE MORE?
OF COURSE!

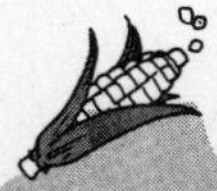

CORN SOUP

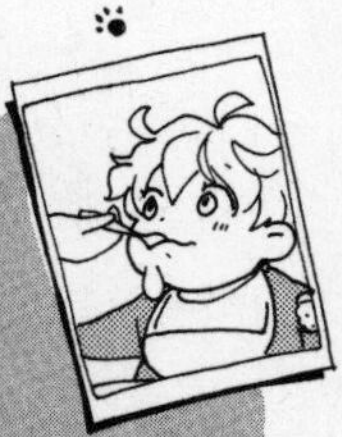

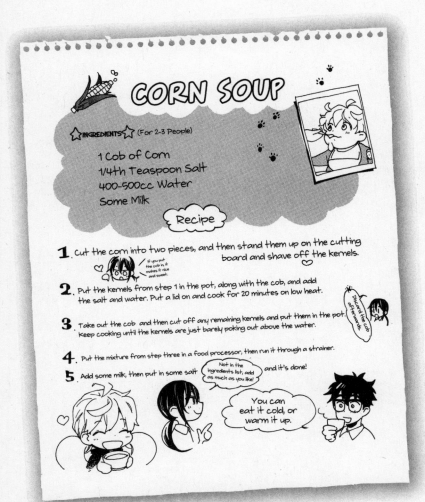

☆INGREDIENTS☆ (For 2-3 People)

1 Cob of Corn
1/4th Teaspoon Salt
400-500cc Water
Some Milk

Recipe

1. Cut the corn into two pieces, and then stand them up on the cutting board and shave off the kernels.

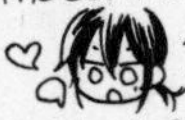
If you put the cob in, it makes it nice and sweet.

2. Put the kernels from step 1 in the pot, along with the cob, and add the salt and water. Put a lid on and cook for 20 minutes on low heat.

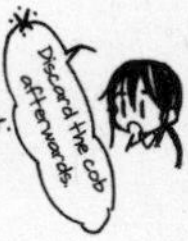
Discard the cob afterwards.

3. Take out the cob and then cut off any remaining kernels and put them in the pot. Keep cooking until the kernels are just barely poking out above the water.

4. Put the mixture from step three in a food processor, then run it through a strainer.

5. Add some milk, then put in some salt (Not in the ingredients list, add as much as you like!) and it's done!

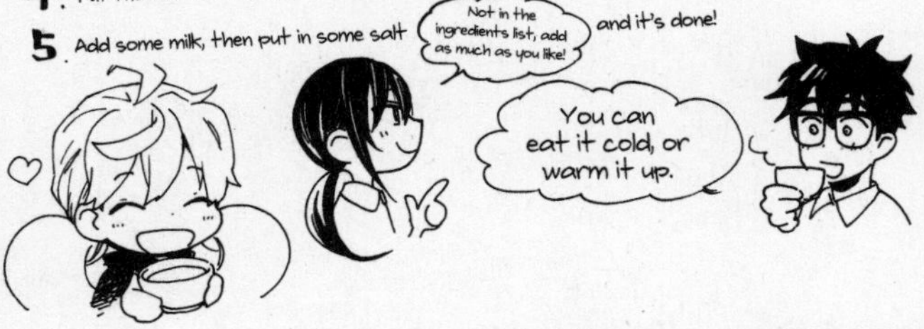
You can eat it cold, or warm it up.

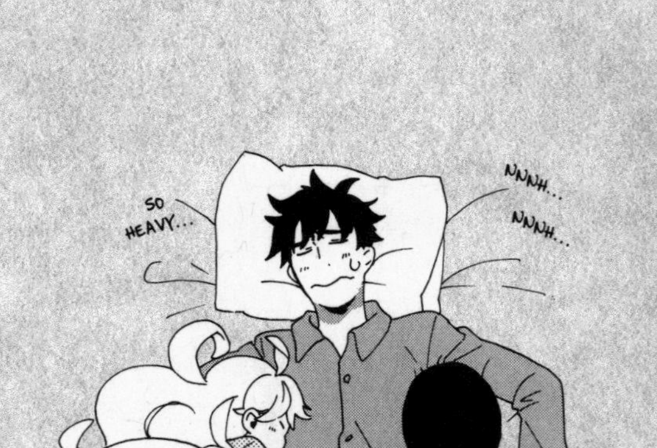
SO HEAVY...
NNNH...
NNNH...

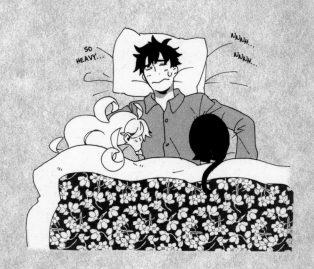

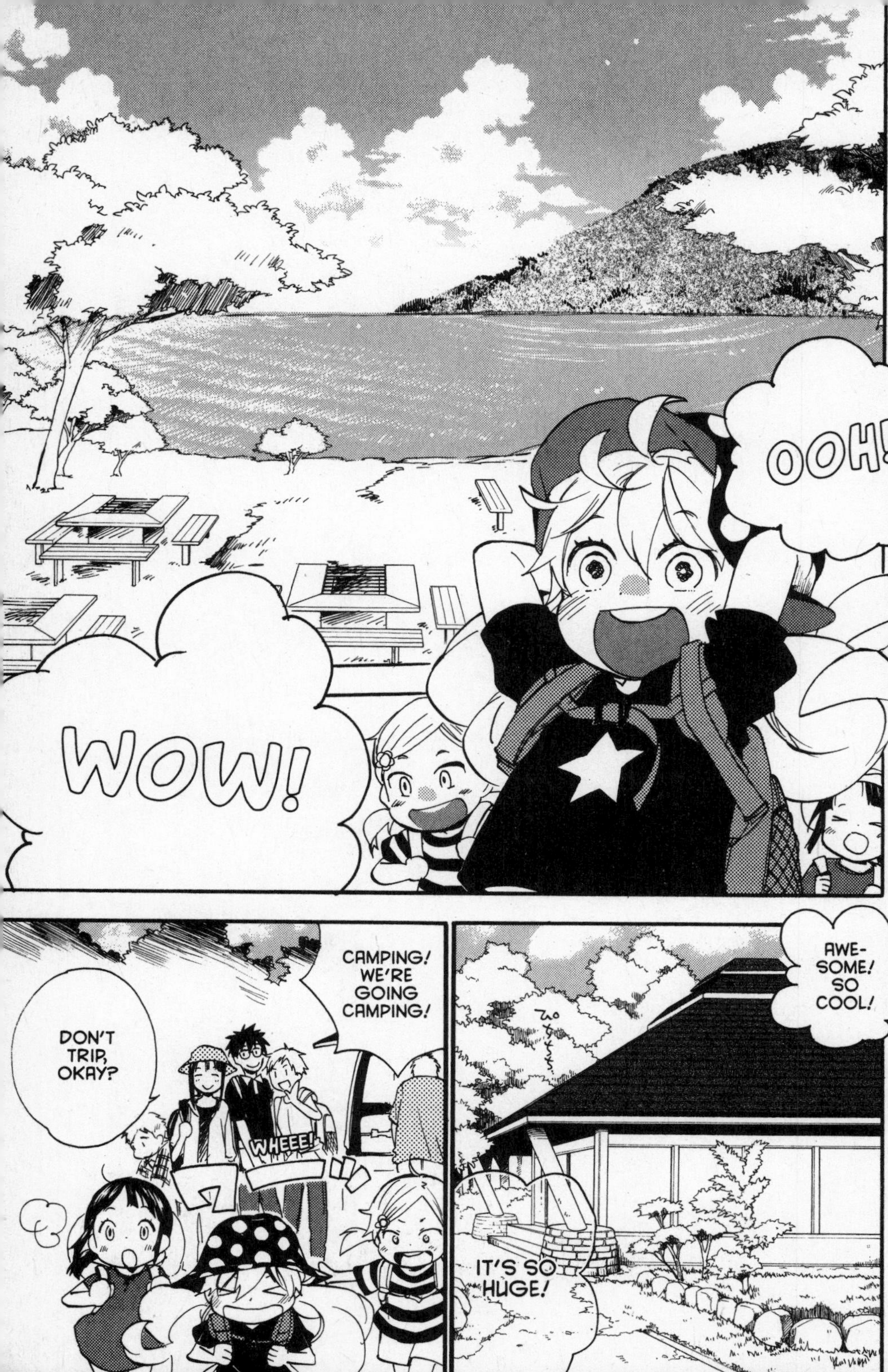
OOH!
WOW!
AWE-SOME! SO COOL!
IT'S SO HUGE!
CAMPING! WE'RE GOING CAMPING!
DON'T TRIP, OKAY?
WHEEE!

Chapter 27: Camping Bread and the Magical Girls

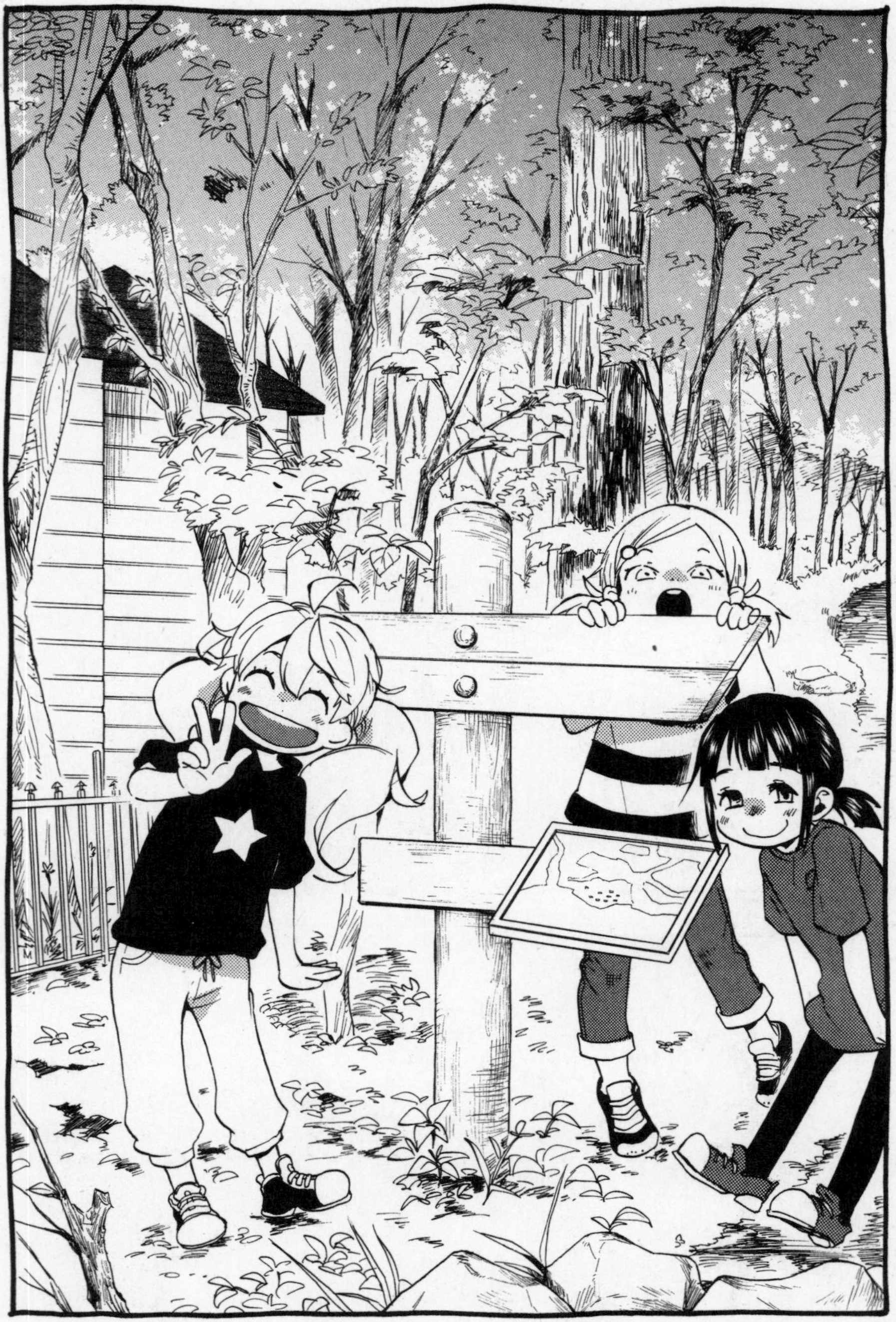

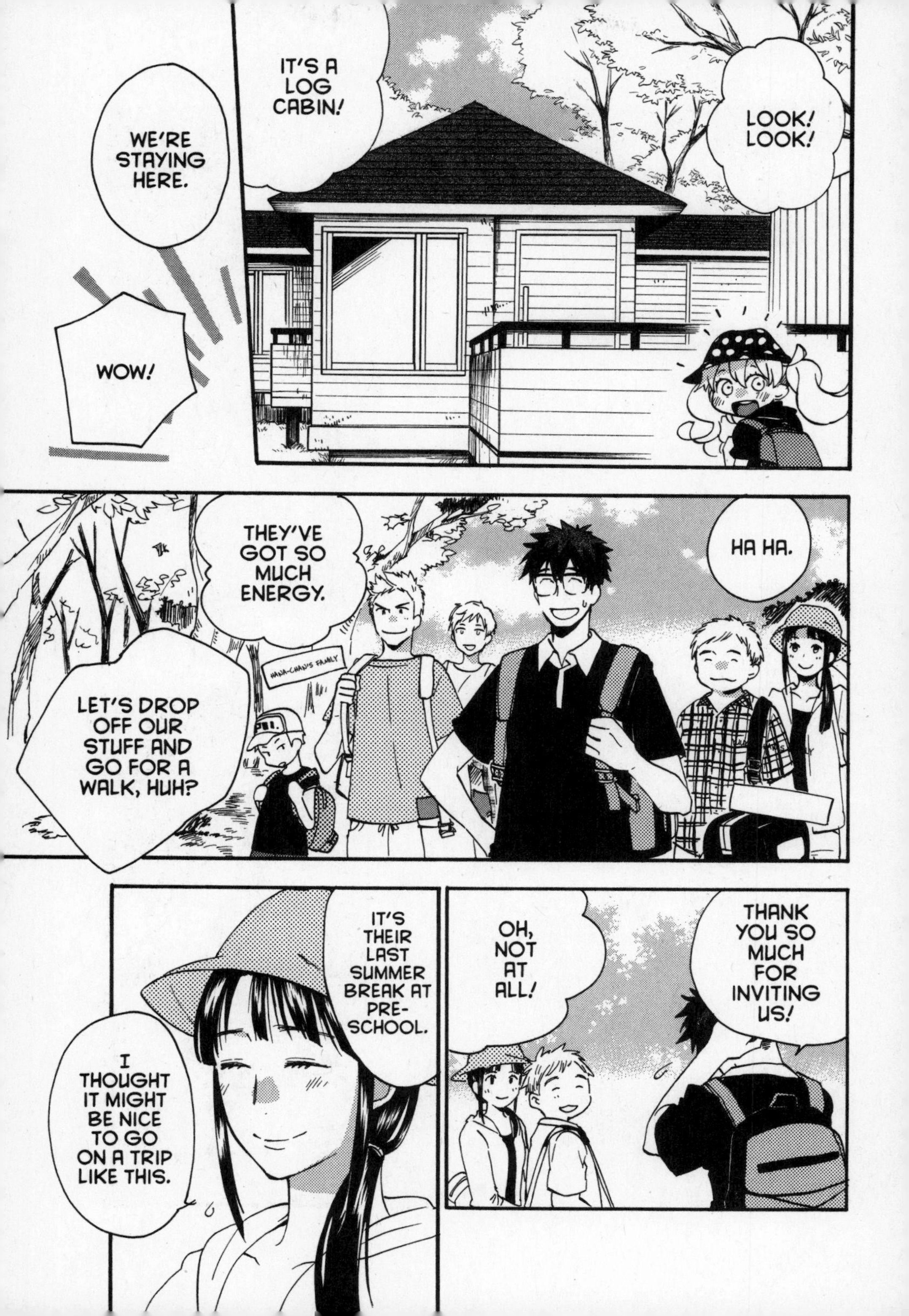
LOOK! LOOK!
IT'S A LOG CABIN!
WE'RE STAYING HERE.
WOW!
HA HA.
THEY'VE GOT SO MUCH ENERGY.
HANA-CHAN'S FAMILY
LET'S DROP OFF OUR STUFF AND GO FOR A WALK, HUH?
THANK YOU SO MUCH FOR INVITING US!
OH, NOT AT ALL!
IT'S THEIR LAST SUMMER BREAK AT PRE-SCHOOL.
I THOUGHT IT MIGHT BE NICE TO GO ON A TRIP LIKE THIS.

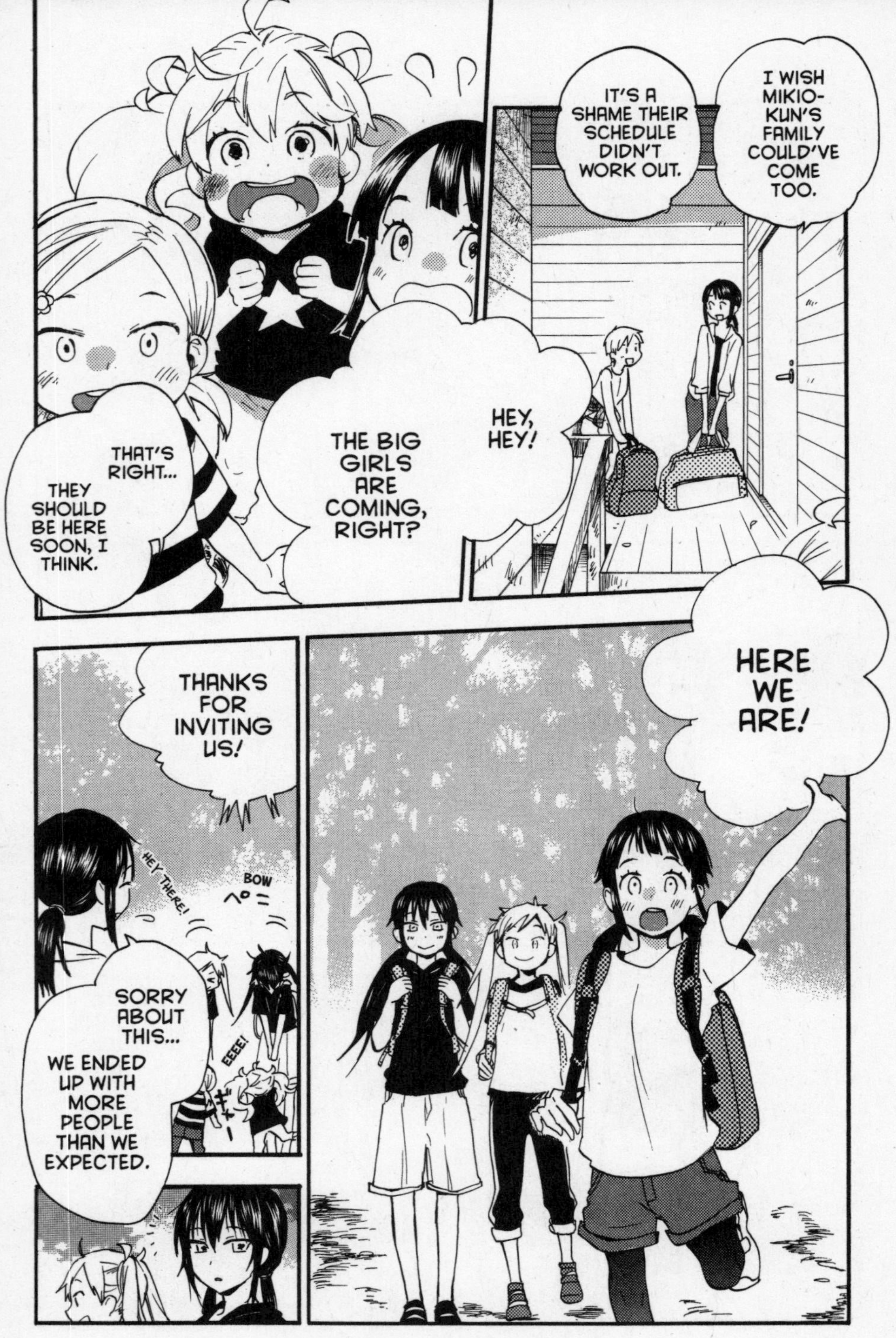
I WISH MIKIO-KUN'S FAMILY COULD'VE COME TOO.
IT'S A SHAME THEIR SCHEDULE DIDN'T WORK OUT.
HEY, HEY!
THE BIG GIRLS ARE COMING, RIGHT?
THAT'S RIGHT... THEY SHOULD BE HERE SOON, I THINK.
HERE WE ARE!
THANKS FOR INVITING US!
HEY THERE!
BOW
EEEE!
SORRY ABOUT THIS... WE ENDED UP WITH MORE PEOPLE THAN WE EXPECTED.

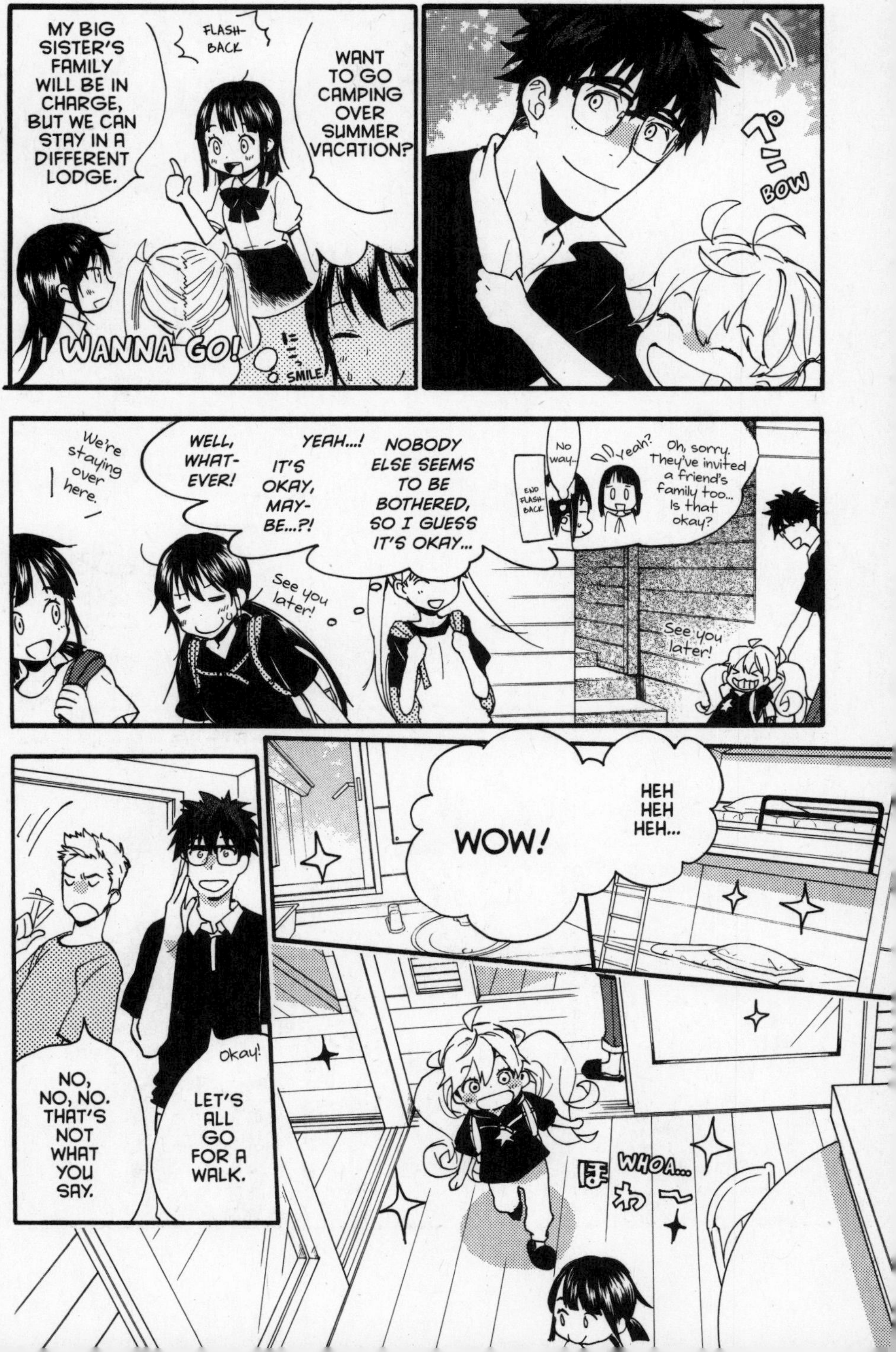
BOW
FLASH-BACK
WANT TO GO CAMPING OVER SUMMER VACATION?
MY BIG SISTER'S FAMILY WILL BE IN CHARGE, BUT WE CAN STAY IN A DIFFERENT LODGE.
I WANNA GO!
SMILE
Oh, sorry. They've invited a friend's family too... Is that okay?
Yeah?
No way...
END FLASH-BACK
See you later!
NOBODY ELSE SEEMS TO BE BOTHERED, SO I GUESS IT'S OKAY...
YEAH...!
IT'S OKAY, MAY-BE...?!
WELL, WHAT-EVER!
See you later!
We're staying over here.
HEH HEH HEH...
WOW!
WHOA...
ほわ～
Okay!
LET'S ALL GO FOR A WALK.
NO, NO, NO. THAT'S NOT WHAT YOU SAY.

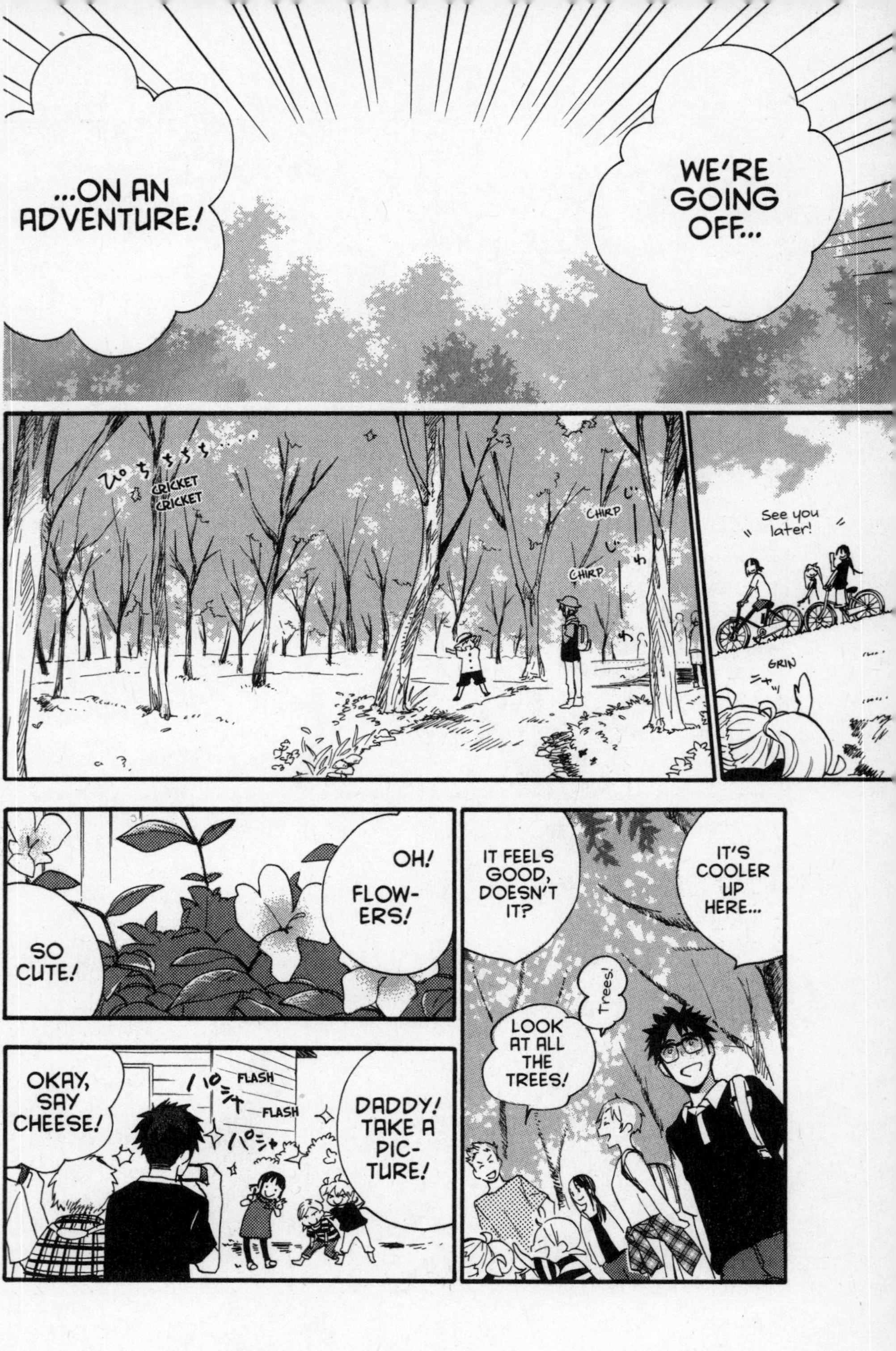
WE'RE GOING OFF...
...ON AN ADVENTURE!
See you later!
GRIN
CRICKET CRICKET
CHIRP
CHIRP
IT'S COOLER UP HERE...
IT FEELS GOOD, DOESN'T IT?
Trees!
LOOK AT ALL THE TREES!
OH! FLOWERS!
SO CUTE!
DADDY! TAKE A PICTURE!
FLASH
FLASH
OKAY, SAY CHEESE!

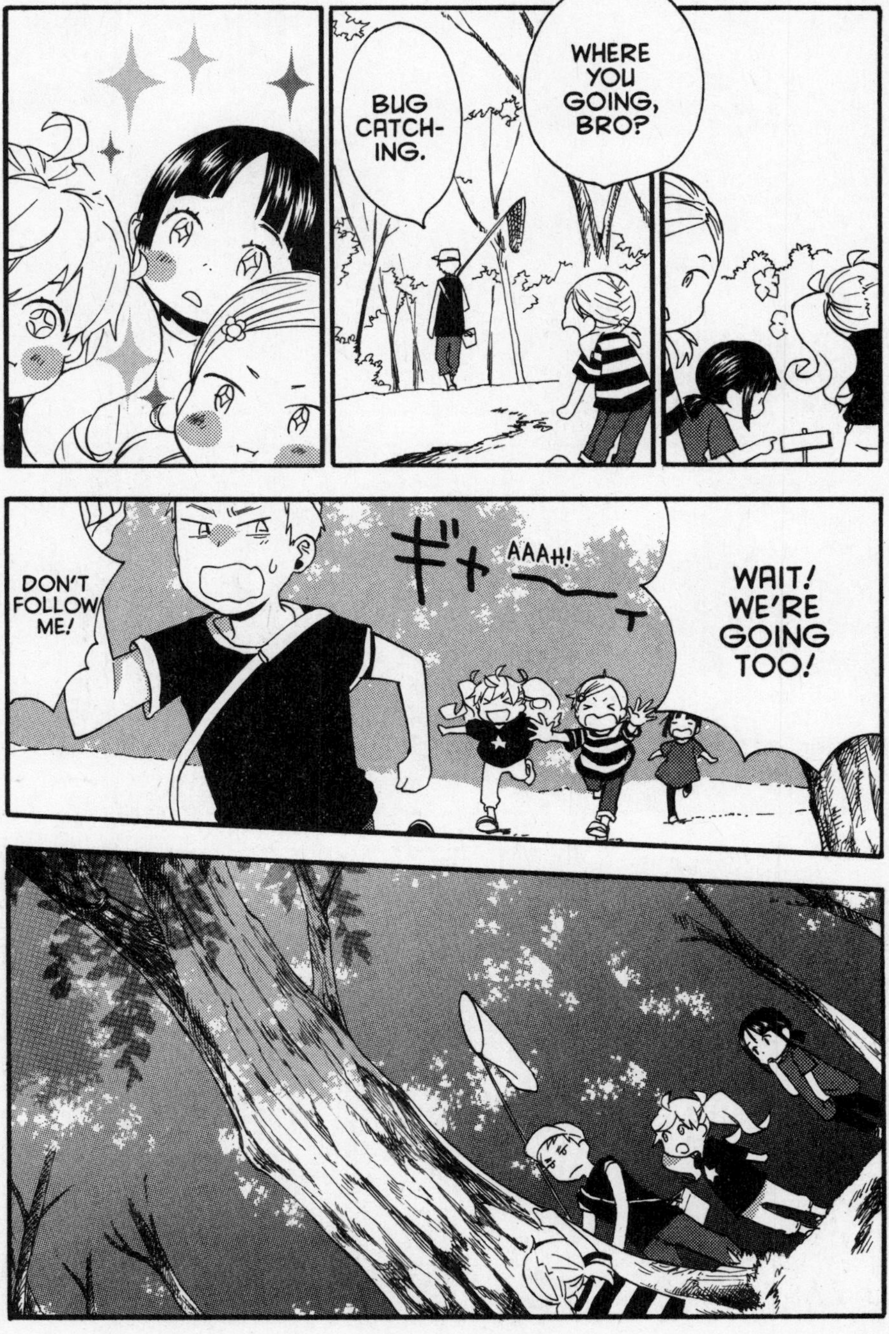
WHERE YOU GOING, BRO?
BUG CATCH-ING.
WAIT! WE'RE GOING TOO!
ギャ～～ッ
AAAH!
DON'T FOLLOW ME!

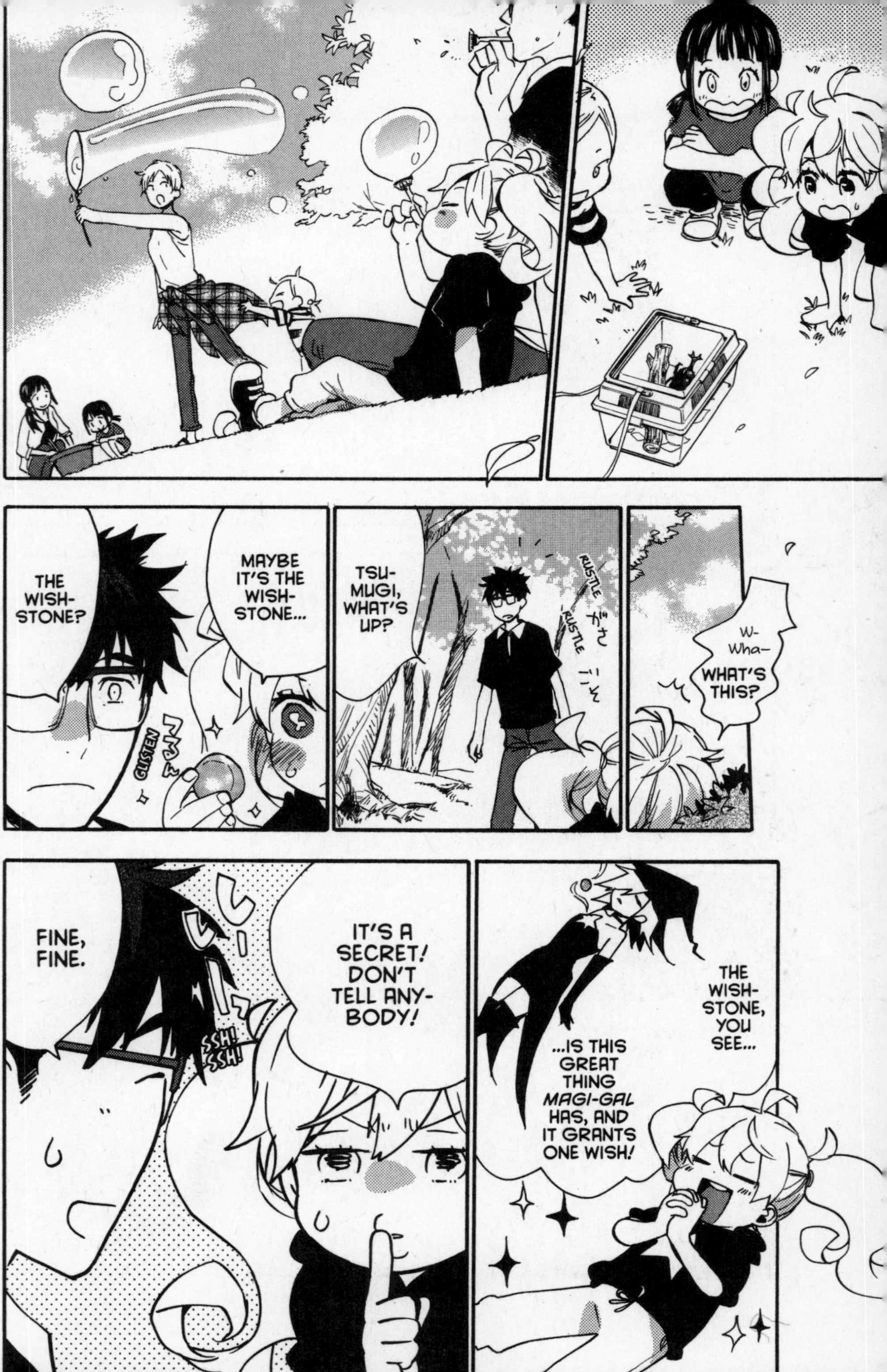
W-
Wha-
WHAT'S THIS?
RUSTLE
RUSTLE
TSU-MUGI, WHAT'S UP?
MAYBE IT'S THE WISH-STONE...
THE WISH-STONE?
GLISTEN
THE WISH-STONE, YOU SEE...
...IS THIS GREAT THING *MAGI-GAL* HAS, AND IT GRANTS ONE WISH!
IT'S A SECRET! DON'T TELL ANY-BODY!
SSH! SSH!
FINE, FINE.

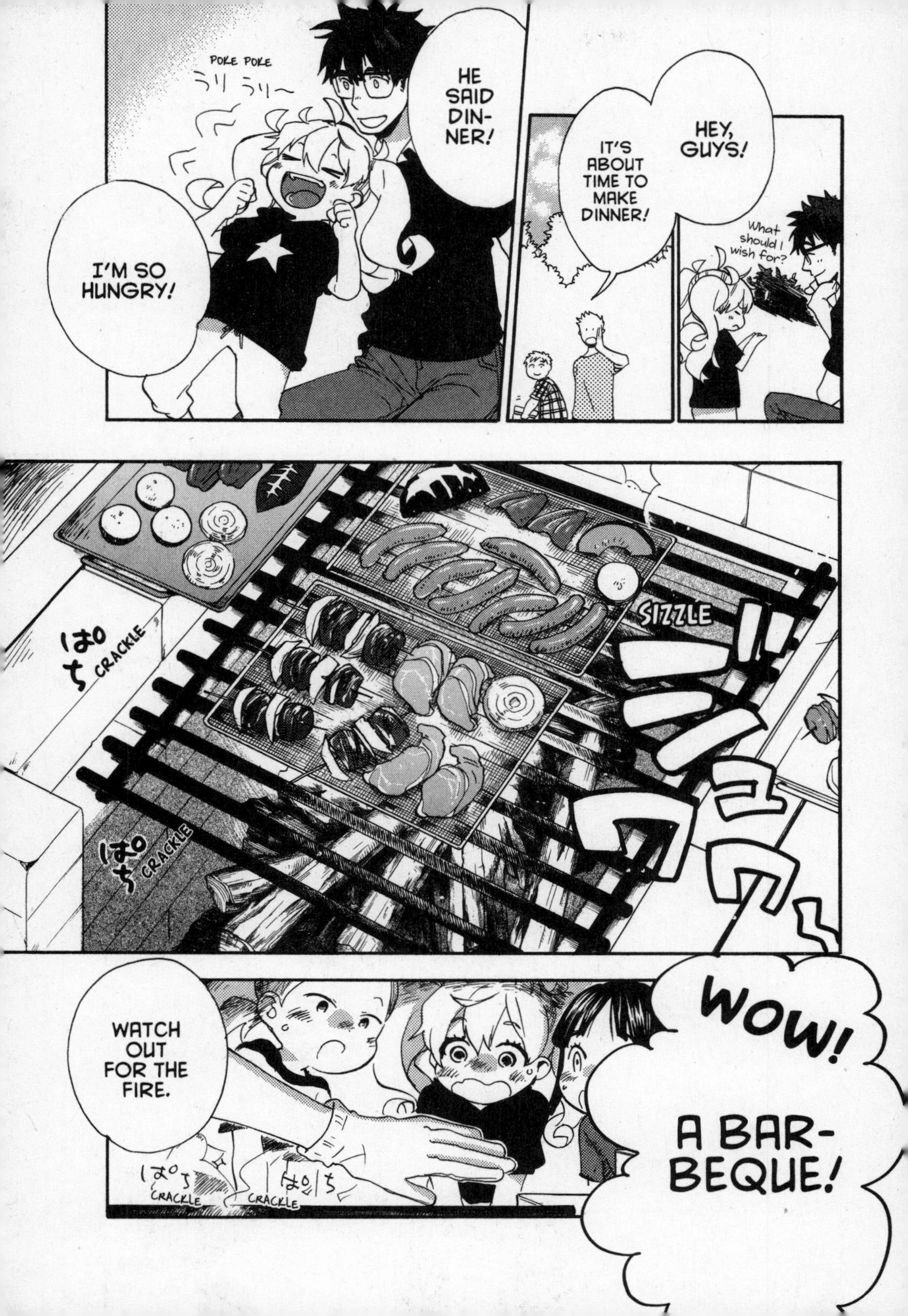
HEY, GUYS!
IT'S ABOUT TIME TO MAKE DINNER!
What should I wish for?
HE SAID DINNER!
POKE POKE
うりうりー
I'M SO HUNGRY!
SIZZLE
CRACKLE
CRACKLE
WOW!
A BARBEQUE!
WATCH OUT FOR THE FIRE.
CRACKLE
CRACKLE

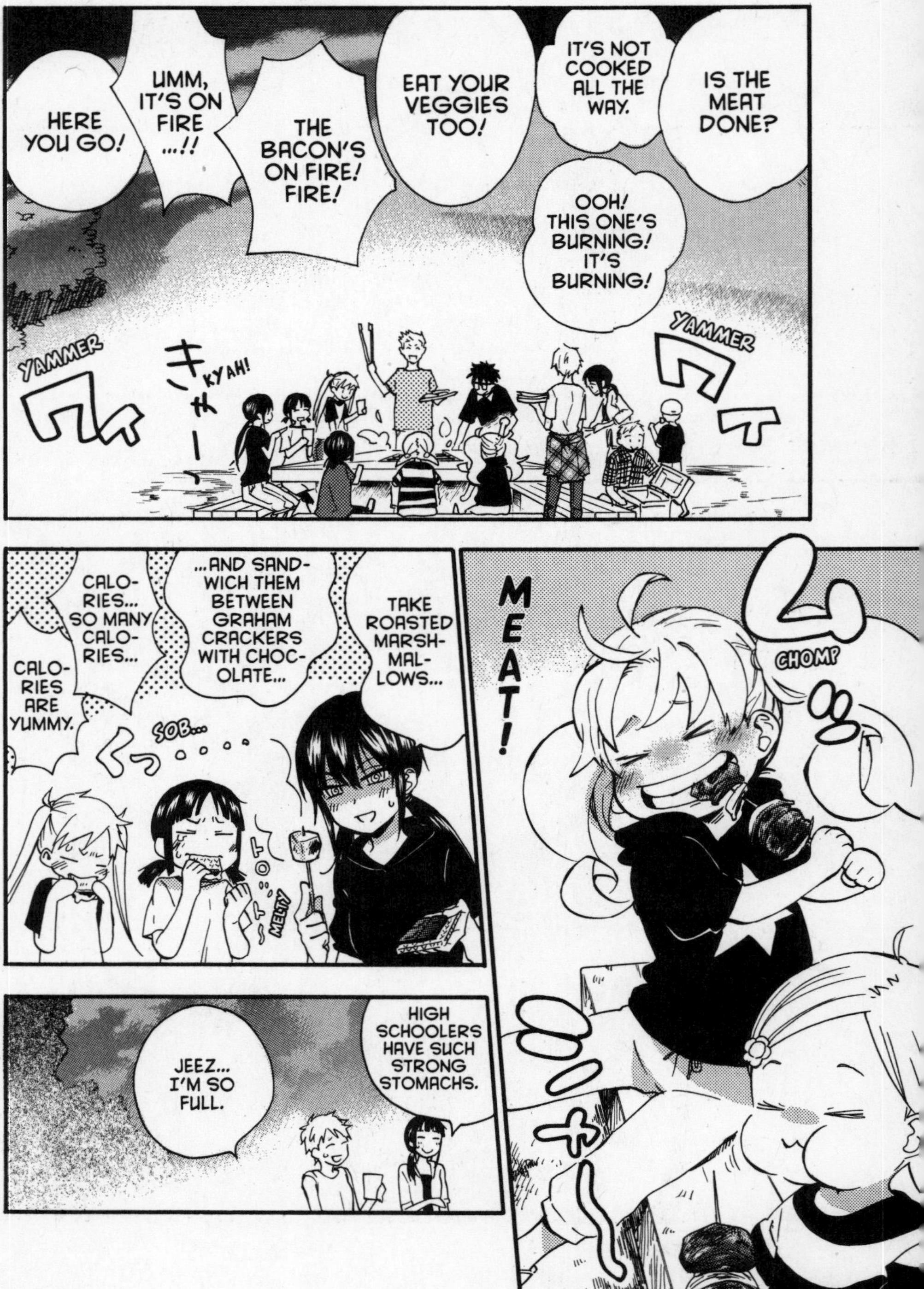
IS THE MEAT DONE?
IT'S NOT COOKED ALL THE WAY.
OOH! THIS ONE'S BURNING! IT'S BURNING!
EAT YOUR VEGGIES TOO!
THE BACON'S ON FIRE! FIRE!
UMM, IT'S ON FIRE ...!!
HERE YOU GO!
YAMMER
KYAH!
YAMMER
MEAT!
CHOMP
TAKE ROASTED MARSHMALLOWS...
...AND SANDWICH THEM BETWEEN GRAHAM CRACKERS WITH CHOCOLATE...
CALORIES... SO MANY CALORIES...
CALORIES ARE YUMMY.
SOB...
MELTY
HIGH SCHOOLERS HAVE SUCH STRONG STOMACHS.
JEEZ... I'M SO FULL.

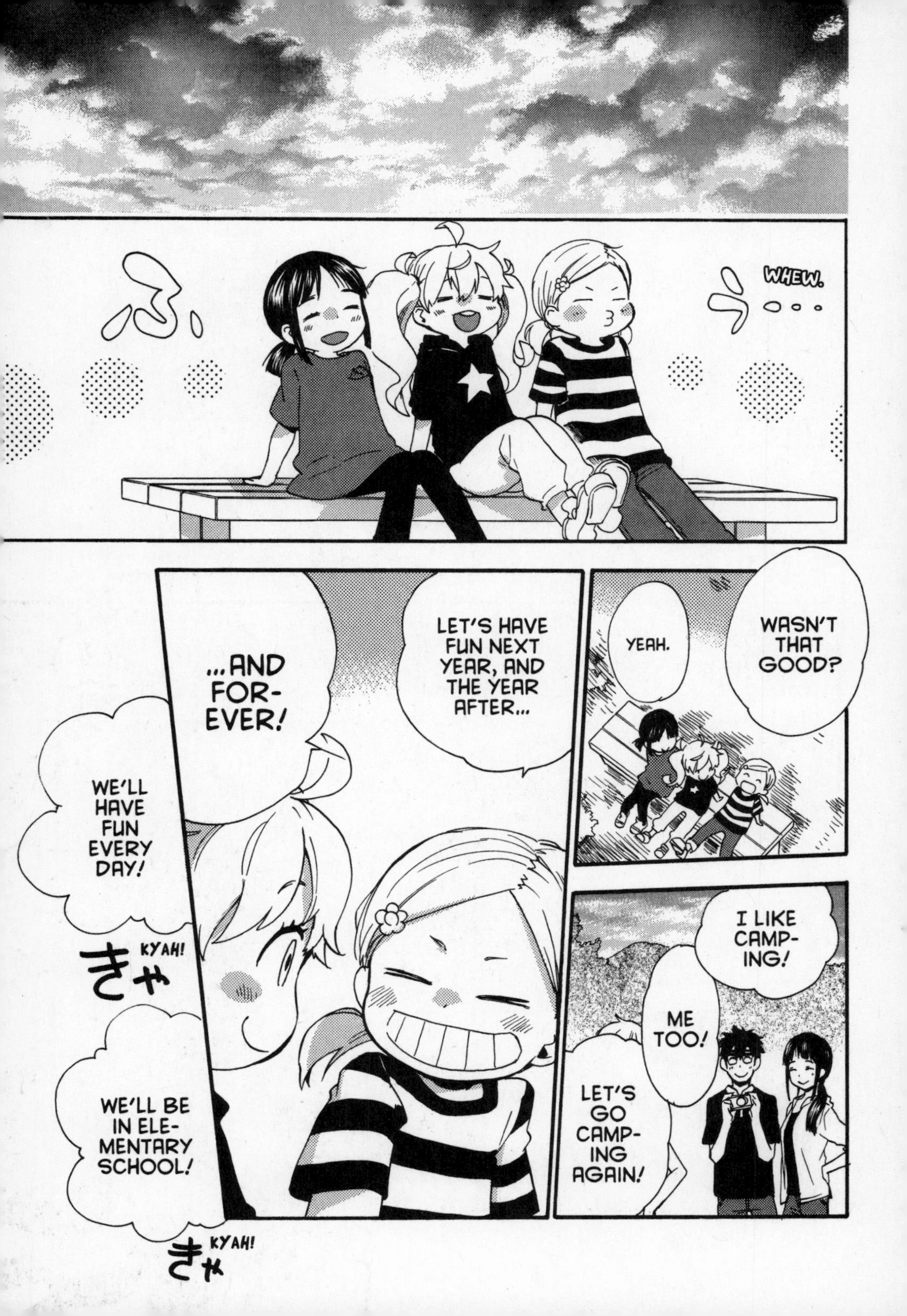

WHEW.
ふ う・・・
WASN'T THAT GOOD?
YEAH.
I LIKE CAMPING!
ME TOO!
LET'S GO CAMPING AGAIN!
LET'S HAVE FUN NEXT YEAR, AND THE YEAR AFTER...
...AND FOREVER!
WE'LL HAVE FUN EVERY DAY!
きゃ KYAH!
WE'LL BE IN ELEMENTARY SCHOOL!
きゃ KYAH!

I MIGHT BE GO-ING...
...TO A DIFFERENT SCHOOL...

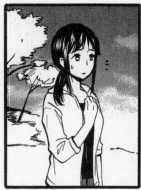

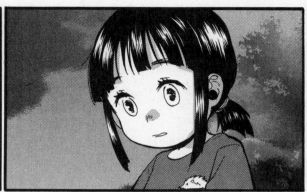

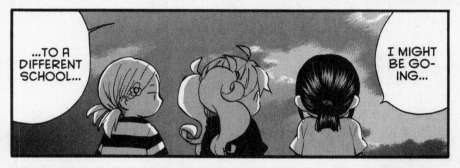

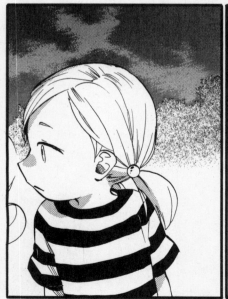

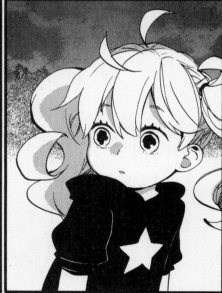

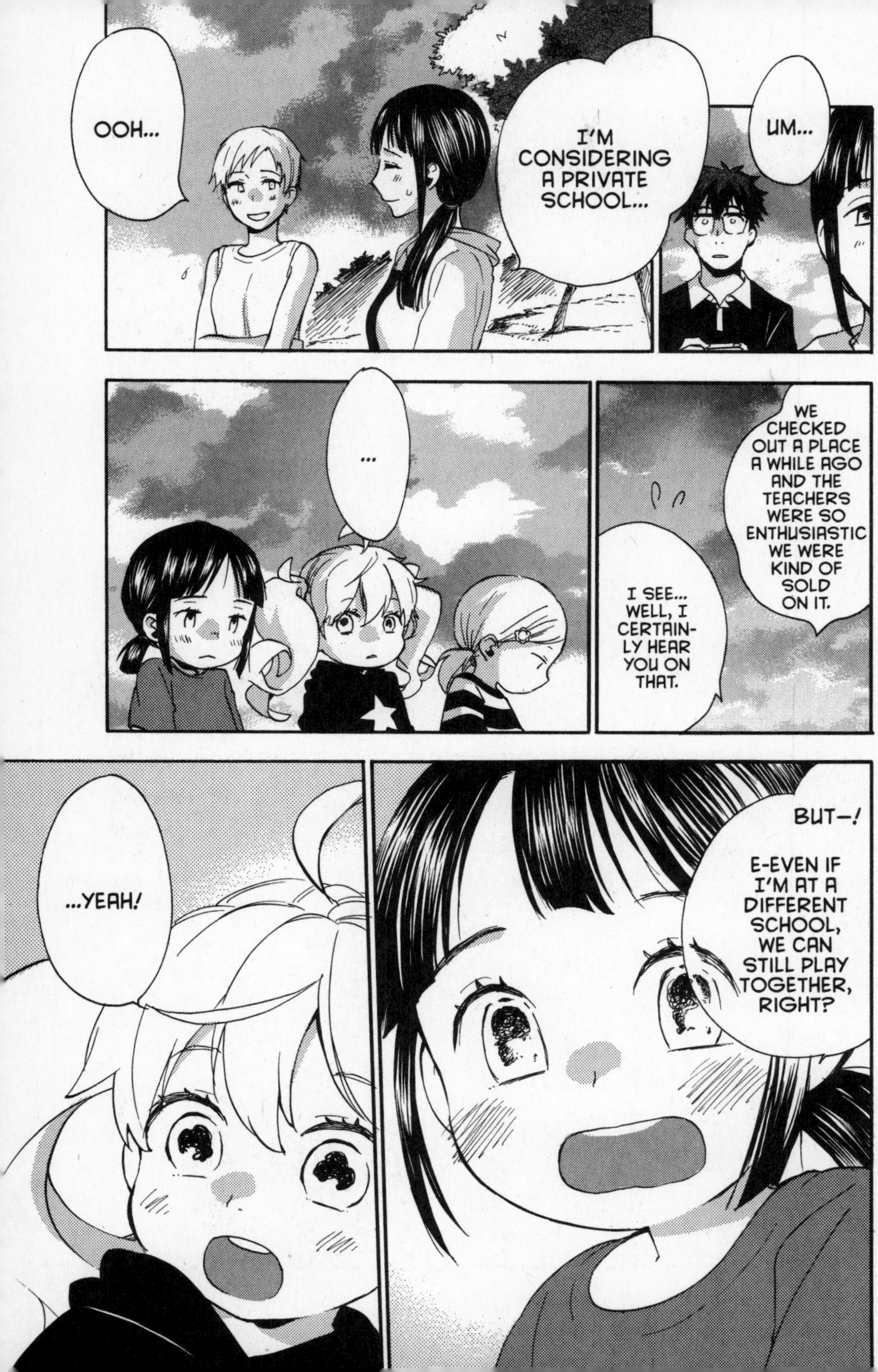
UM...
I'M CONSIDERING A PRIVATE SCHOOL...
OOH...
WE CHECKED OUT A PLACE A WHILE AGO AND THE TEACHERS WERE SO ENTHUSIASTIC WE WERE KIND OF SOLD ON IT.
I SEE... WELL, I CERTAINLY HEAR YOU ON THAT.
...
BUT—!
E-EVEN IF I'M AT A DIFFERENT SCHOOL, WE CAN STILL PLAY TOGETHER, RIGHT?
...YEAH!

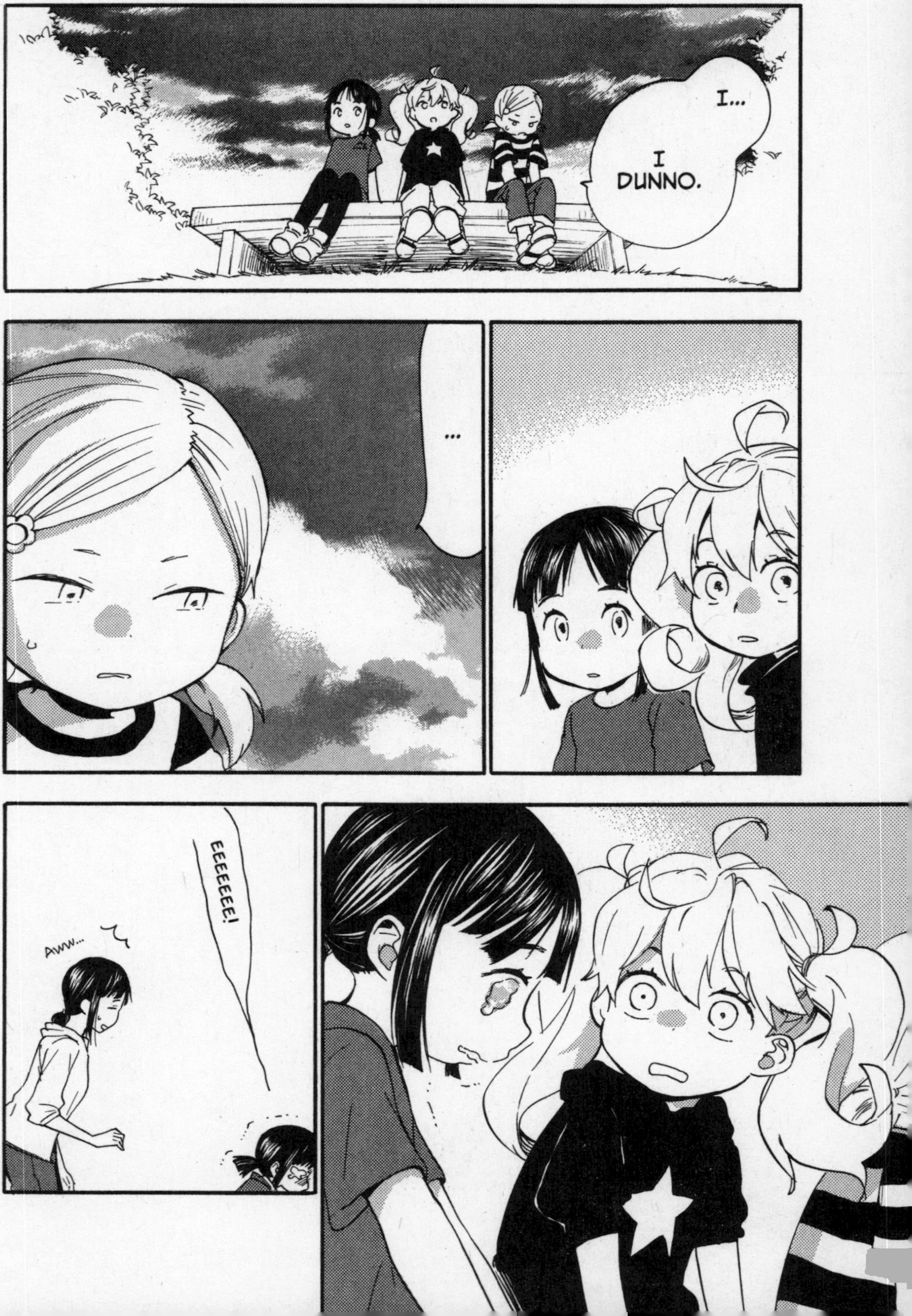
I...
I DUNNO.
...
EEEEEEE!
AWW...

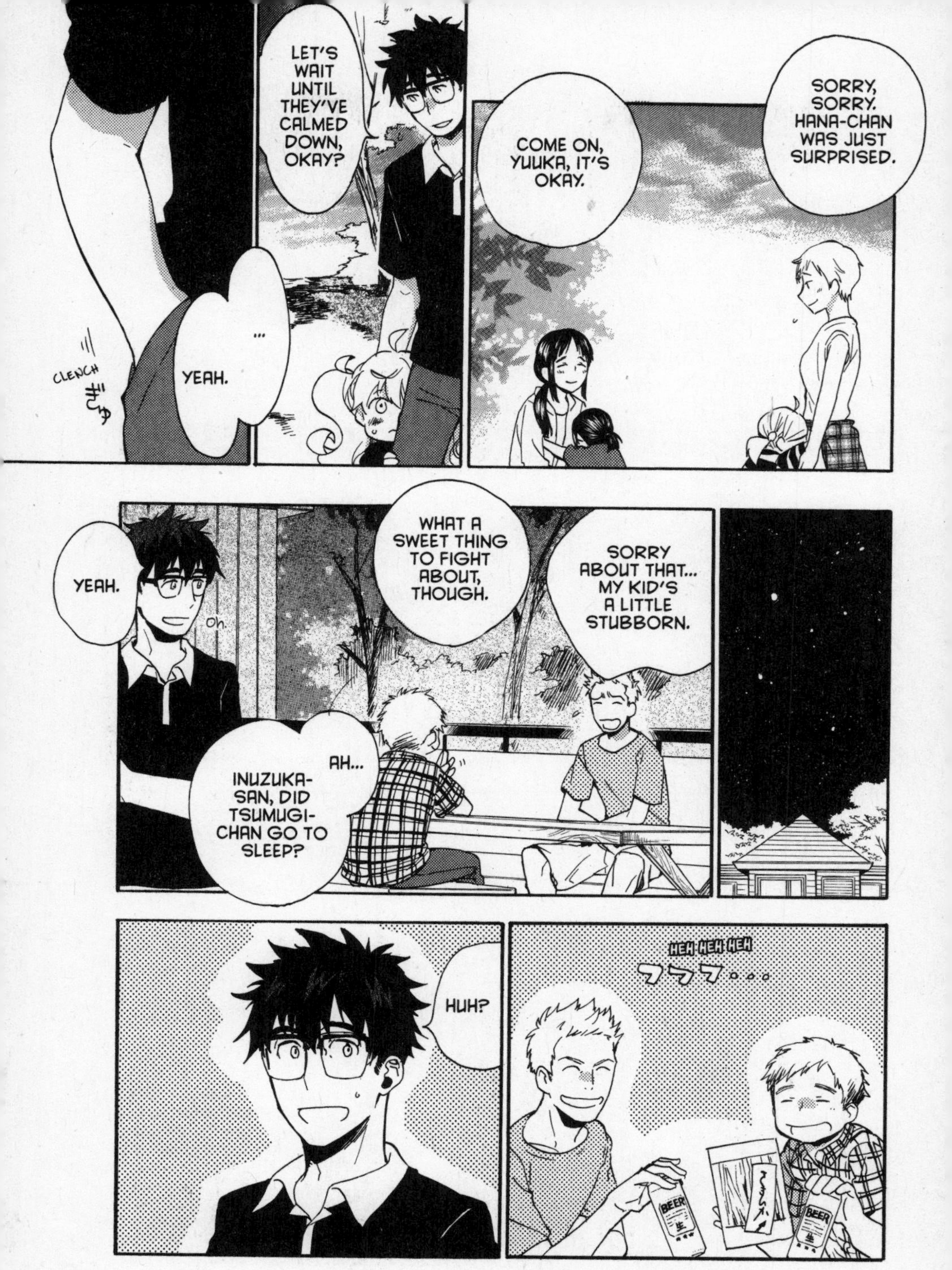
SORRY, SORRY. HANA-CHAN WAS JUST SURPRISED.
COME ON, YUUKA, IT'S OKAY.
LET'S WAIT UNTIL THEY'VE CALMED DOWN, OKAY?
... YEAH.
CLENCH
SORRY ABOUT THAT... MY KID'S A LITTLE STUBBORN.
WHAT A SWEET THING TO FIGHT ABOUT, THOUGH.
YEAH.
Oh.
AH... INUZUKA-SAN, DID TSUMUGI-CHAN GO TO SLEEP?
HEH HEH HEH
BEER
BEER
HUH?

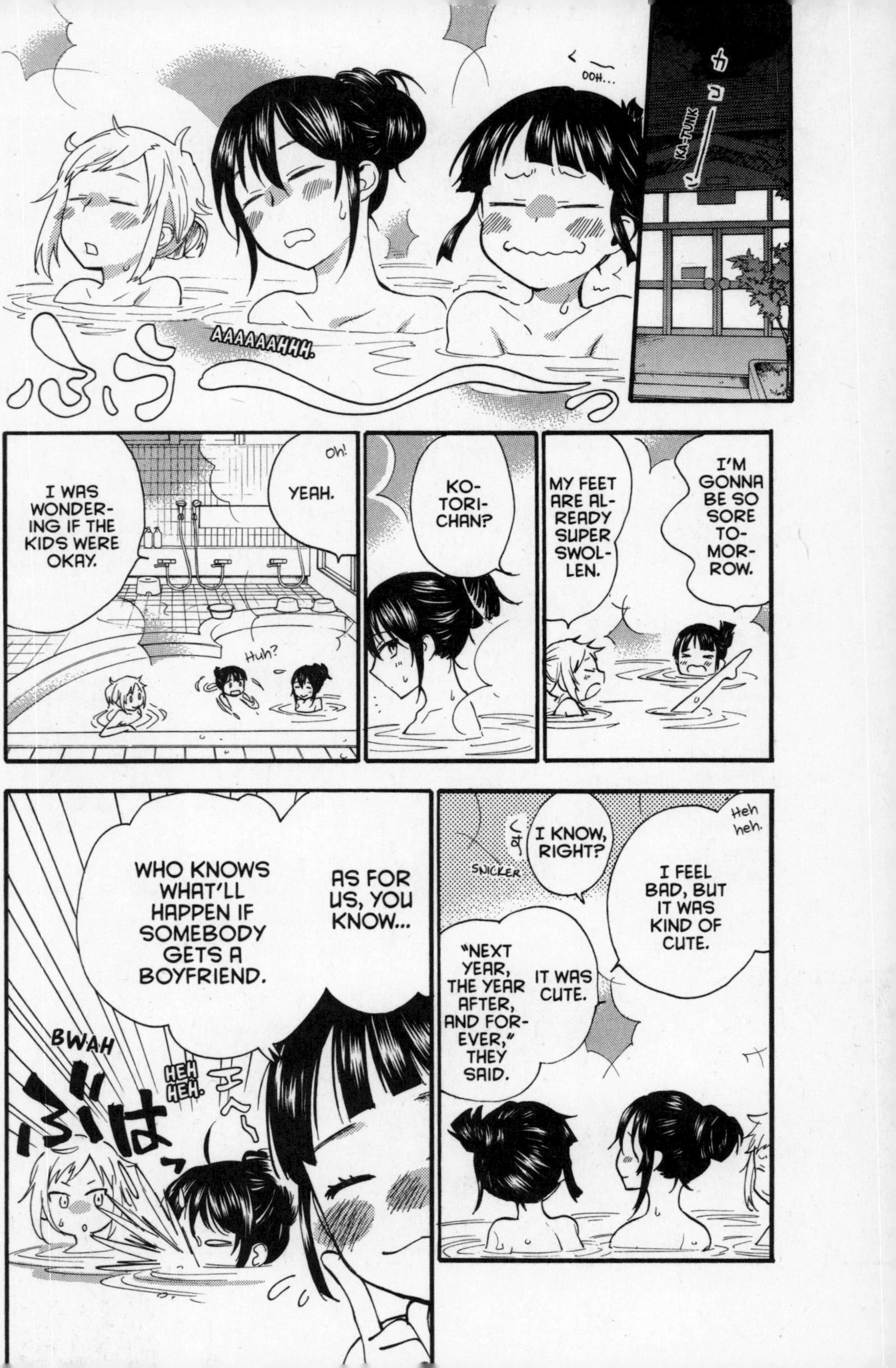
カコ
KA-TUNK
くー
OOH...
ふう
AAAAAAHHH.
I'M GONNA BE SO SORE TO-MOR-ROW.
MY FEET ARE AL-READY SUPER SWOL-LEN.
KO-TORI-CHAN?
Oh!
YEAH.
I WAS WONDER-ING IF THE KIDS WERE OKAY.
Huh?
Heh heh.
I FEEL BAD, BUT IT WAS KIND OF CUTE.
I KNOW, RIGHT?
くす
SNICKER
IT WAS CUTE.
"NEXT YEAR, THE YEAR AFTER, AND FOR-EVER," THEY SAID.
AS FOR US, YOU KNOW...
WHO KNOWS WHAT'LL HAPPEN IF SOMEBODY GETS A BOYFRIEND.
エヘ
HEH HEH.
ぶはっ
BWAH

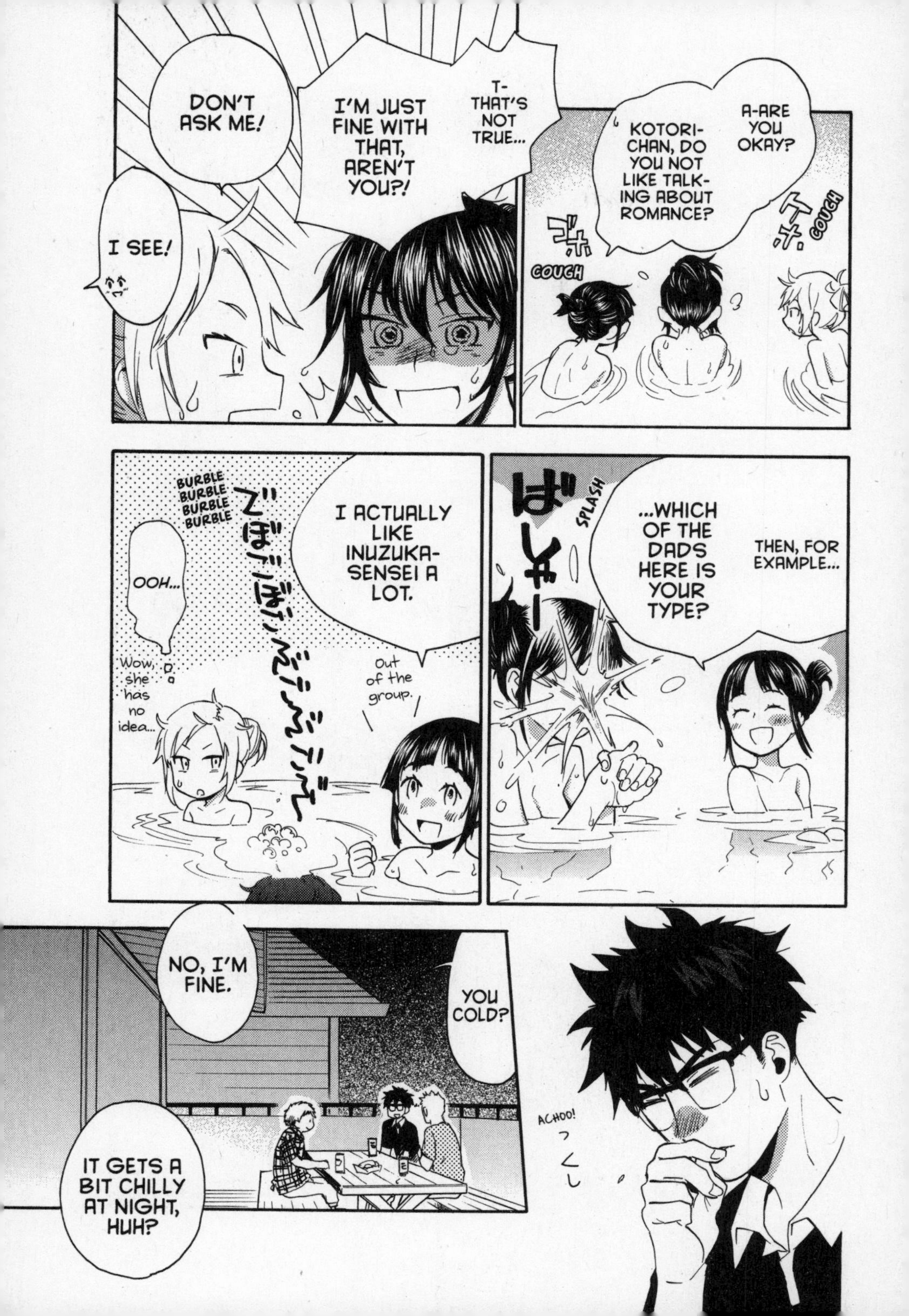
A-ARE YOU OKAY?
KOTORI-CHAN, DO YOU NOT LIKE TALKING ABOUT ROMANCE?
COUGH
COUGH
T-THAT'S NOT TRUE...
I'M JUST FINE WITH THAT, AREN'T YOU?!
DON'T ASK ME!
I SEE!
THEN, FOR EXAMPLE...
...WHICH OF THE DADS HERE IS YOUR TYPE?
SPLASH
I ACTUALLY LIKE INUZUKA-SENSEI A LOT.
Out of the group.
BURBLE BURBLE BURBLE BURBLE
OOH...
Wow, she has no idea...
ACHOO!
YOU COLD?
NO, I'M FINE.
IT GETS A BIT CHILLY AT NIGHT, HUH?

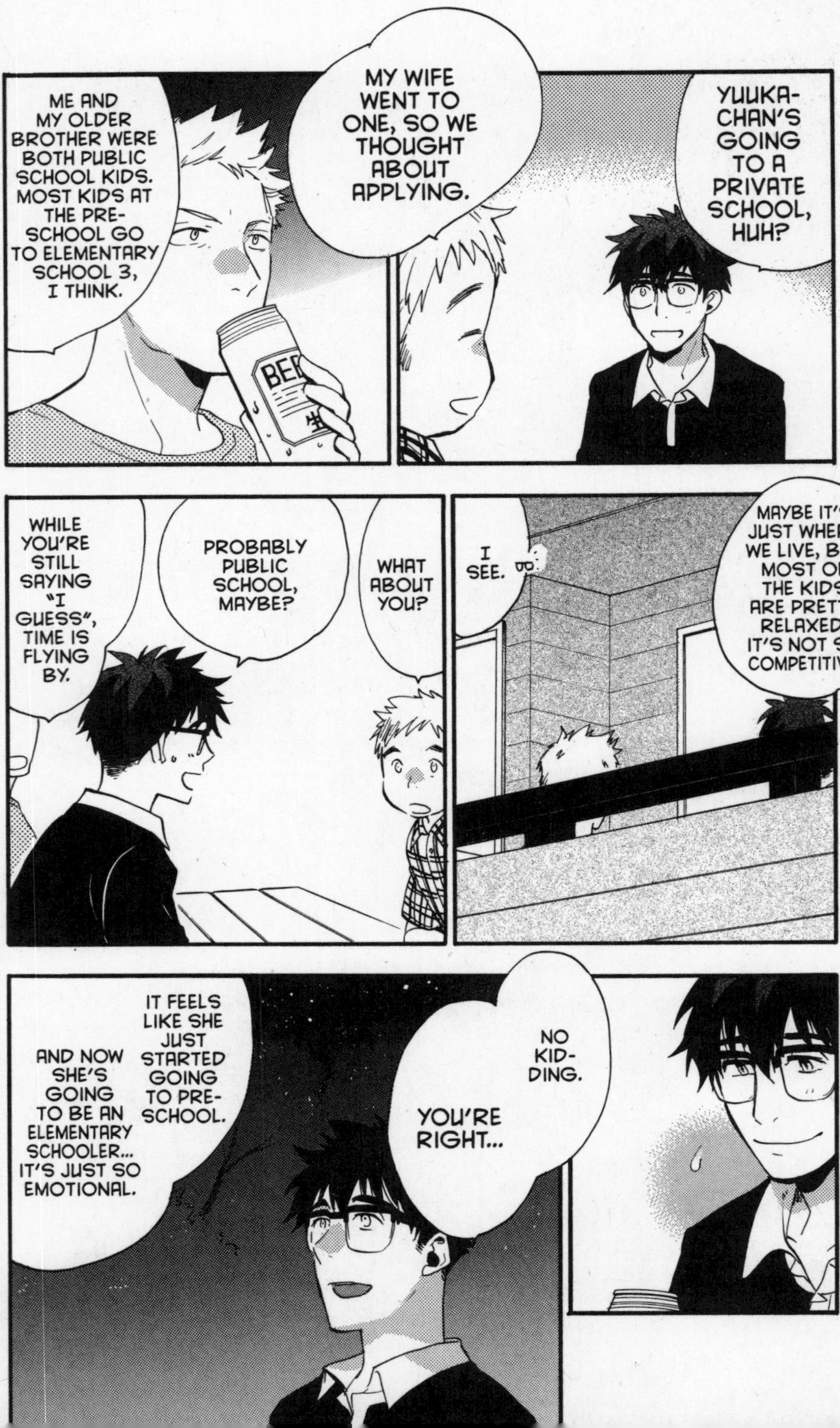
YUUKA-CHAN'S GOING TO A PRIVATE SCHOOL, HUH?
MY WIFE WENT TO ONE, SO WE THOUGHT ABOUT APPLYING.
ME AND MY OLDER BROTHER WERE BOTH PUBLIC SCHOOL KIDS. MOST KIDS AT THE PRE-SCHOOL GO TO ELEMENTARY SCHOOL 3, I THINK.
MAYBE IT'S JUST WHERE WE LIVE, BUT MOST OF THE KIDS ARE PRETTY RELAXED. IT'S NOT SO COMPETITIVE.
I SEE.
WHAT ABOUT YOU?
PROBABLY PUBLIC SCHOOL, MAYBE?
WHILE YOU'RE STILL SAYING "I GUESS", TIME IS FLYING BY.
NO KID-DING.
YOU'RE RIGHT...
IT FEELS LIKE SHE JUST STARTED GOING TO PRE-SCHOOL.
AND NOW SHE'S GOING TO BE AN ELEMENTARY SCHOOLER... IT'S JUST SO EMOTIONAL.

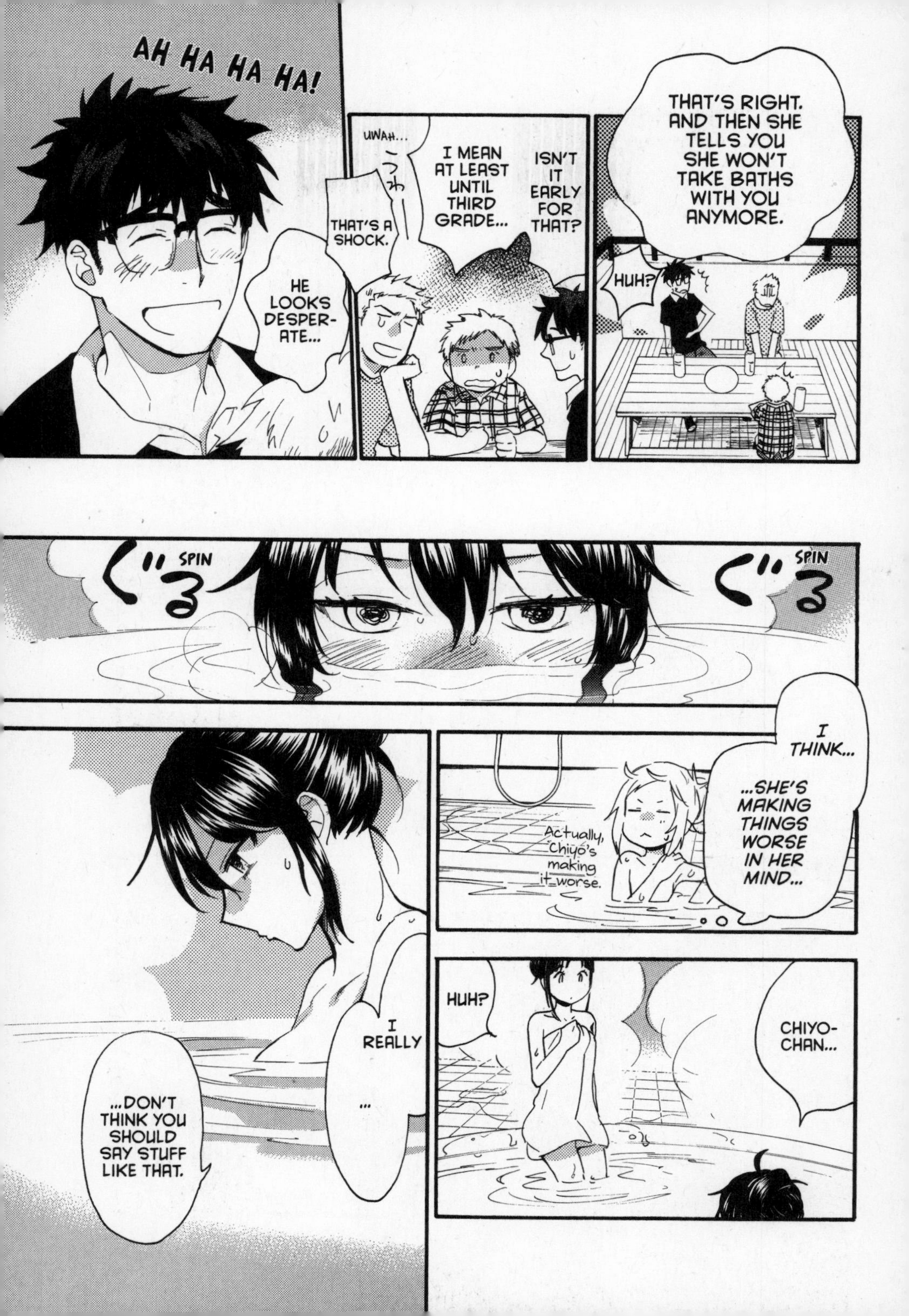
THAT'S RIGHT. AND THEN SHE TELLS YOU SHE WON'T TAKE BATHS WITH YOU ANYMORE.
HUH?
ISN'T IT EARLY FOR THAT?
I MEAN AT LEAST UNTIL THIRD GRADE...
UWAH...
うわ
THAT'S A SHOCK.
AH HA HA HA!
HE LOOKS DESPERATE...
ぐる SPIN
ぐる SPIN
I THINK...
...SHE'S MAKING THINGS WORSE IN HER MIND...
Actually, Chiyo's making it worse.
CHIYO-CHAN...
HUH?
I REALLY
...
...DON'T THINK YOU SHOULD SAY STUFF LIKE THAT.

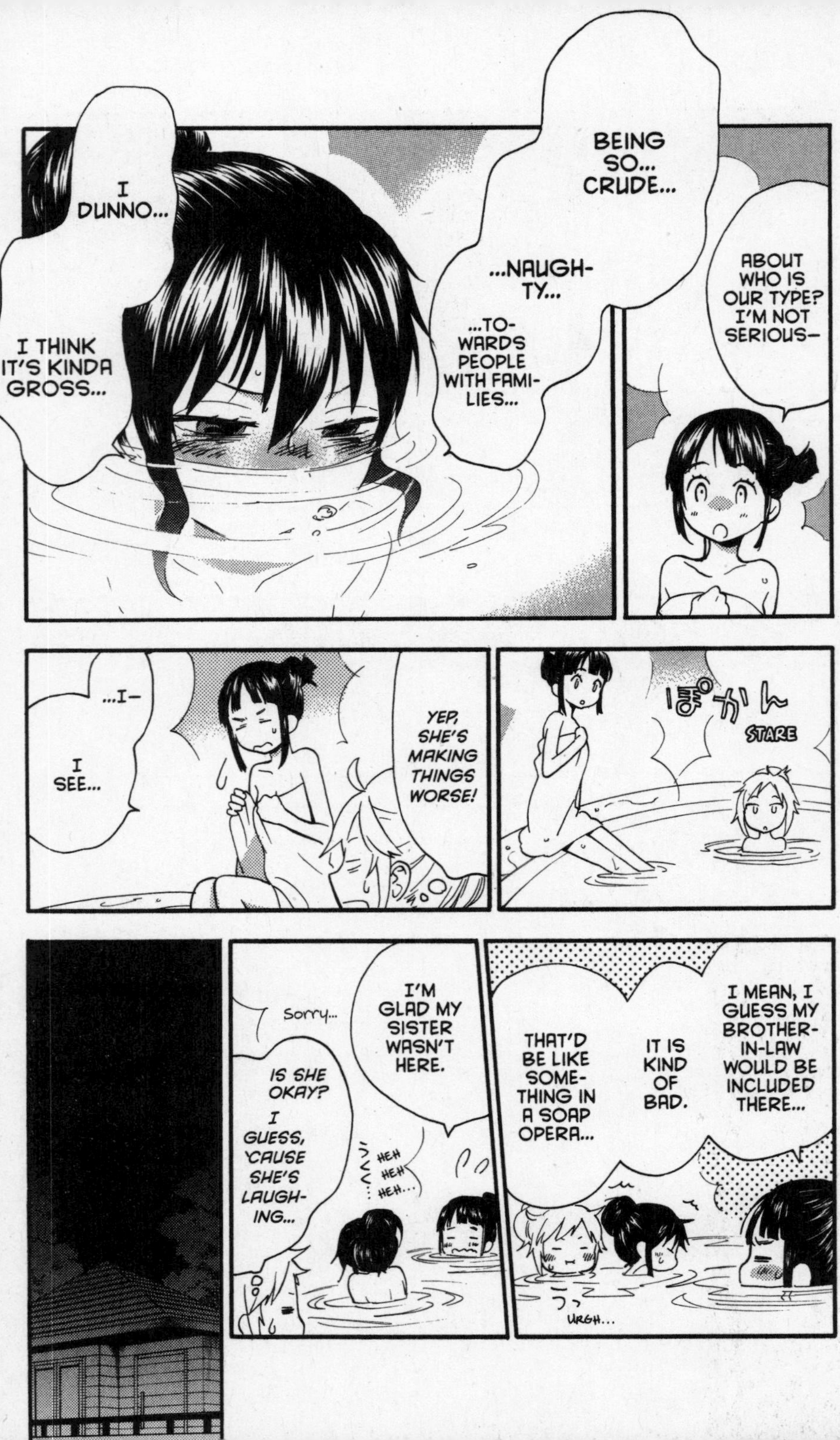
ABOUT WHO IS OUR TYPE? I'M NOT SERIOUS—
BEING SO... CRUDE...
...NAUGH-TY...
...TO-WARDS PEOPLE WITH FAMI-LIES...
I DUNNO...
I THINK IT'S KINDA GROSS...
ぽかん
STARE
YEP, SHE'S MAKING THINGS WORSE!
...I—
I SEE...
I MEAN, I GUESS MY BROTHER-IN-LAW WOULD BE INCLUDED THERE...
IT IS KIND OF BAD.
THAT'D BE LIKE SOME-THING IN A SOAP OPERA...
URGH...
I'M GLAD MY SISTER WASN'T HERE.
Sorry...
HEH HEH HEH...
IS SHE OKAY?
I GUESS, 'CAUSE SHE'S LAUGH-ING...

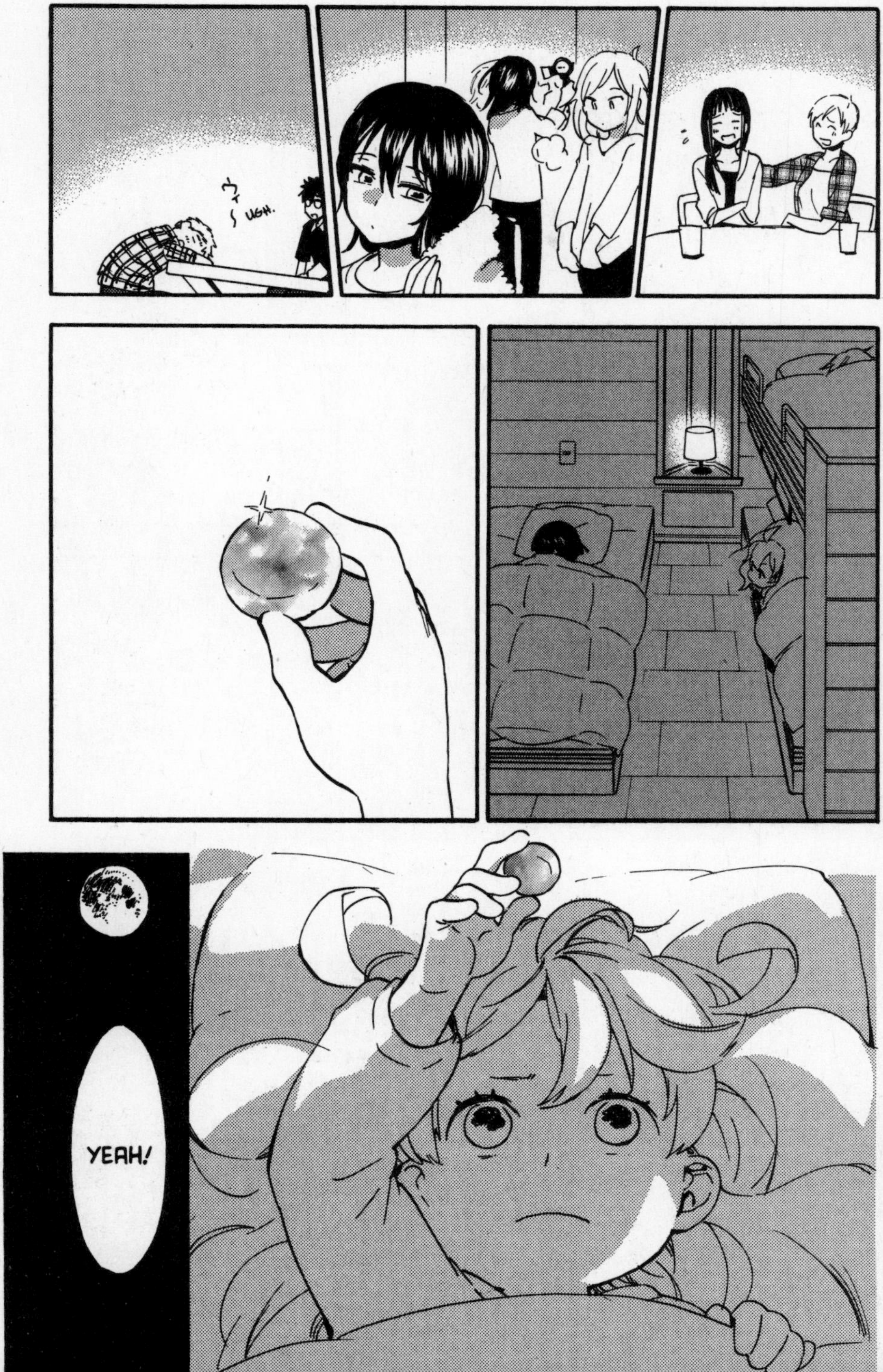
UGH.
YEAH!

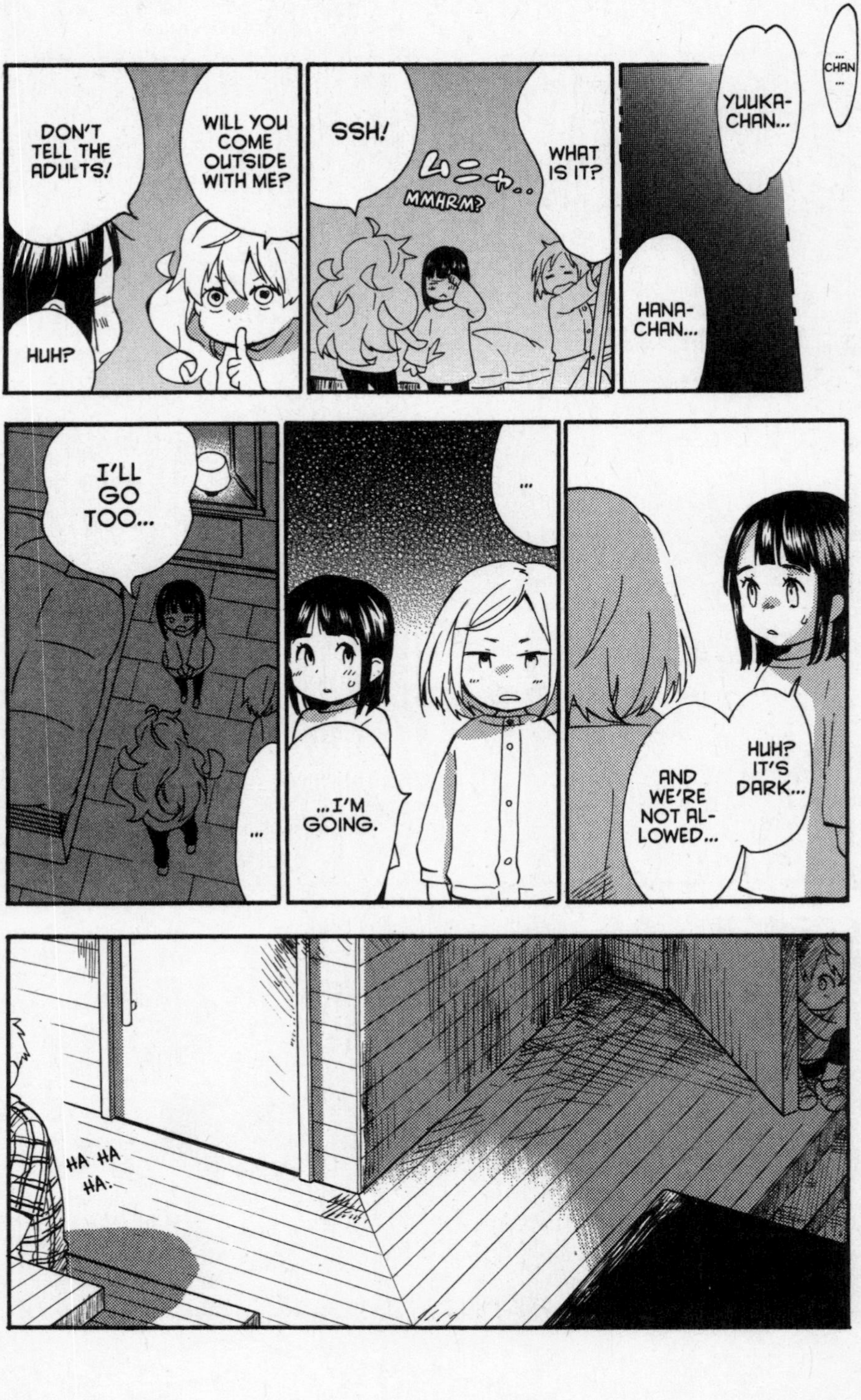
...CHAN...
YUUKA-CHAN...
HANA-CHAN...
WHAT IS IT?
ムニャ..
MMHRM?
SSH!
WILL YOU COME OUTSIDE WITH ME?
DON'T TELL THE ADULTS!
HUH?
HUH? IT'S DARK...
AND WE'RE NOT AL-LOWED...
...
...I'M GOING.
I'LL GO TOO...
...
HA HA HA.

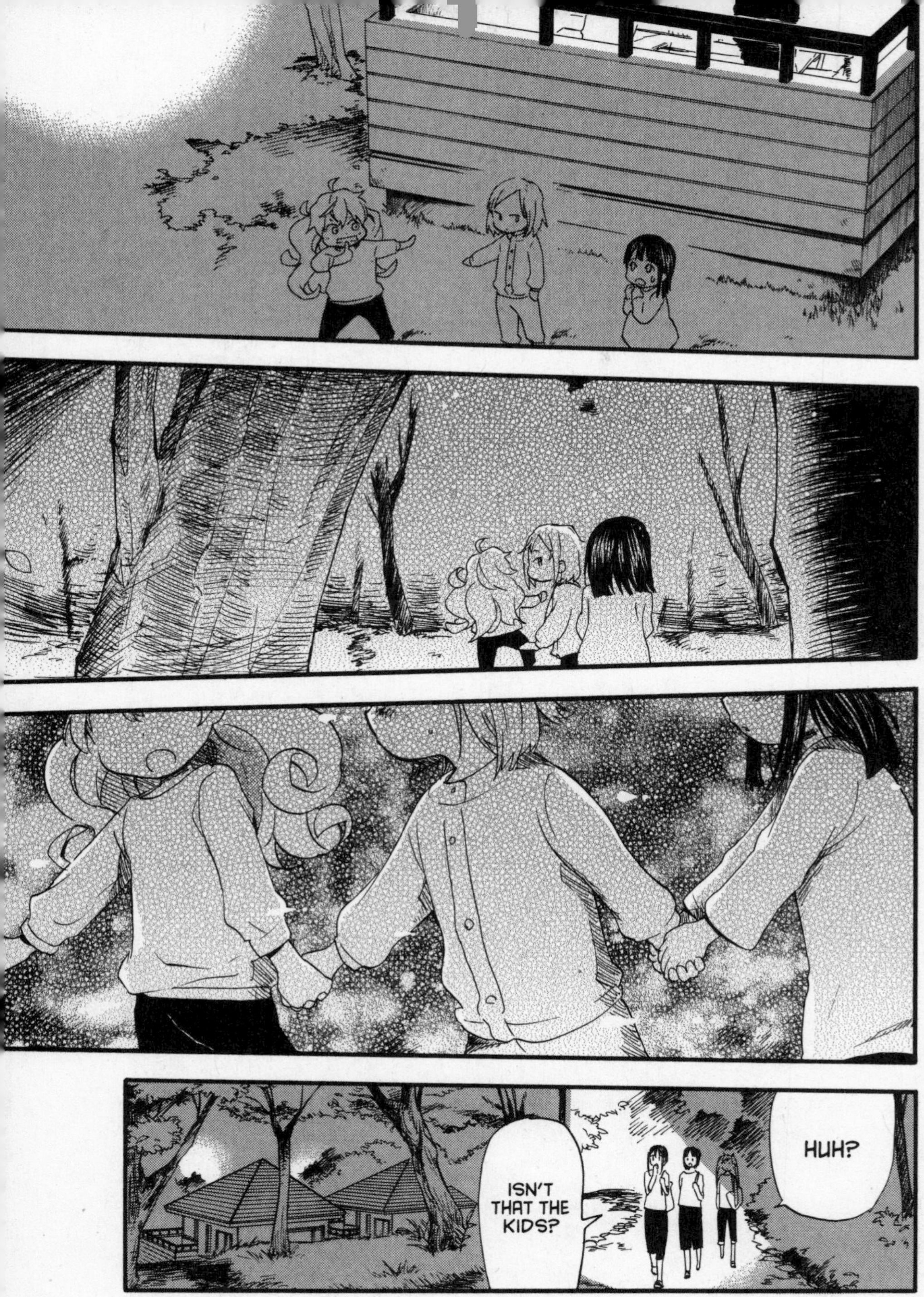
HUH?
ISN'T THAT THE KIDS?

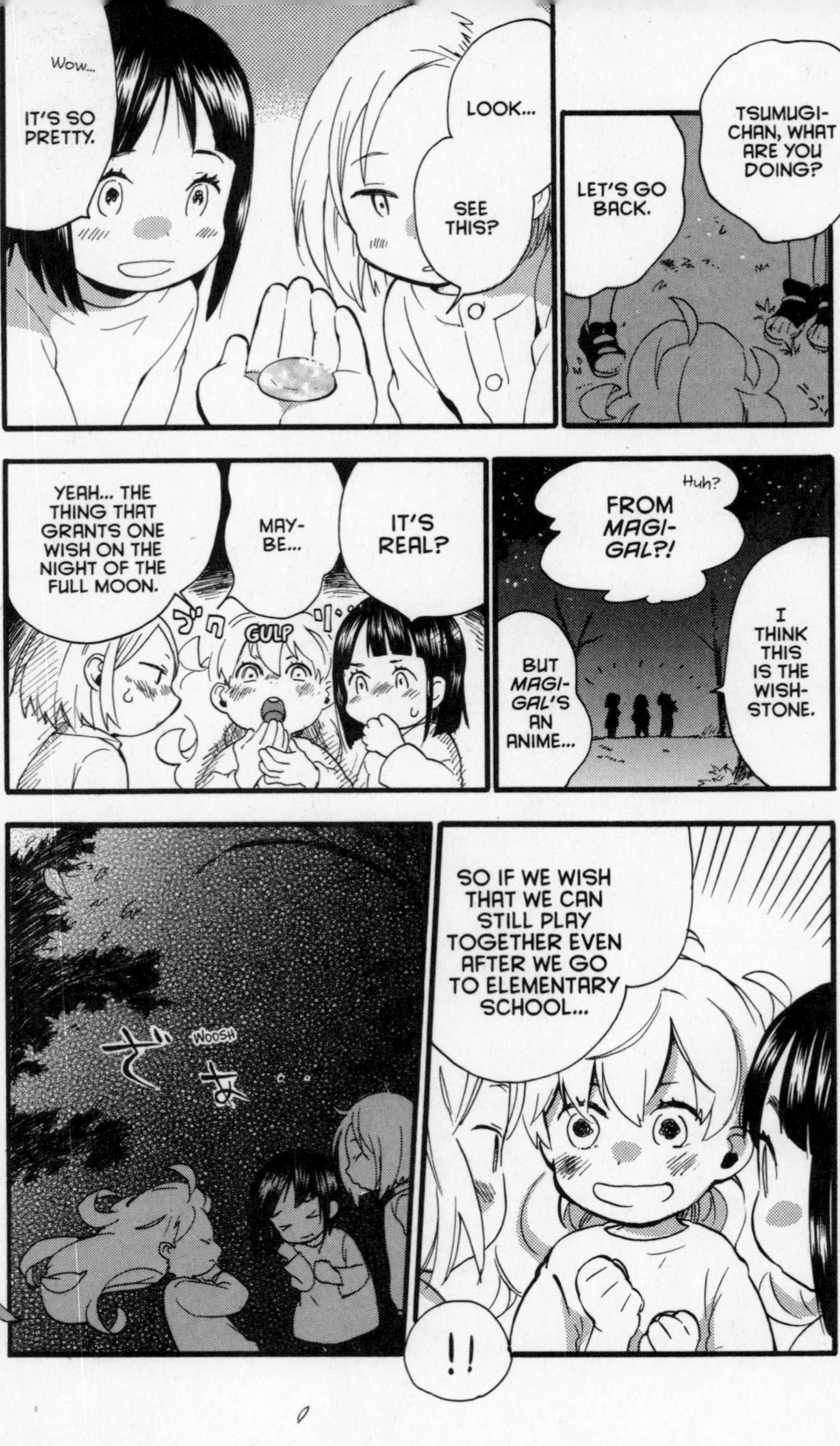
TSUMUGI-CHAN, WHAT ARE YOU DOING?
LET'S GO BACK.
LOOK...
SEE THIS?
Wow...
IT'S SO PRETTY.
Huh?
FROM MAGI-GAL?!
I THINK THIS IS THE WISH-STONE.
BUT MAGI-GAL'S AN ANIME...
IT'S REAL?
MAY-BE...
YEAH... THE THING THAT GRANTS ONE WISH ON THE NIGHT OF THE FULL MOON.
GULP
SO IF WE WISH THAT WE CAN STILL PLAY TOGETHER EVEN AFTER WE GO TO ELEMENTARY SCHOOL...
!!
WOOSH

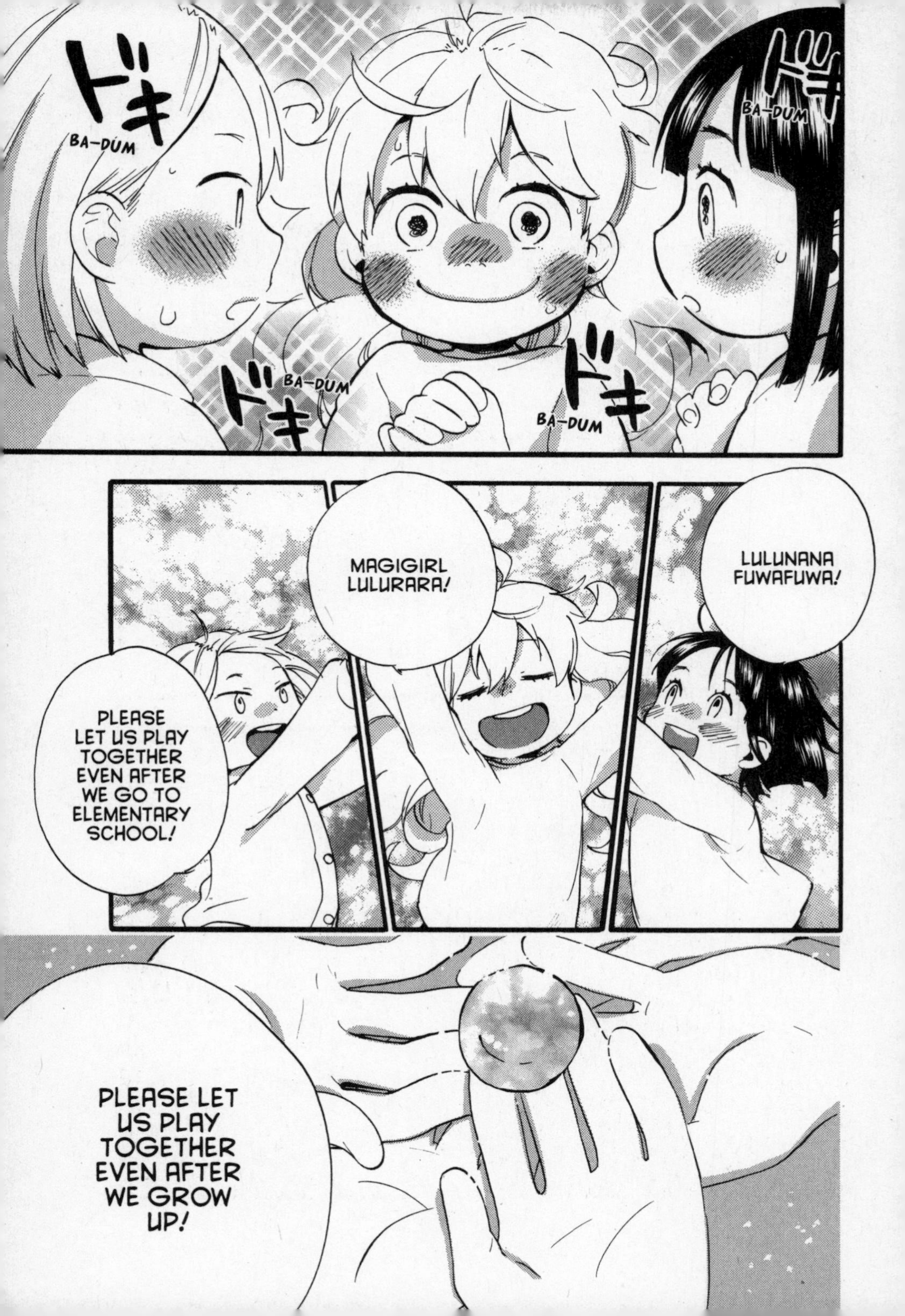
ドキ
BA-DUM
ドキ
BA-DUM
ドキ
BA-DUM
ドキ
BA-DUM
LULUNANA FUWAFUWA!
MAGIGIRL LULURARA!
PLEASE LET US PLAY TOGETHER EVEN AFTER WE GO TO ELEMENTARY SCHOOL!
PLEASE LET US PLAY TOGETHER EVEN AFTER WE GROW UP!

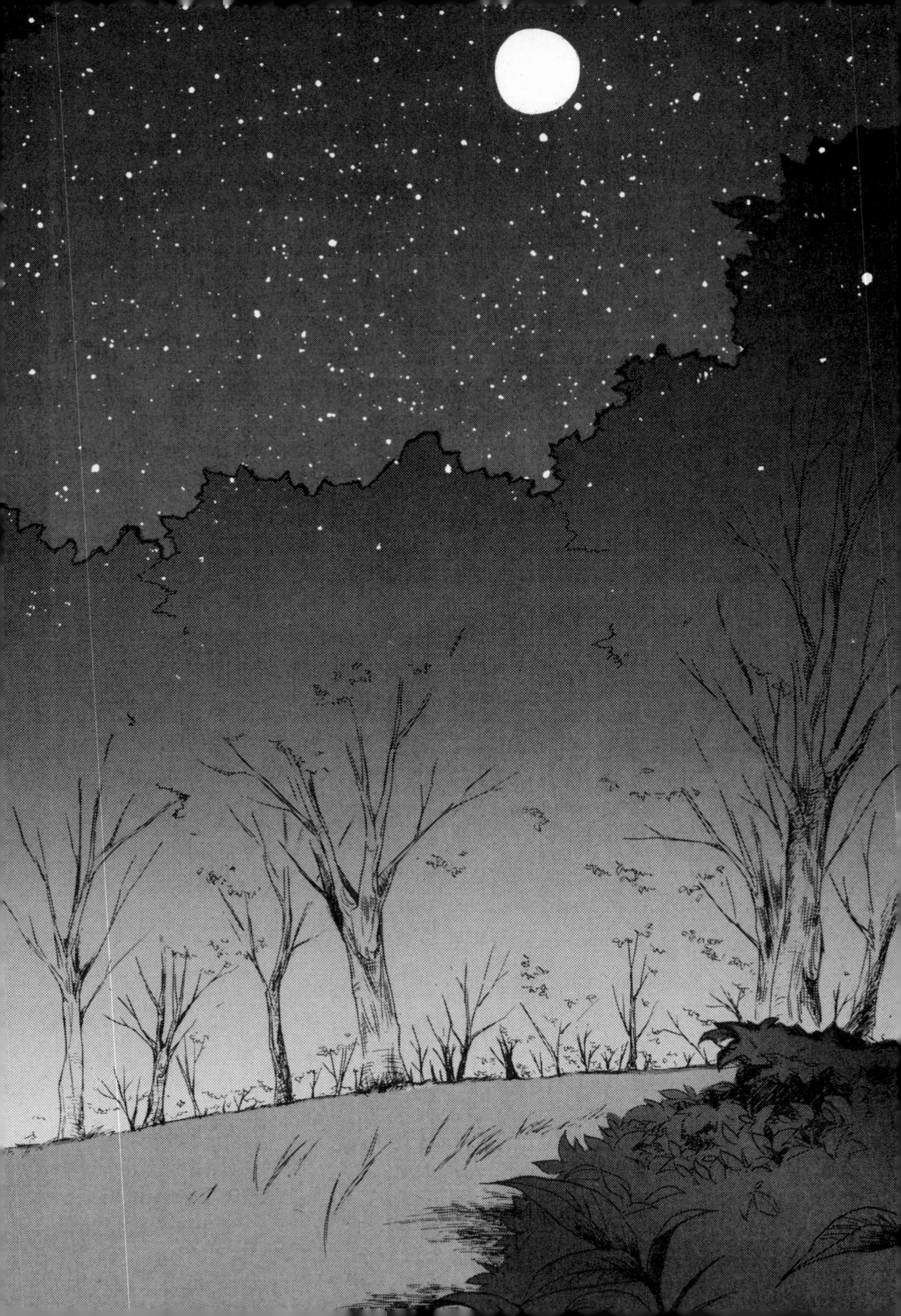

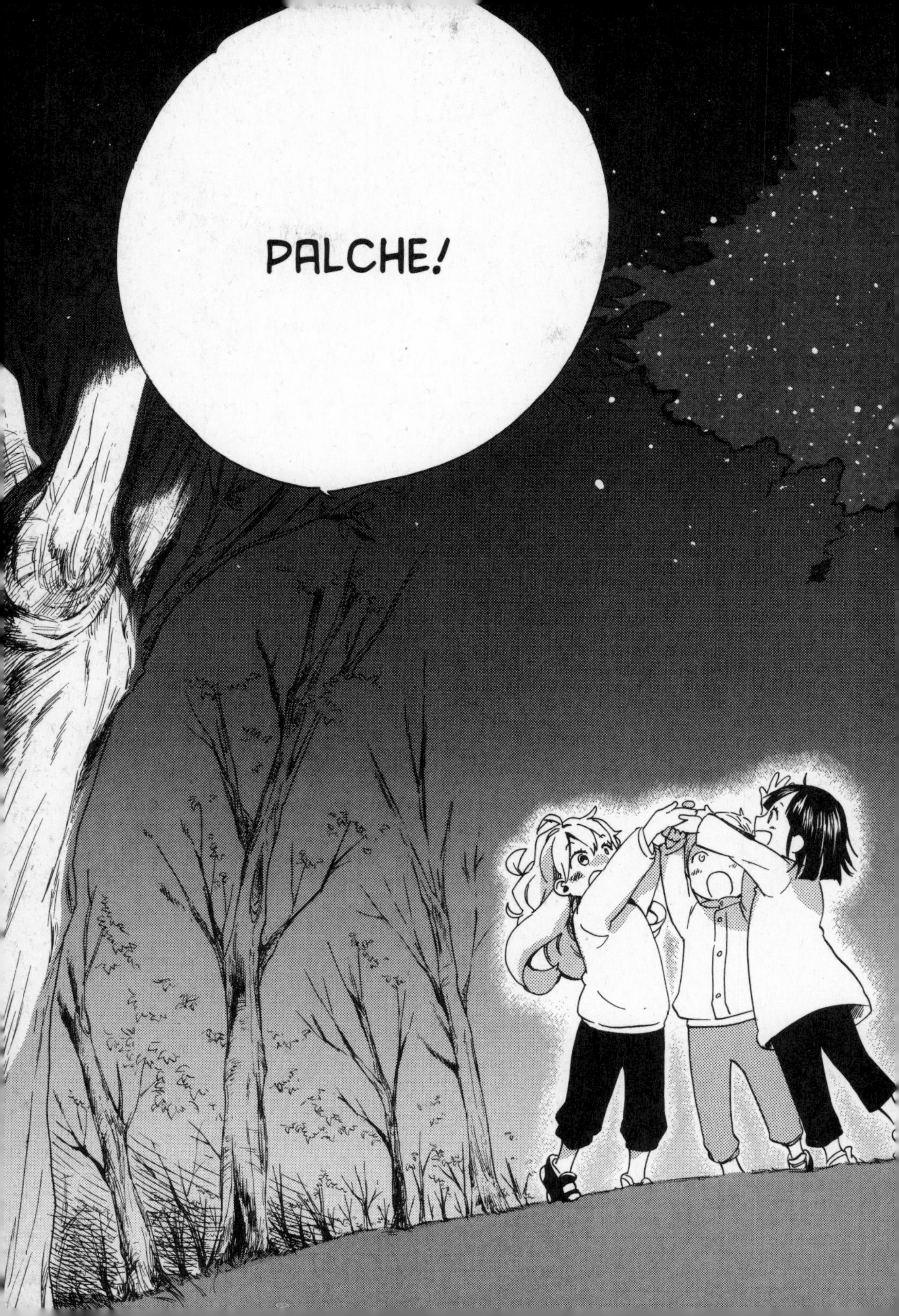
PALCHE!

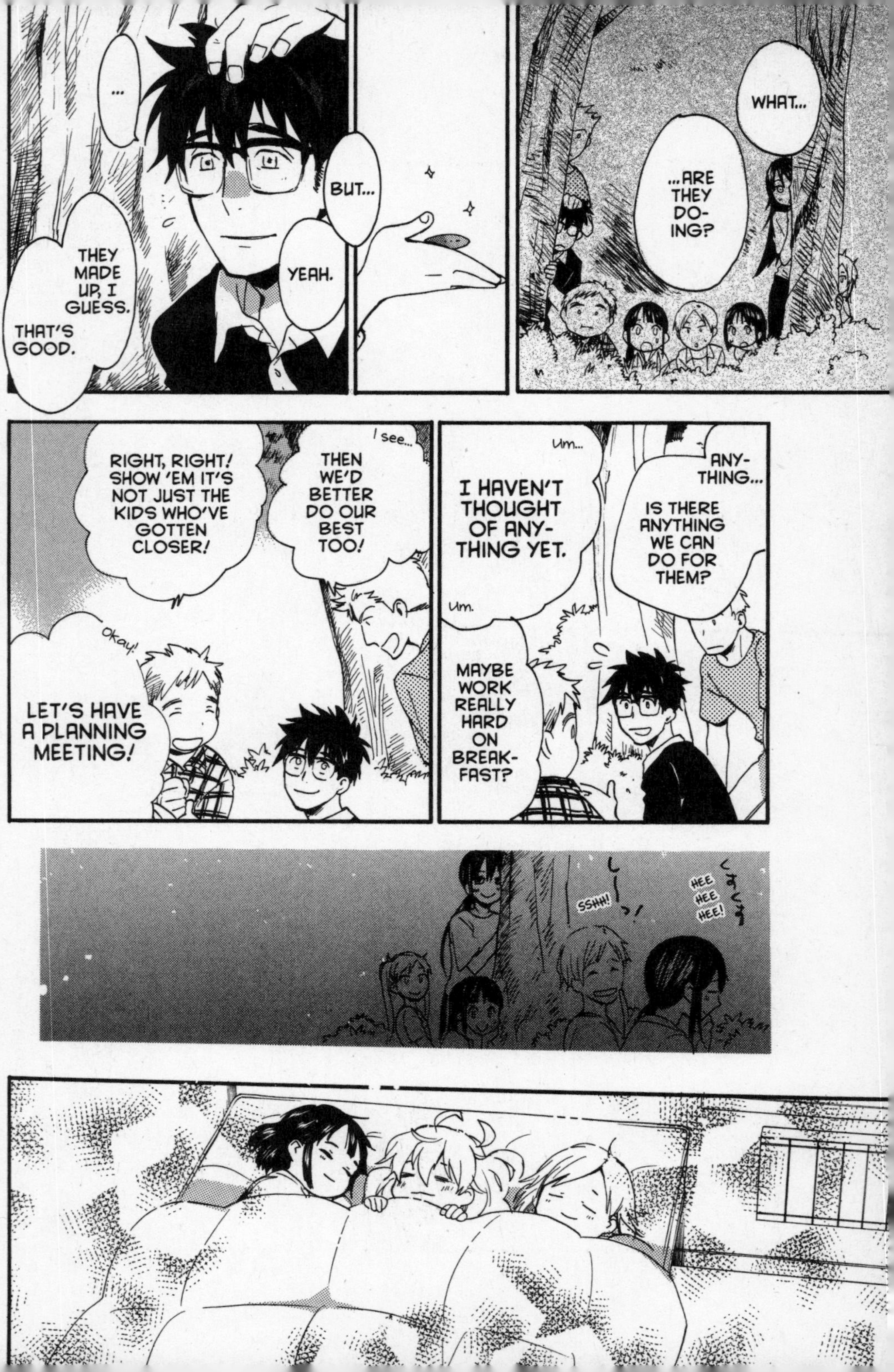
WHAT...
...ARE THEY DOING?
BUT...
YEAH.
...
THEY MADE UP, I GUESS. THAT'S GOOD.
ANYTHING...
IS THERE ANYTHING WE CAN DO FOR THEM?
Um...
I HAVEN'T THOUGHT OF ANYTHING YET.
Um.
MAYBE WORK REALLY HARD ON BREAKFAST?
I see...
THEN WE'D BETTER DO OUR BEST TOO!
RIGHT, RIGHT! SHOW 'EM IT'S NOT JUST THE KIDS WHO'VE GOTTEN CLOSER!
Okay!
LET'S HAVE A PLANNING MEETING!
くすくす
HEE HEE HEE!
しーっ!
SSHH!

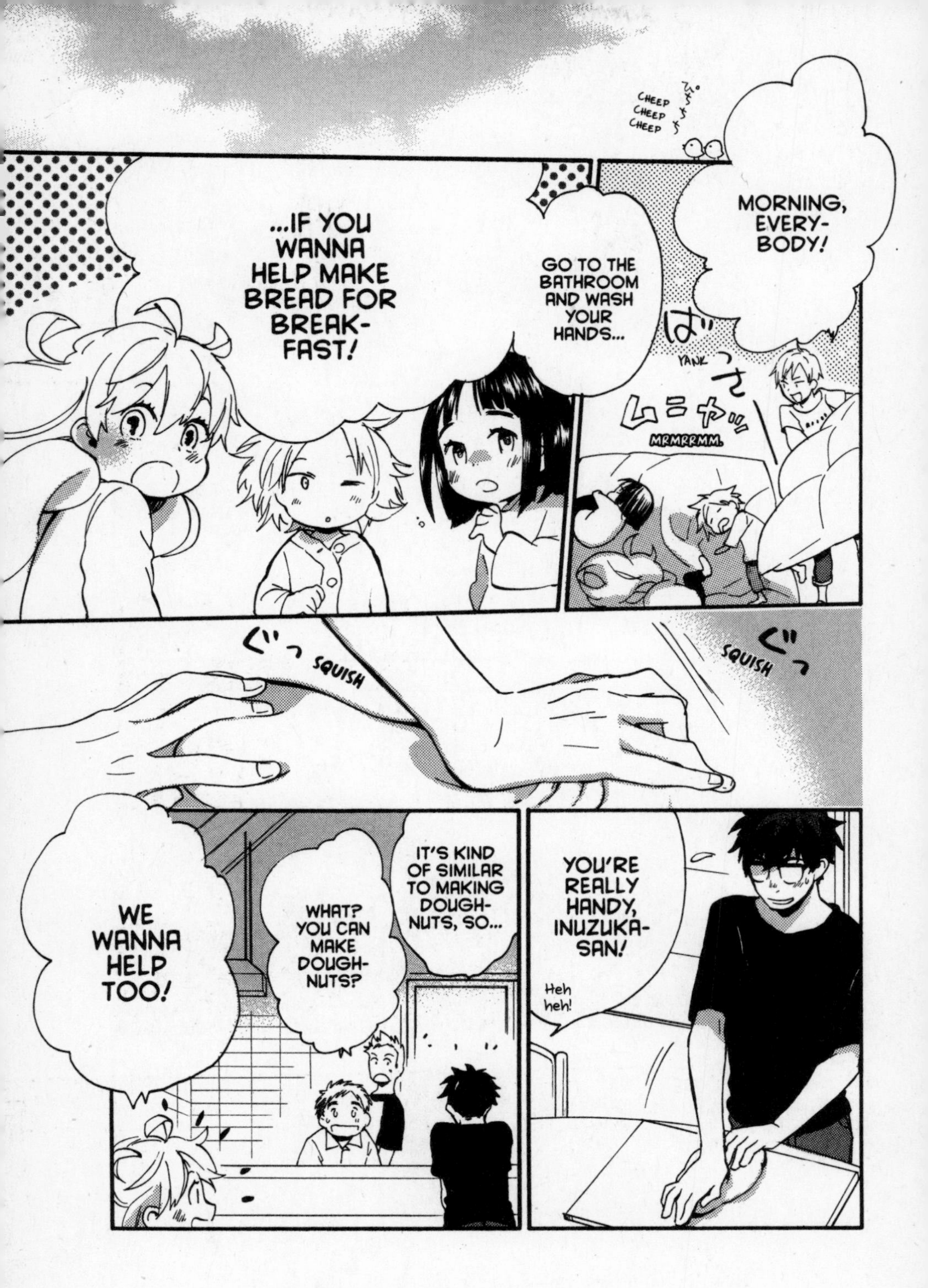
CHEEP
CHEEP
CHEEP
MORNING, EVERY-BODY!
ばっ
YANK
ムニャ
MRMRRMM.
GO TO THE BATHROOM AND WASH YOUR HANDS...
...IF YOU WANNA HELP MAKE BREAD FOR BREAK-FAST!
ぐっ
SQUISH
ぐっ
SQUISH
YOU'RE REALLY HANDY, INUZUKA-SAN!
Heh heh!
IT'S KIND OF SIMILAR TO MAKING DOUGH-NUTS, SO...
WHAT? YOU CAN MAKE DOUGH-NUTS?
WE WANNA HELP TOO!

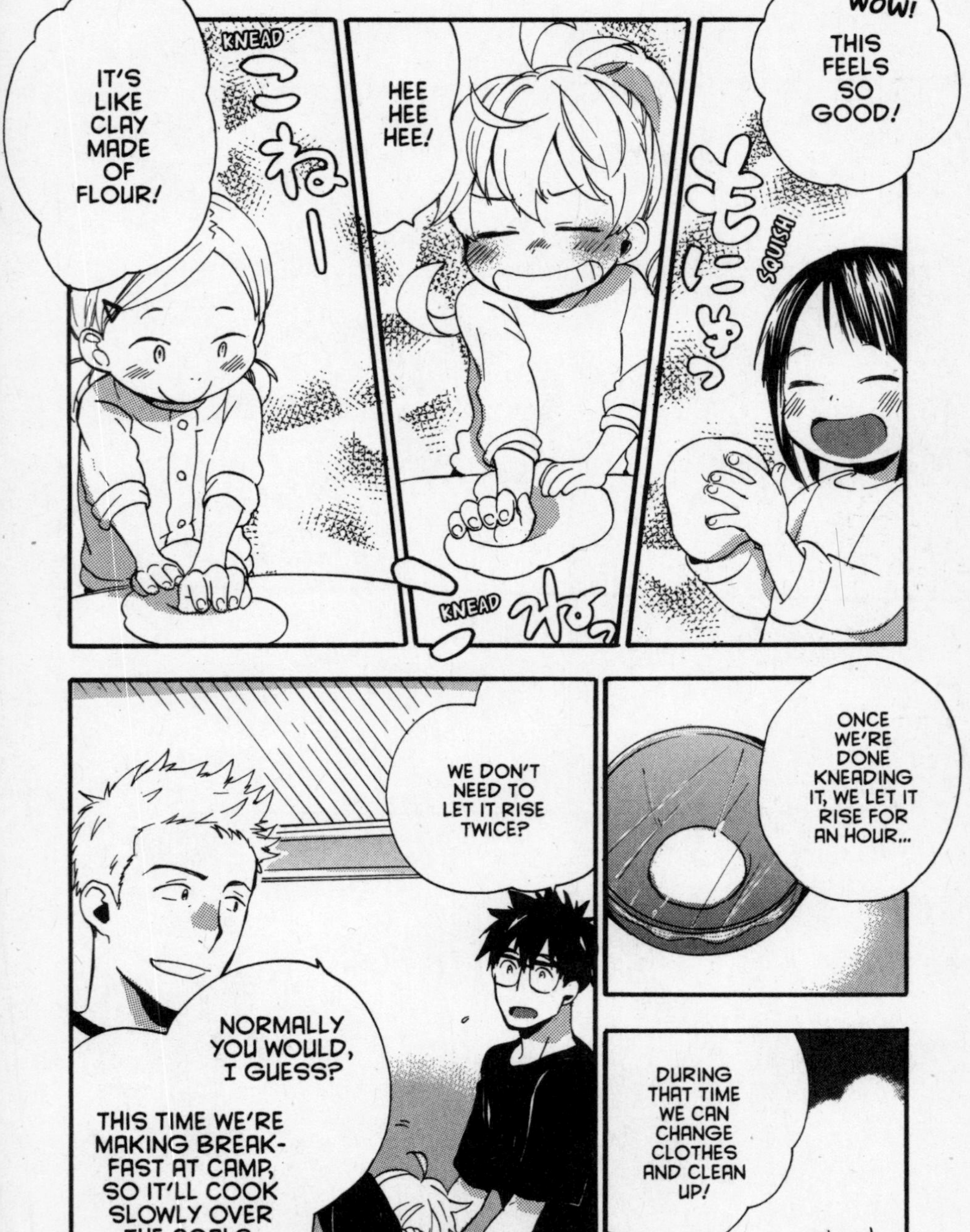
WOW!
THIS FEELS SO GOOD!
SQUISH
HEE HEE HEE!
KNEAD
IT'S LIKE CLAY MADE OF FLOUR!
KNEAD
ONCE WE'RE DONE KNEADING IT, WE LET IT RISE FOR AN HOUR...
DURING THAT TIME WE CAN CHANGE CLOTHES AND CLEAN UP!
Okay!
WE DON'T NEED TO LET IT RISE TWICE?
NORMALLY YOU WOULD, I GUESS?
THIS TIME WE'RE MAKING BREAK-FAST AT CAMP, SO IT'LL COOK SLOWLY OVER THE COALS.

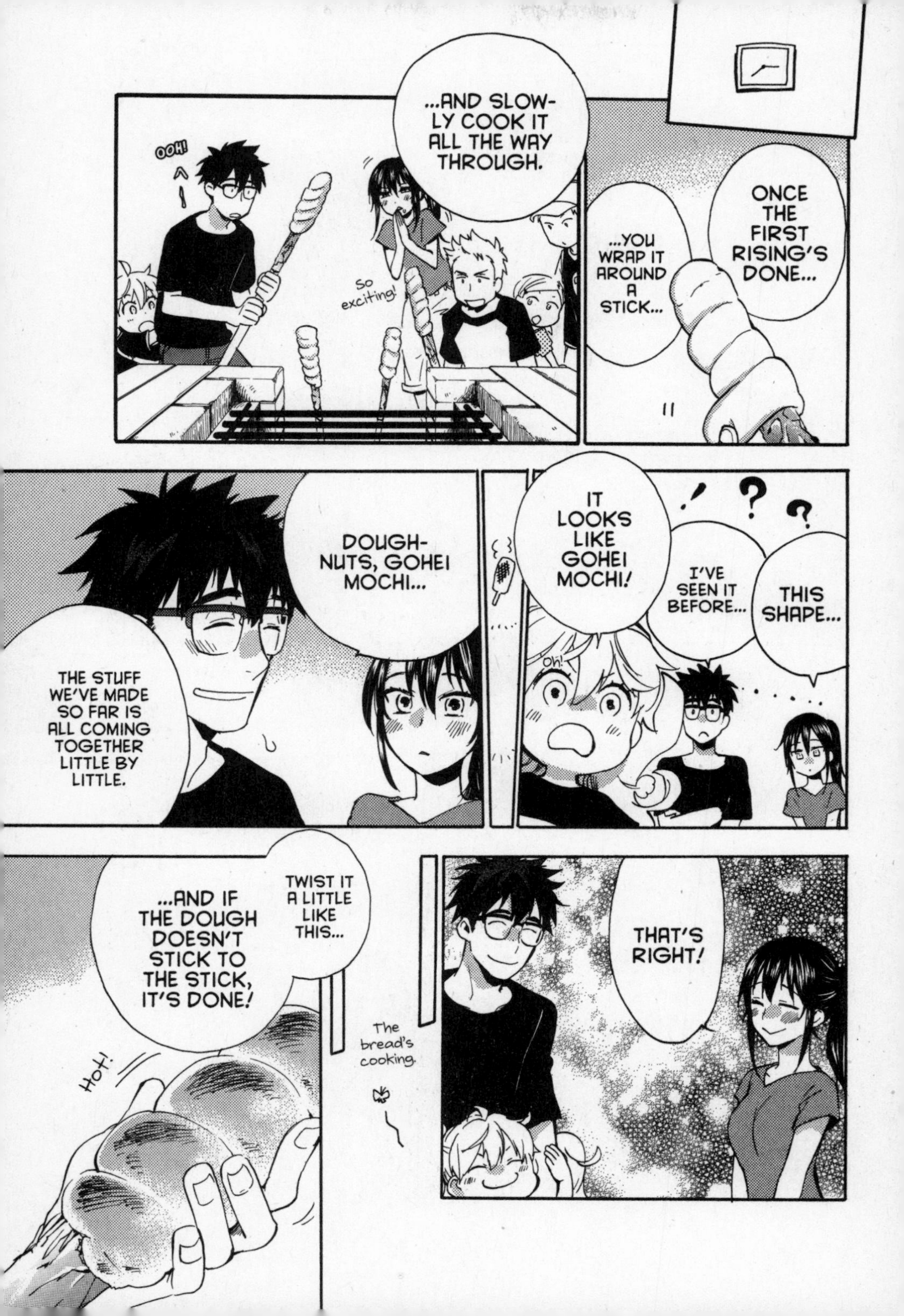
ONCE THE FIRST RISING'S DONE...
...YOU WRAP IT AROUND A STICK...
...AND SLOW-LY COOK IT ALL THE WAY THROUGH.
OOH!
So exciting!
THIS SHAPE...
I'VE SEEN IT BEFORE...
IT LOOKS LIKE GOHEI MOCHI!
Oh!
DOUGH-NUTS, GOHEI MOCHI...
THE STUFF WE'VE MADE SO FAR IS ALL COMING TOGETHER LITTLE BY LITTLE.
THAT'S RIGHT!
The bread's cooking.
TWIST IT A LITTLE LIKE THIS...
...AND IF THE DOUGH DOESN'T STICK TO THE STICK, IT'S DONE!
Hot!

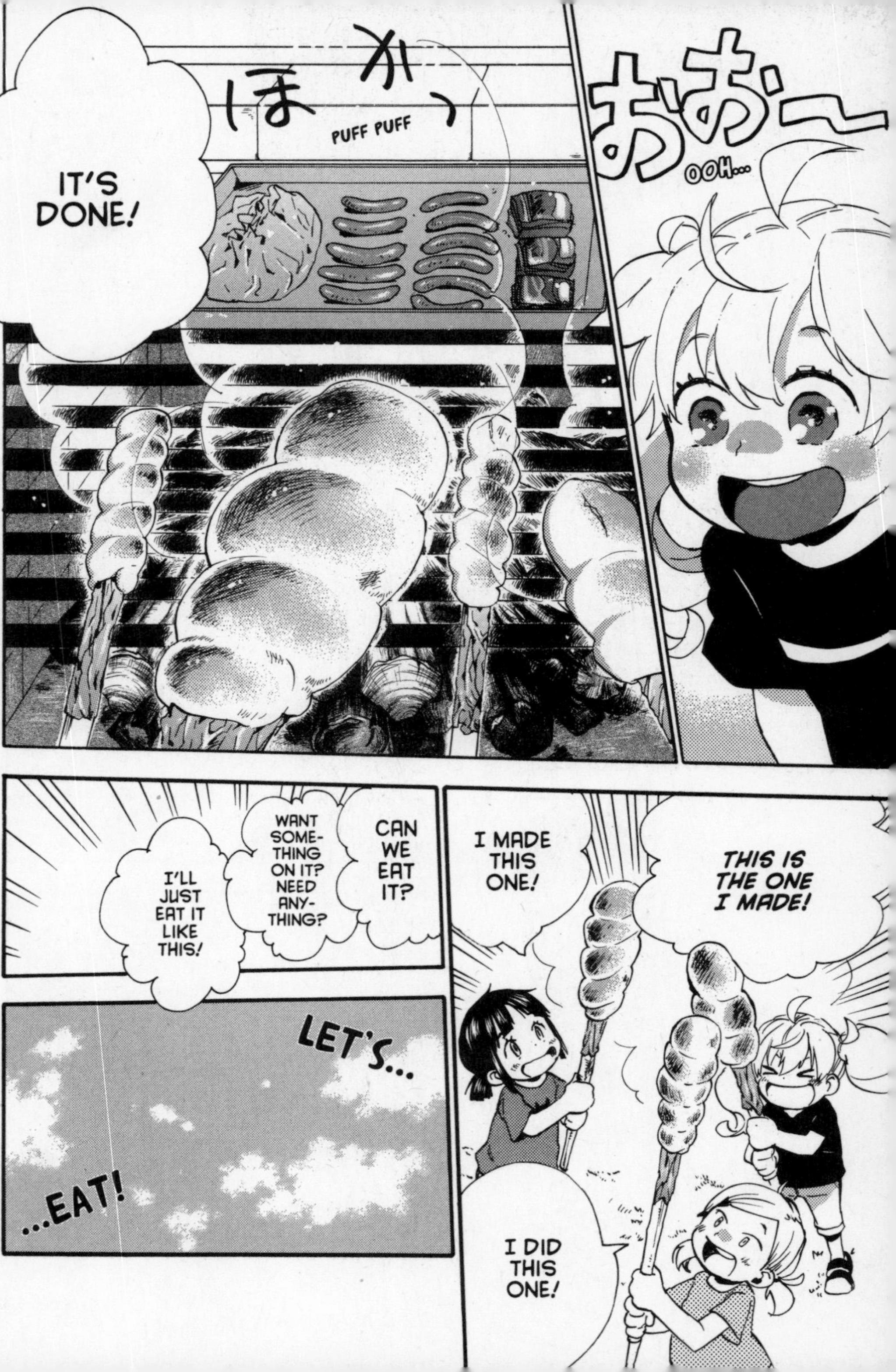
おお〜
OOH...
ほかっ
PUFF PUFF
IT'S DONE!
THIS IS THE ONE I MADE!
I MADE THIS ONE!
I DID THIS ONE!
CAN WE EAT IT?
WANT SOMETHING ON IT? NEED ANYTHING?
I'LL JUST EAT IT LIKE THIS!
LET'S...
...EAT!

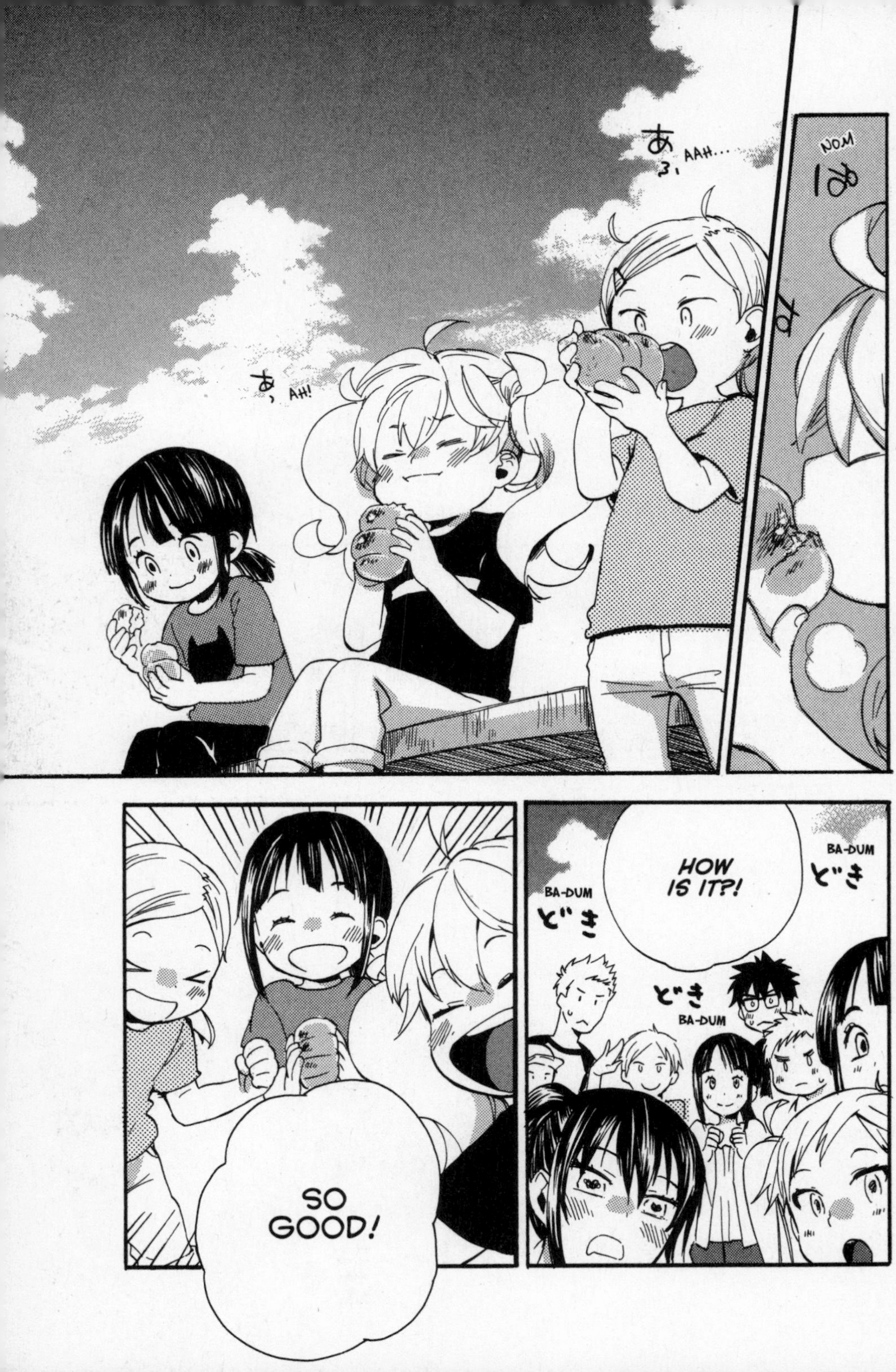
NOM
ぱ
あ、ふ、AAH...
あ、AH!
BA-DUM
どき
HOW IS IT?!
BA-DUM
どき
どき
BA-DUM
SO GOOD!

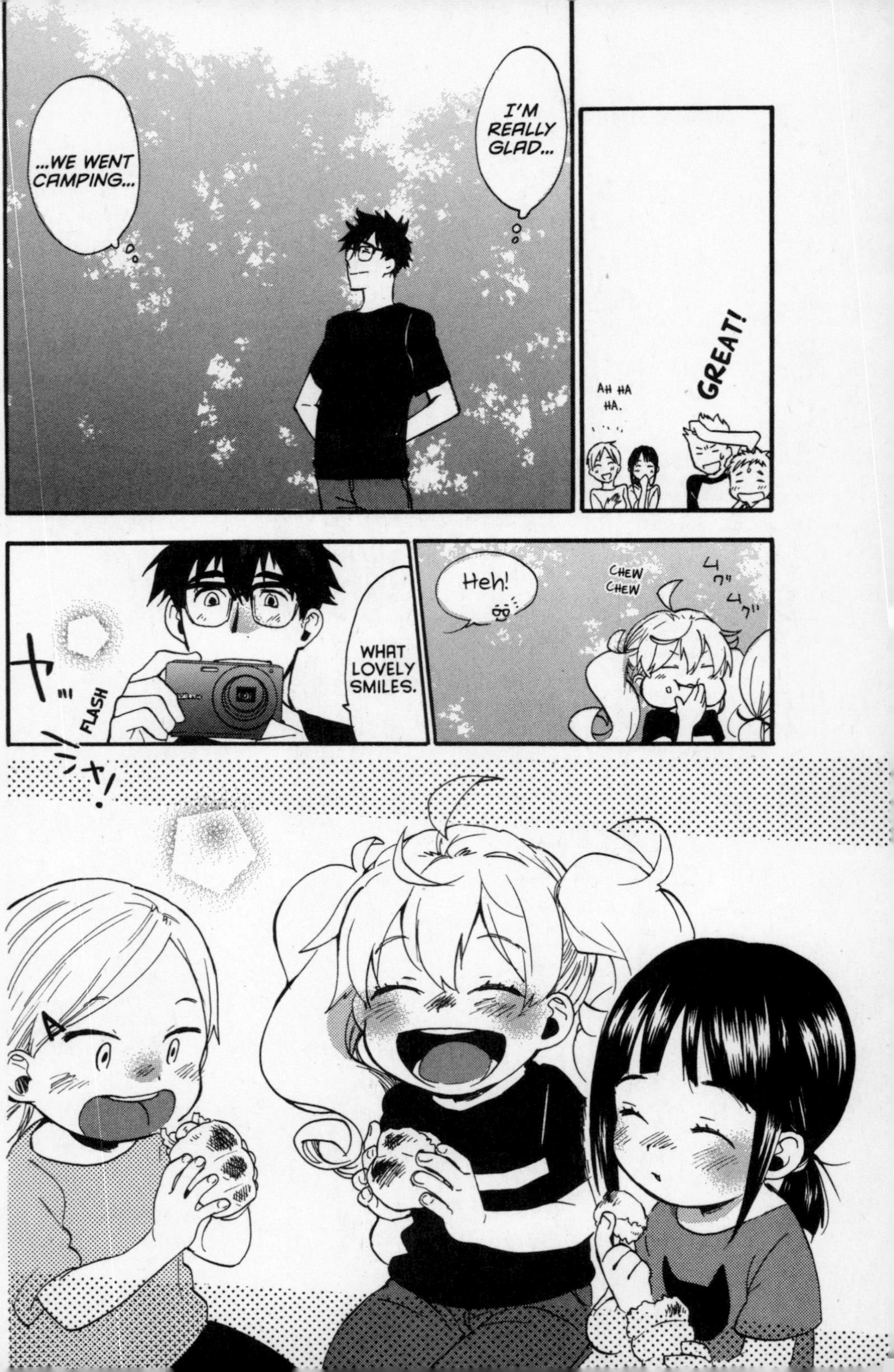
GREAT!
AH HA HA.
I'M REALLY GLAD...
...WE WENT CAMPING...
CHEW CHEW
Heh!
WHAT LOVELY SMILES.
FLASH

BREAD STICKS

☆ INGREDIENTS ☆ (For 6 Breadsticks)

300g Strong Flour
20g Butter
180cc Lukewarm Water
Ⓐ 30g Sugar 5g Salt 6g Dry Yeast

Recipe

1. Run the strong flour through a sieve and then mix in the ingredients from A, then add in water and stir. Warm the butter to room temperature.

2. Knead and mix the dough from 1 with your hands and bring it all together in a ball. When you can easily remove it from the bowl, move it to a surface that's been lightly dusted with flour.

3. Push down on it, then spread it out with your hands, and then fold it back over and push it down and spread it out again. Repeat this. Once it's smooth and easily removed from the surface, fold in the butter and knead some more.

At first you'll get sticky, but don't worry about it and keep kneading!

4. Once the butter has been thoroughly mixed in and the dough stays together after it's lifted off the surface, lift it up and then smack it into the surface, and then roll it up away from you. Change direction and repeat. Do this for 20 minutes, until you can stretch the dough with your fingers and it forms a thin film without breaking.

5. Coat a big bowl with a thin film of vegetable oil (not listed in the ingredients), then put in the dough from step 4 and cover with plastic wrap. Allow the dough to rise for one hour by either placing it in a warm place, or a bowl of lukewarm water.

6. Dust your index finger with flour and then use it to poke a hole in the dough. the hole remains even after the finger is removed, it's done rising!

This is called a finger check!

7. Cut the dough from step 6 into 6 equal parts, then press down on them softly. Then fold the edges you cut inwards, while you pull down the dough from the top down to roll it up. Pinch the point where the top touches the bottom with your fingers to close it, then move the dough to a cooking sheet with the pinched part facing down.

Roll

8. Cover the dough with a wet cloth that's been thoroughly wrung out for 15 minutes to let it rest.

9. Place the dough on a surface, then press down slightly and use a rolling pin to roll it out into a long shape.

Stretch

10. Put the edge of the dough on a bamboo stick, then pull slightly as you wrap the rest of it around.
Pinch the edges to make sure they're stuck on tight.

Wrap Wrap

✦ POINT If the dough is thick, it won't cook right, so be careful!

11. Cook on a charcoal grill. Once the bread is easily removed from the stick, it's done!

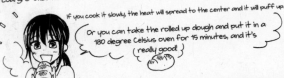

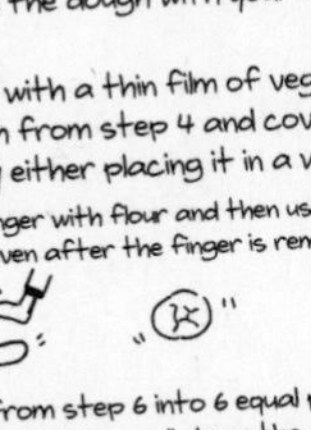

If you cook it slowly, the heat will spread to the center and it will puff up.

Or you can take the rolled up dough and put it in a 180 degree Celsius oven for 15 minutes, and it's really good!

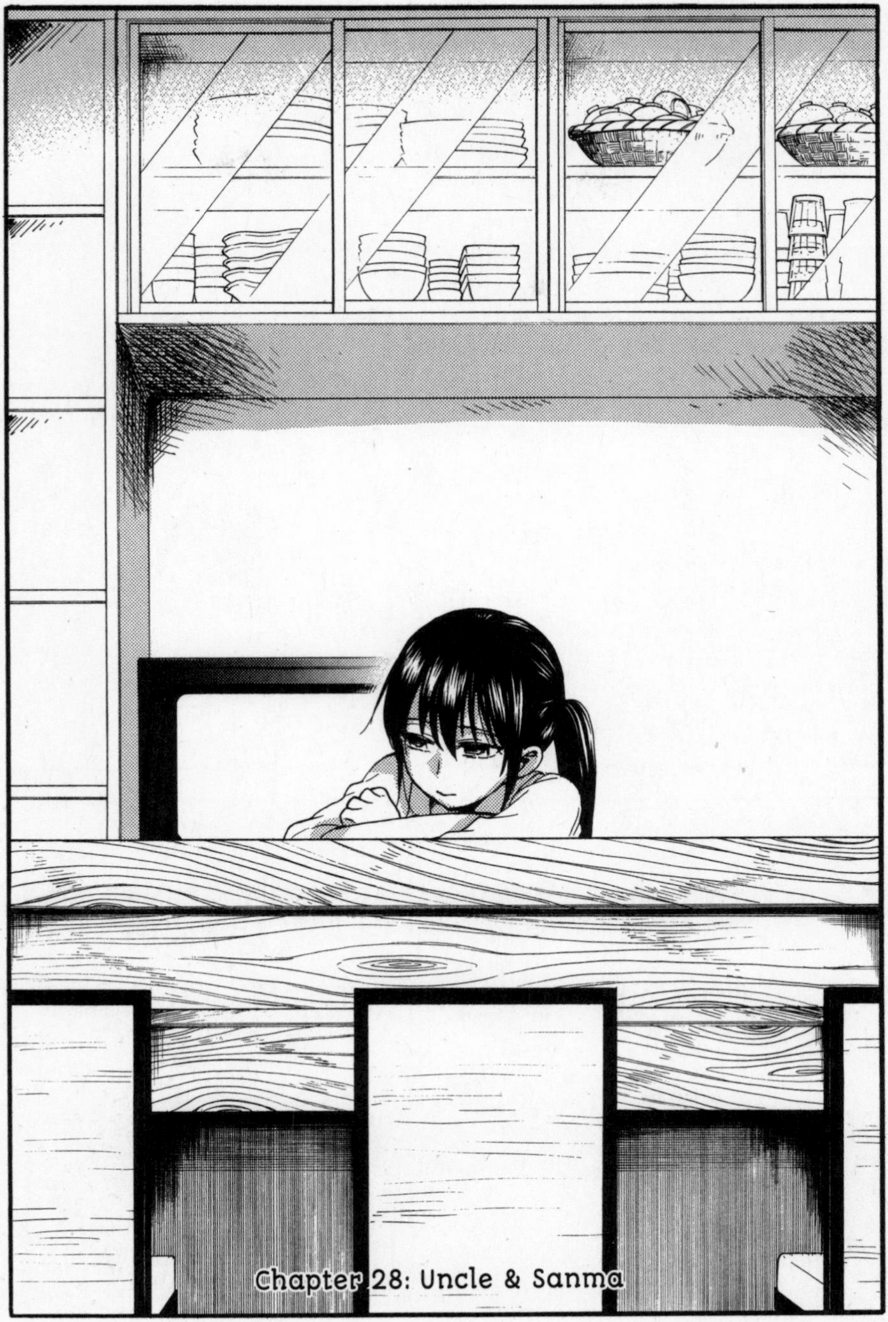
Chapter 28: Uncle & Sanma

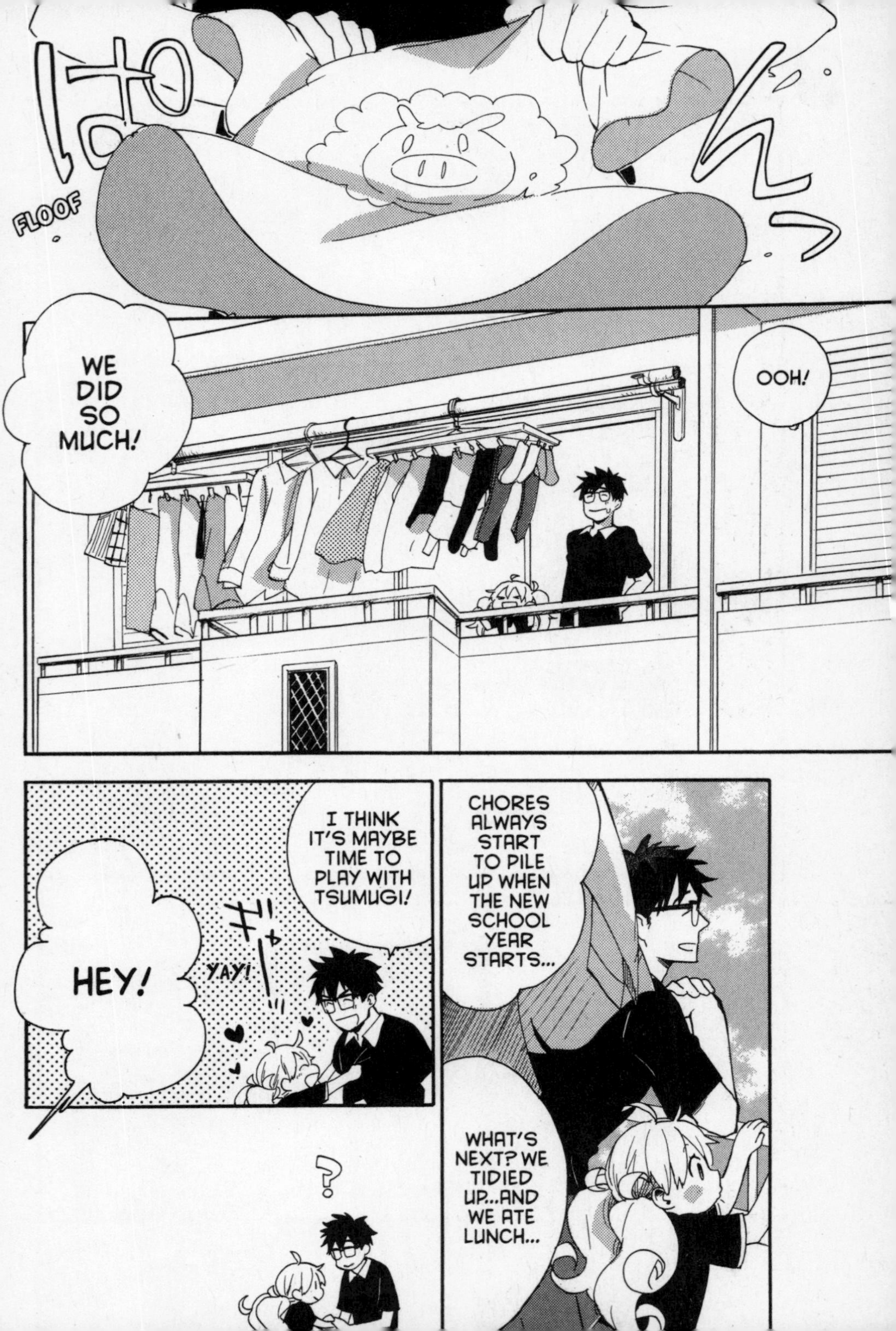
FLOOF
OOH!
WE DID SO MUCH!
CHORES ALWAYS START TO PILE UP WHEN THE NEW SCHOOL YEAR STARTS...
WHAT'S NEXT? WE TIDIED UP...AND WE ATE LUNCH...
?
I THINK IT'S MAYBE TIME TO PLAY WITH TSUMUGI!
YAY!
HEY!

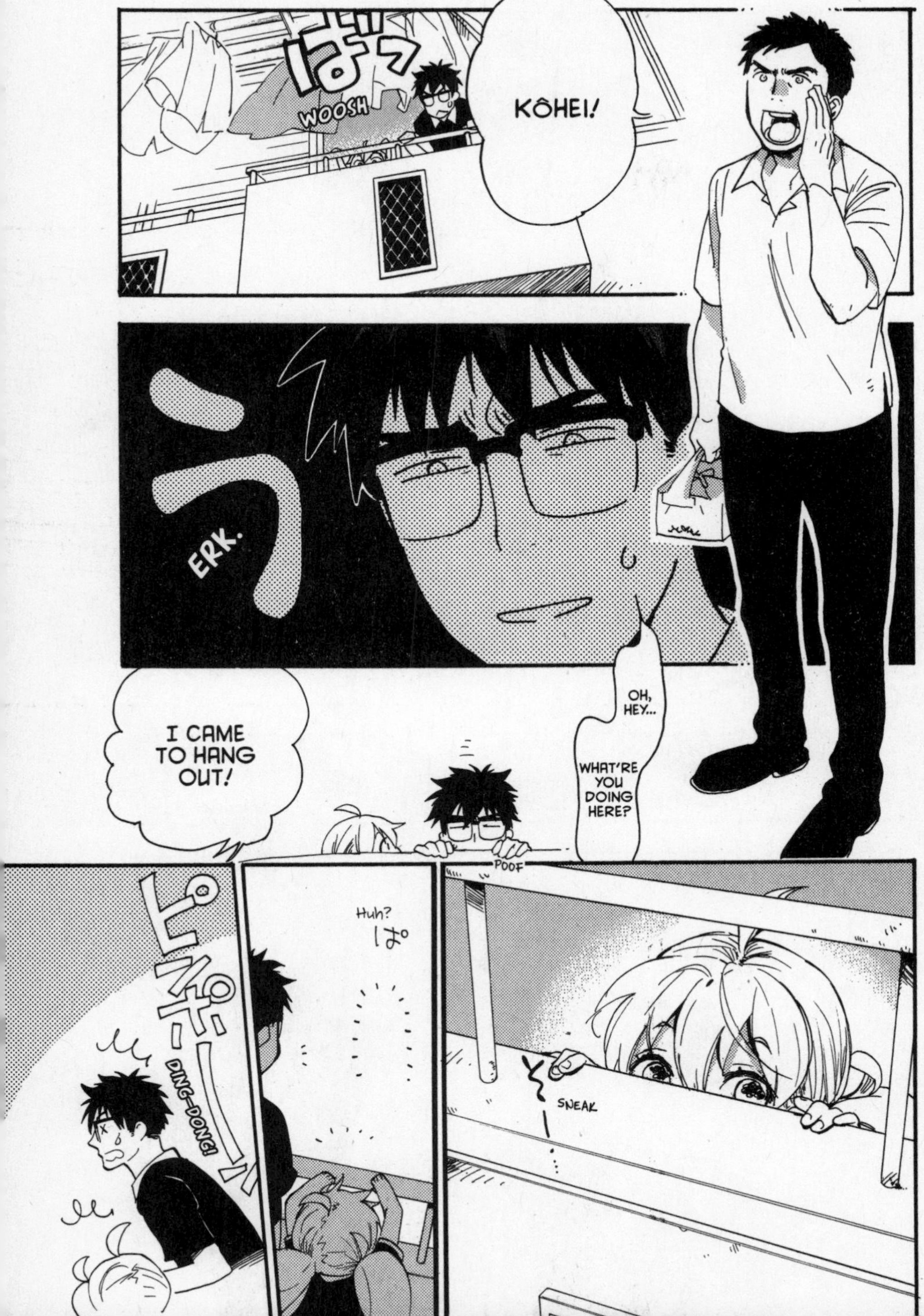
KÔHEI!
ばっ
WOOSH
う
ERK.
OH, HEY...
WHAT'RE YOU DOING HERE?
I CAME TO HANG OUT!
POOF
そ
SNEAK
Huh?
ぱ
ピンポーン
DING-DONG!

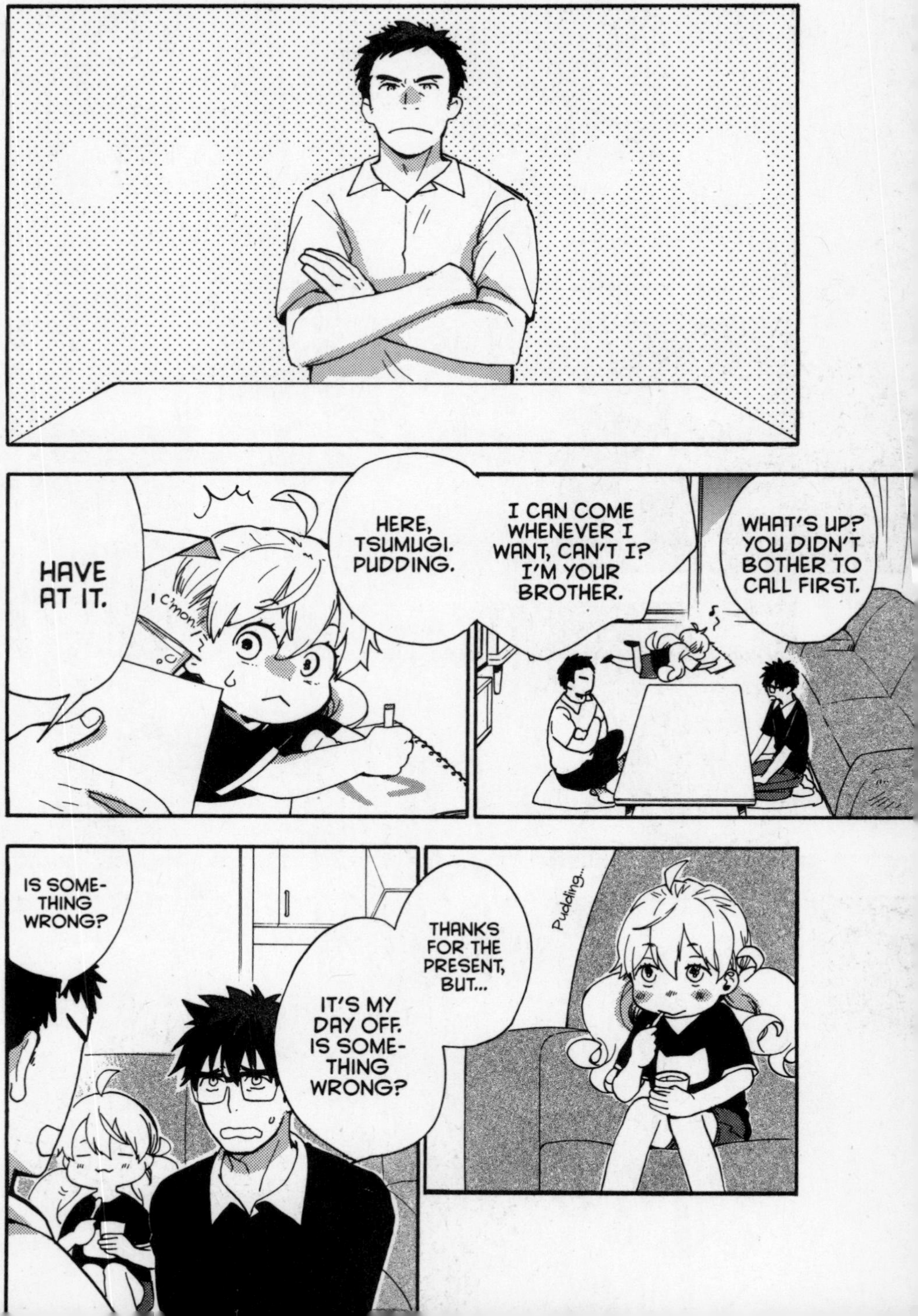
WHAT'S UP? YOU DIDN'T BOTHER TO CALL FIRST.
I CAN COME WHENEVER I WANT, CAN'T I? I'M YOUR BROTHER.
HERE, TSUMUGI. PUDDING.
C'mon
HAVE AT IT.
Pudding...
THANKS FOR THE PRESENT, BUT...
IT'S MY DAY OFF. IS SOME-THING WRONG?
IS SOME-THING WRONG?

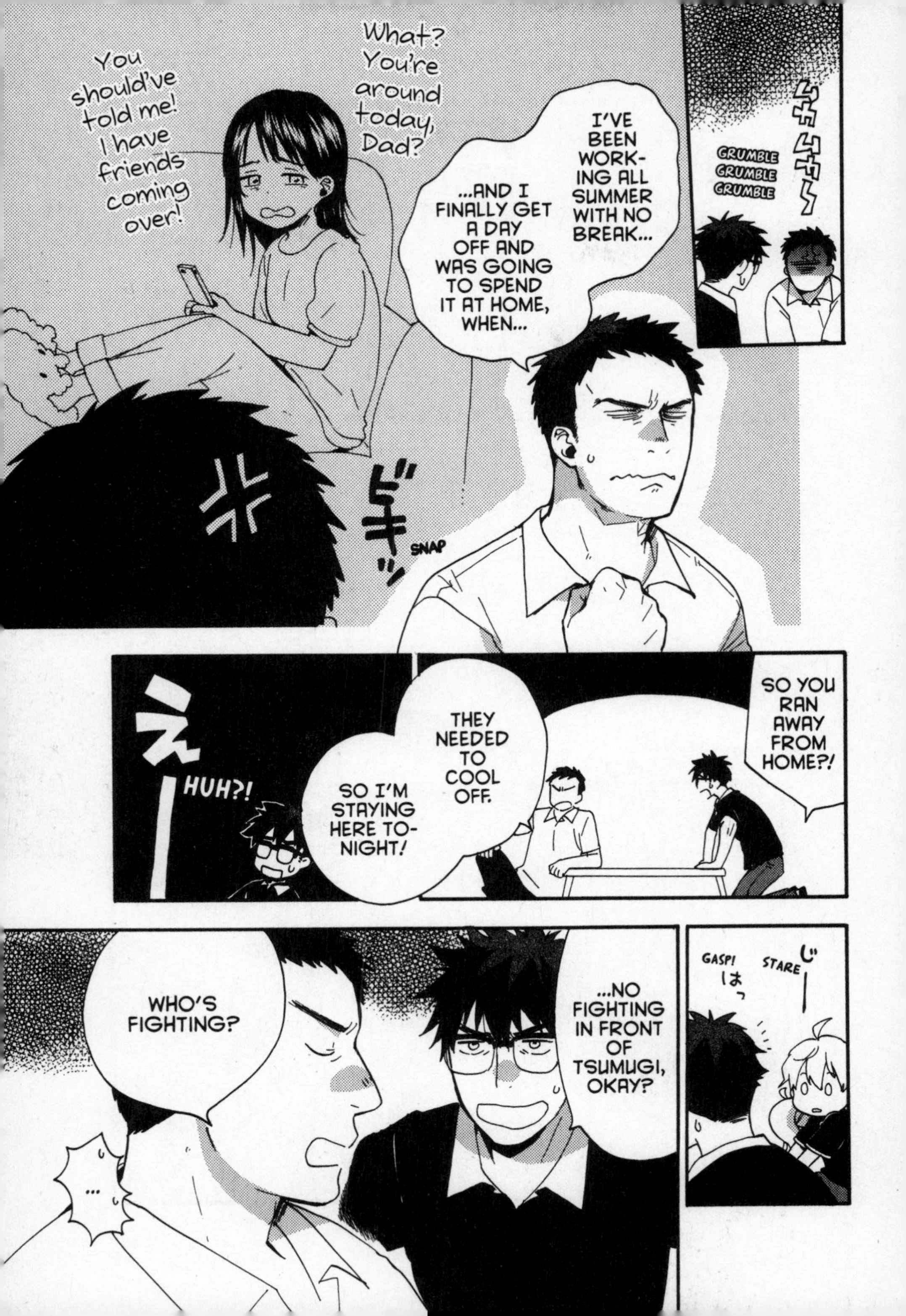
ムカムカ
GRUMBLE GRUMBLE GRUMBLE
I'VE BEEN WORKING ALL SUMMER WITH NO BREAK...
...AND I FINALLY GET A DAY OFF AND WAS GOING TO SPEND IT AT HOME, WHEN...
What? You're around today, Dad?
You should've told me! I have friends coming over!
ビキッ
SNAP
SO YOU RAN AWAY FROM HOME?!
THEY NEEDED TO COOL OFF.
SO I'M STAYING HERE TO-NIGHT!
え
HUH?!
じー
STARE
はっ
GASP!
...NO FIGHTING IN FRONT OF TSUMUGI, OKAY?
WHO'S FIGHTING?
...

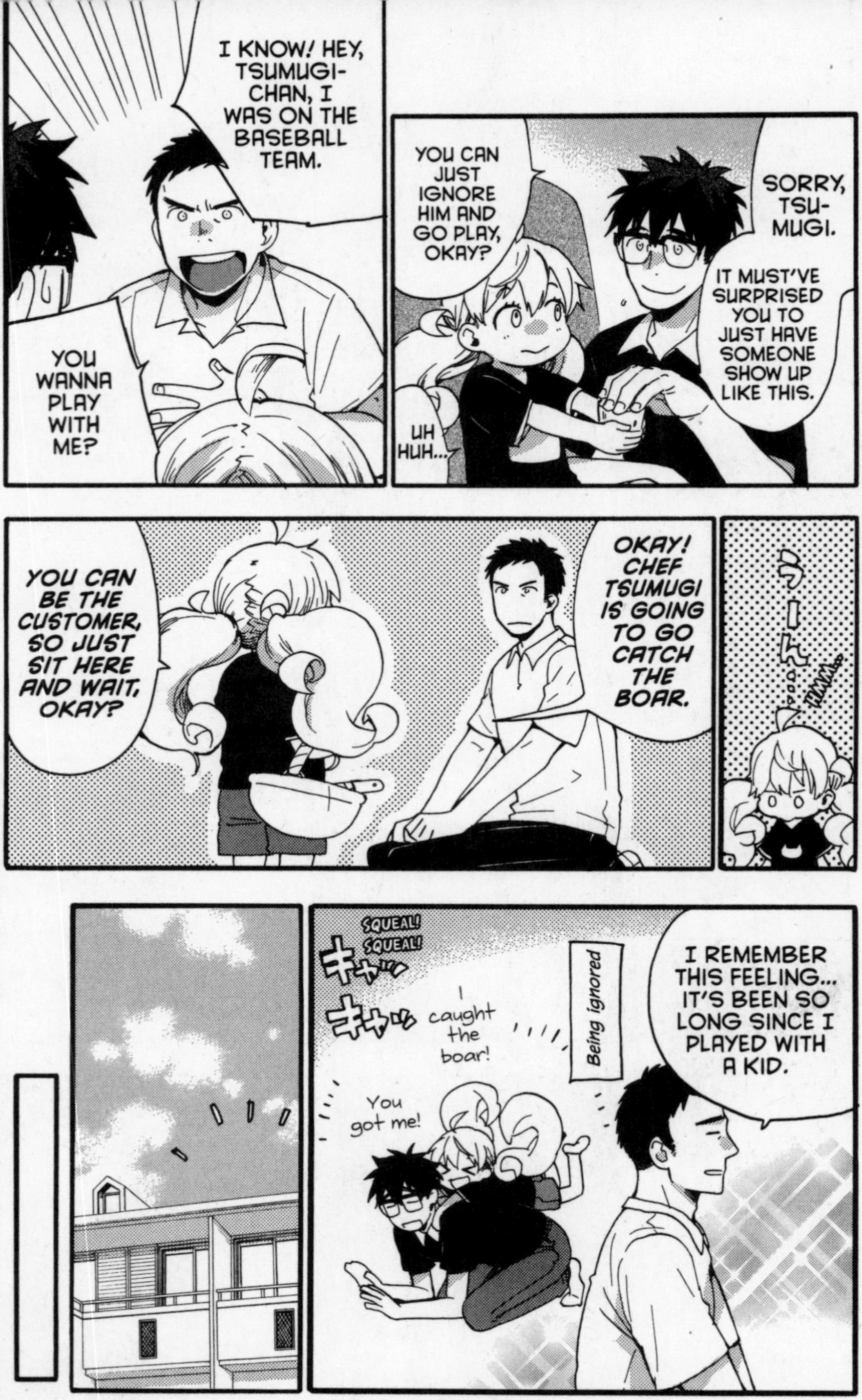
SORRY, TSUMUGI.
IT MUST'VE SURPRISED YOU TO JUST HAVE SOMEONE SHOW UP LIKE THIS.
YOU CAN JUST IGNORE HIM AND GO PLAY, OKAY?
UH HUH...
I KNOW! HEY, TSUMUGI-CHAN, I WAS ON THE BASEBALL TEAM.
YOU WANNA PLAY WITH ME?
うーん…
HMMM...
OKAY! CHEF TSUMUGI IS GOING TO GO CATCH THE BOAR.
YOU CAN BE THE CUSTOMER, SO JUST SIT HERE AND WAIT, OKAY?
I REMEMBER THIS FEELING... IT'S BEEN SO LONG SINCE I PLAYED WITH A KID.
Being ignored
I caught the boar!
キャッ キャッ
SQUEAL! SQUEAL!
You got me!

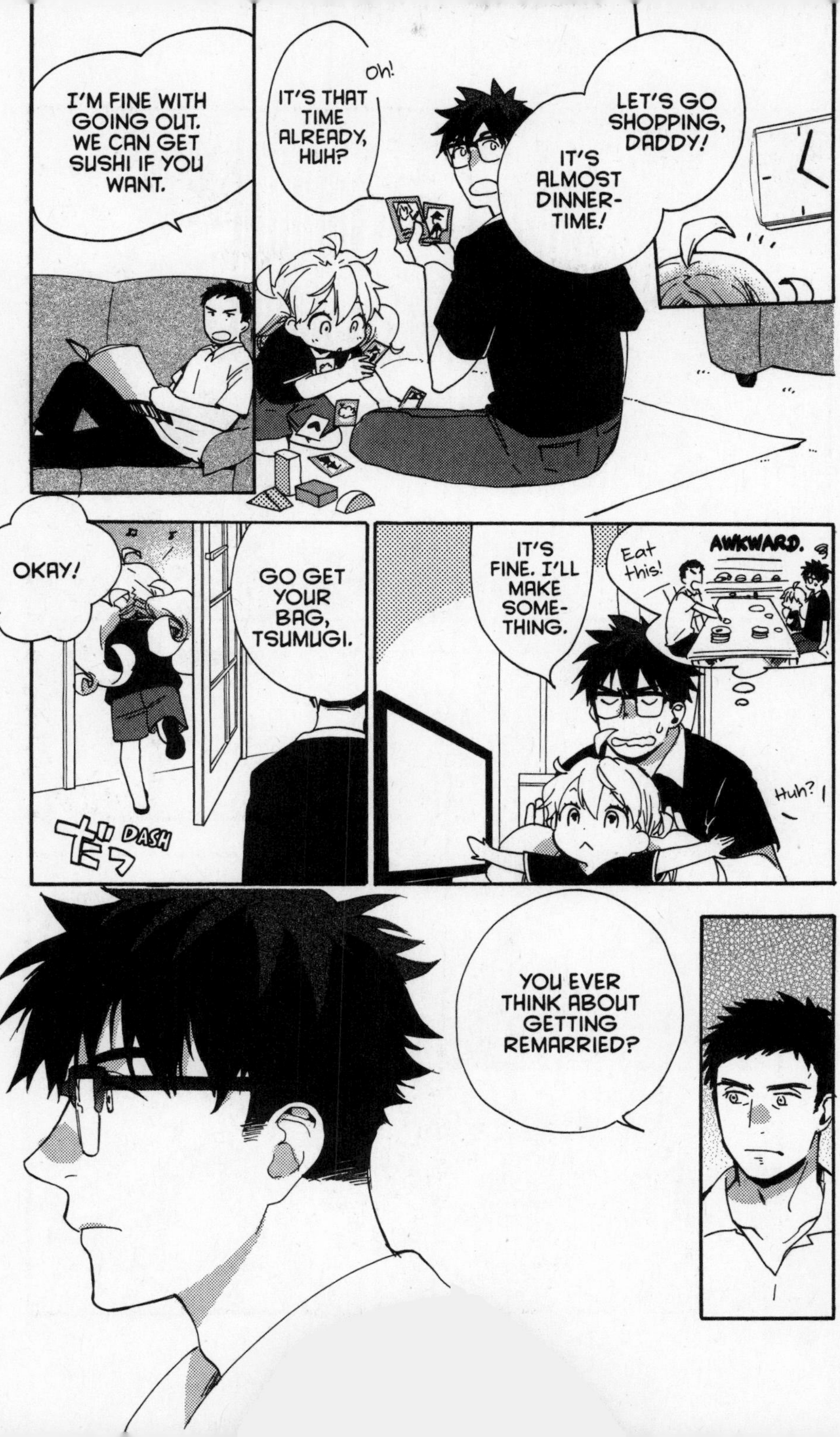
LET'S GO SHOPPING, DADDY!
IT'S ALMOST DINNER-TIME!
Oh!
IT'S THAT TIME ALREADY, HUH?
I'M FINE WITH GOING OUT. WE CAN GET SUSHI IF YOU WANT.
IT'S FINE. I'LL MAKE SOME-THING.
AWKWARD.
Eat this!
Huh?
GO GET YOUR BAG, TSUMUGI.
OKAY!
ダッ DASH
YOU EVER THINK ABOUT GETTING REMARRIED?

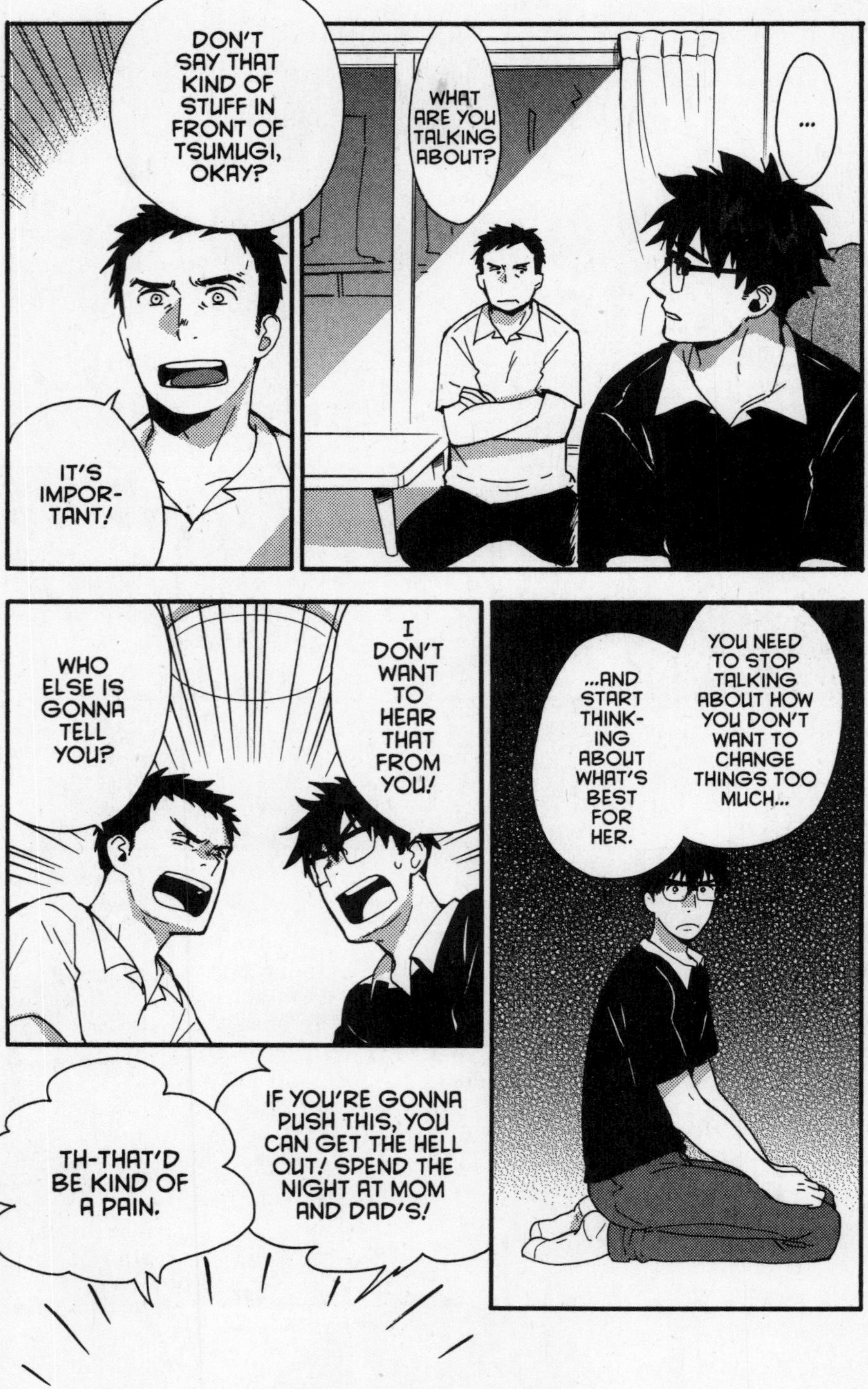
...
WHAT ARE YOU TALKING ABOUT?
DON'T SAY THAT KIND OF STUFF IN FRONT OF TSUMUGI, OKAY?
IT'S IMPORTANT!
YOU NEED TO STOP TALKING ABOUT HOW YOU DON'T WANT TO CHANGE THINGS TOO MUCH...
...AND START THINKING ABOUT WHAT'S BEST FOR HER.
I DON'T WANT TO HEAR THAT FROM YOU!
WHO ELSE IS GONNA TELL YOU?
IF YOU'RE GONNA PUSH THIS, YOU CAN GET THE HELL OUT! SPEND THE NIGHT AT MOM AND DAD'S!
TH-THAT'D BE KIND OF A PAIN.

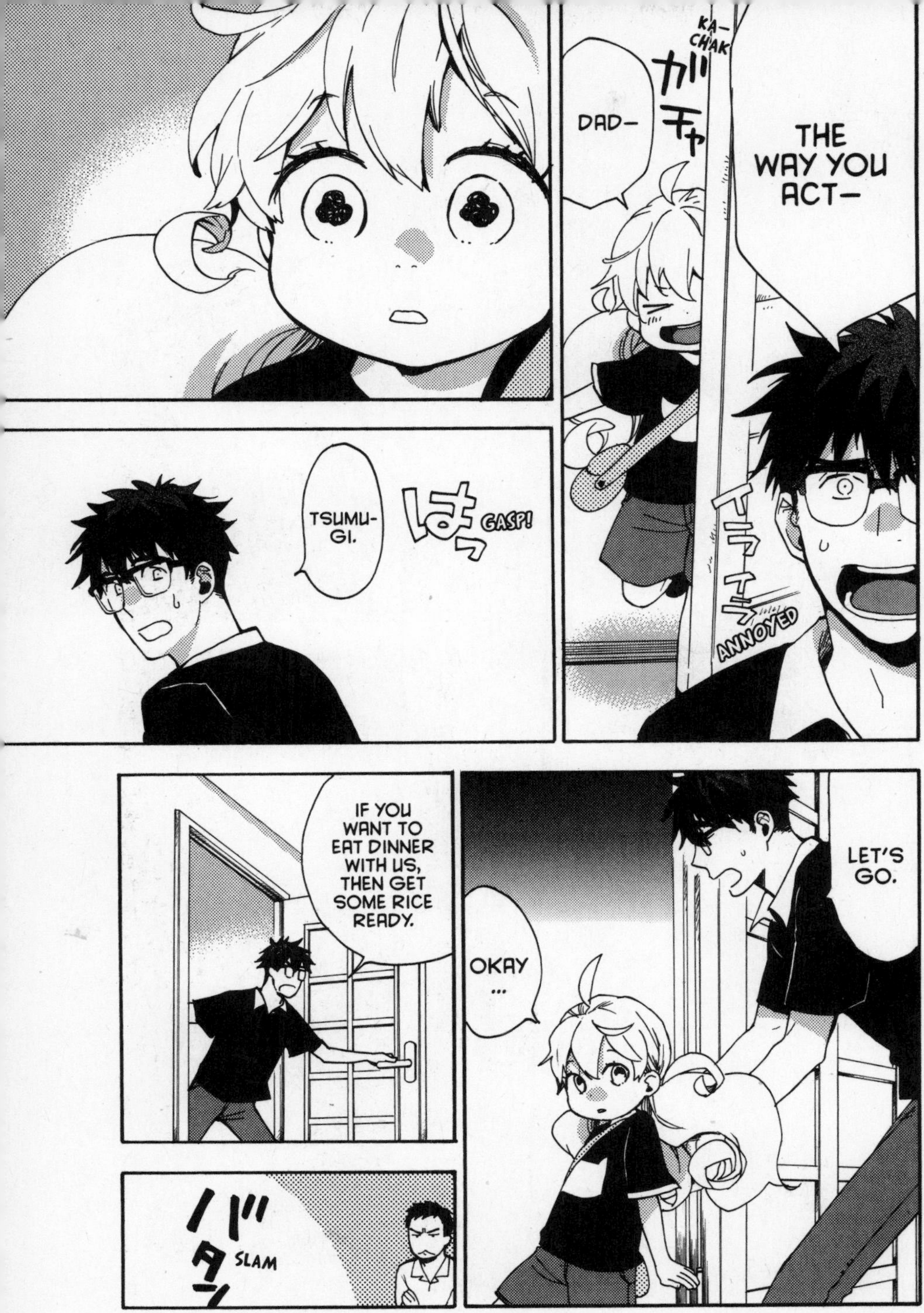
KA-CHAK
ガチャ
DAD—
THE WAY YOU ACT—
イライラ
ANNOYED
TSUMUGI.
はっ
GASP!
LET'S GO.
OKAY ...
IF YOU WANT TO EAT DINNER WITH US, THEN GET SOME RICE READY.
バタン
SLAM

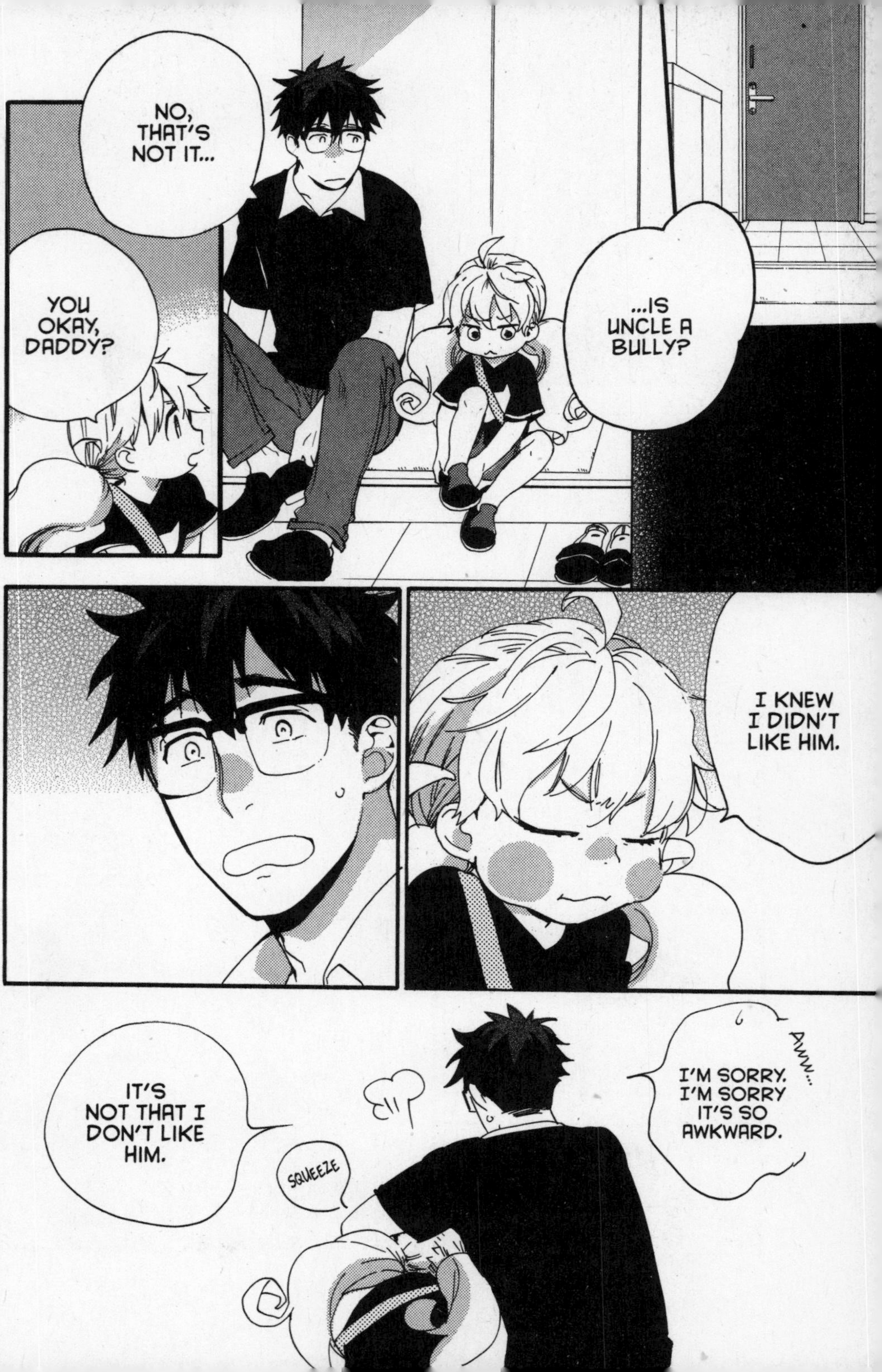
...IS UNCLE A BULLY?
NO, THAT'S NOT IT...
YOU OKAY, DADDY?
I KNEW I DIDN'T LIKE HIM.
AWW...
I'M SORRY. I'M SORRY IT'S SO AWKWARD.
IT'S NOT THAT I DON'T LIKE HIM.
SQUEEZE

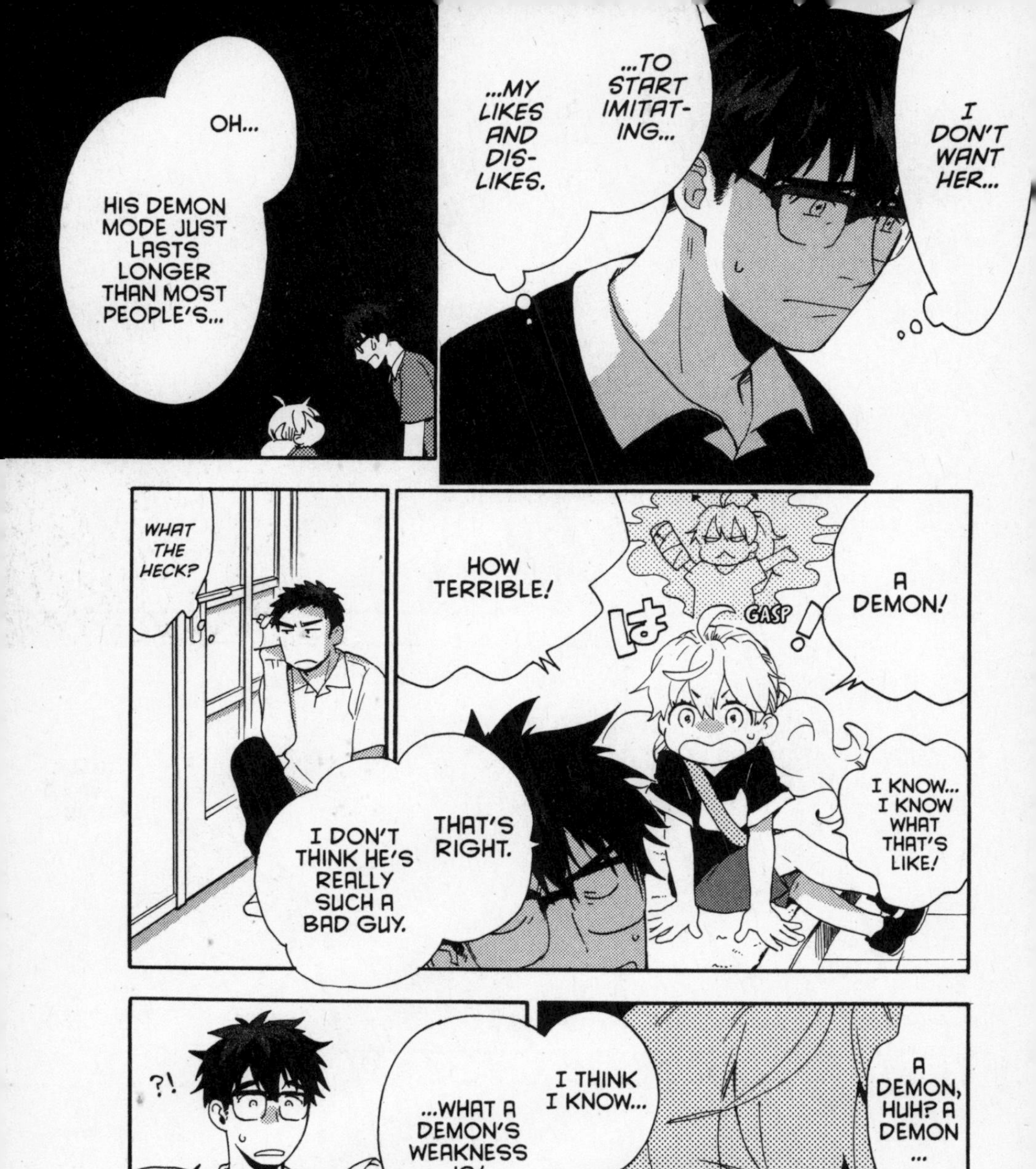
I DON'T WANT HER...
...TO START IMITATING...
...MY LIKES AND DISLIKES.
OH...
HIS DEMON MODE JUST LASTS LONGER THAN MOST PEOPLE'S...
A DEMON!
HOW TERRIBLE!
は
GASP
!
I KNOW... I KNOW WHAT THAT'S LIKE!
THAT'S RIGHT.
I DON'T THINK HE'S REALLY SUCH A BAD GUY.
WHAT THE HECK?
A DEMON, HUH? A DEMON...
I THINK I KNOW...
...WHAT A DEMON'S WEAKNESS IS!
?!
HUH? WHAT IS IT?
HEH!

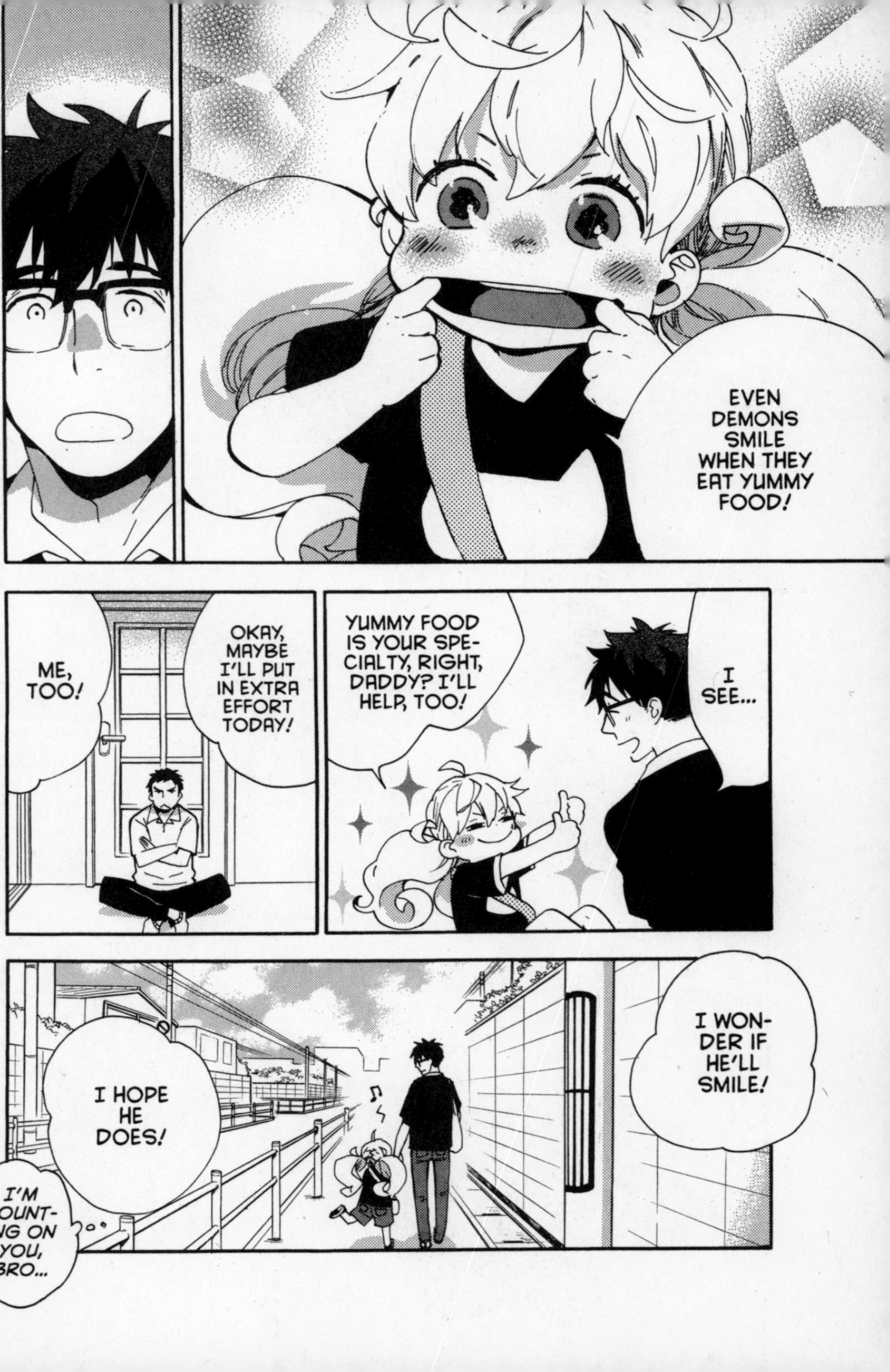
EVEN DEMONS SMILE WHEN THEY EAT YUMMY FOOD!
I SEE...
YUMMY FOOD IS YOUR SPE-CIALTY, RIGHT, DADDY? I'LL HELP, TOO!
OKAY, MAYBE I'LL PUT IN EXTRA EFFORT TODAY!
ME, TOO!
I WON-DER IF HE'LL SMILE!
I HOPE HE DOES!
I'M COUNT-ING ON YOU, BRO...

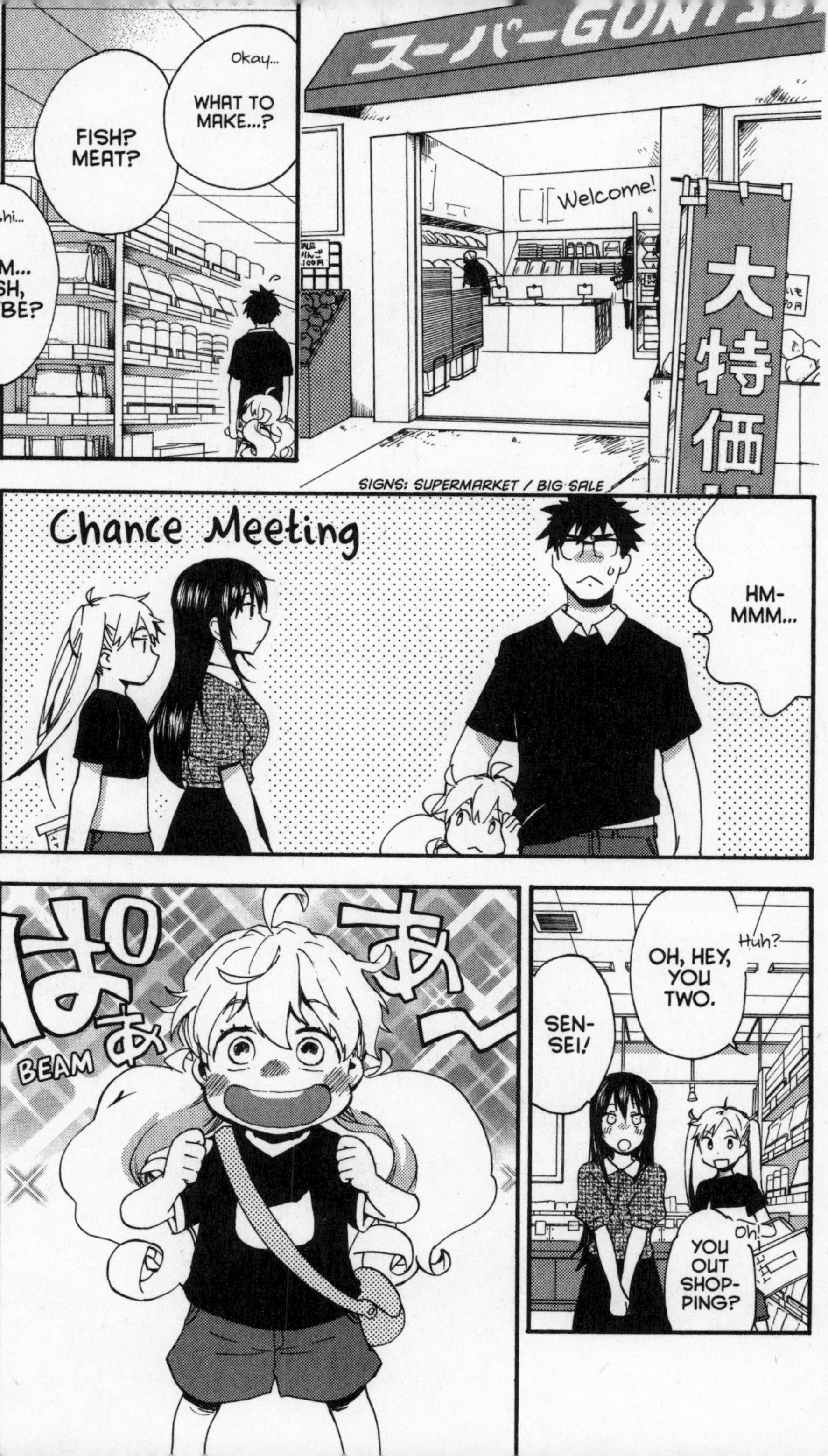
スーパー
Welcome!
大特価
SIGNS: SUPERMARKET / BIG SALE
Okay...
WHAT TO MAKE...?
FISH? MEAT?
Sushi...
HMM... FISH, MAYBE?
Chance Meeting
HM-MMM...
Huh?
OH, HEY, YOU TWO.
SEN-SEI!
Oh!
YOU OUT SHOP-PING?
ぱぁ
あ～
BEAM

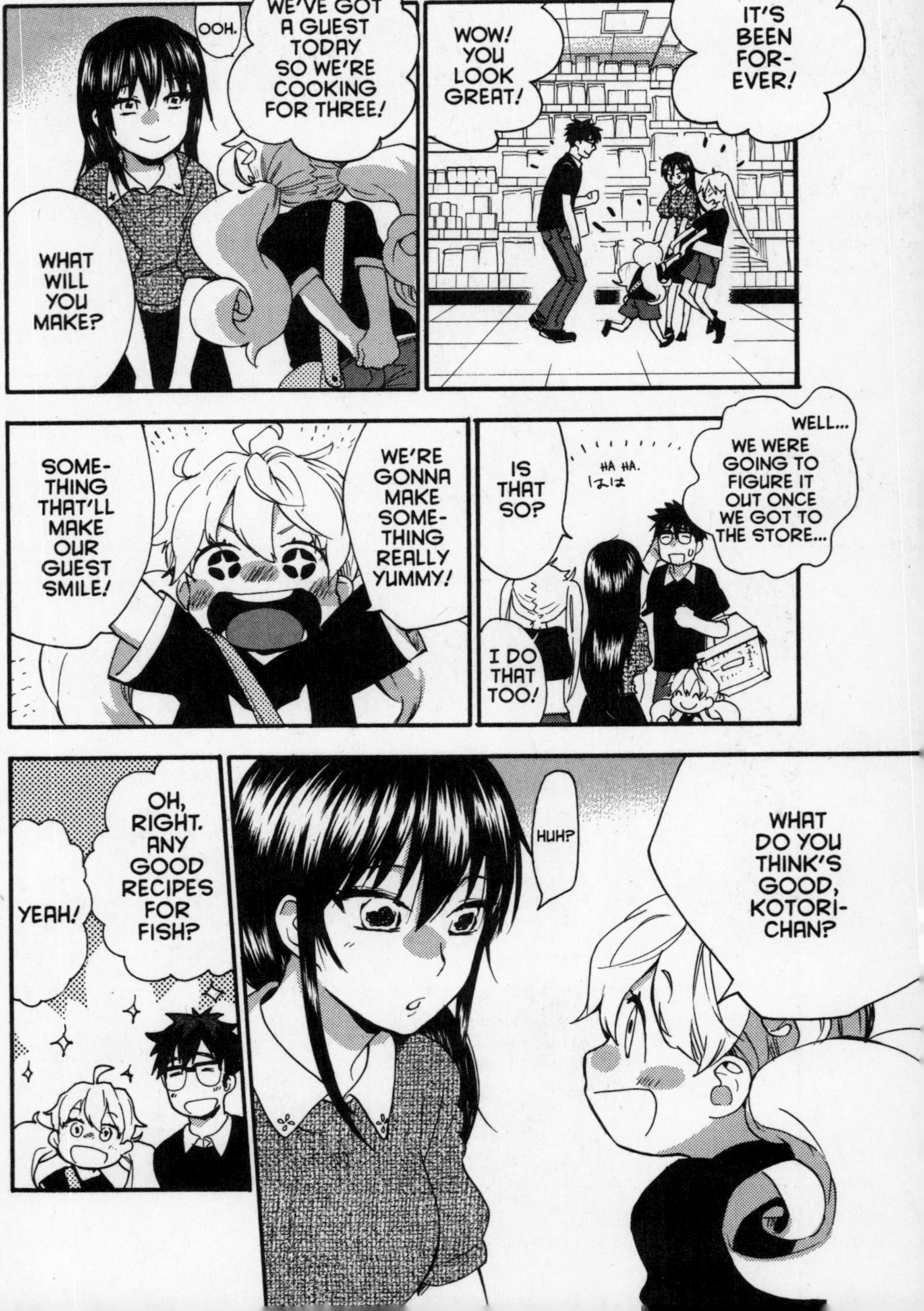
IT'S BEEN FOR-EVER!
WOW! YOU LOOK GREAT!
WE'VE GOT A GUEST TODAY SO WE'RE COOKING FOR THREE!
OOH.
WHAT WILL YOU MAKE?
WELL... WE WERE GOING TO FIGURE IT OUT ONCE WE GOT TO THE STORE...
HA HA. はは
IS THAT SO?
I DO THAT TOO!
WE'RE GONNA MAKE SOME-THING REALLY YUMMY!
SOME-THING THAT'LL MAKE OUR GUEST SMILE!
WHAT DO YOU THINK'S GOOD, KOTORI-CHAN?
HUH?
OH, RIGHT. ANY GOOD RECIPES FOR FISH?
YEAH!

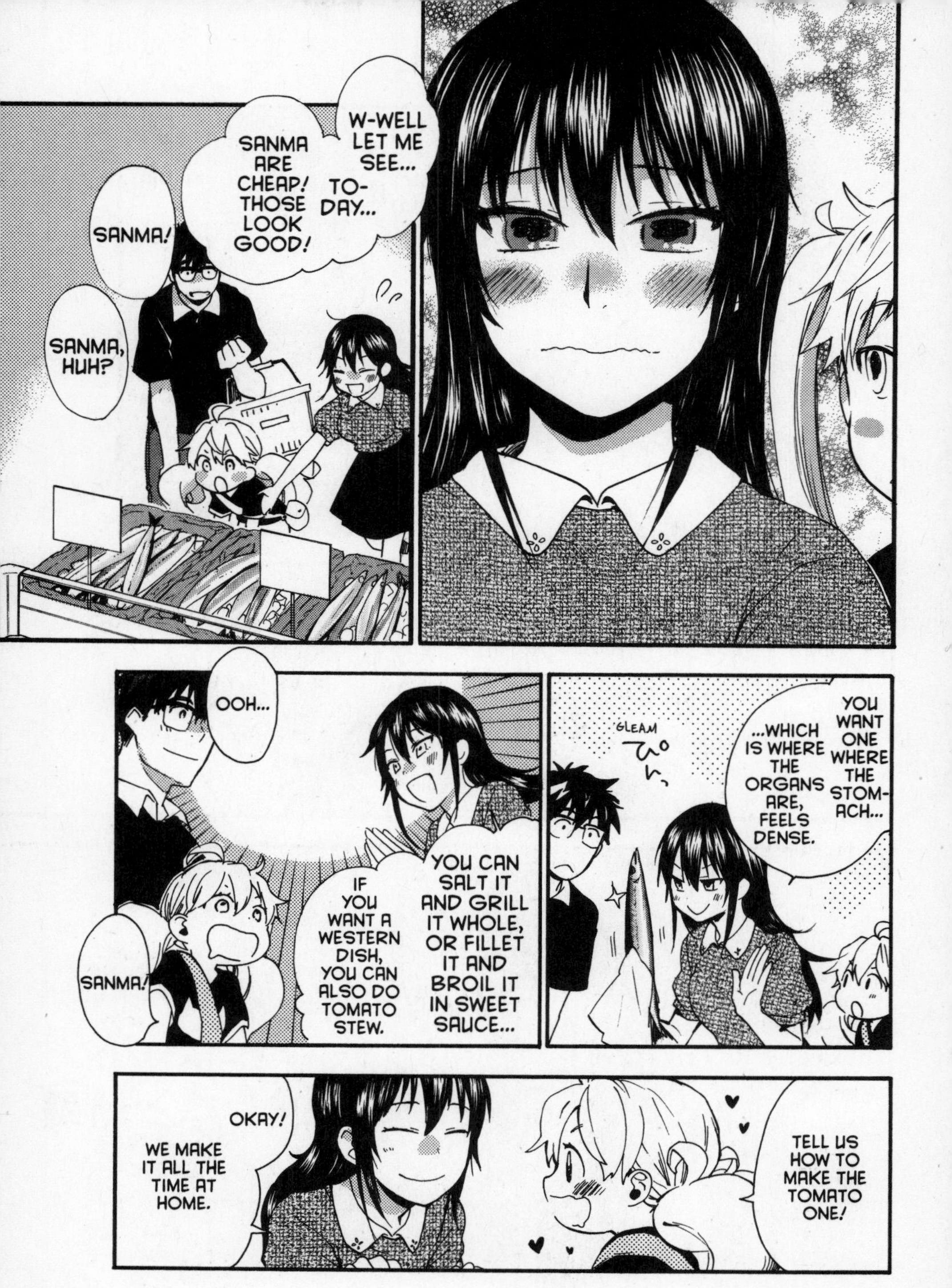
W-WELL LET ME SEE... TO-DAY...
SANMA ARE CHEAP! THOSE LOOK GOOD!
SANMA!
SANMA, HUH?
YOU WANT ONE WHERE THE STOMACH...
...WHICH IS WHERE THE ORGANS ARE, FEELS DENSE.
GLEAM
YOU CAN SALT IT AND GRILL IT WHOLE, OR FILLET IT AND BROIL IT IN SWEET SAUCE...
IF YOU WANT A WESTERN DISH, YOU CAN ALSO DO TOMATO STEW.
OOH...
SANMA!
TELL US HOW TO MAKE THE TOMATO ONE!
OKAY!
WE MAKE IT ALL THE TIME AT HOME.

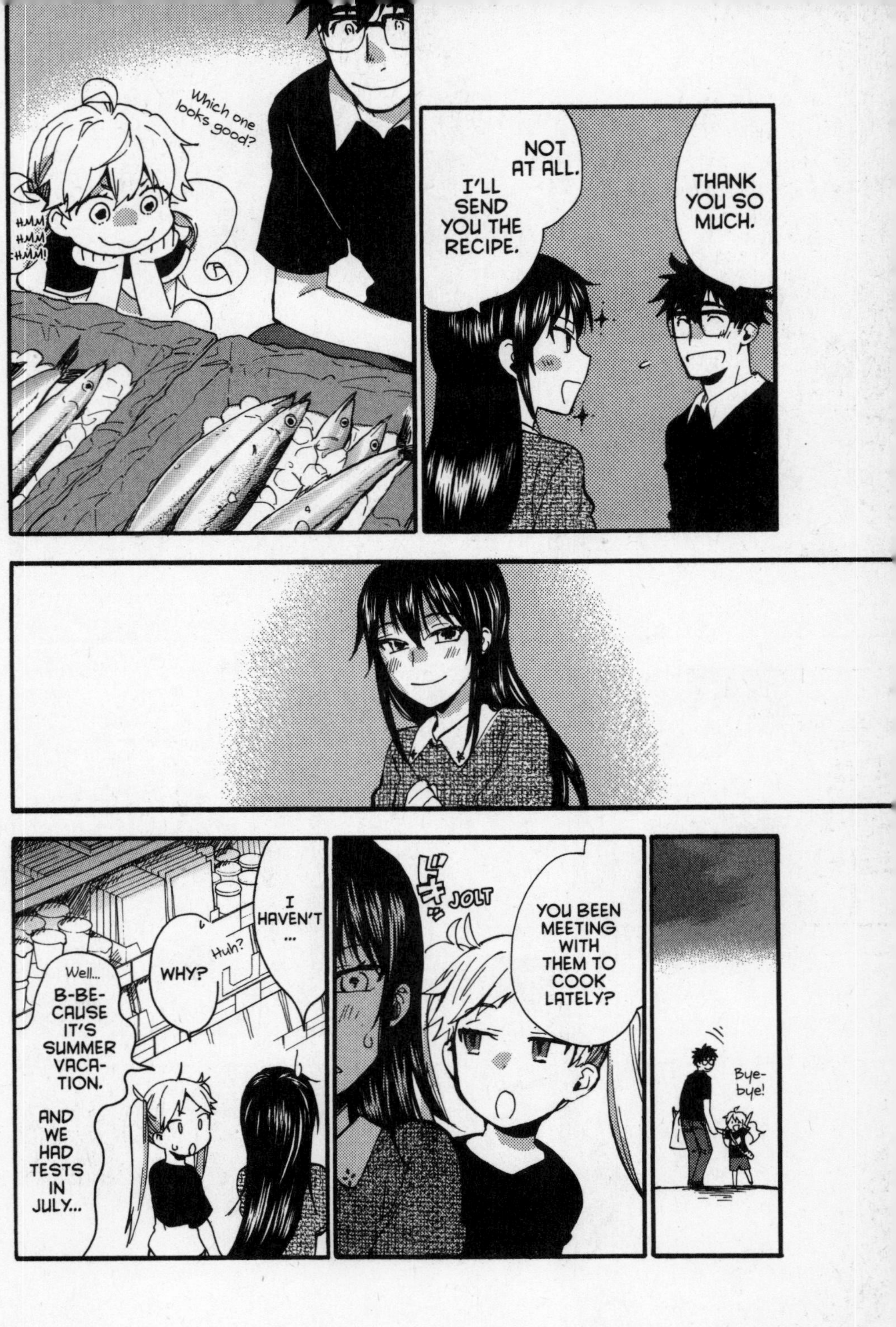
THANK YOU SO MUCH.
NOT AT ALL.
I'LL SEND YOU THE RECIPE.
Which one looks good?
HMM HMM HMM!
Bye-bye!
ドキッ
JOLT
YOU BEEN MEETING WITH THEM TO COOK LATELY?
I HAVEN'T ...
Huh?
WHY?
Well...
B-BECAUSE IT'S SUMMER VACATION.
AND WE HAD TESTS IN JULY...

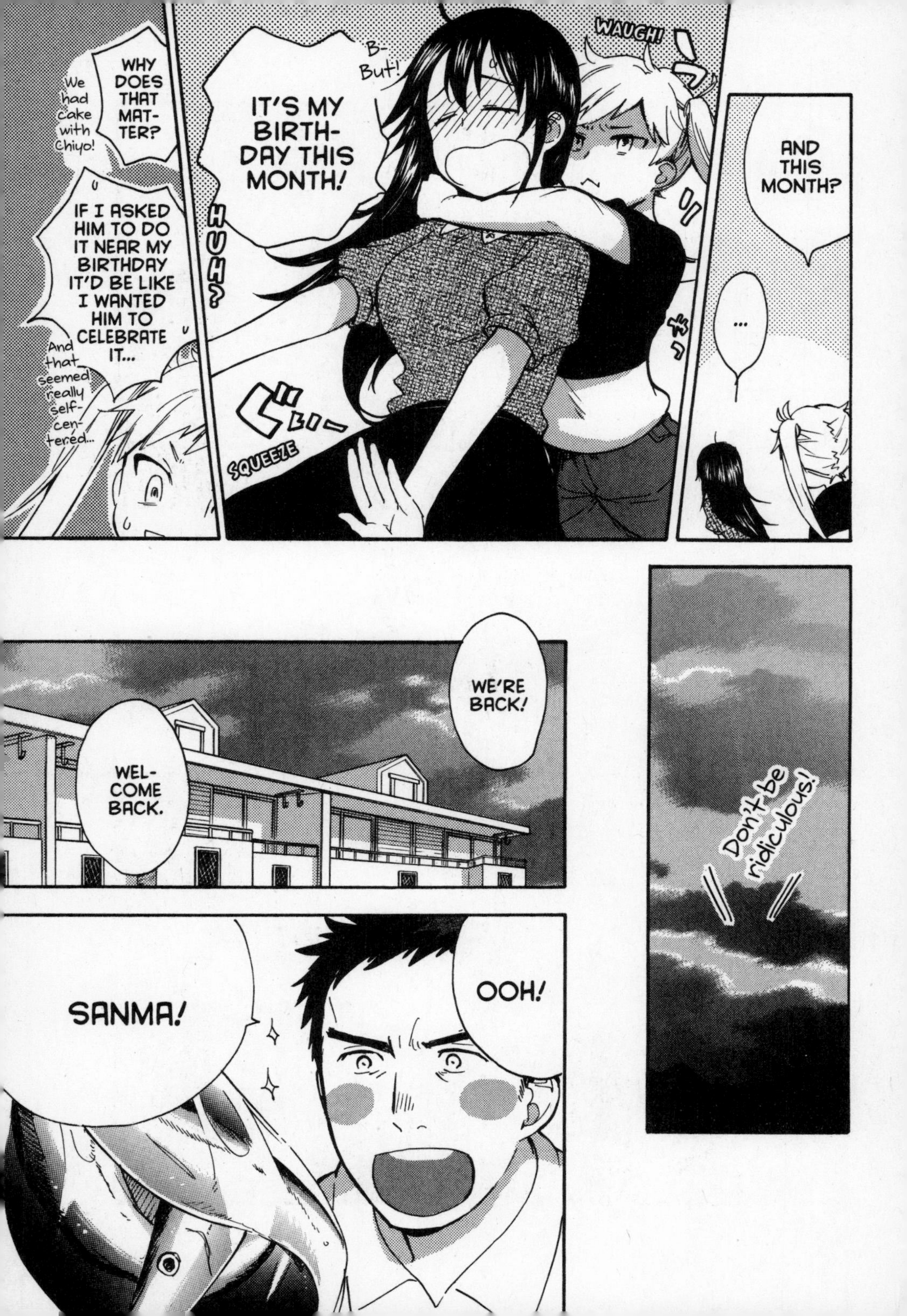
AND THIS MONTH?
...
WAUGH!
B-But!
IT'S MY BIRTHDAY THIS MONTH!
HUH?
SQUEEZE
WHY DOES THAT MATTER?
We had cake with Chiyo!
IF I ASKED HIM TO DO IT NEAR MY BIRTHDAY IT'D BE LIKE I WANTED HIM TO CELEBRATE IT...
And that seemed really self-centered...
Don't be ridiculous!
WE'RE BACK!
WELCOME BACK.
OOH!
SANMA!

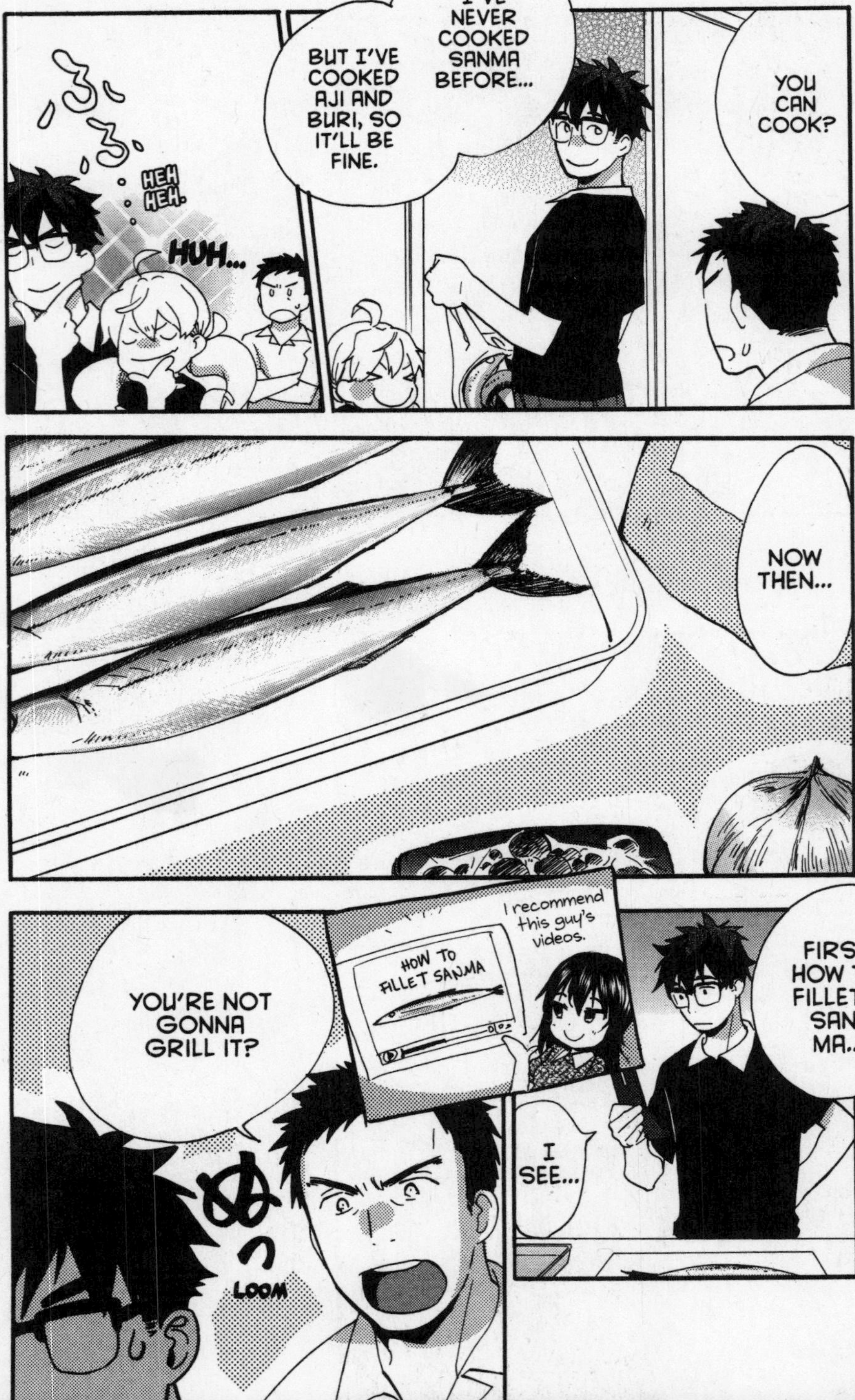
YOU CAN COOK?
I'VE NEVER COOKED SANMA BEFORE...
BUT I'VE COOKED AJI AND BURI, SO IT'LL BE FINE.
ふふ
HEH HEH.
HUH...
NOW THEN...
FIRST, HOW TO FILLET A SAN-MA...
I recommend this guy's videos.
HOW TO FILLET SANMA
I SEE...
YOU'RE NOT GONNA GRILL IT?
ぬっ
LOOM

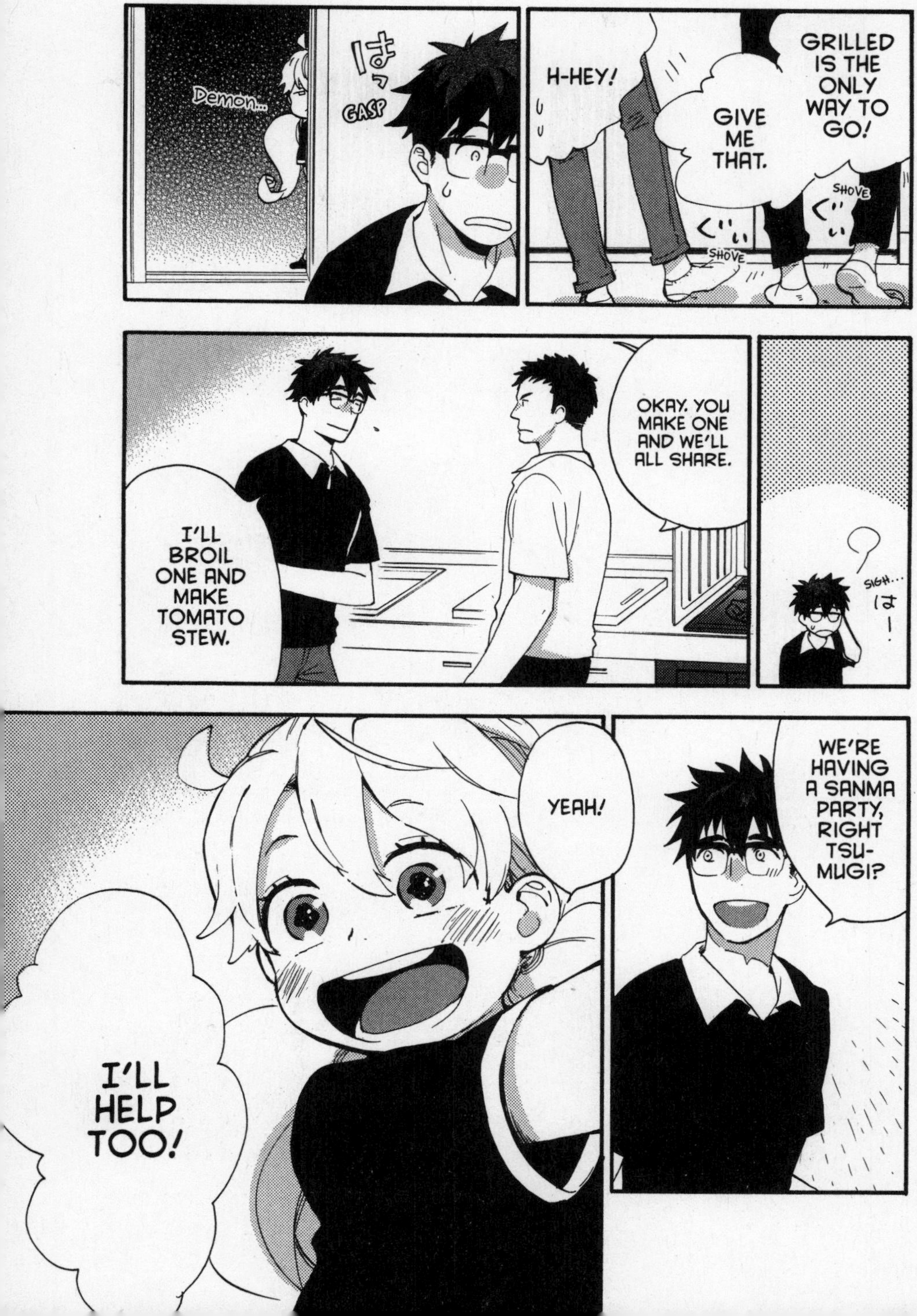
GRILLED IS THE ONLY WAY TO GO!
GIVE ME THAT.
H-HEY!
SHOVE
ぐい
SHOVE
ぐい
はっ
GASP
Demon...
SIGH...
は
OKAY. YOU MAKE ONE AND WE'LL ALL SHARE.
I'LL BROIL ONE AND MAKE TOMATO STEW.
WE'RE HAVING A SANMA PARTY, RIGHT TSU-MUGI?
YEAH!
I'LL HELP TOO!

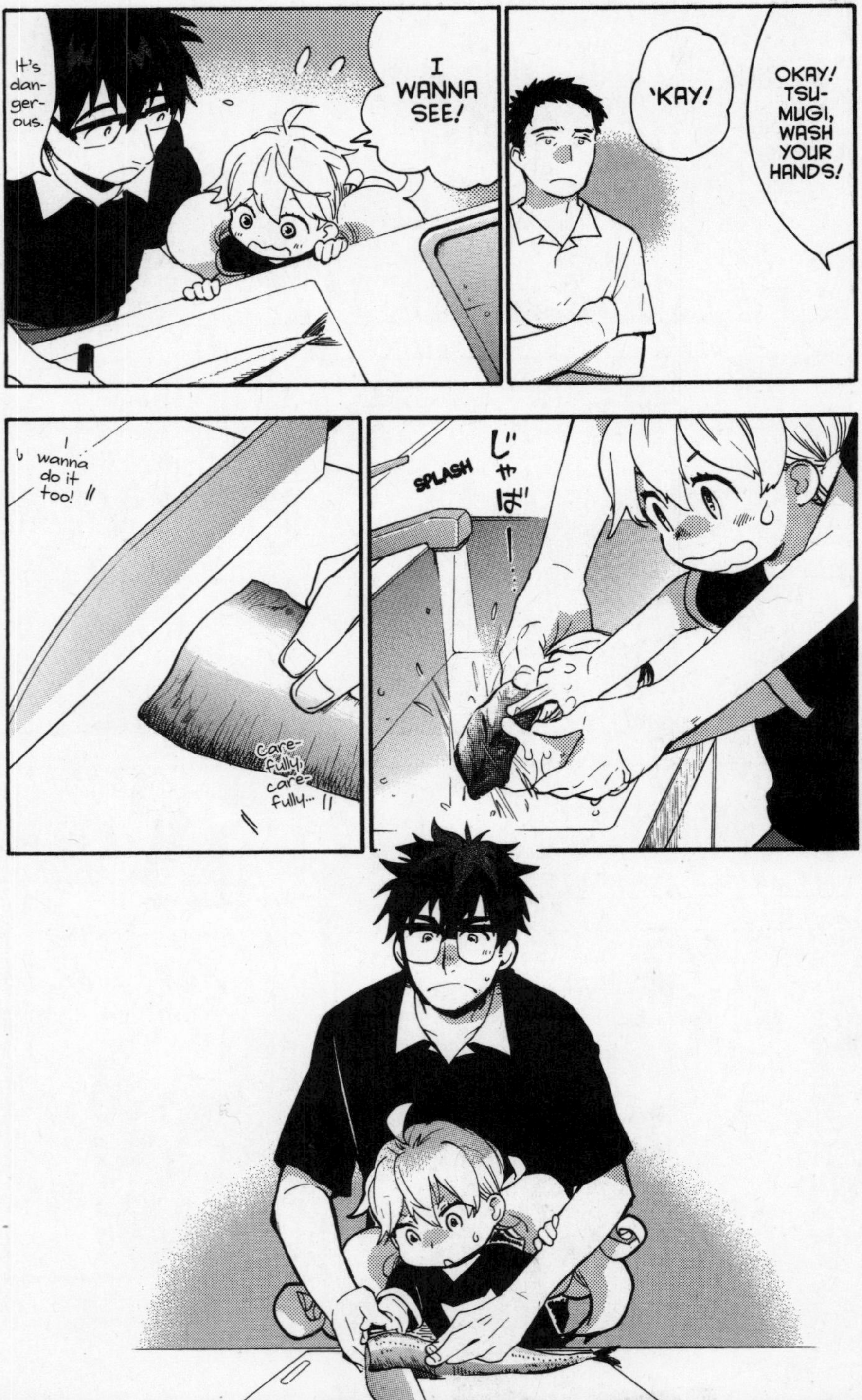
OKAY! TSU-MUGI, WASH YOUR HANDS!
'KAY!
I WANNA SEE!
It's dan-ger-ous.
SPLASH
じゃばー…
I wanna do it too!
care-fully, care-fully...

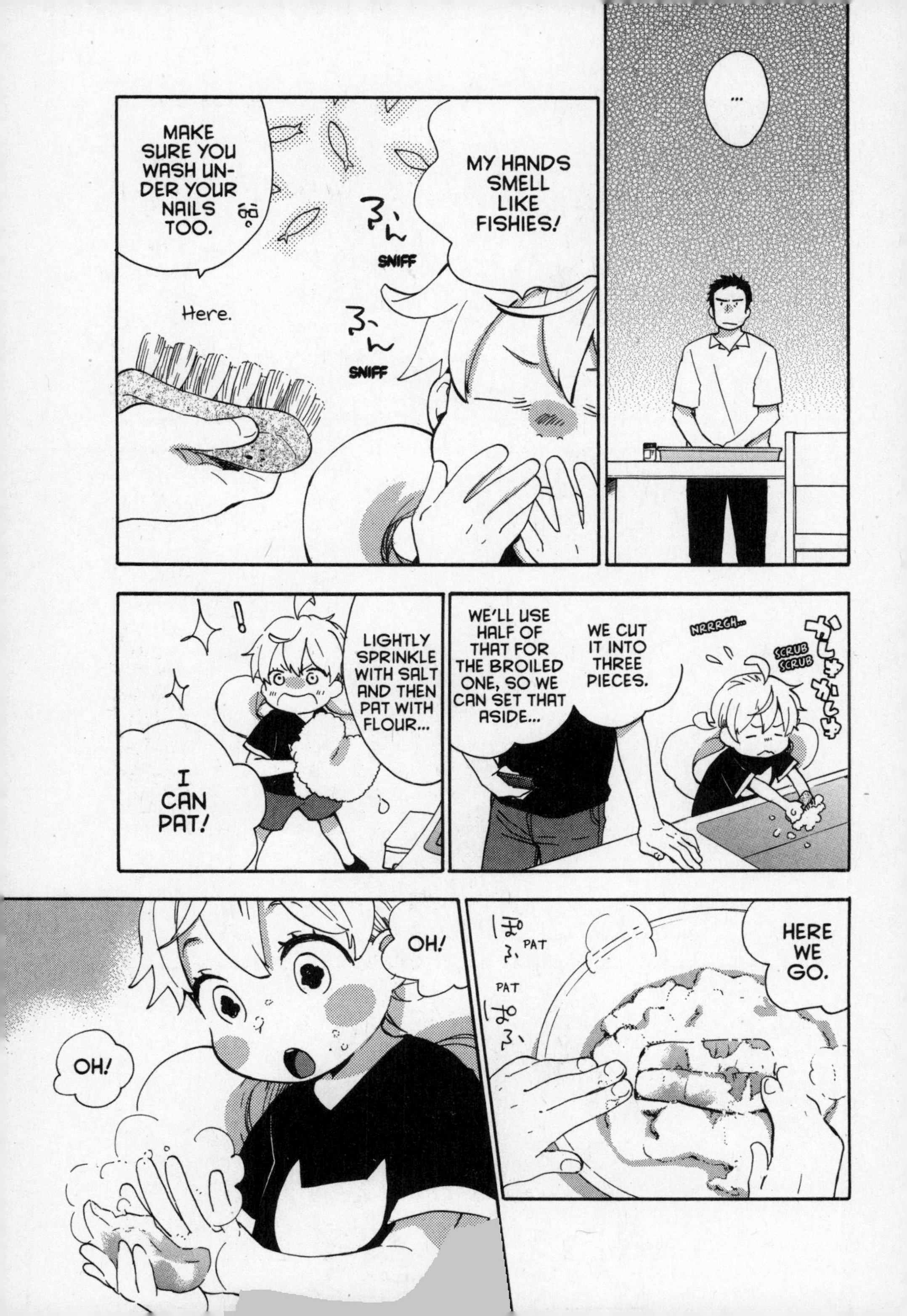
...
MY HANDS SMELL LIKE FISHIES!
SNIFF
SNIFF
MAKE SURE YOU WASH UNDER YOUR NAILS TOO.
Here.
NRRRGH...
SCRUB SCRUB
WE CUT IT INTO THREE PIECES.
WE'LL USE HALF OF THAT FOR THE BROILED ONE, SO WE CAN SET THAT ASIDE...
!
LIGHTLY SPRINKLE WITH SALT AND THEN PAT WITH FLOUR...
I CAN PAT!
HERE WE GO.
PAT
PAT
OH!
OH!

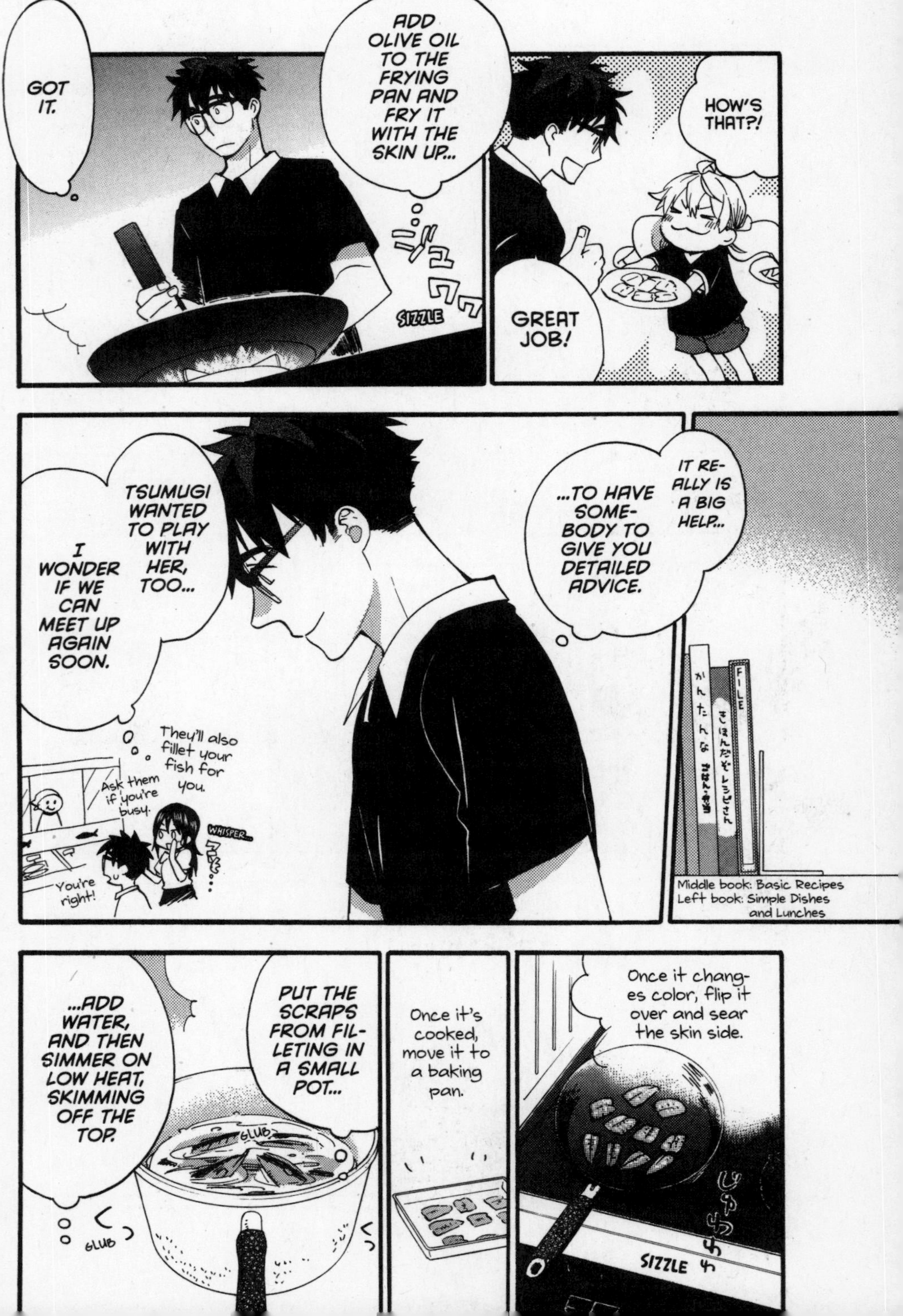
HOW'S THAT?!
GREAT JOB!
ADD OLIVE OIL TO THE FRYING PAN AND FRY IT WITH THE SKIN UP...
GOT IT.
SIZZLE
Middle book: Basic Recipes
Left book: Simple Dishes and Lunches
IT REALLY IS A BIG HELP...
...TO HAVE SOMEBODY TO GIVE YOU DETAILED ADVICE.
TSUMUGI WANTED TO PLAY WITH HER, TOO...
I WONDER IF WE CAN MEET UP AGAIN SOON.
They'll also fillet your fish for you.
Ask them if you're busy.
WHISPER...
You're right!
Once it changes color, flip it over and sear the skin side.
SIZZLE
Once it's cooked, move it to a baking pan.
PUT THE SCRAPS FROM FILLETING IN A SMALL POT...
...ADD WATER, AND THEN SIMMER ON LOW HEAT, SKIMMING OFF THE TOP.
GLUB
GLUB

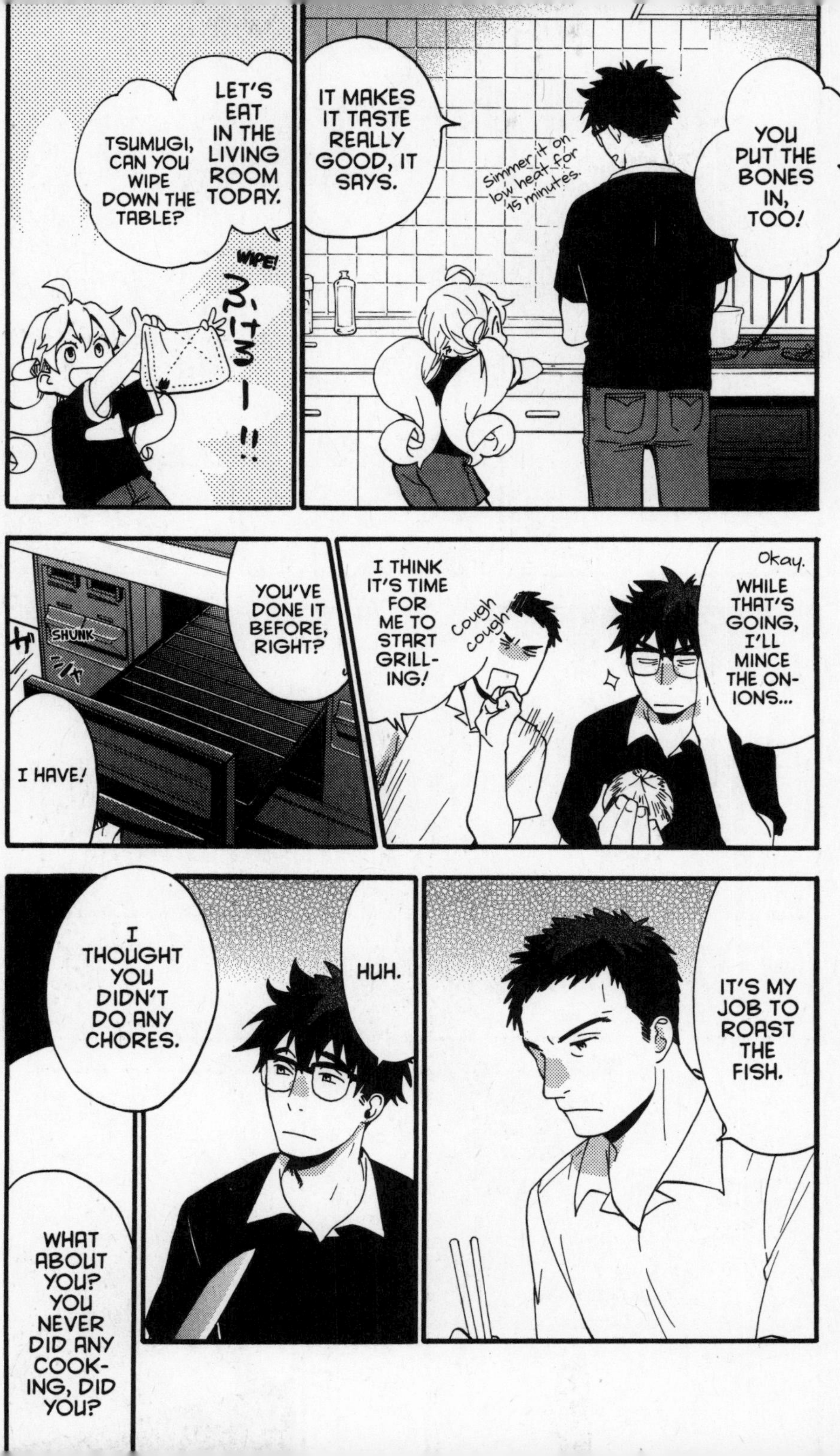
YOU PUT THE BONES IN, TOO!
Simmer it on low heat for 15 minutes.
IT MAKES IT TASTE REALLY GOOD, IT SAYS.
LET'S EAT IN THE LIVING ROOM TODAY.
TSUMUGI, CAN YOU WIPE DOWN THE TABLE?
WIPE!
ふけるー!!
Okay.
WHILE THAT'S GOING, I'LL MINCE THE ON-IONS...
I THINK IT'S TIME FOR ME TO START GRILL-ING!
cough cough
YOU'VE DONE IT BEFORE, RIGHT?
SHUNK
I HAVE!
IT'S MY JOB TO ROAST THE FISH.
HUH.
I THOUGHT YOU DIDN'T DO ANY CHORES.
WHAT ABOUT YOU? YOU NEVER DID ANY COOKING, DID YOU?

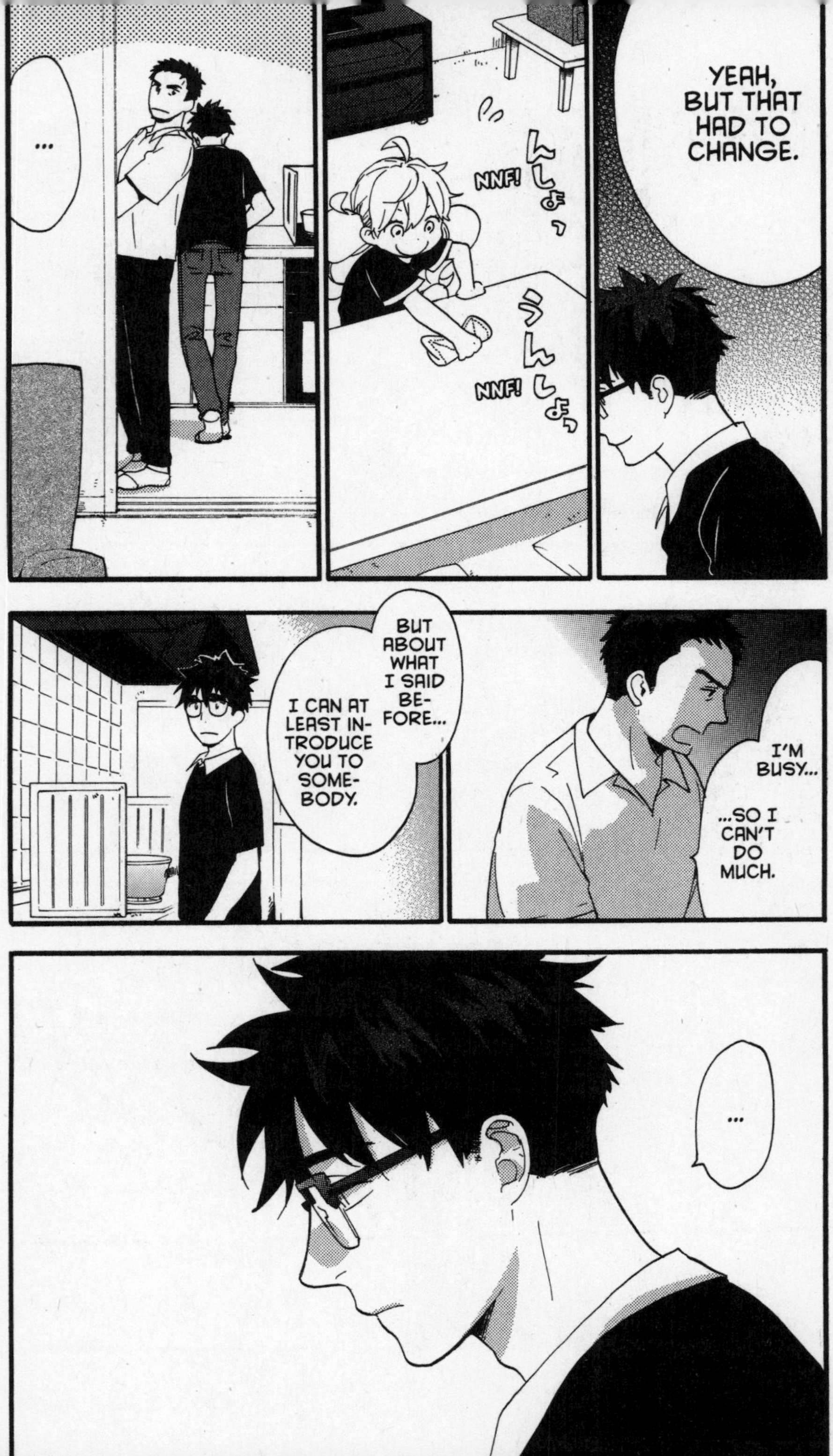
YEAH, BUT THAT HAD TO CHANGE.
んしょっ
NNF!
うんしょっ
NNF!
...
I'M BUSY...
...SO I CAN'T DO MUCH.
BUT ABOUT WHAT I SAID BEFORE...
I CAN AT LEAST INTRODUCE YOU TO SOMEBODY.
...

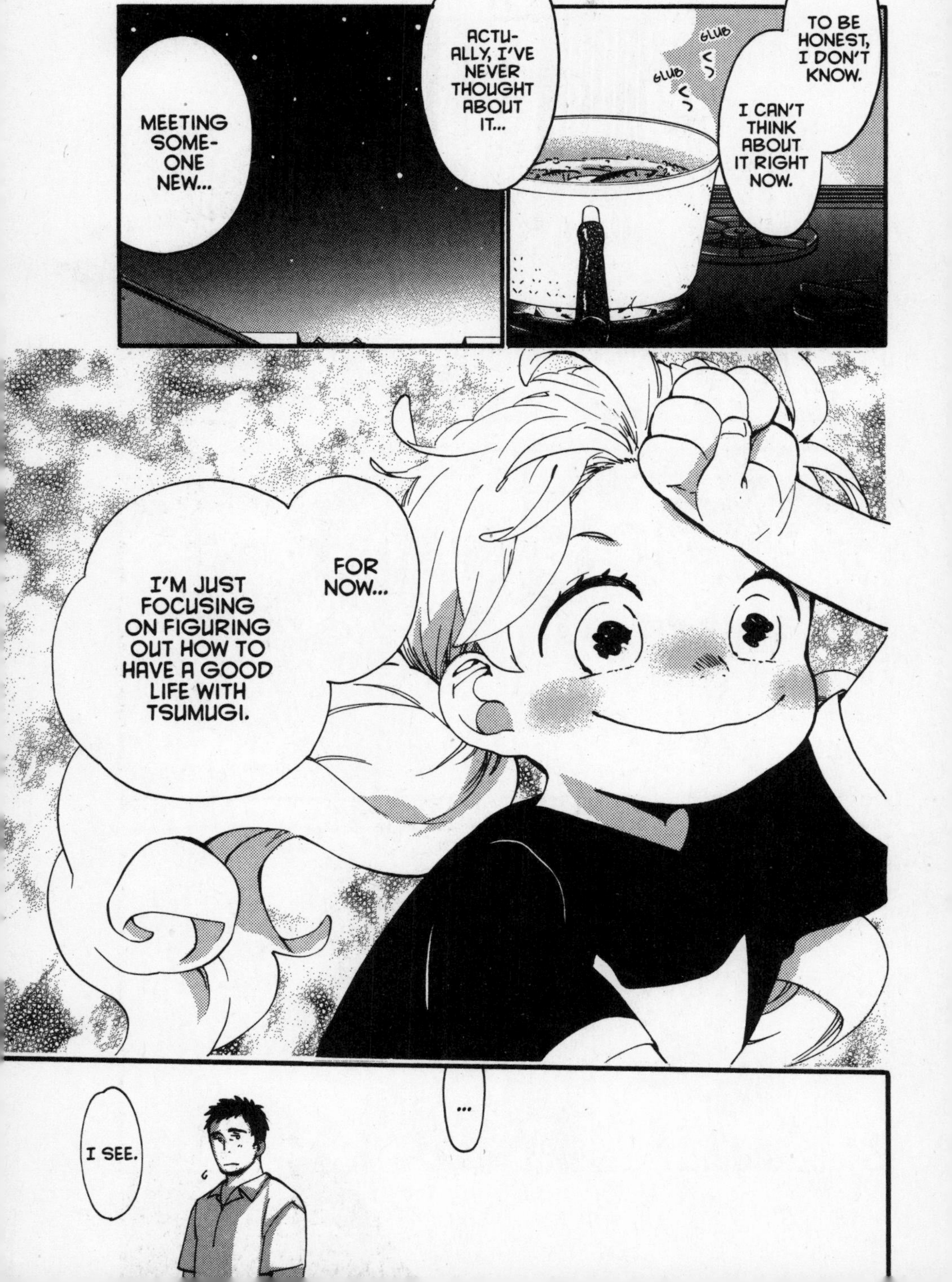
TO BE HONEST, I DON'T KNOW.
I CAN'T THINK ABOUT IT RIGHT NOW.
GLUB
GLUB
ACTUALLY, I'VE NEVER THOUGHT ABOUT IT...
MEETING SOMEONE NEW...
FOR NOW...
I'M JUST FOCUSING ON FIGURING OUT HOW TO HAVE A GOOD LIFE WITH TSUMUGI.
...
I SEE.

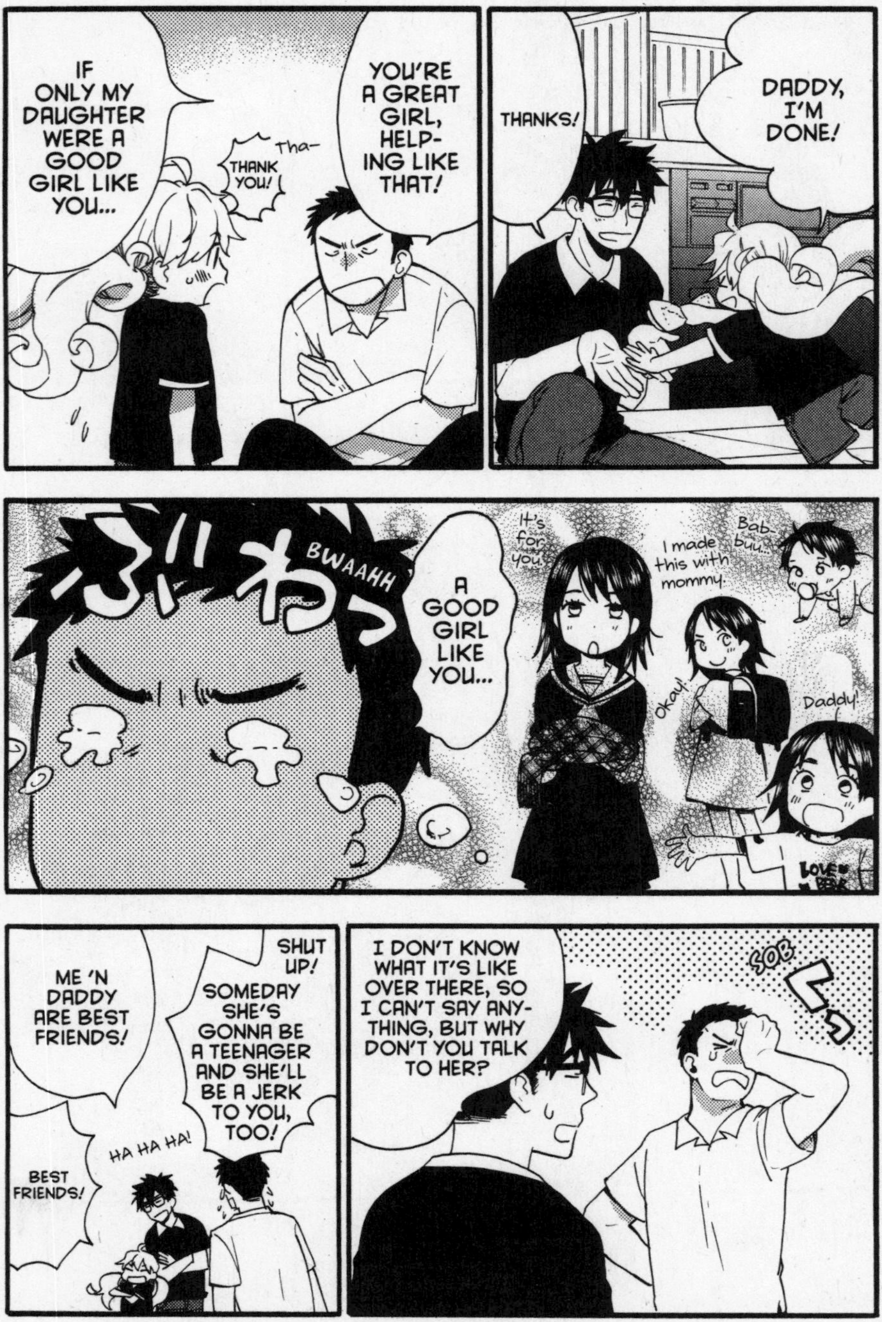
DADDY, I'M DONE!
THANKS!
YOU'RE A GREAT GIRL, HELPING LIKE THAT!
Tha-
THANK YOU!
IF ONLY MY DAUGHTER WERE A GOOD GIRL LIKE YOU...
Bab-buu...
Daddy!
I made this with mommy.
Okay!
It's for you.
A GOOD GIRL LIKE YOU...
ぶわっ
BWAAHH
SOB
I DON'T KNOW WHAT IT'S LIKE OVER THERE, SO I CAN'T SAY ANYTHING, BUT WHY DON'T YOU TALK TO HER?
SHUT UP!
SOMEDAY SHE'S GONNA BE A TEENAGER AND SHE'LL BE A JERK TO YOU, TOO!
ME 'N DADDY ARE BEST FRIENDS!
HA HA HA!
BEST FRIENDS!

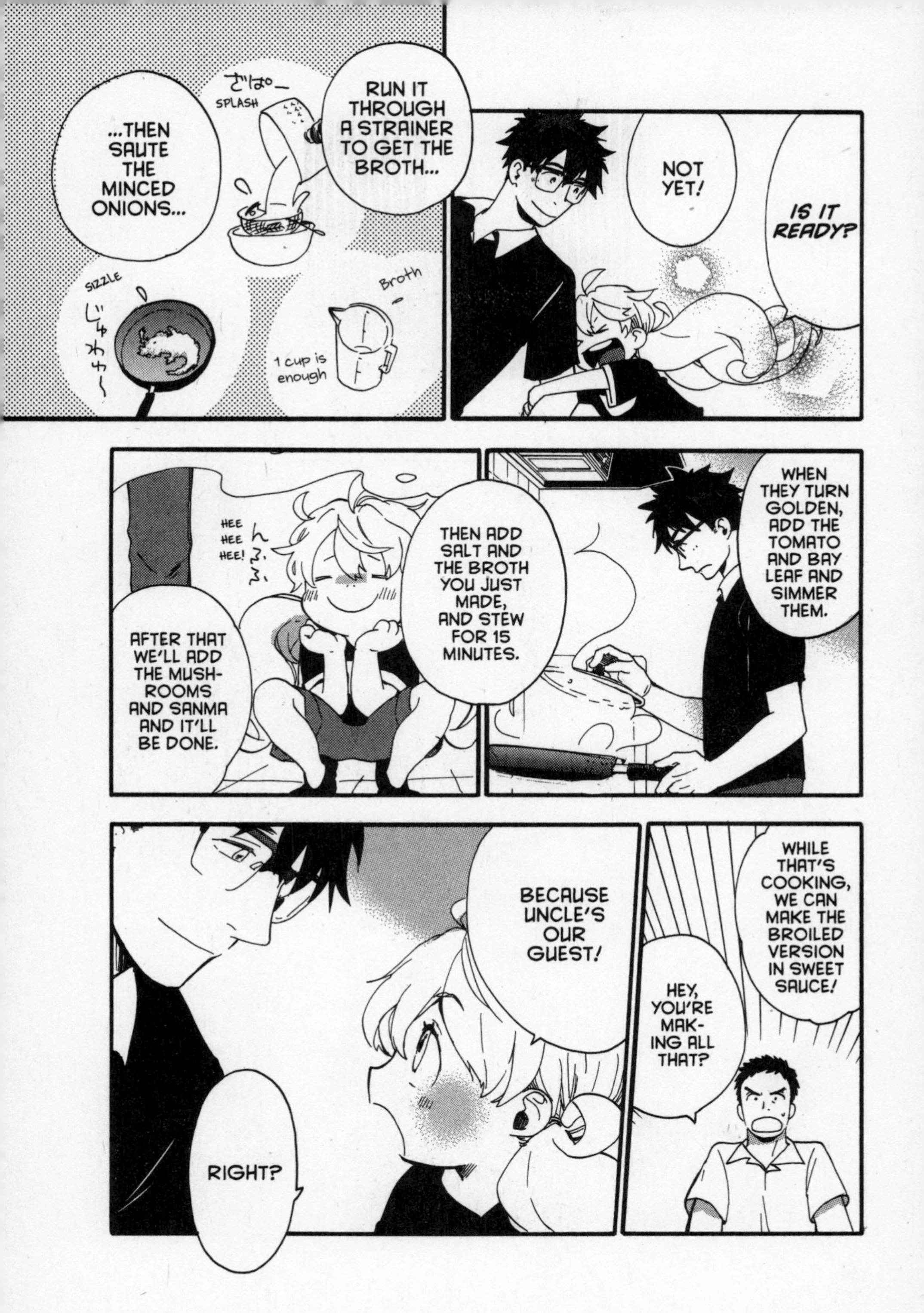
IS IT READY?
NOT YET!
RUN IT THROUGH A STRAINER TO GET THE BROTH...
ざばー
SPLASH
...THEN SAUTE THE MINCED ONIONS...
Broth
1 cup is enough
SIZZLE
じゅわ〜
WHEN THEY TURN GOLDEN, ADD THE TOMATO AND BAY LEAF AND SIMMER THEM.
THEN ADD SALT AND THE BROTH YOU JUST MADE, AND STEW FOR 15 MINUTES.
HEE HEE HEE!
んふふ
AFTER THAT WE'LL ADD THE MUSH-ROOMS AND SANMA AND IT'LL BE DONE.
WHILE THAT'S COOKING, WE CAN MAKE THE BROILED VERSION IN SWEET SAUCE!
HEY, YOU'RE MAK-ING ALL THAT?
BECAUSE UNCLE'S OUR GUEST!
RIGHT?

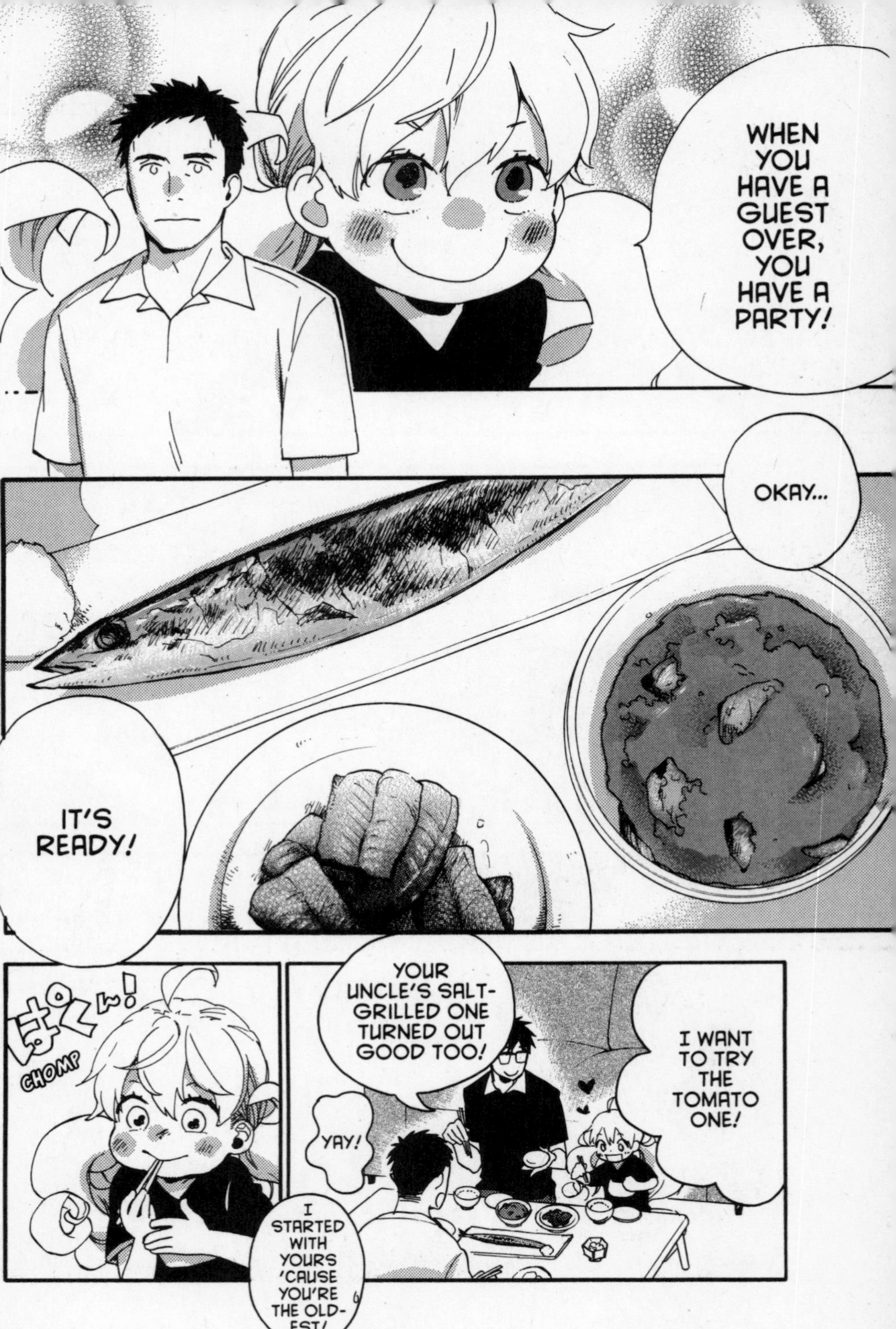
WHEN YOU HAVE A GUEST OVER, YOU HAVE A PARTY!
OKAY...
IT'S READY!
I WANT TO TRY THE TOMATO ONE!
YOUR UNCLE'S SALT-GRILLED ONE TURNED OUT GOOD TOO!
YAY!
I STARTED WITH YOURS 'CAUSE YOU'RE THE OLD-EST!
CHOMP

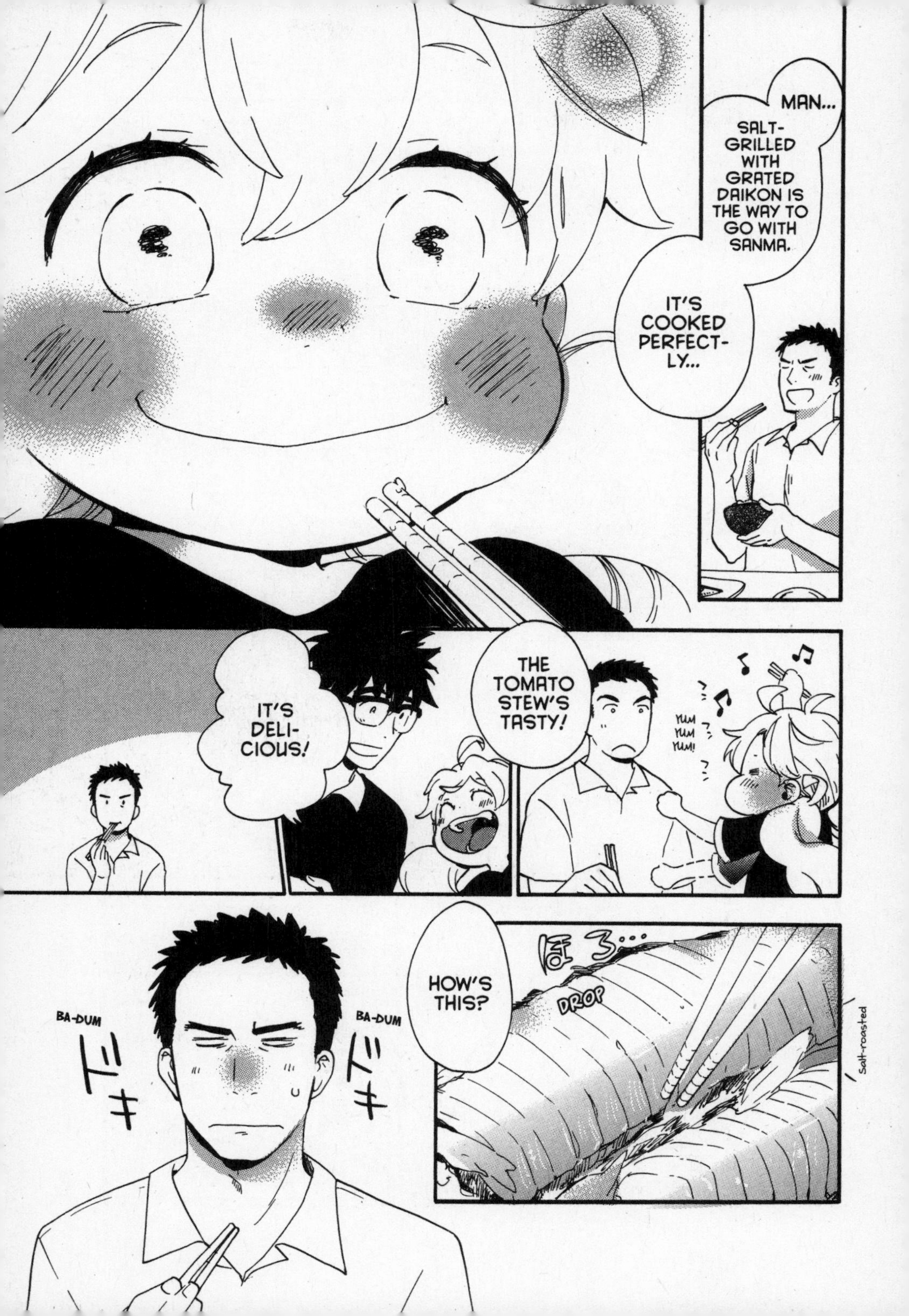
MAN...
SALT-GRILLED WITH GRATED DAIKON IS THE WAY TO GO WITH SANMA.
IT'S COOKED PERFECTLY...
YUM YUM YUM!
THE TOMATO STEW'S TASTY!
IT'S DELICIOUS!
ほろ...
DROP
HOW'S THIS?
Salt-roasted
BA-DUM
ドキ
BA-DUM
ドキ

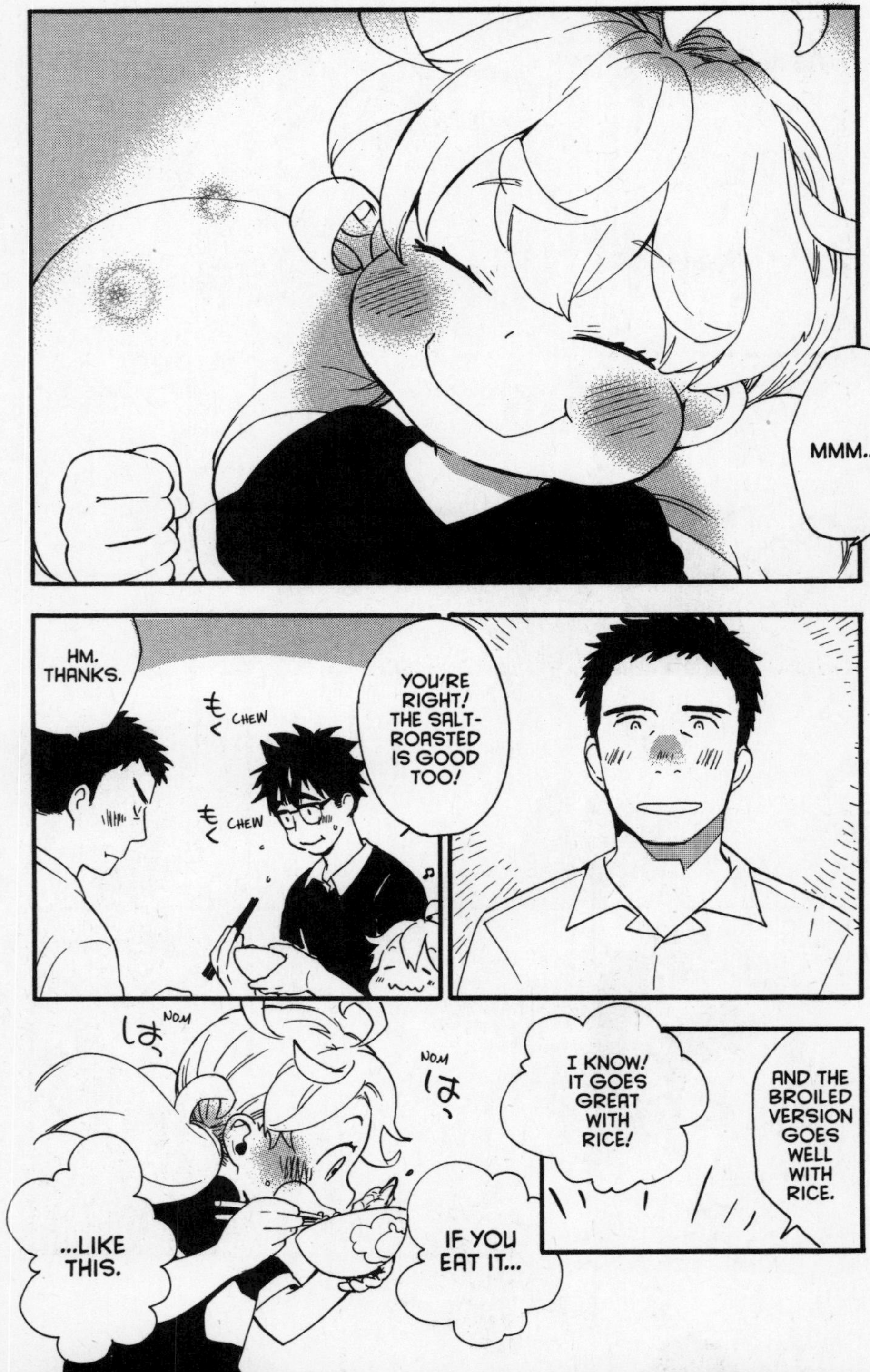
MMM...
YOU'RE RIGHT! THE SALT-ROASTED IS GOOD TOO!
HM. THANKS.
もく CHEW
もく CHEW
AND THE BROILED VERSION GOES WELL WITH RICE.
I KNOW! IT GOES GREAT WITH RICE!
NOM は、
は、NOM
IF YOU EAT IT...
...LIKE THIS.

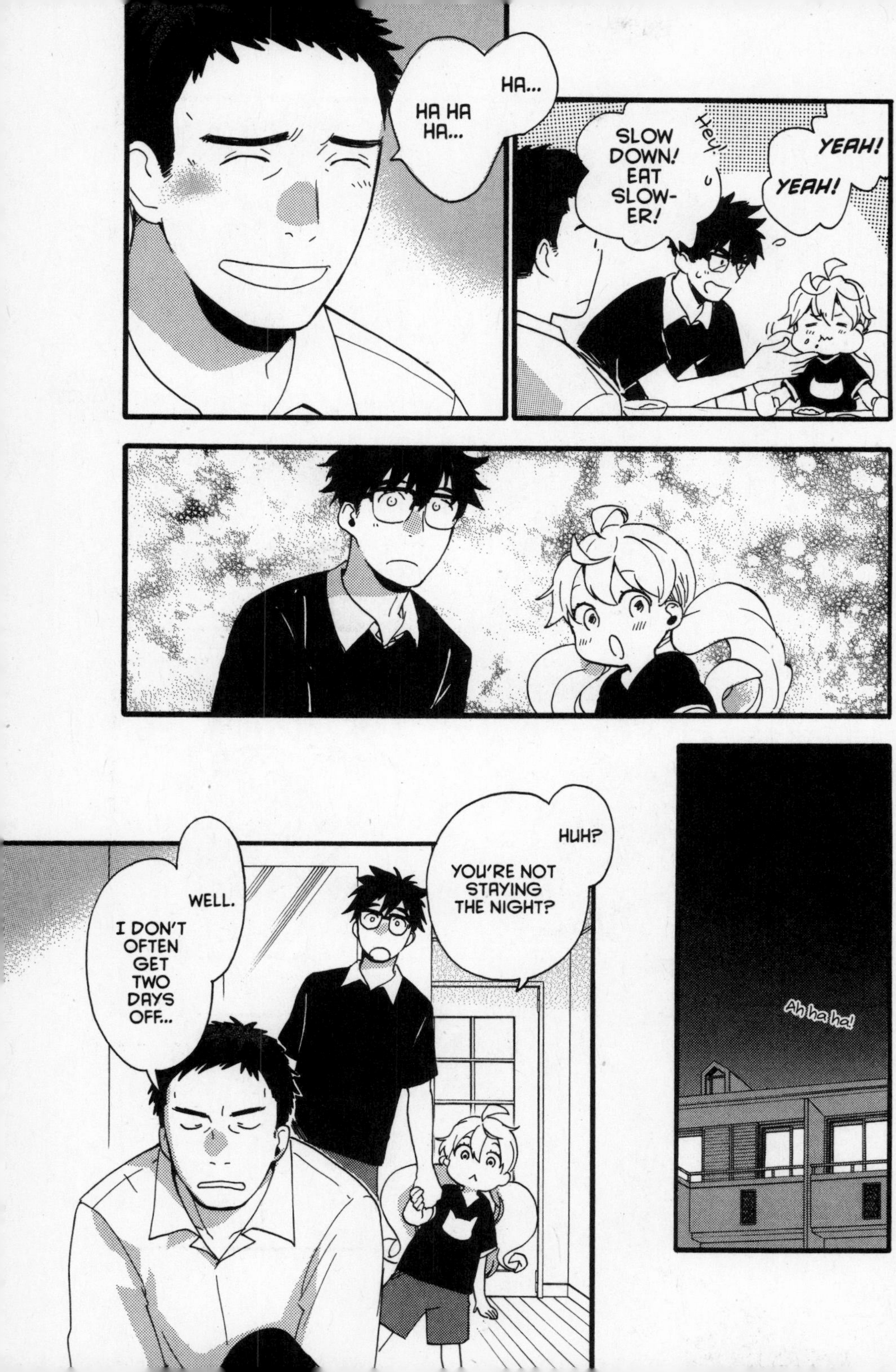
YEAH!
YEAH!
Hey!
SLOW DOWN! EAT SLOWER!
HA...
HA HA HA...
Ah ha ha!
HUH?
YOU'RE NOT STAYING THE NIGHT?
WELL.
I DON'T OFTEN GET TWO DAYS OFF...

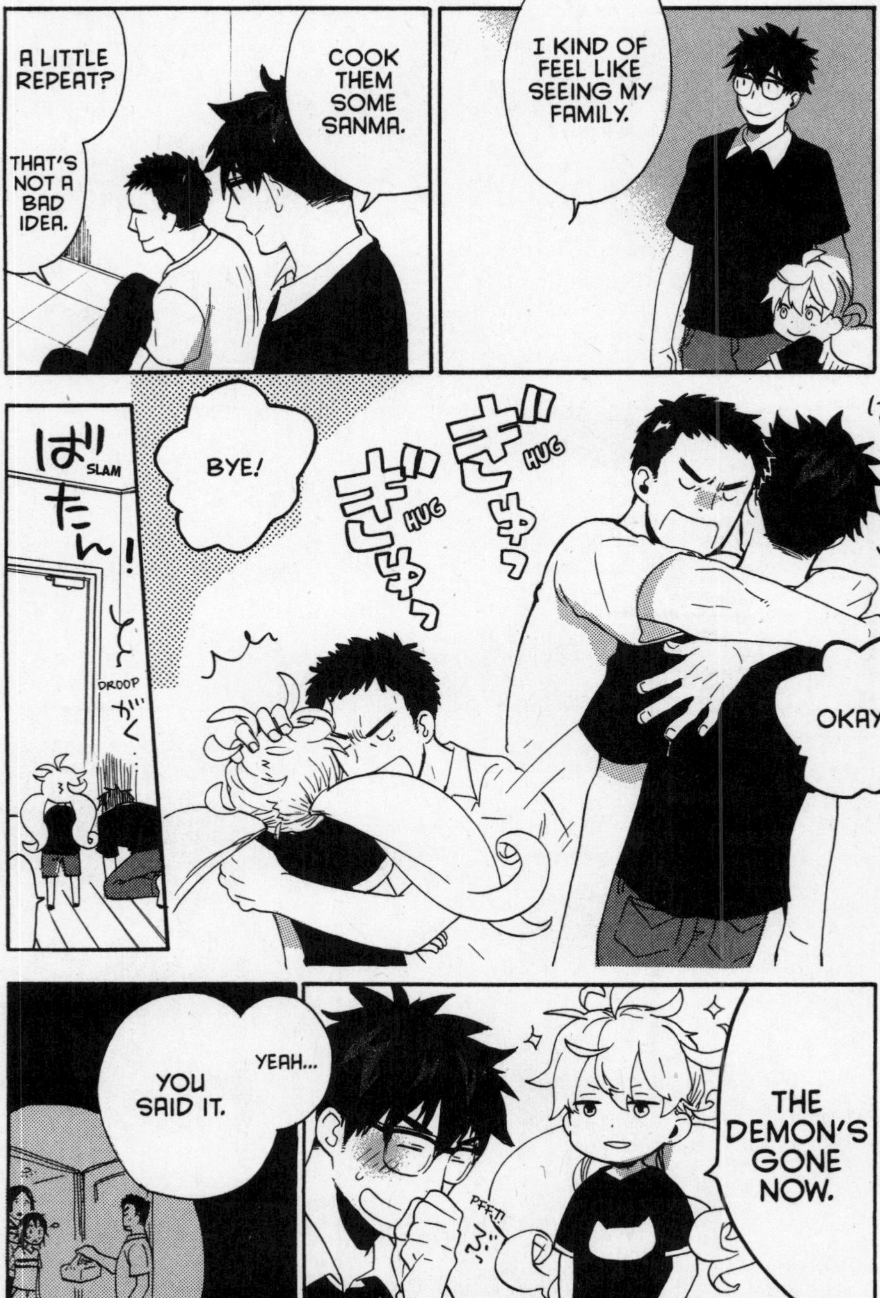
I KIND OF FEEL LIKE SEEING MY FAMILY.
COOK THEM SOME SANMA.
A LITTLE REPEAT?
THAT'S NOT A BAD IDEA.
ばしばし PAT PAT
ぎゅっ HUG
ぎゅっ HUG
BYE!
OKAY!
ばたん! SLAM
がく DROOP
THE DEMON'S GONE NOW.
ぷっ PFFT!
YEAH...
YOU SAID IT.

MACKEREL PIKE STEWED IN TOMATOES

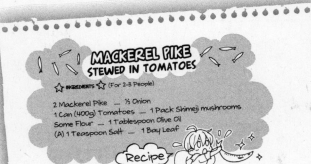

☆ INGREDIENTS ☆ (For 2-3 People)

2 Mackerel Pike ..... ½ Onion
1 Can (400g) Tomatoes ..... 1 Pack Shimeji mushrooms
Some Flour ..... 1 Tablespoon Olive Oil
(A) 1 Teaspoon Salt ..... 1 Bay Leaf

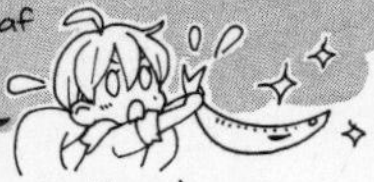

Recipe

1. Fillet the pike. Remove the ara (the head and bones), and cut the meat into three equal pieces. Mince the onions.
2. Put the head and bones into a small pot. Put in enough water to thoroughly cover them and cook on high until they boil.

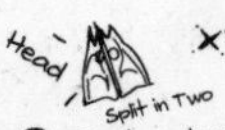
Head
Split in Two

POINT: Remove the gills on the head and split it into two pieces. Cut the backbone around the center. Wash both thoroughly to remove the blood. Use the rib bones that you scraped off, too.

3. Cook on low heat for 15 minutes, continually skimming off the scum. Strain in a strainer and save about a cup of soup.
4. Lightly salt (salt not listed in ingredients) the pike and add the flour. Put down olive oil in the frying pan and fry on medium heat, skin facing up.
5. Once it gets a nice color, flip it and fry the skin side, then remove.
6. Put the onions from step 1 into the frying pan from step 5 and fry them. Once they're browned add the canned tomatoes, the soup from step 3, and the ingredients in A. Once it starts to boil turn to low head and put a lid on it.
7. Let cook for 20 minutes before adding the shimeji mushrooms and boil for 5 more minutes. Add in the pike you removed from step 5.
8. Once it's nice and warm, add salt to taste and it's done!

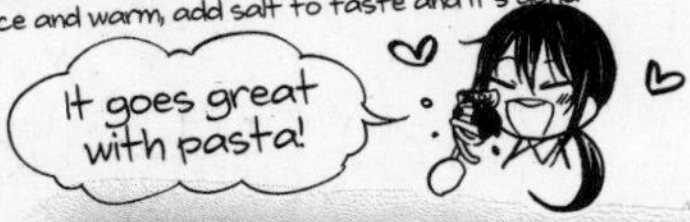
It goes great with pasta!

MACKEREL PIKE KABA-YAKI

☆ INGREDIENTS ☆ (For 2 People)

2 Mackerel Pike
Some Flour ..... ½ Tablespoon Salad Oil

(A) 2 Tablespoons Soy Sauce ..... 2 Tablespoons Mirin
2 Tablespoons Sake ..... 1 Tablespoon Sugar

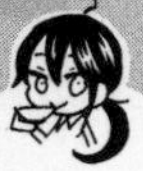

Recipe

1. Fillet the pike, and cut the meat into two equal pieces. Dust with flour.
2. Put vegetable oil in the frying pan and heat, then cook the pike skin side down first.
3. Once both sides have grill marks on them, add in A.
4. Once it's started to boil for a bit, it's done!

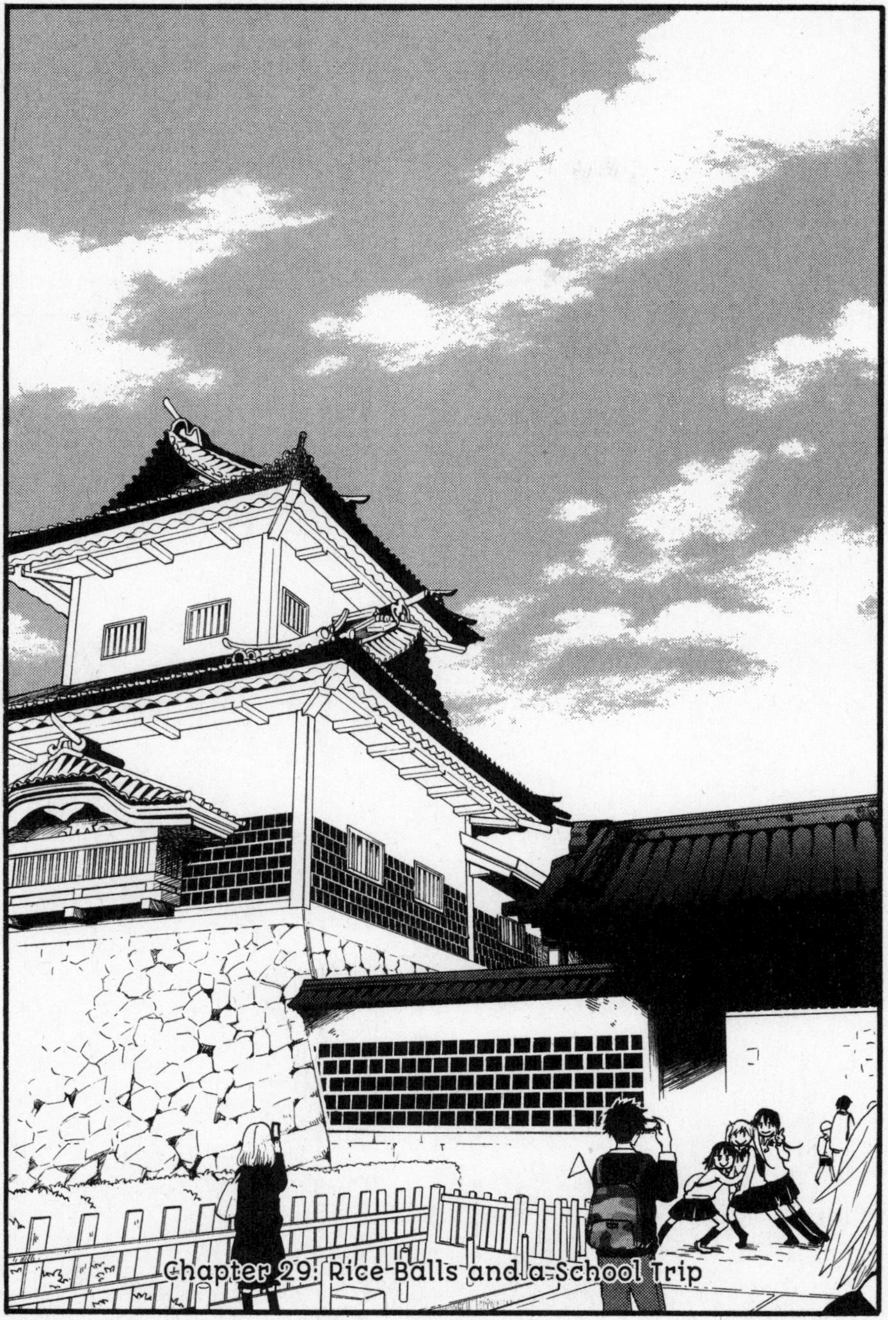
Chapter 29: Rice Balls and a School Trip

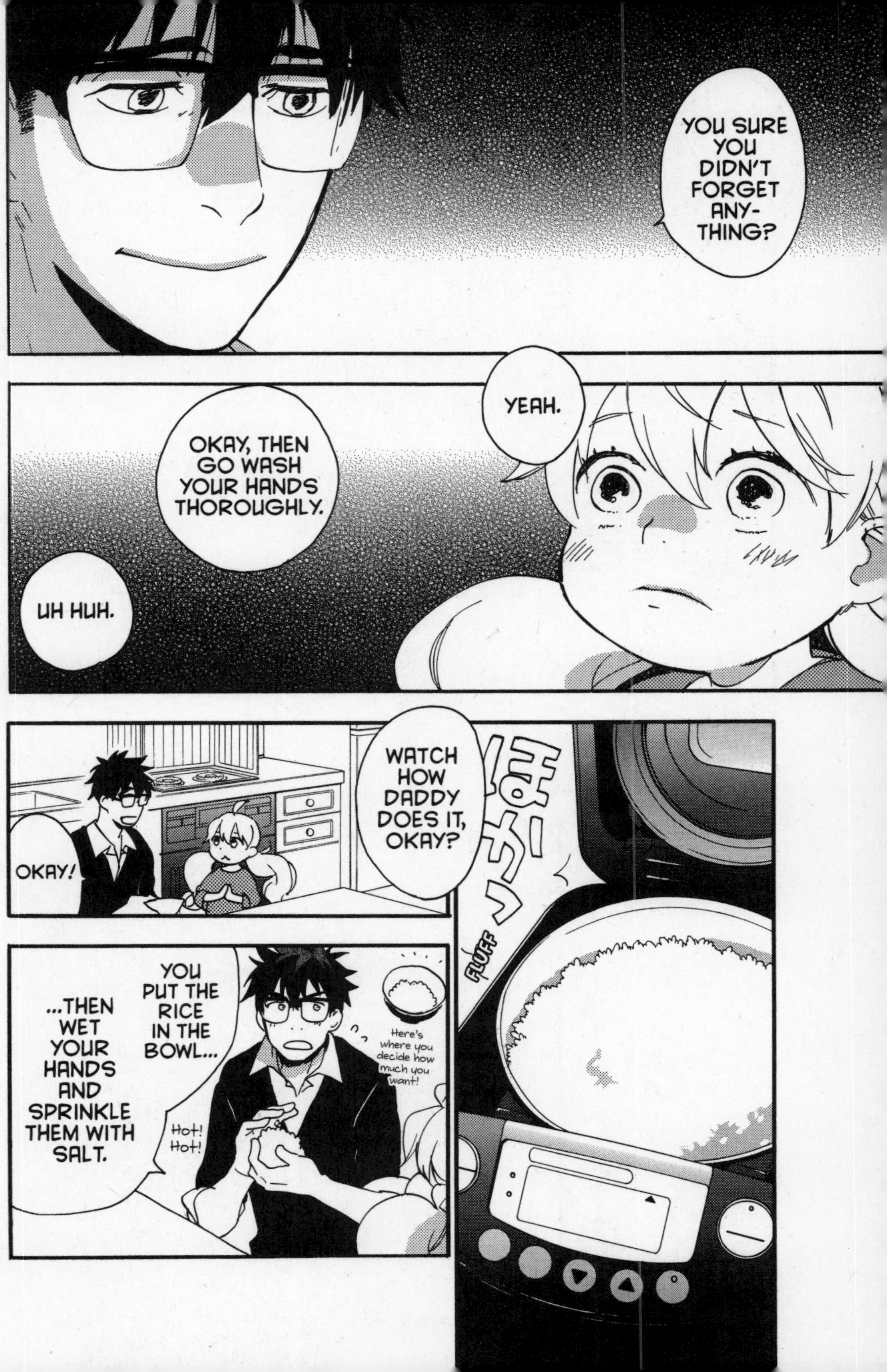
YOU SURE YOU DIDN'T FORGET ANY-THING?
YEAH.
OKAY, THEN GO WASH YOUR HANDS THOROUGHLY.
UH HUH.
WATCH HOW DADDY DOES IT, OKAY?
FLUFF
OKAY!
YOU PUT THE RICE IN THE BOWL...
...THEN WET YOUR HANDS AND SPRINKLE THEM WITH SALT.
Here's where you decide how much you want!
Hot! Hot!

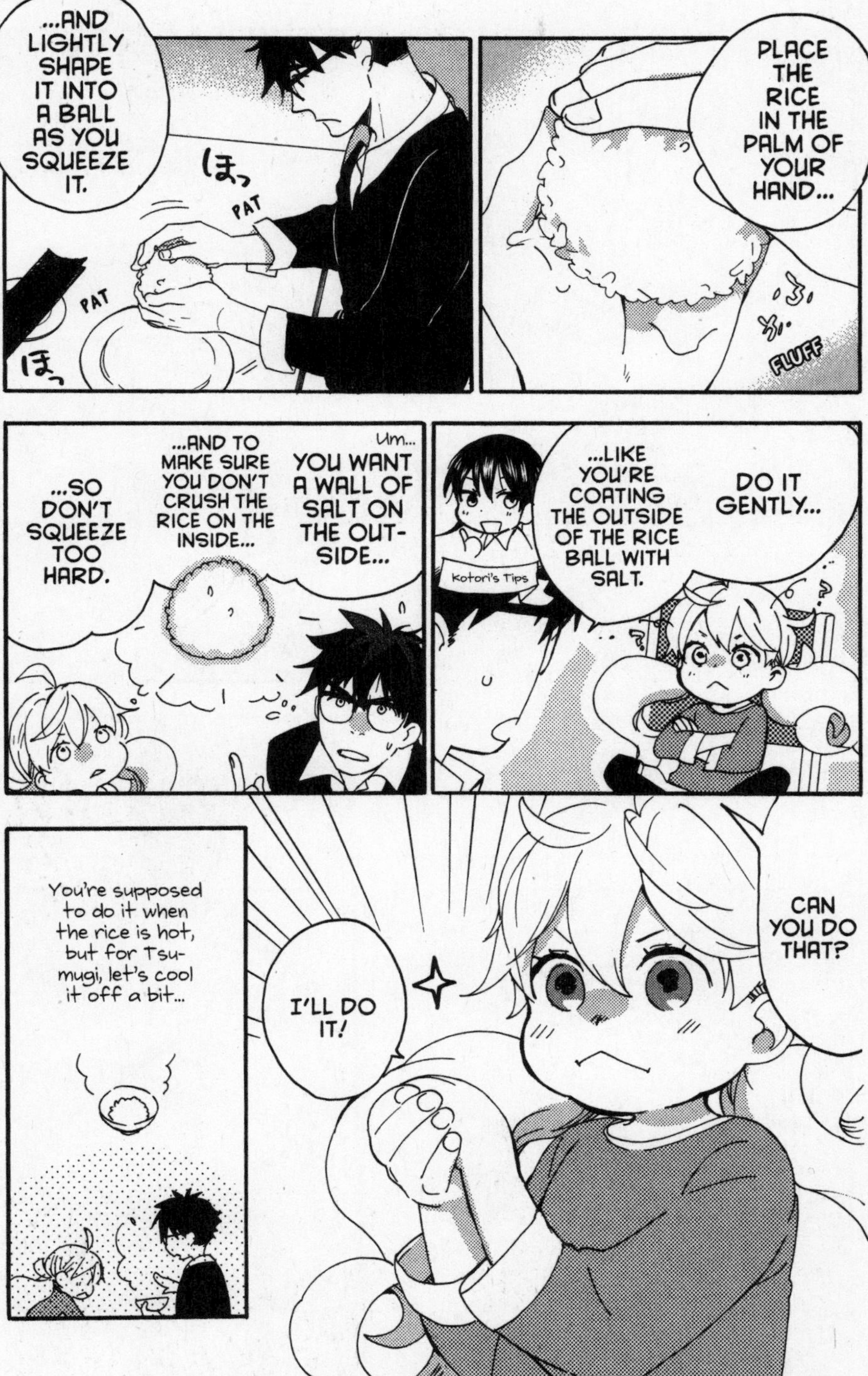
PLACE THE RICE IN THE PALM OF YOUR HAND...
ふわ
ふわ
FLUFF
...AND LIGHTLY SHAPE IT INTO A BALL AS YOU SQUEEZE IT.
ほっ
PAT
PAT
ほっ
DO IT GENTLY...
...LIKE YOU'RE COATING THE OUTSIDE OF THE RICE BALL WITH SALT.
Kotori's Tips
Um...
YOU WANT A WALL OF SALT ON THE OUT-SIDE...
...AND TO MAKE SURE YOU DON'T CRUSH THE RICE ON THE INSIDE...
...SO DON'T SQUEEZE TOO HARD.
CAN YOU DO THAT?
I'LL DO IT!
You're supposed to do it when the rice is hot, but for Tsu-mugi, let's cool it off a bit...

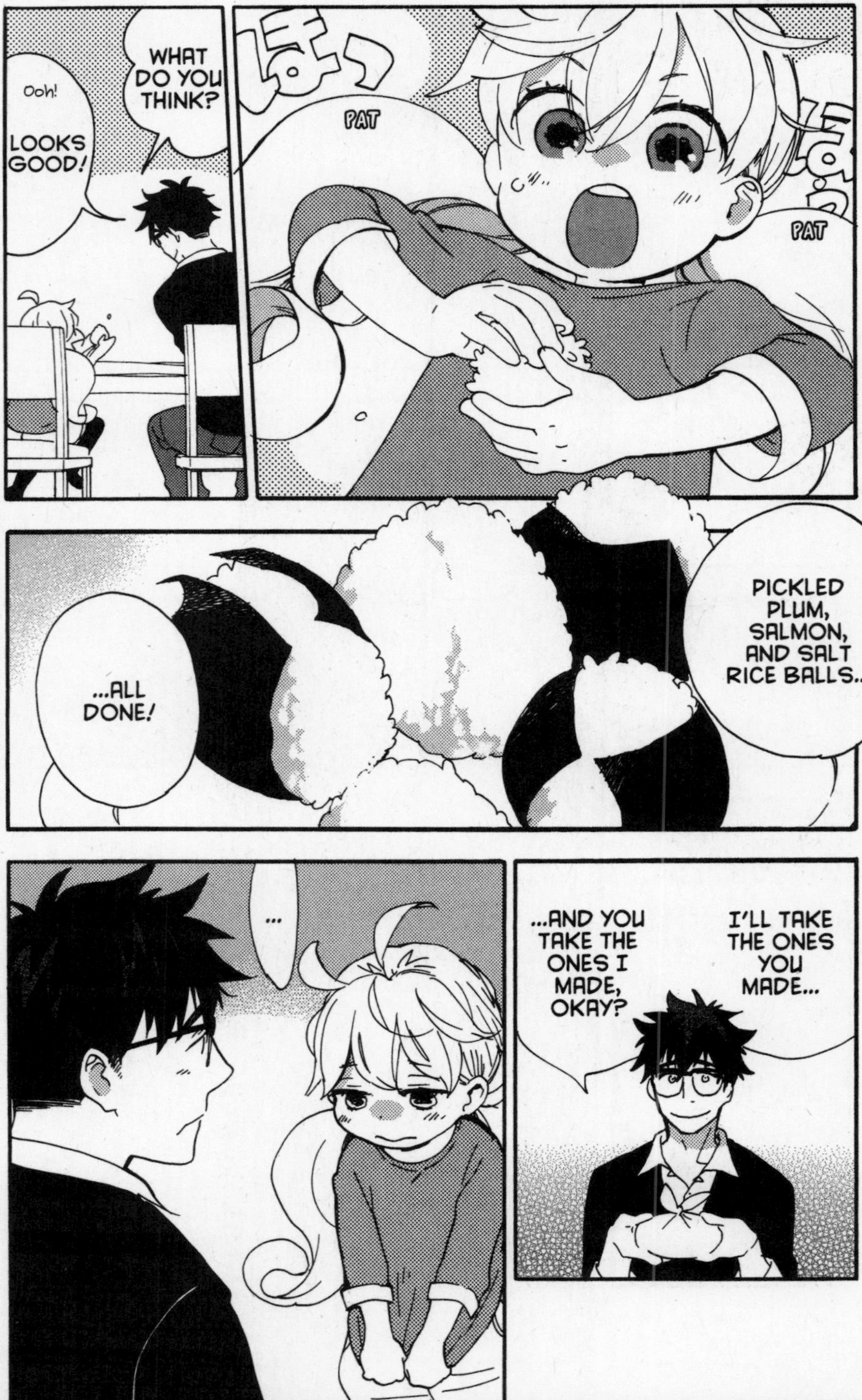
ほっ
PAT
ほっ
PAT
WHAT DO YOU THINK?
Ooh!
LOOKS GOOD!
PICKLED PLUM, SALMON, AND SALT RICE BALLS...
...ALL DONE!
I'LL TAKE THE ONES YOU MADE...
...AND YOU TAKE THE ONES I MADE, OKAY?
...

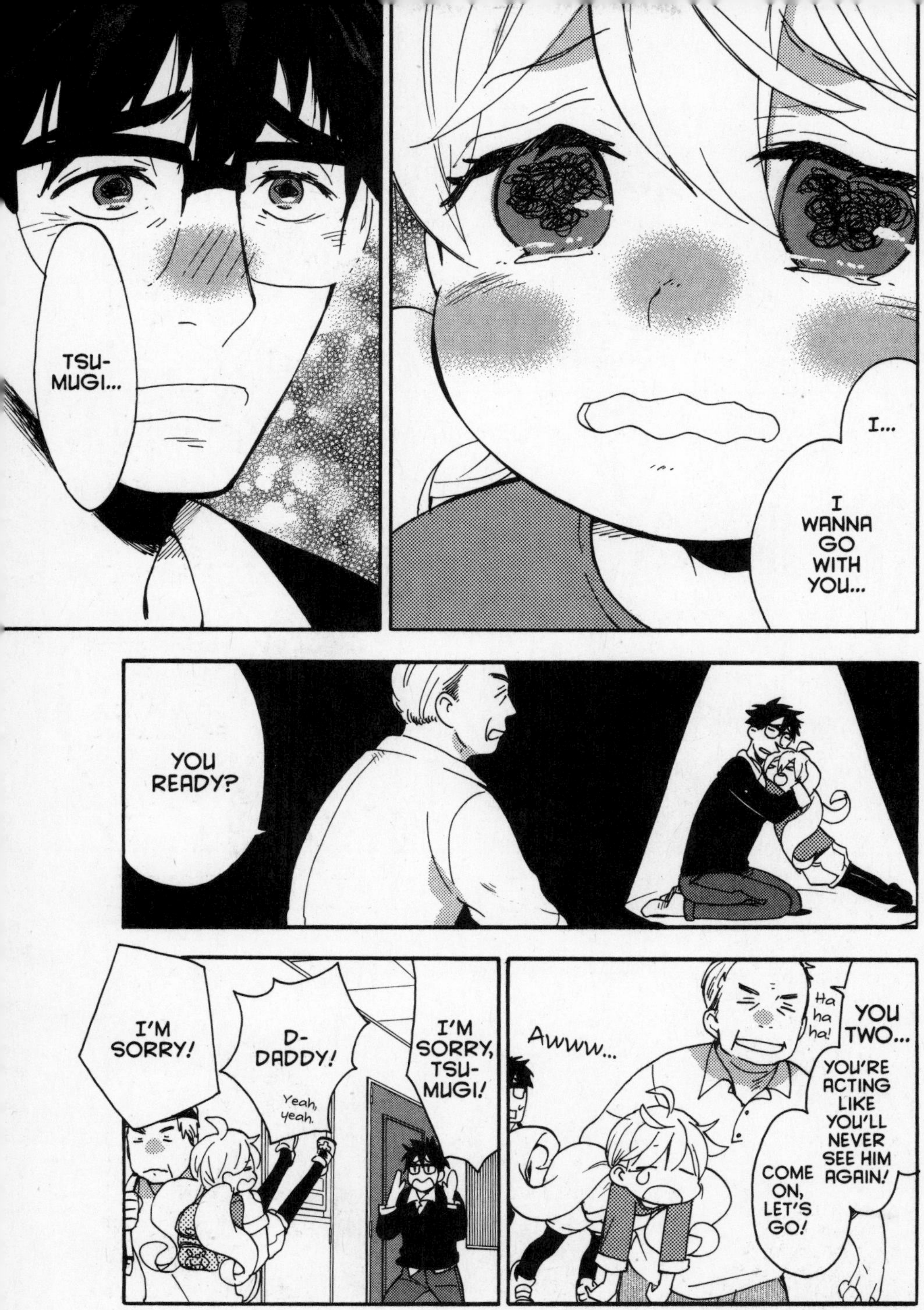
I...
I WANNA GO WITH YOU...
TSU-MUGI...
YOU READY?
Ha ha ha!
YOU TWO...
YOU'RE ACTING LIKE YOU'LL NEVER SEE HIM AGAIN!
COME ON, LET'S GO!
Awww...
I'M SORRY, TSU-MUGI!
D-DADDY!
Yeah, yeah.
I'M SORRY!

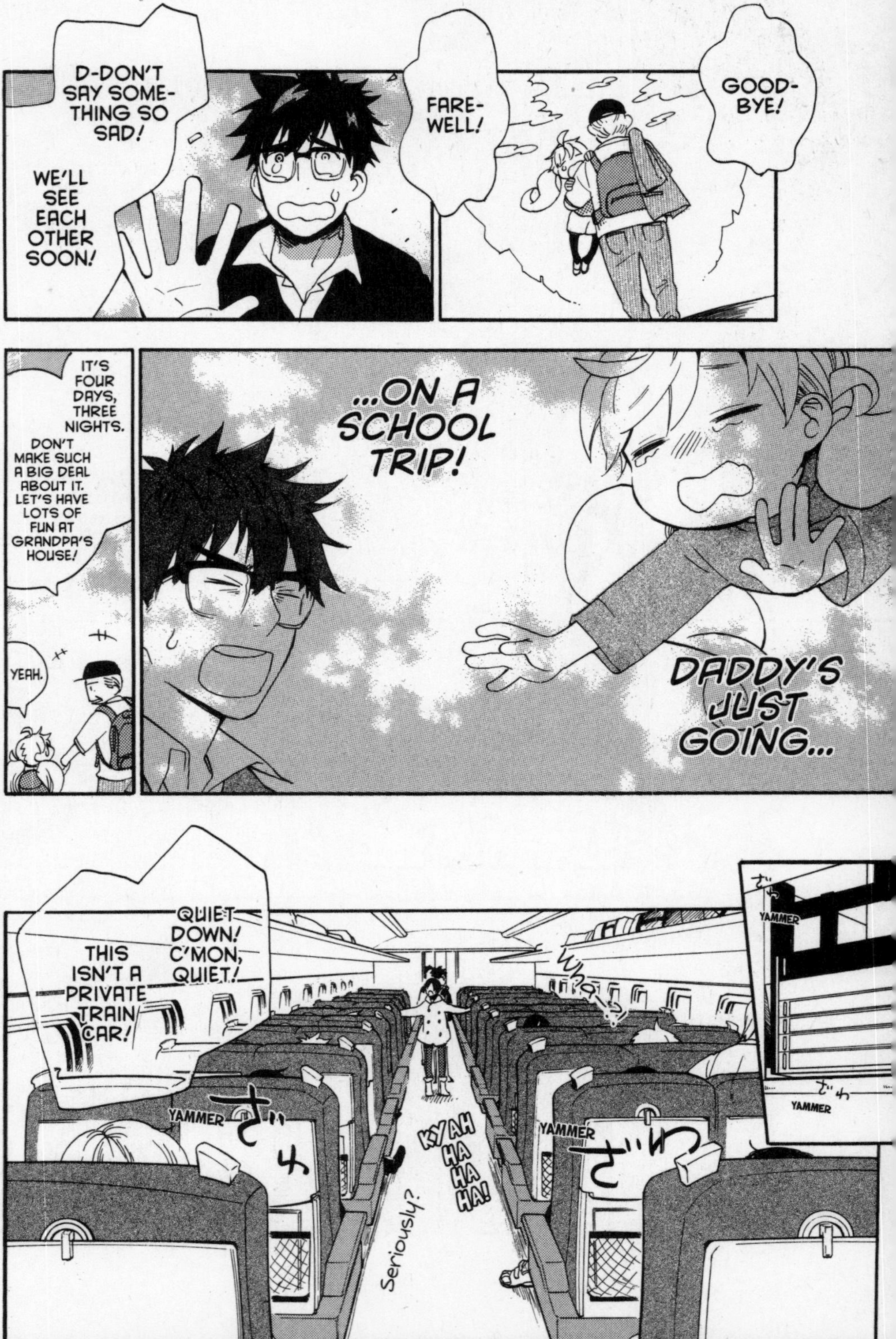

GOOD-BYE!
FARE-WELL!
D-DON'T SAY SOME-THING SO SAD!
WE'LL SEE EACH OTHER SOON!
DADDY'S JUST GOING...
...ON A SCHOOL TRIP!
IT'S FOUR DAYS, THREE NIGHTS.
DON'T MAKE SUCH A BIG DEAL ABOUT IT. LET'S HAVE LOTS OF FUN AT GRANDPA'S HOUSE!
YEAH.
YAMMER
ざわ
YAMMER
ざわ
QUIET DOWN! C'MON, QUIET!
THIS ISN'T A PRIVATE TRAIN CAR!
YAMMER
ざわ
YAMMER
ざわ
KYAH HA HA HA HA!
Seriously?

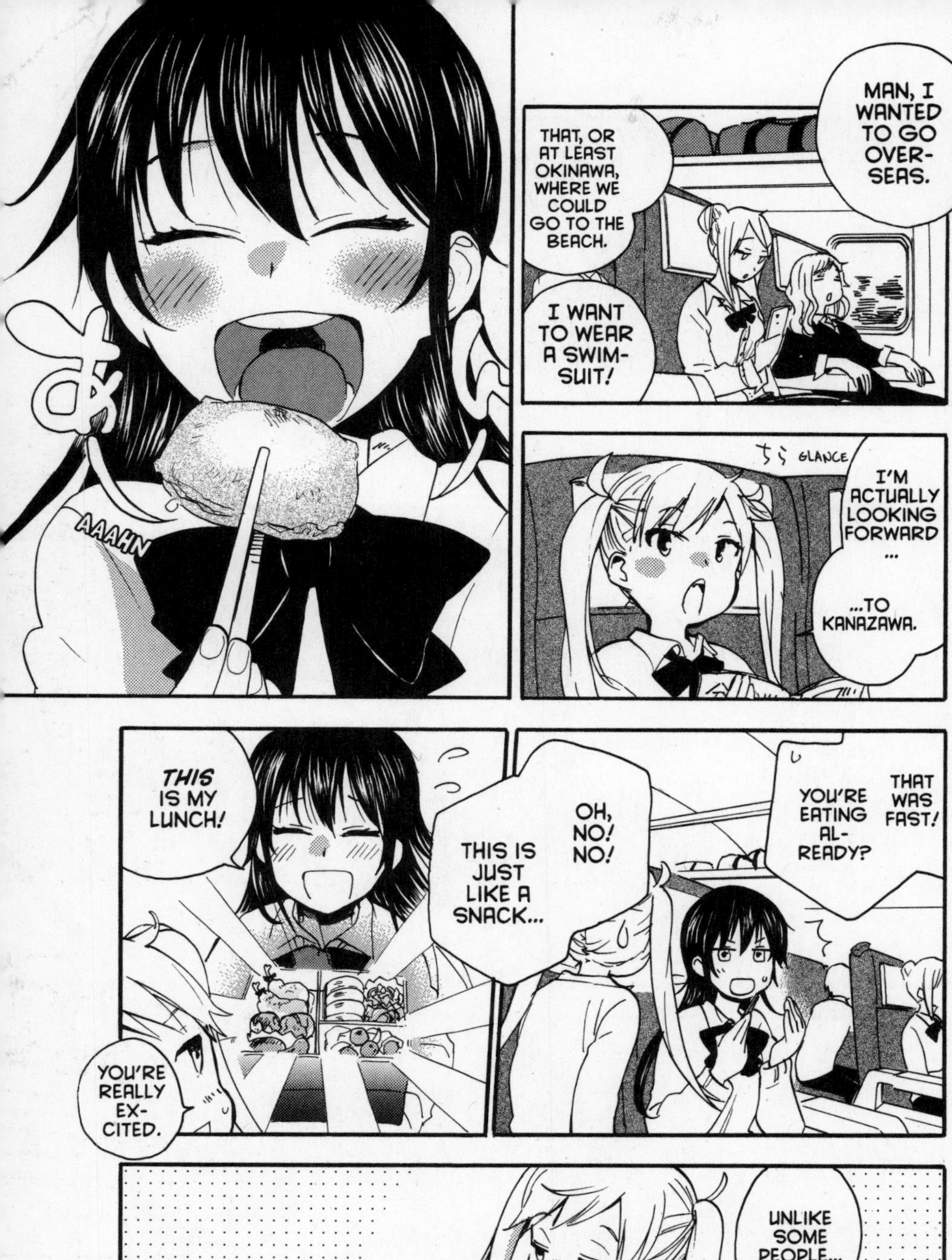
MAN, I WANTED TO GO OVERSEAS.
THAT, OR AT LEAST OKINAWA, WHERE WE COULD GO TO THE BEACH.
I WANT TO WEAR A SWIMSUIT!
ちら GLANCE
I'M ACTUALLY LOOKING FORWARD...
...TO KANAZAWA.
AAAHN
THAT WAS FAST!
YOU'RE EATING ALREADY?
OH, NO! NO!
THIS IS JUST LIKE A SNACK...
THIS IS MY LUNCH!
YOU'RE REALLY EXCITED.
UNLIKE SOME PEOPLE...

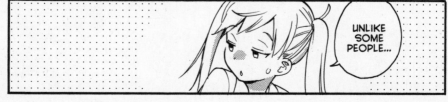

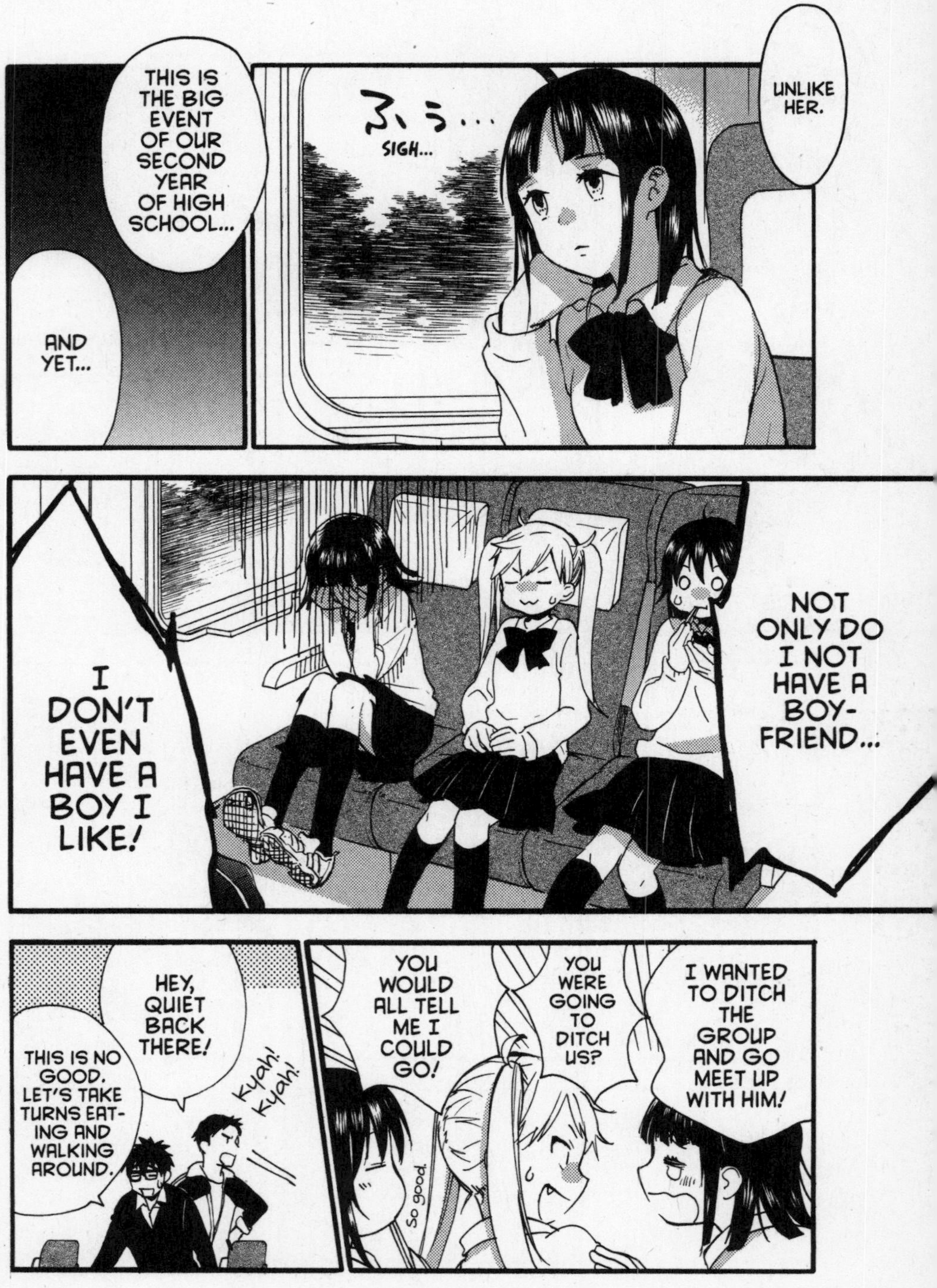
UNLIKE HER.
ふぅ...
SIGH...
THIS IS THE BIG EVENT OF OUR SECOND YEAR OF HIGH SCHOOL...
AND YET...
NOT ONLY DO I NOT HAVE A BOY-FRIEND...
I DON'T EVEN HAVE A BOY I LIKE!
I WANTED TO DITCH THE GROUP AND GO MEET UP WITH HIM!
YOU WERE GOING TO DITCH US?
YOU WOULD ALL TELL ME I COULD GO!
So good.
HEY, QUIET BACK THERE!
Kyah! Kyah!
THIS IS NO GOOD. LET'S TAKE TURNS EAT-ING AND WALKING AROUND.

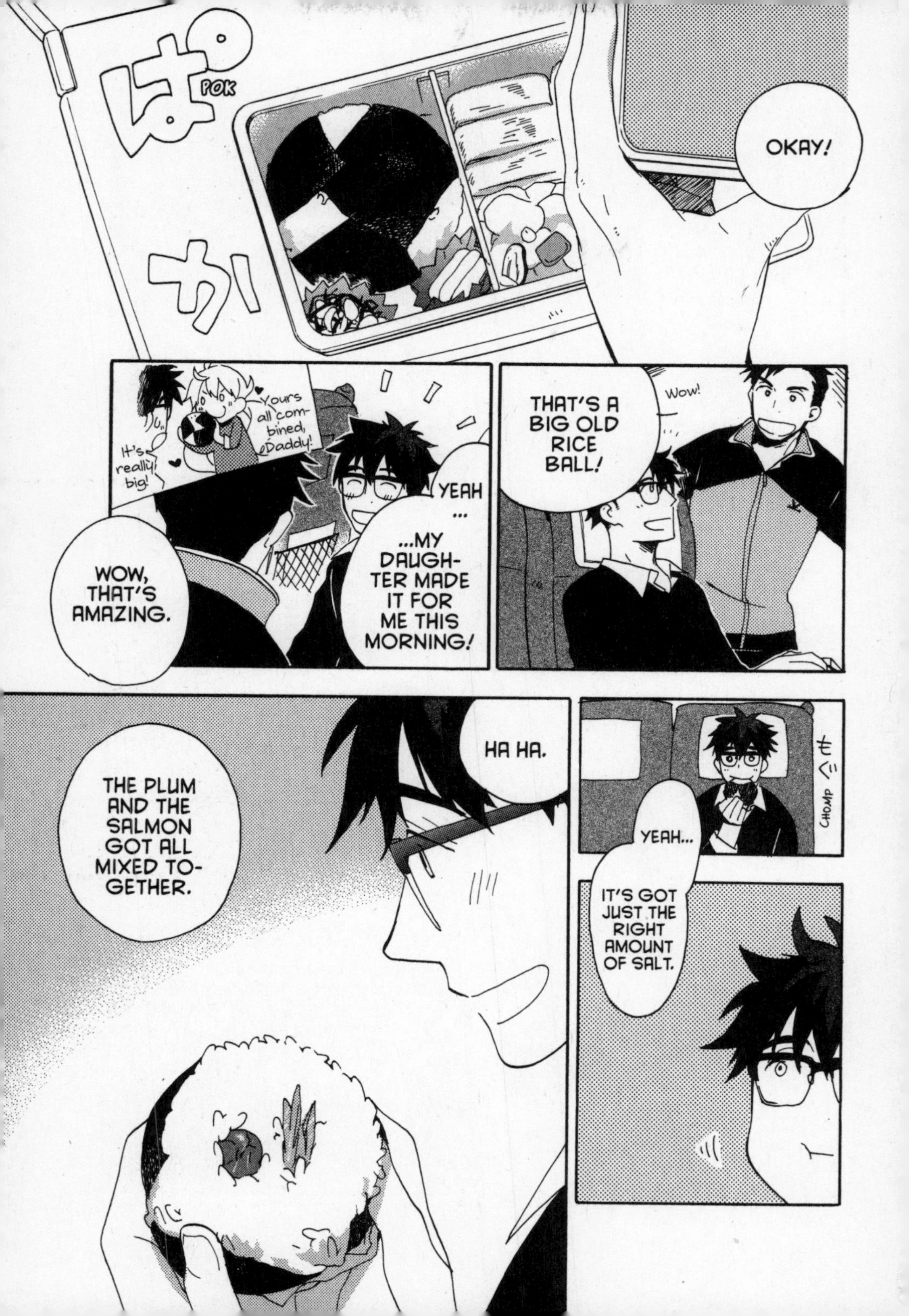
OKAY!
ぱか
POK
Wow!
THAT'S A BIG OLD RICE BALL!
YEAH ...
...MY DAUGH-TER MADE IT FOR ME THIS MORNING!
WOW, THAT'S AMAZING.
Yours all com-bined, Daddy!
It's really big!
もぐ
CHOMP
YEAH...
IT'S GOT JUST THE RIGHT AMOUNT OF SALT.
HA HA.
THE PLUM AND THE SALMON GOT ALL MIXED TO-GETHER.

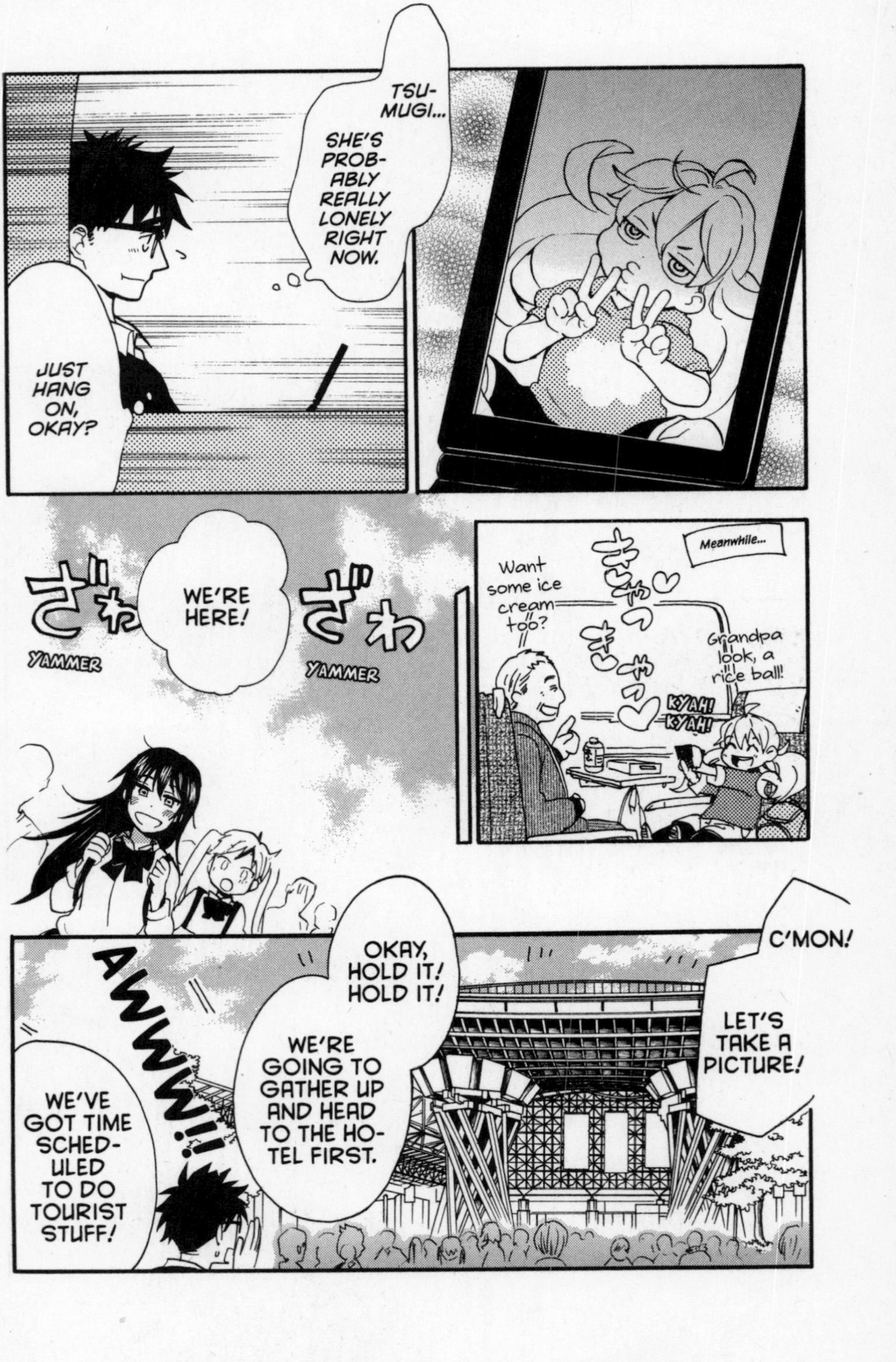
TSU-MUGI...
SHE'S PROBABLY REALLY LONELY RIGHT NOW.
JUST HANG ON, OKAY?
Meanwhile...
きゃっきゃっ
KYAH! KYAH!
Want some ice cream too?
Grandpa look, a rice ball!
ざわ
YAMMER
WE'RE HERE!
ざわ
YAMMER
C'MON!
LET'S TAKE A PICTURE!
OKAY, HOLD IT! HOLD IT!
WE'RE GOING TO GATHER UP AND HEAD TO THE HOTEL FIRST.
AWWW!!!
WE'VE GOT TIME SCHEDULED TO DO TOURIST STUFF!

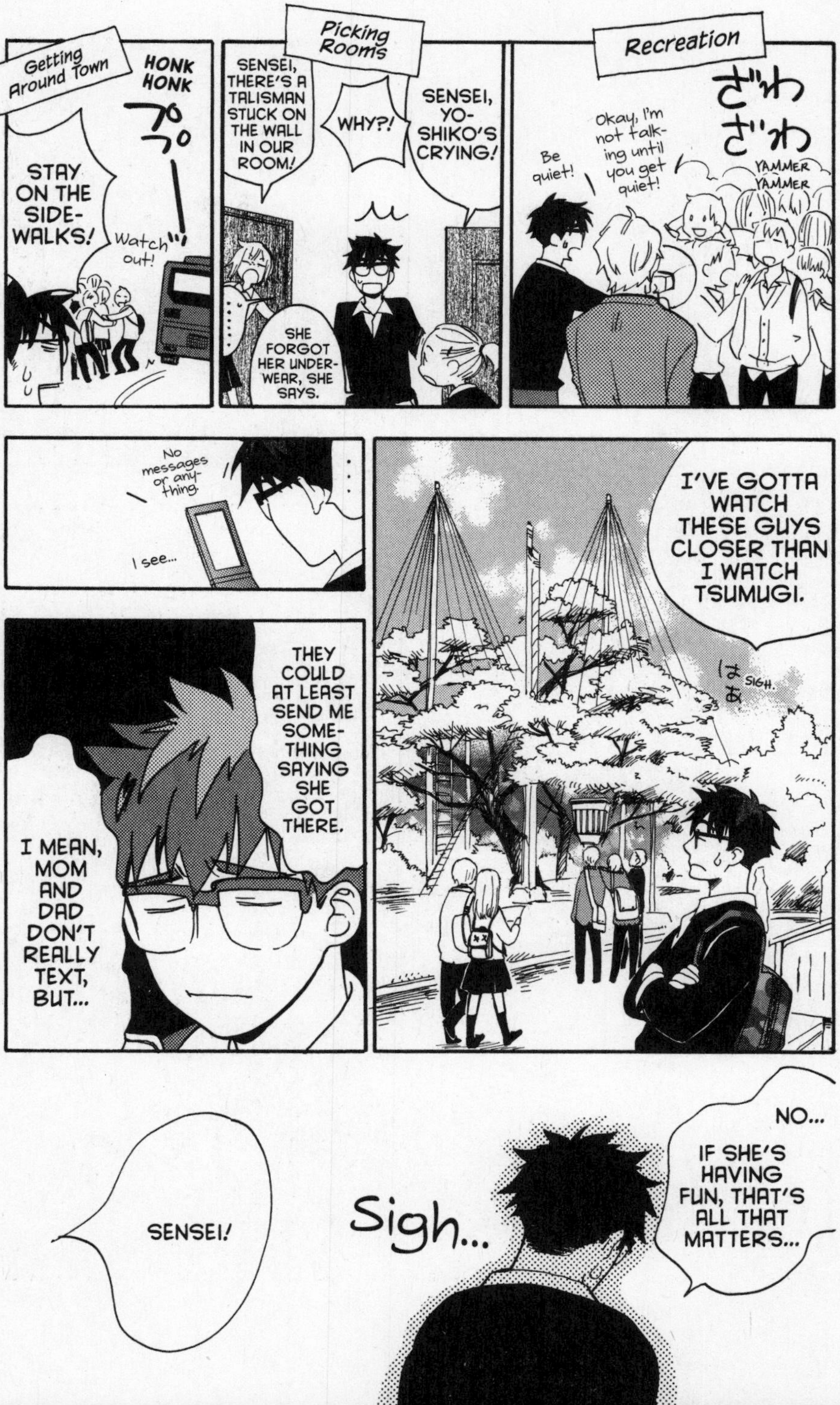
Recreation
ざわざわ
YAMMER YAMMER
Okay, I'm not talk-ing until you get quiet!
Be quiet!
Picking Rooms
SENSEI, YO-SHIKO'S CRYING!
WHY?!
SENSEI, THERE'S A TALISMAN STUCK ON THE WALL IN OUR ROOM!
SHE FORGOT HER UNDER-WEAR, SHE SAYS.
Getting Around Town
HONK HONK
プップー
STAY ON THE SIDE-WALKS!
Watch out!
I'VE GOTTA WATCH THESE GUYS CLOSER THAN I WATCH TSUMUGI.
はあ SIGH.
No messages or any-thing.
I see...
THEY COULD AT LEAST SEND ME SOME-THING SAYING SHE GOT THERE.
I MEAN, MOM AND DAD DON'T REALLY TEXT, BUT...
NO...
IF SHE'S HAVING FUN, THAT'S ALL THAT MATTERS...
Sigh...
SENSEI!

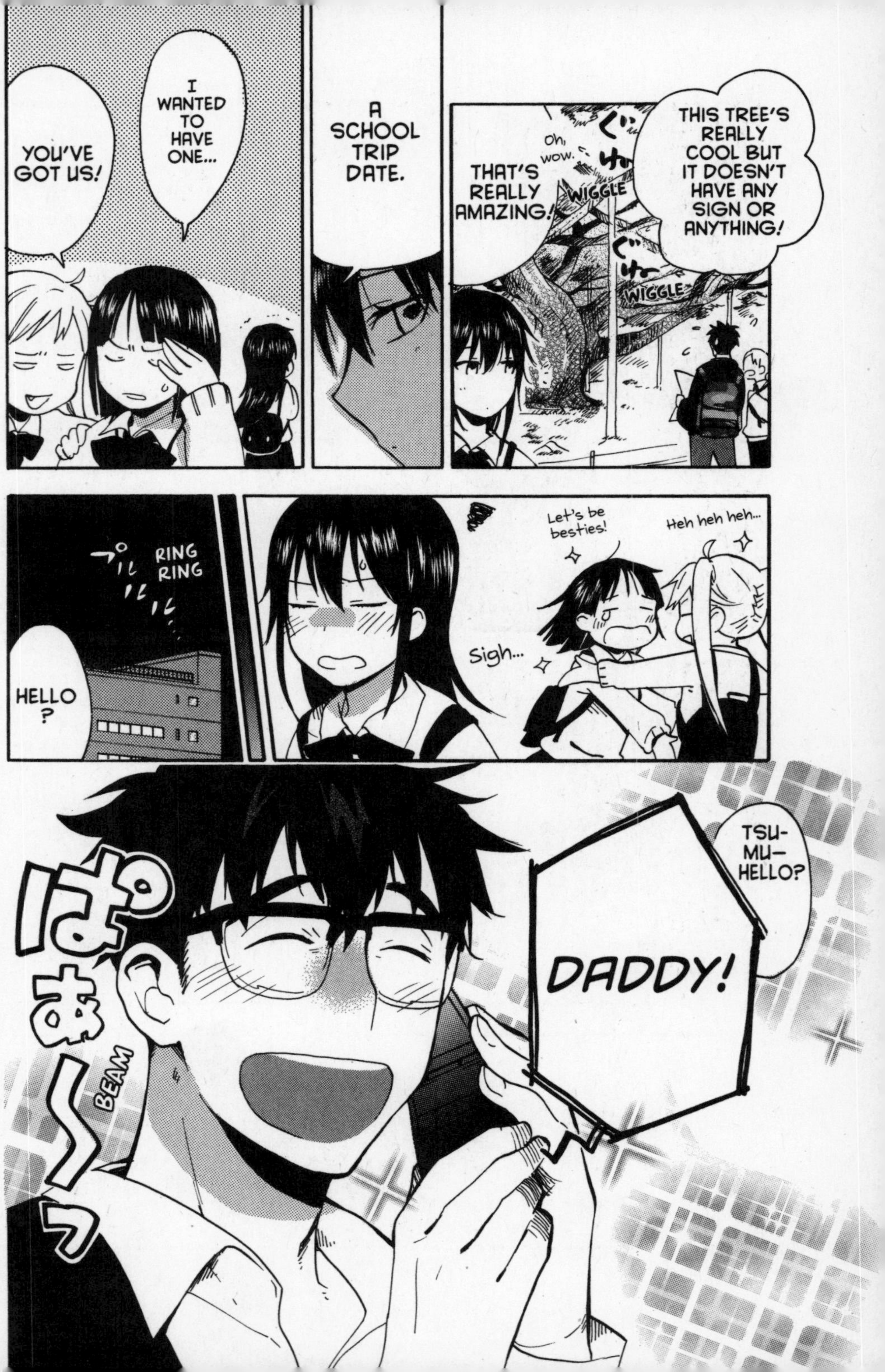
THIS TREE'S REALLY COOL BUT IT DOESN'T HAVE ANY SIGN OR ANYTHING!
WIGGLE
Oh, wow.
THAT'S REALLY AMAZING!
WIGGLE
A SCHOOL TRIP DATE.
I WANTED TO HAVE ONE...
YOU'VE GOT US!
Heh heh heh...
Let's be besties!
Sigh...
RING RING
HELLO?
TSU-MU-HELLO?
DADDY!
ぱぁ～っ
BEAM

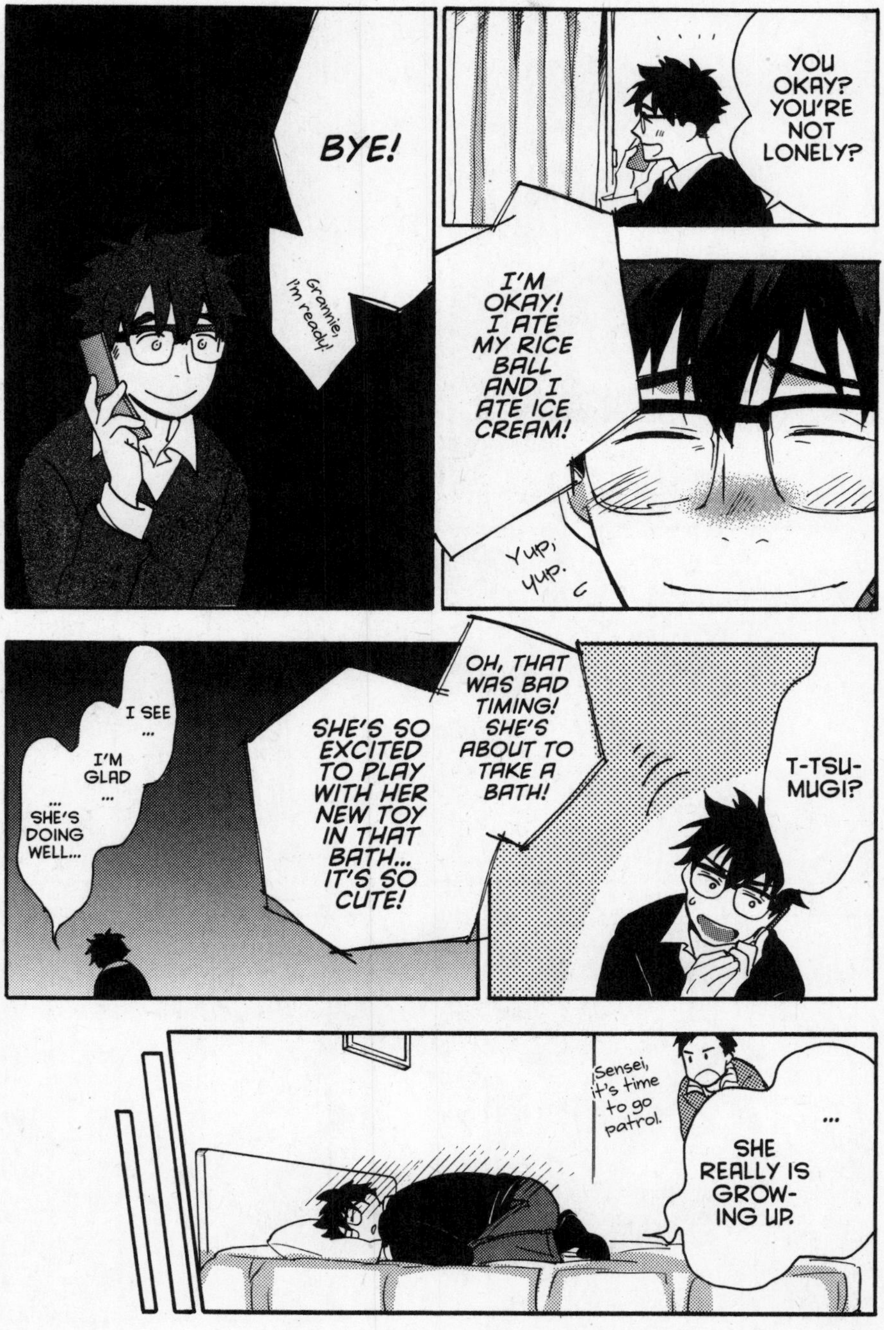
YOU OKAY? YOU'RE NOT LONELY?
I'M OKAY! I ATE MY RICE BALL AND I ATE ICE CREAM!
Yup, yup.
BYE!
Grammie, I'm ready!
T-TSU-MUGI?
OH, THAT WAS BAD TIMING! SHE'S ABOUT TO TAKE A BATH!
SHE'S SO EXCITED TO PLAY WITH HER NEW TOY IN THAT BATH... IT'S SO CUTE!
I SEE ... I'M GLAD ... SHE'S DOING WELL...
... SHE REALLY IS GROWING UP.
Sensei, it's time to go patrol.

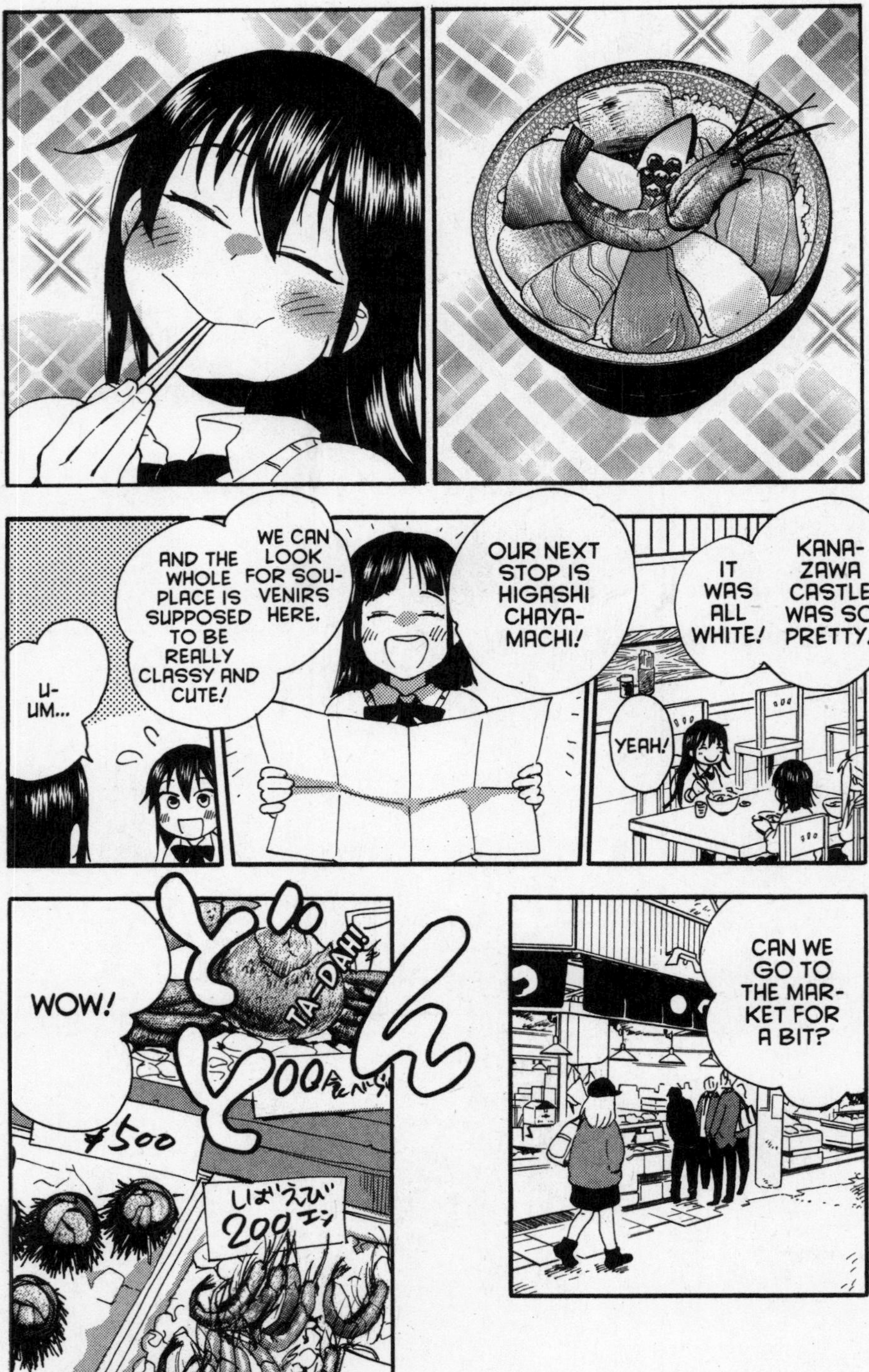
KANA-ZAWA CASTLE WAS SO PRETTY!
IT WAS ALL WHITE!
YEAH!
OUR NEXT STOP IS HIGASHI CHAYA-MACHI!
WE CAN LOOK FOR SOU-VENIRS HERE.
AND THE WHOLE PLACE IS SUPPOSED TO BE REALLY CLASSY AND CUTE!
U-UM...
CAN WE GO TO THE MAR-KET FOR A BIT?
WOW!
TA-DAH!
¥500
しばえび 200エン
Sign: Shiba-Ebi Shrimp 200 Yen

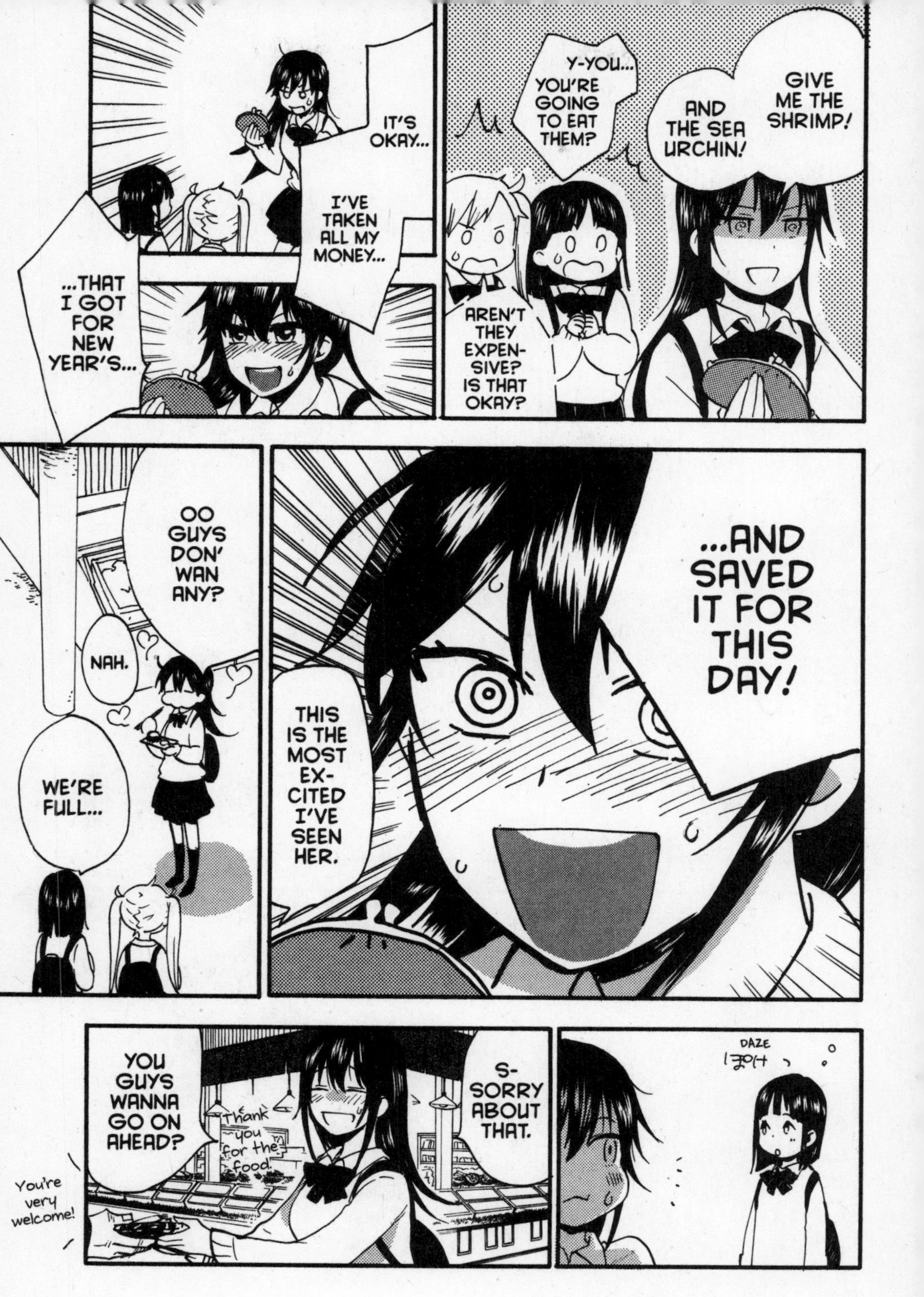
GIVE ME THE SHRIMP!
AND THE SEA URCHIN!
Y-YOU... YOU'RE GOING TO EAT THEM?
AREN'T THEY EXPENSIVE? IS THAT OKAY?
IT'S OKAY...
I'VE TAKEN ALL MY MONEY...
...THAT I GOT FOR NEW YEAR'S...
...AND SAVED IT FOR THIS DAY!
THIS IS THE MOST EXCITED I'VE SEEN HER.
OO GUYS DON' WAN ANY?
NAH.
WE'RE FULL...
DAZE
S-SORRY ABOUT THAT.
YOU GUYS WANNA GO ON AHEAD?
Thank you for the food
You're very welcome!

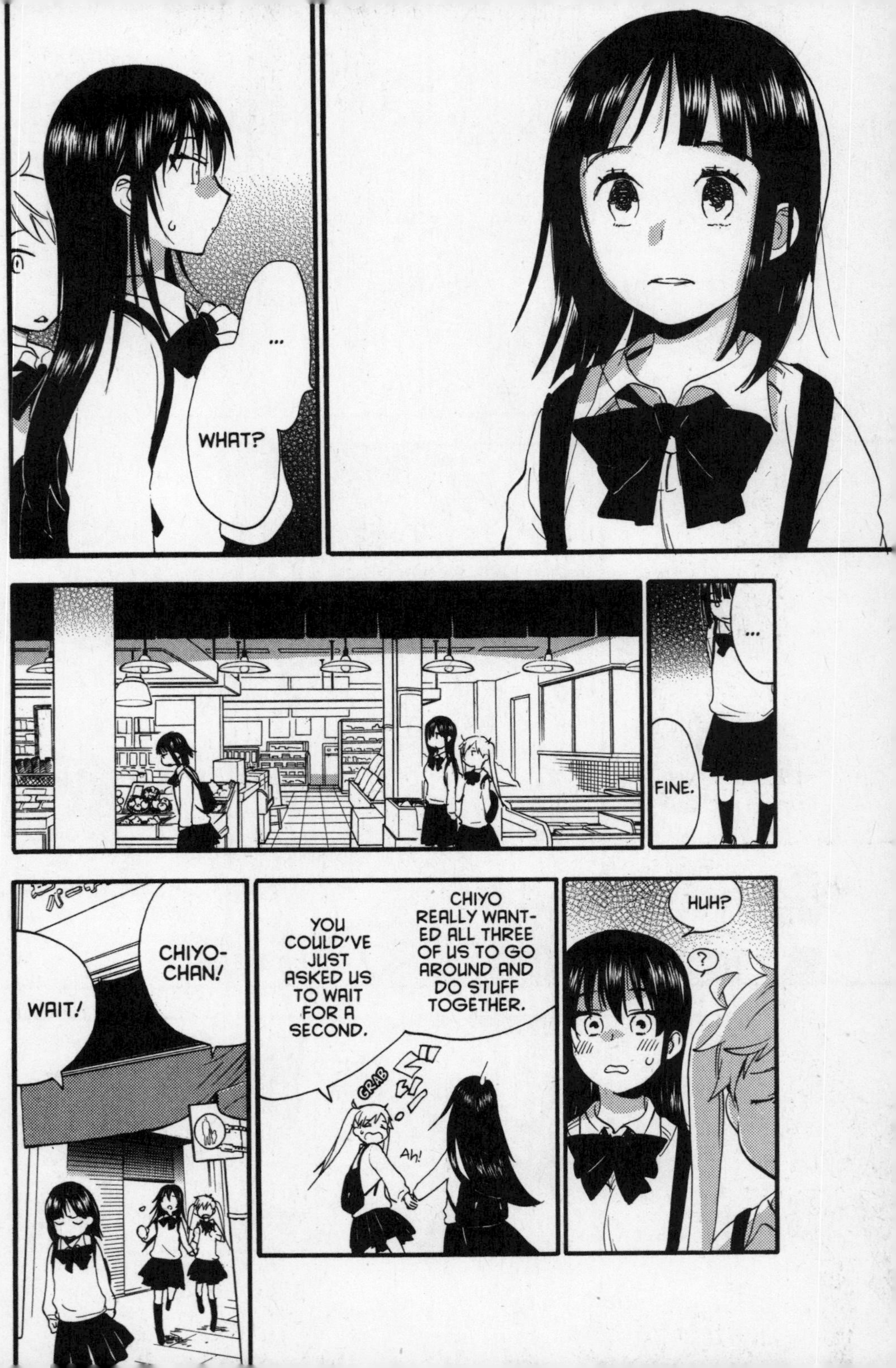
...
WHAT?
...
FINE.
HUH?
?
CHIYO REALLY WANTED ALL THREE OF US TO GO AROUND AND DO STUFF TOGETHER.
YOU COULD'VE JUST ASKED US TO WAIT FOR A SECOND.
GRAB
Ah!
CHIYO-CHAN!
WAIT!

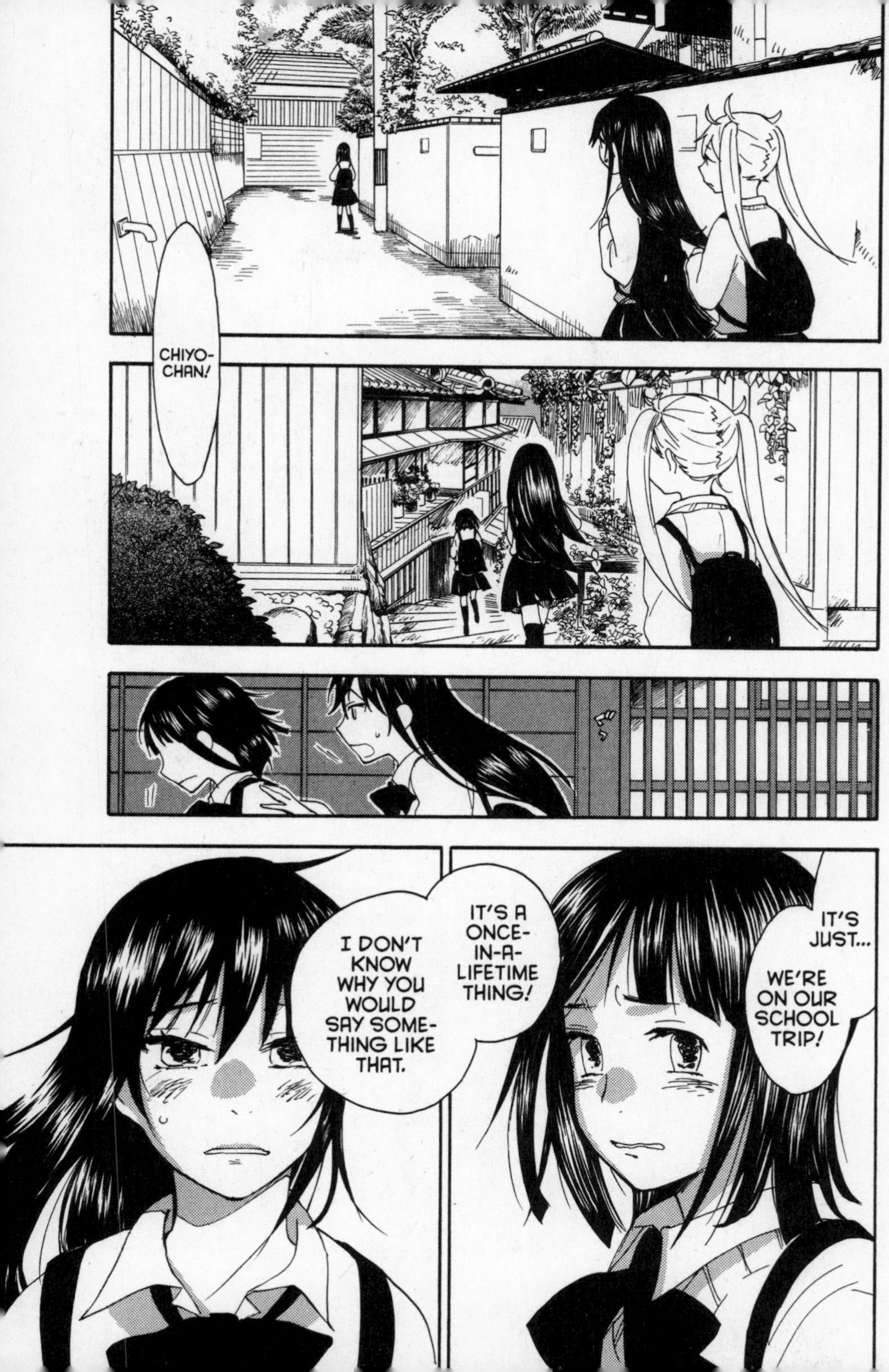
CHIYO-CHAN!
IT'S JUST...
WE'RE ON OUR SCHOOL TRIP!
IT'S A ONCE-IN-A-LIFETIME THING!
I DON'T KNOW WHY YOU WOULD SAY SOME-THING LIKE THAT.

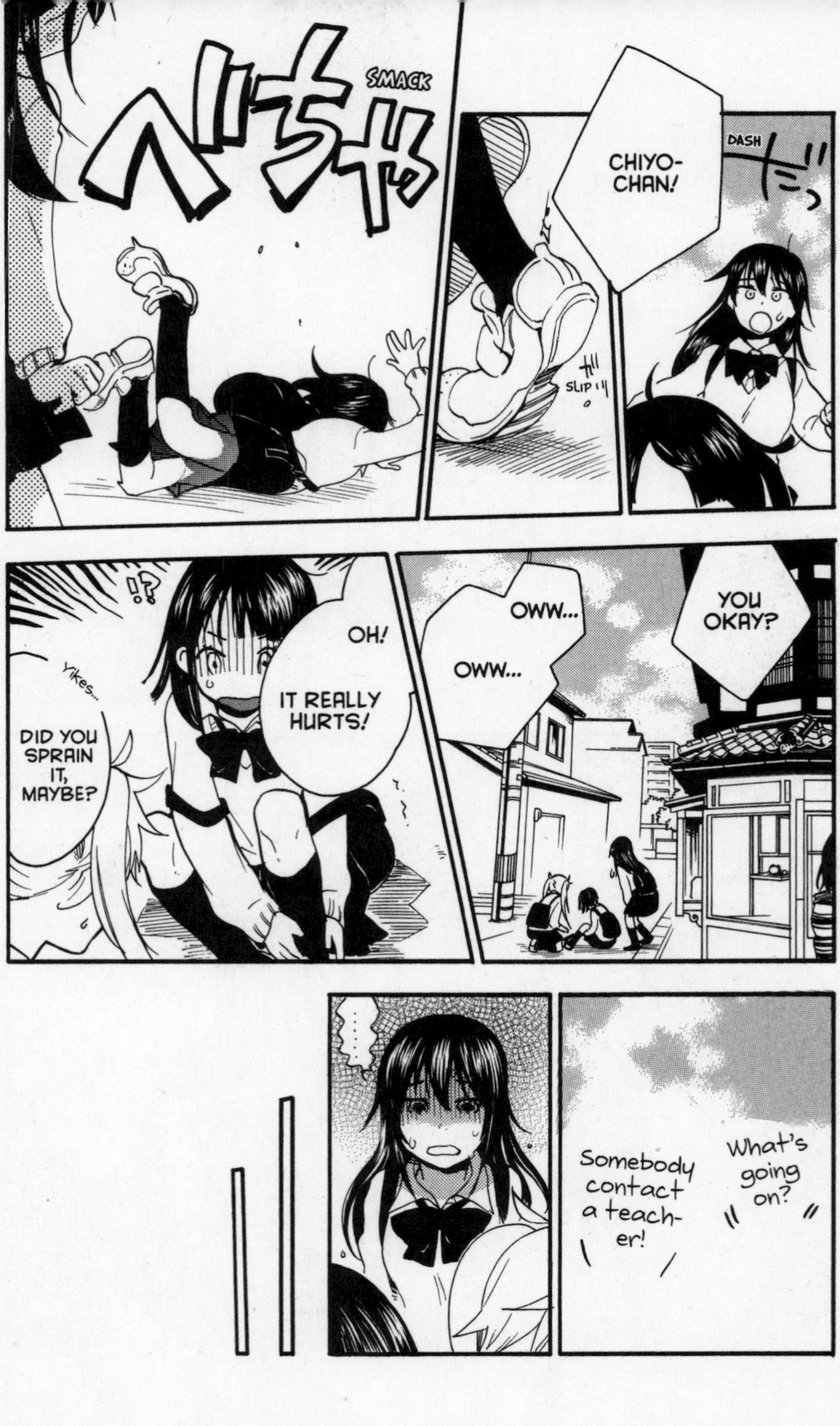
DASH
CHIYO-CHAN!
SLIP
SMACK
YOU OKAY?
OWW...
OWW...
OH!
IT REALLY HURTS!
!?
Yikes...
DID YOU SPRAIN IT, MAYBE?
What's going on?
Somebody contact a teach-er!
...

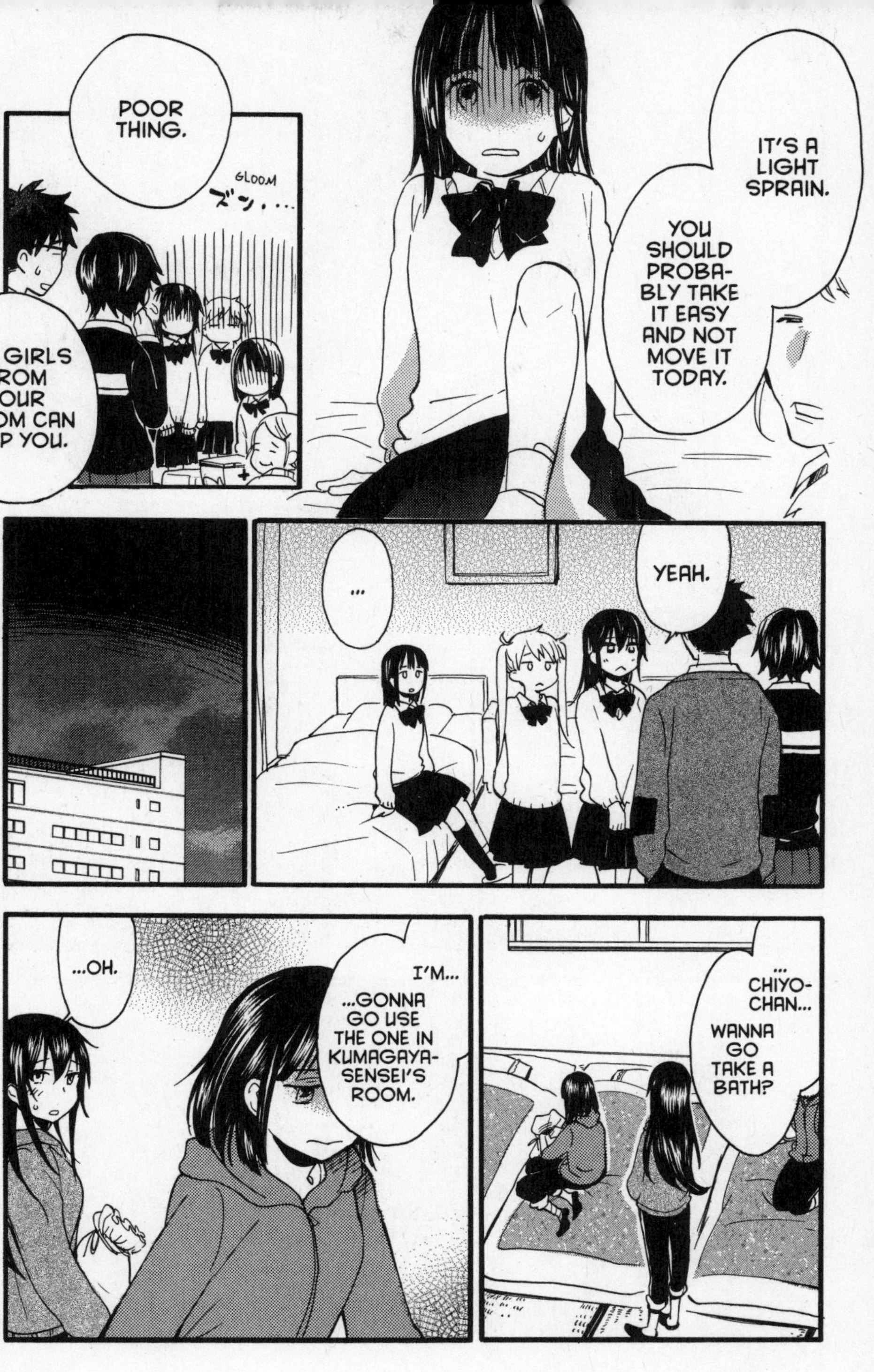
IT'S A LIGHT SPRAIN.
YOU SHOULD PROBA-BLY TAKE IT EASY AND NOT MOVE IT TODAY.
POOR THING.
GLOOM
ズーン・・・
THE GIRLS FROM YOUR ROOM CAN HELP YOU.
YEAH.
...
... CHIYO-CHAN...
WANNA GO TAKE A BATH?
I'M...
...GONNA GO USE THE ONE IN KUMAGAYA-SENSEI'S ROOM.
...OH.

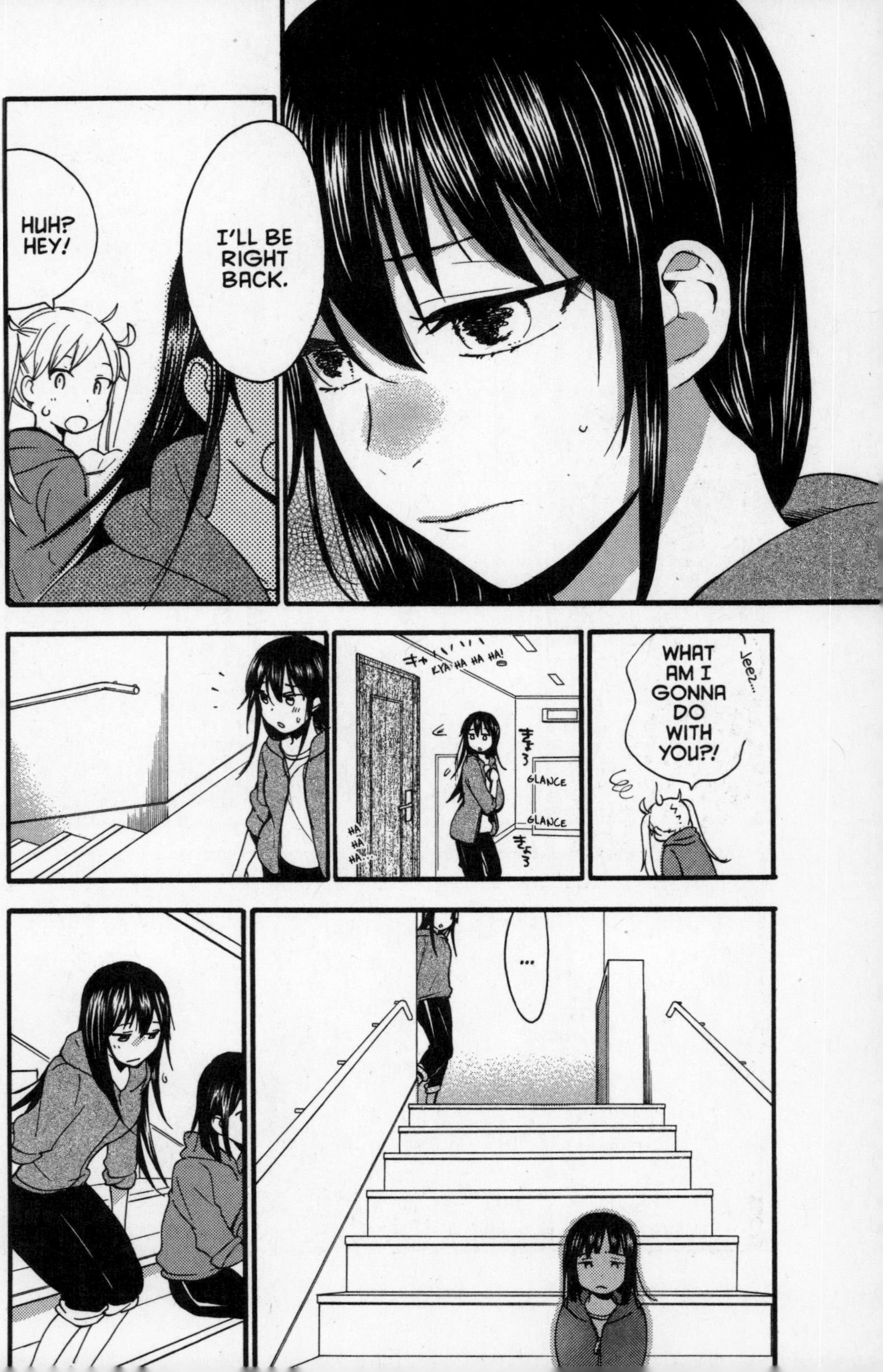
I'LL BE RIGHT BACK.
HUH? HEY!
Jeez...
WHAT AM I GONNA DO WITH YOU?!
KYA HA HA HA!
HA HA HA...
GLANCE
GLANCE
...

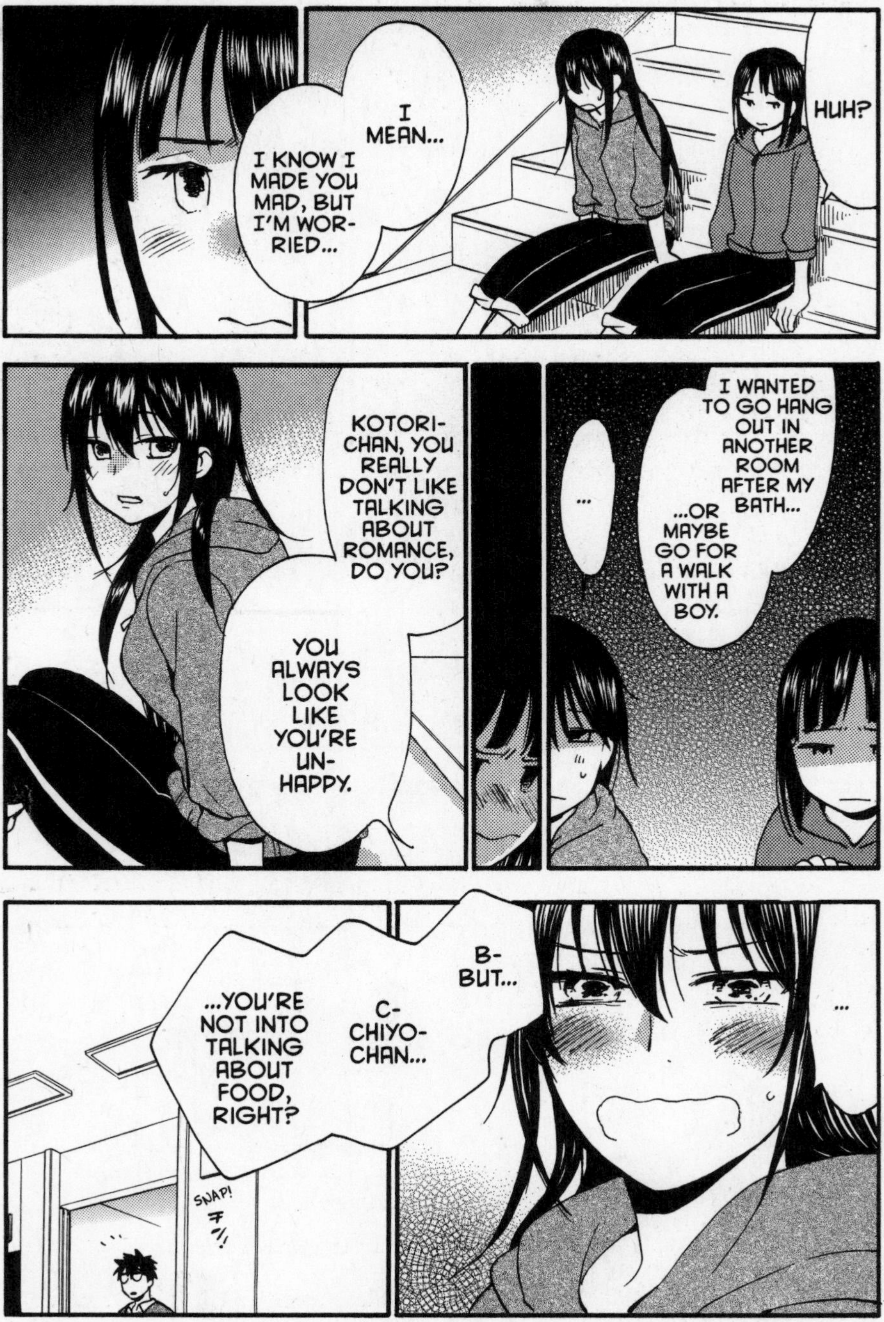
HUH?
I MEAN...
I KNOW I MADE YOU MAD, BUT I'M WOR-RIED...
I WANTED TO GO HANG OUT IN ANOTHER ROOM AFTER MY BATH...
...OR MAYBE GO FOR A WALK WITH A BOY.
...
KOTORI-CHAN, YOU REALLY DON'T LIKE TALKING ABOUT ROMANCE, DO YOU?
YOU ALWAYS LOOK LIKE YOU'RE UN-HAPPY.
...
B-BUT...
C-CHIYO-CHAN...
...YOU'RE NOT INTO TALKING ABOUT FOOD, RIGHT?
SNAP!

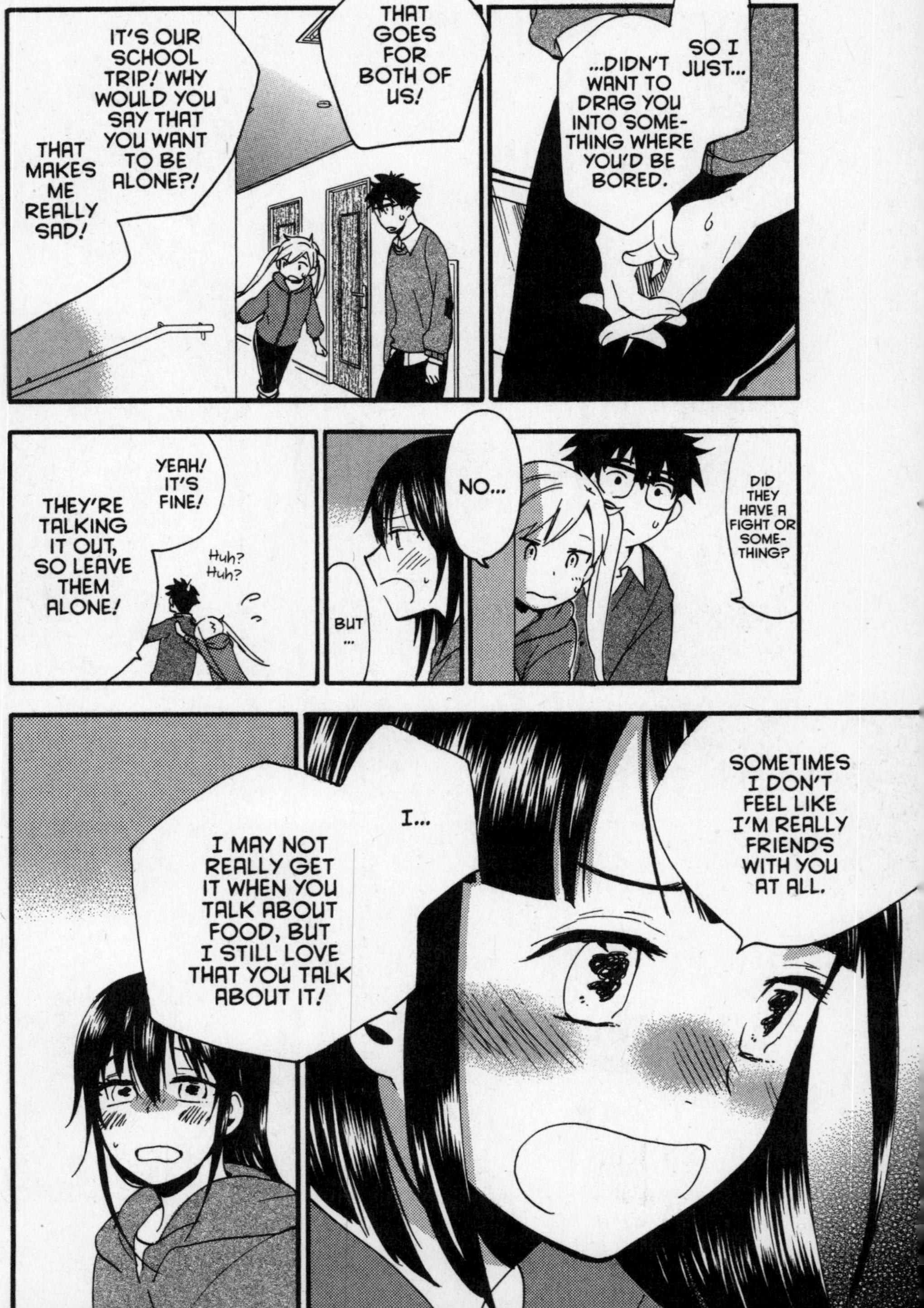
SO I JUST...
...DIDN'T WANT TO DRAG YOU INTO SOMETHING WHERE YOU'D BE BORED.
THAT GOES FOR BOTH OF US!
IT'S OUR SCHOOL TRIP! WHY WOULD YOU SAY THAT YOU WANT TO BE ALONE?!
THAT MAKES ME REALLY SAD!
DID THEY HAVE A FIGHT OR SOMETHING?
NO...
BUT ...
YEAH! IT'S FINE!
THEY'RE TALKING IT OUT, SO LEAVE THEM ALONE!
Huh? Huh?
SOMETIMES I DON'T FEEL LIKE I'M REALLY FRIENDS WITH YOU AT ALL.
I...
I MAY NOT REALLY GET IT WHEN YOU TALK ABOUT FOOD, BUT I STILL LOVE THAT YOU TALK ABOUT IT!

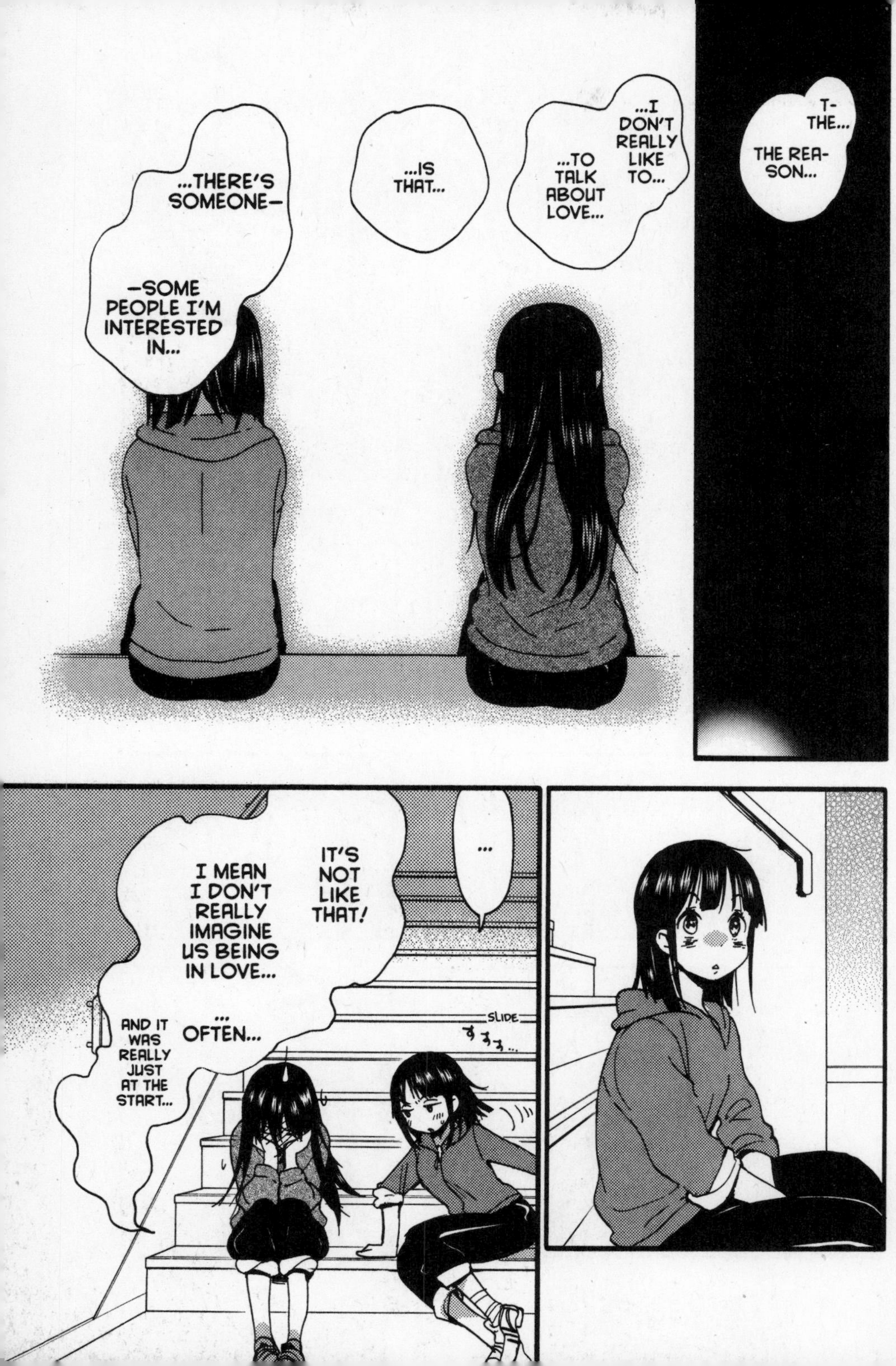
T-THE...
THE REASON...
...I DON'T REALLY LIKE TO...
...TO TALK ABOUT LOVE...
...IS THAT...
...THERE'S SOMEONE—
—SOME PEOPLE I'M INTERESTED IN...
...
IT'S NOT LIKE THAT!
I MEAN I DON'T REALLY IMAGINE US BEING IN LOVE...
...OFTEN...
AND IT WAS REALLY JUST AT THE START...
SLIDE

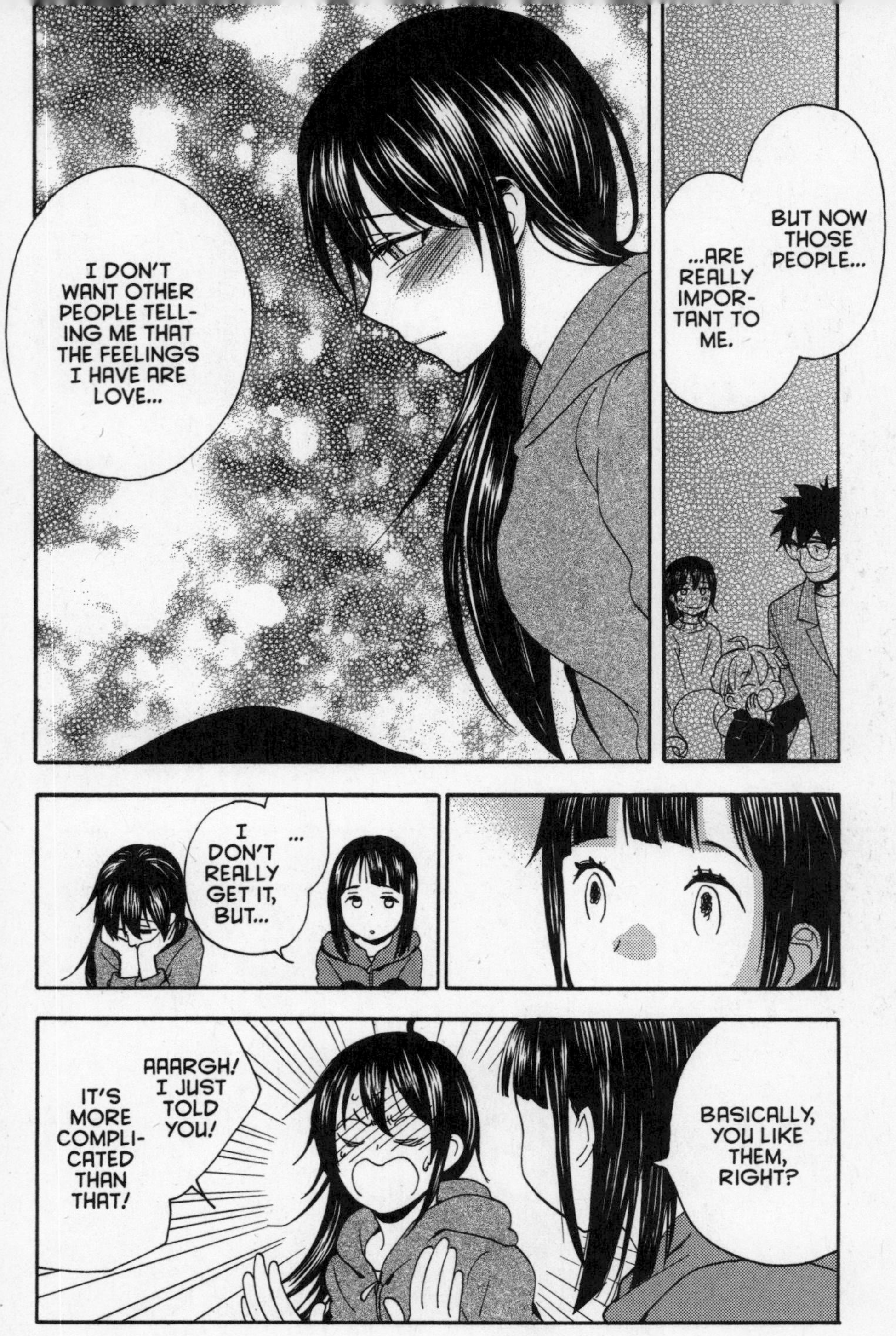
BUT NOW THOSE PEOPLE...
...ARE REALLY IMPORTANT TO ME.
I DON'T WANT OTHER PEOPLE TELLING ME THAT THE FEELINGS I HAVE ARE LOVE...
...
I DON'T REALLY GET IT, BUT...
BASICALLY, YOU LIKE THEM, RIGHT?
AAARGH! I JUST TOLD YOU!
IT'S MORE COMPLICATED THAN THAT!

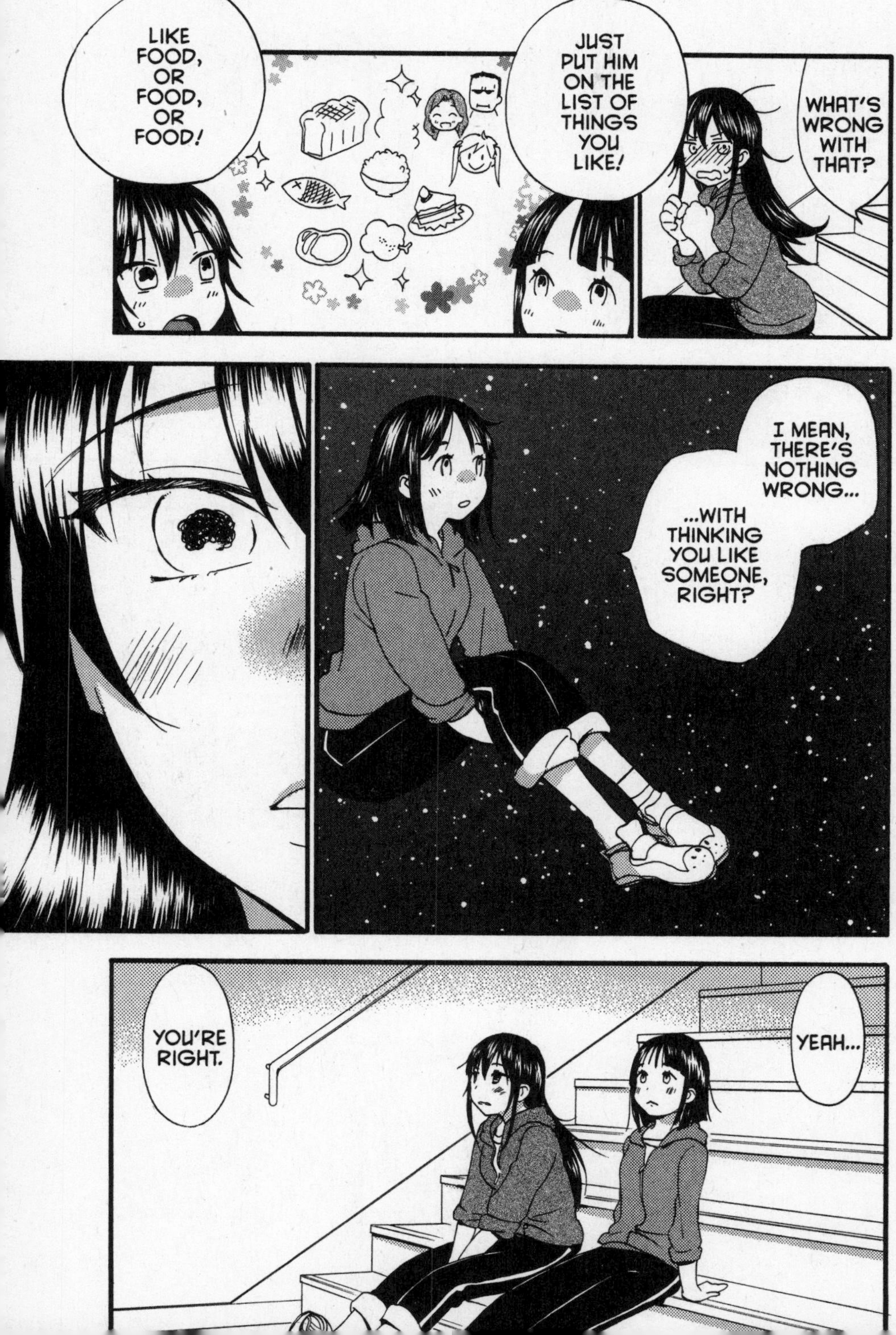
WHAT'S WRONG WITH THAT?
JUST PUT HIM ON THE LIST OF THINGS YOU LIKE!
LIKE FOOD, OR FOOD, OR FOOD!
I MEAN, THERE'S NOTHING WRONG...
...WITH THINKING YOU LIKE SOMEONE, RIGHT?
YEAH...
YOU'RE RIGHT.

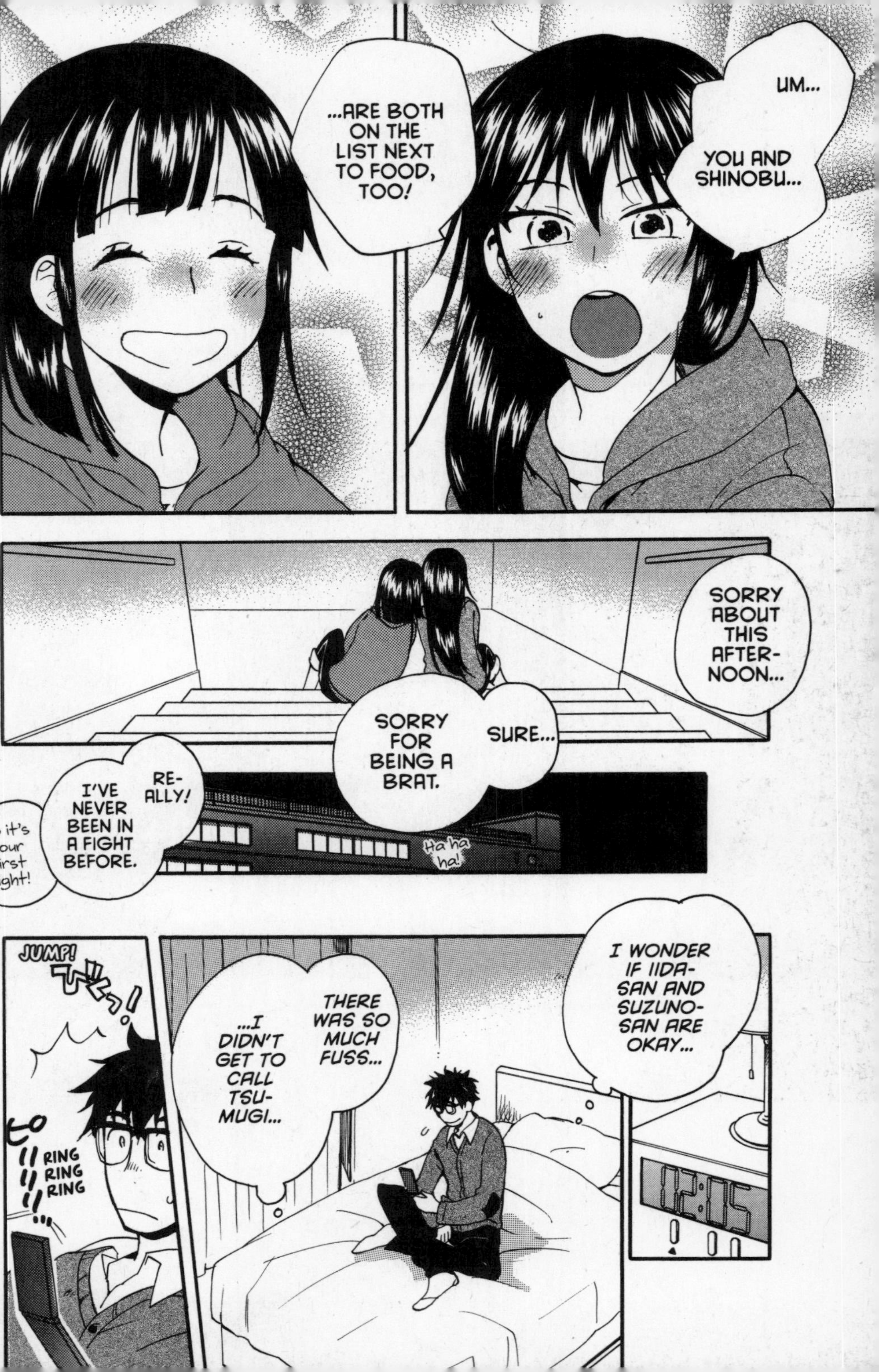
UM...
YOU AND SHINOBU...
...ARE BOTH ON THE LIST NEXT TO FOOD, TOO!
SORRY ABOUT THIS AFTERNOON...
SURE...
SORRY FOR BEING A BRAT.
Ha ha ha!
RE-ALLY!
I'VE NEVER BEEN IN A FIGHT BEFORE.
So it's your first fight!
I WONDER IF IIDA-SAN AND SUZUNO-SAN ARE OKAY...
THERE WAS SO MUCH FUSS...
...I DIDN'T GET TO CALL TSU-MUGI...
12:05
JUMP!
RING RING RING

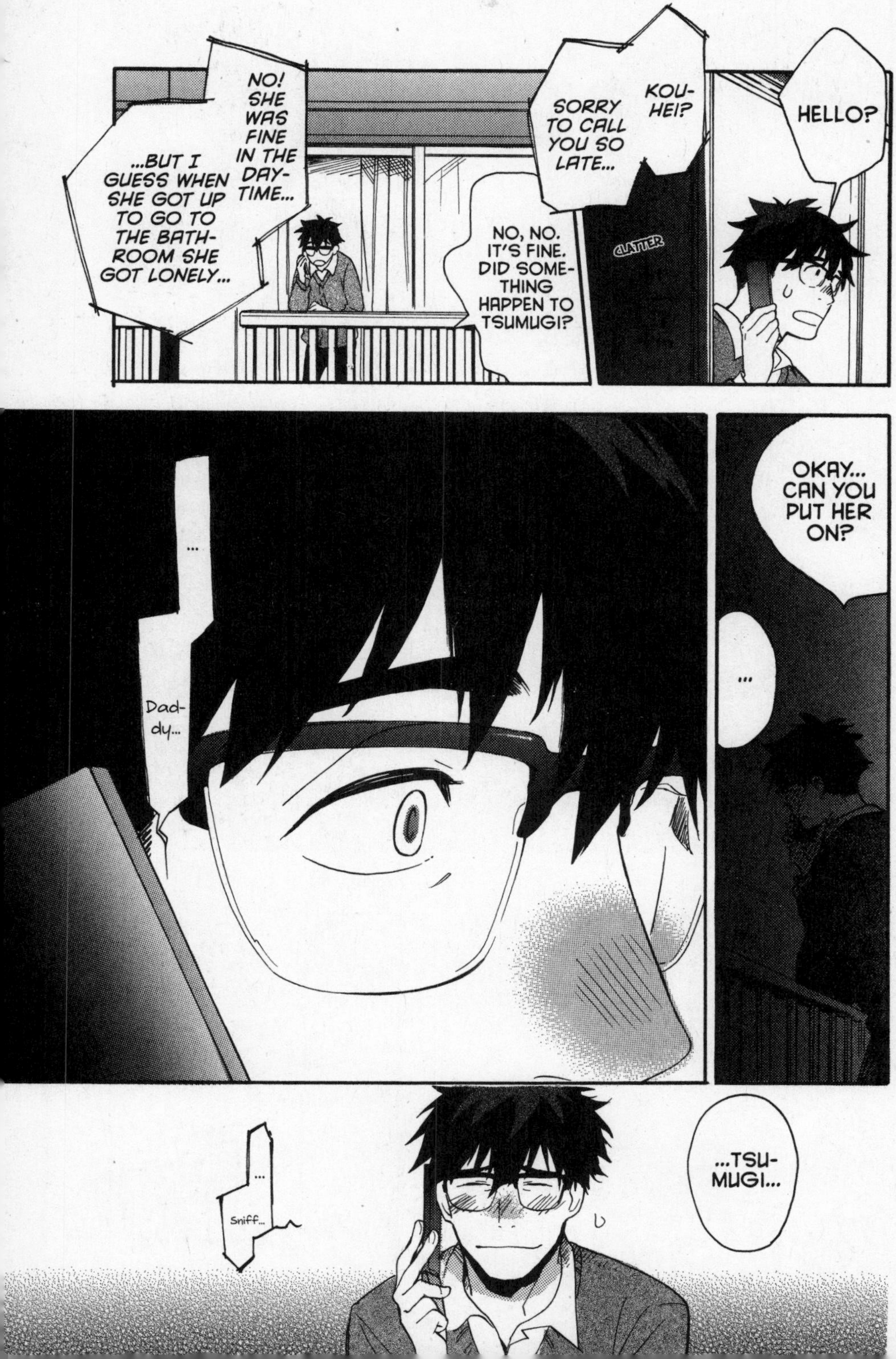
HELLO?
CLATTER
KOU-HEI?
SORRY TO CALL YOU SO LATE...
NO, NO. IT'S FINE. DID SOMETHING HAPPEN TO TSUMUGI?
NO! SHE WAS FINE IN THE DAYTIME...
...BUT I GUESS WHEN SHE GOT UP TO GO TO THE BATHROOM SHE GOT LONELY...
OKAY... CAN YOU PUT HER ON?
...
...
Daddy...
...TSUMUGI...
...
Sniff...

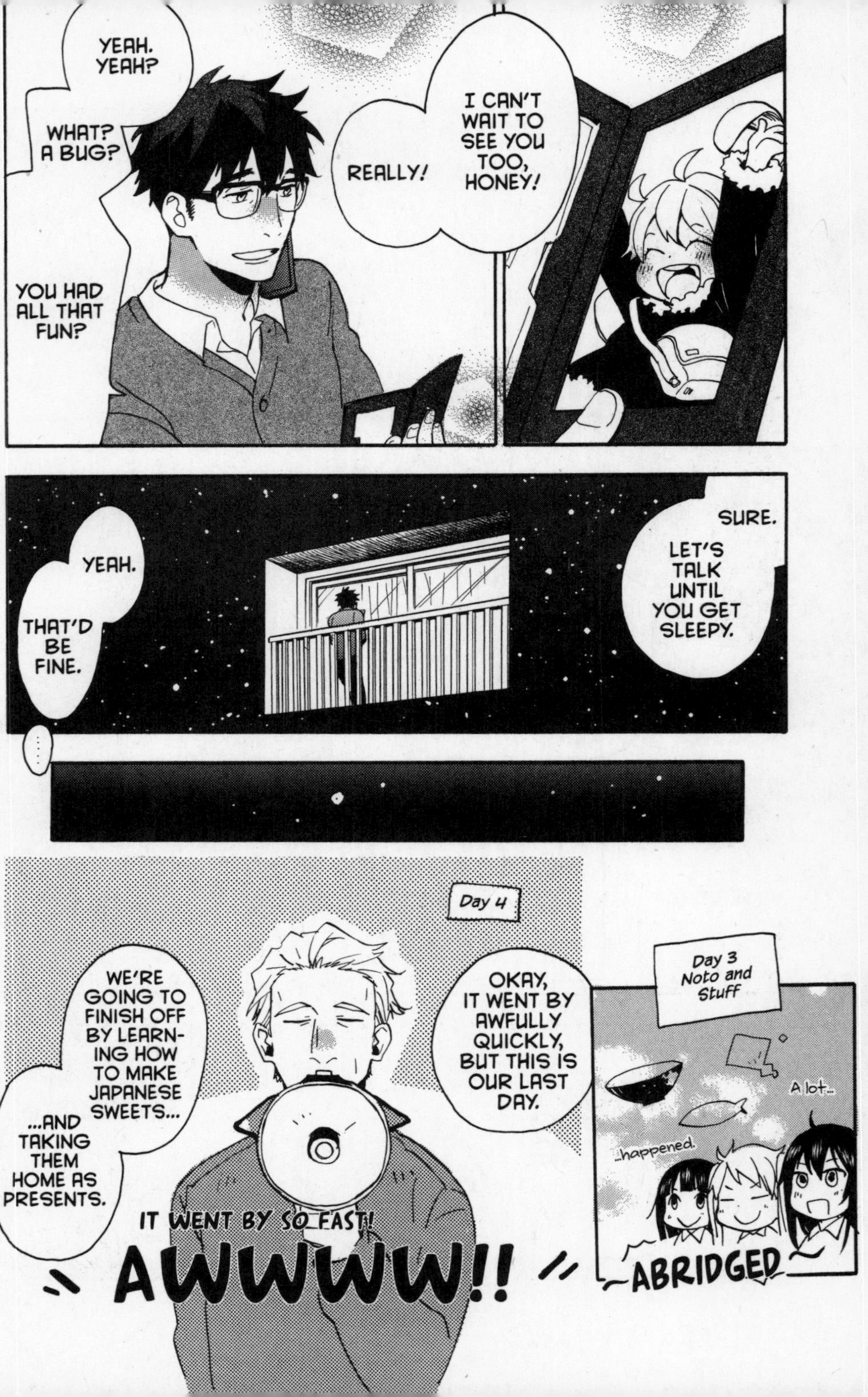
I CAN'T WAIT TO SEE YOU TOO, HONEY!
REALLY!
YEAH. YEAH?
WHAT? A BUG?
YOU HAD ALL THAT FUN?
SURE.
LET'S TALK UNTIL YOU GET SLEEPY.
YEAH.
THAT'D BE FINE.
......
Day 3 Noto and Stuff
A lot...
...happened.
ABRIDGED
Day 4
OKAY, IT WENT BY AWFULLY QUICKLY, BUT THIS IS OUR LAST DAY.
WE'RE GOING TO FINISH OFF BY LEARNING HOW TO MAKE JAPANESE SWEETS...
...AND TAKING THEM HOME AS PRESENTS.
IT WENT BY SO FAST!
AWWWW!!

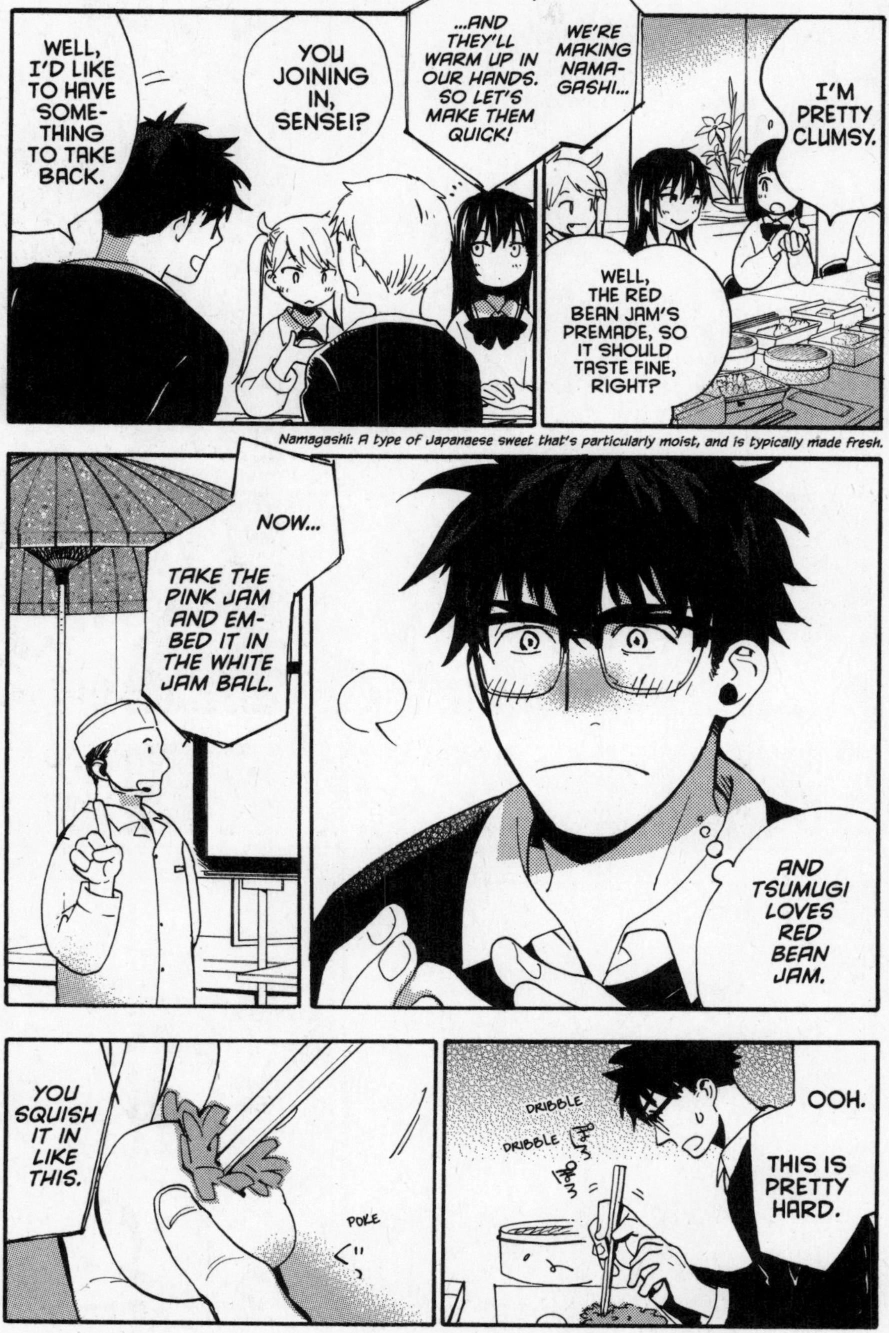
I'M PRETTY CLUMSY.
WE'RE MAKING NAMA-GASHI...
...AND THEY'LL WARM UP IN OUR HANDS. SO LET'S MAKE THEM QUICK!
WELL, THE RED BEAN JAM'S PREMADE, SO IT SHOULD TASTE FINE, RIGHT?
YOU JOINING IN, SENSEI?
WELL, I'D LIKE TO HAVE SOME-THING TO TAKE BACK.
AND TSUMUGI LOVES RED BEAN JAM.
NOW...
TAKE THE PINK JAM AND EM-BED IT IN THE WHITE JAM BALL.
OOH.
THIS IS PRETTY HARD.
DRIBBLE
DRIBBLE
YOU SQUISH IT IN LIKE THIS.
POKE

Namagashi: A type of Japanaese sweet that's particularly moist, and is typically made fresh.

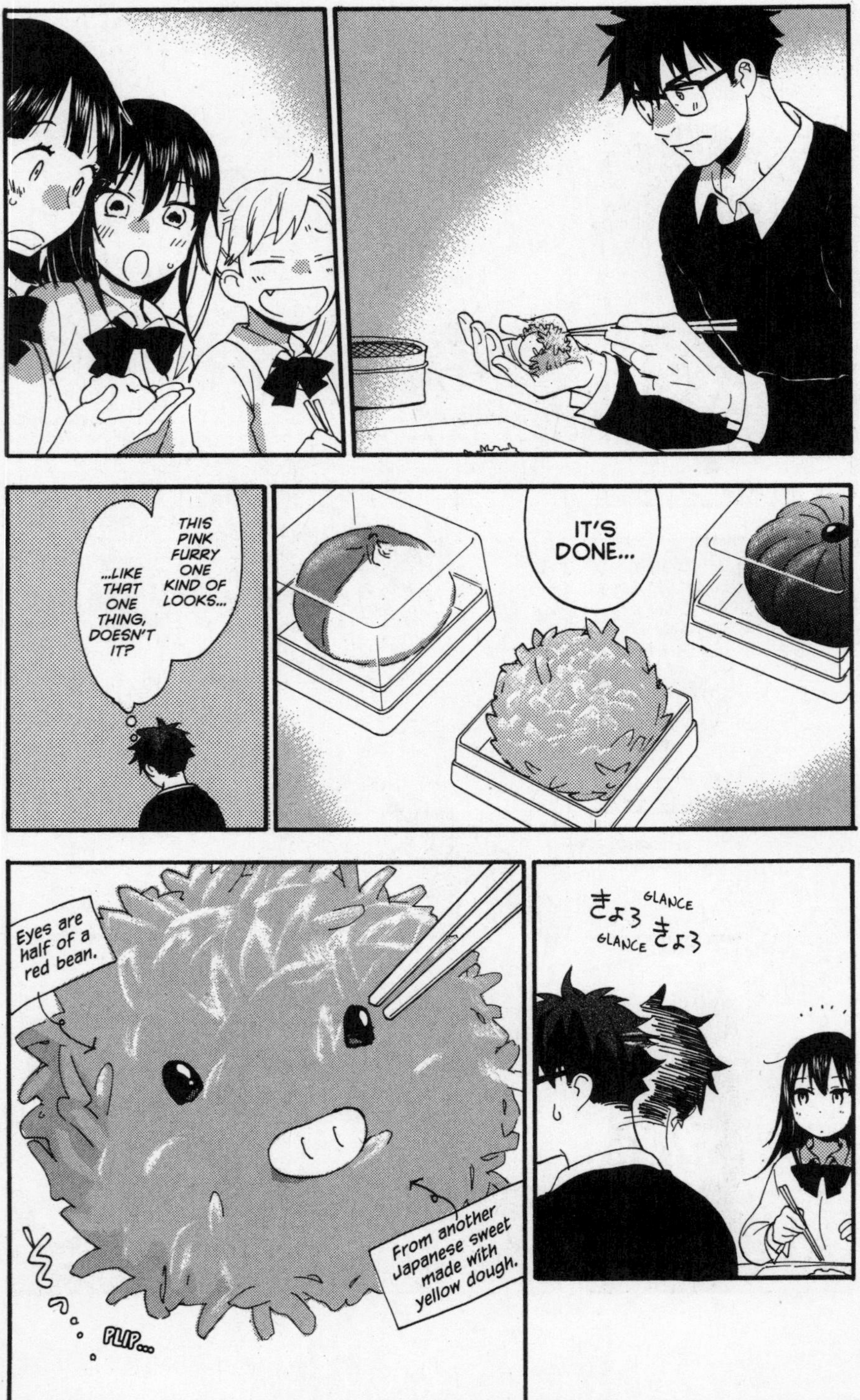
IT'S DONE...
THIS PINK FURRY ONE KIND OF LOOKS...
...LIKE THAT ONE THING, DOESN'T IT?
きょろ GLANCE きょろ GLANCE
....
Eyes are half of a red bean.
From another Japanese sweet made with yellow dough.
PLIP...

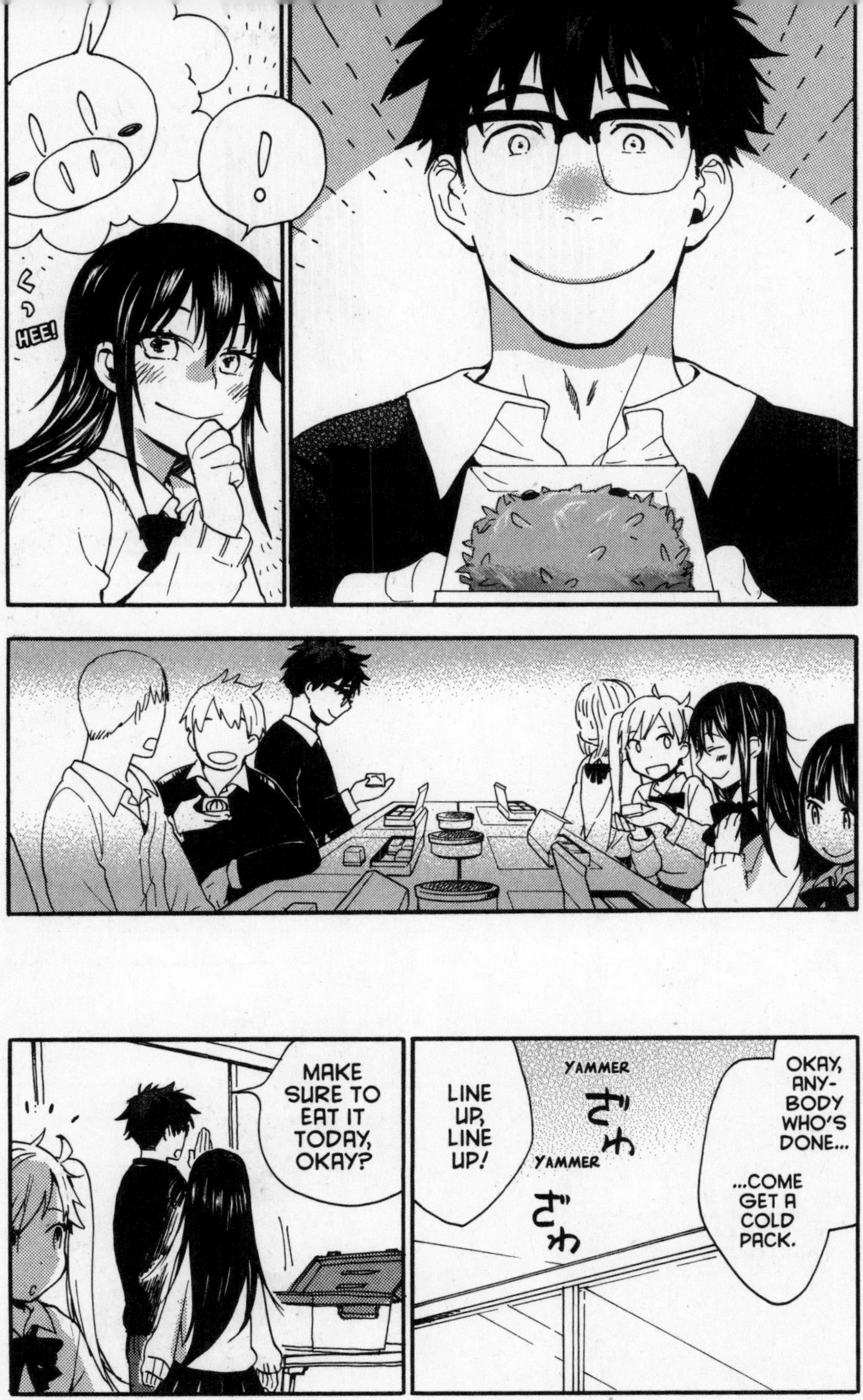
!
くっ
HEE!
OKAY, ANY-BODY WHO'S DONE...
...COME GET A COLD PACK.
YAMMER
ざわ
YAMMER
ざわ
LINE UP, LINE UP!
MAKE SURE TO EAT IT TODAY, OKAY?

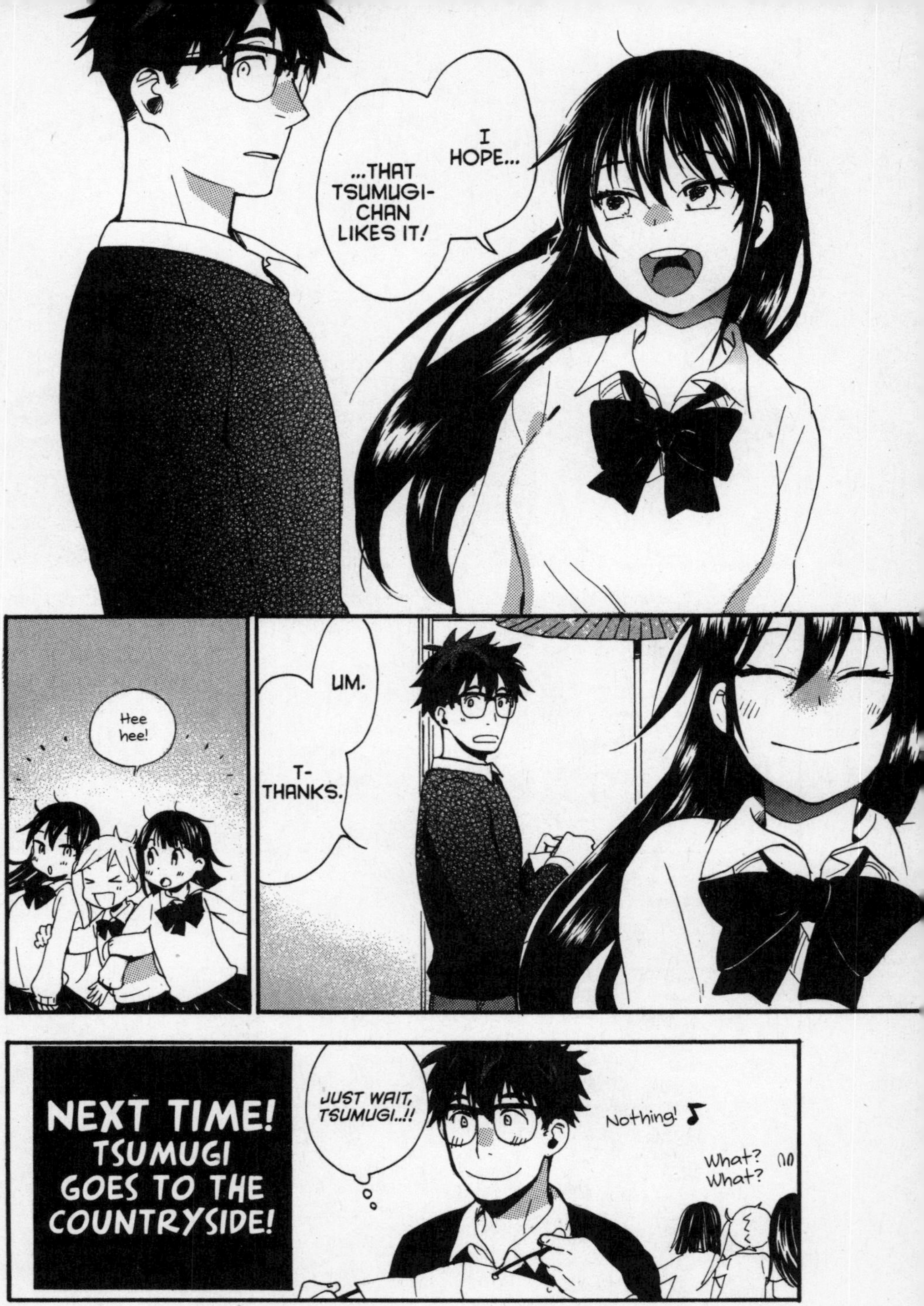
I HOPE...
...THAT TSUMUGI-CHAN LIKES IT!
UM.
T-THANKS.
Hee hee!
Nothing! ♪
What? What?
JUST WAIT, TSUMUGI...!!
NEXT TIME! TSUMUGI GOES TO THE COUNTRYSIDE!

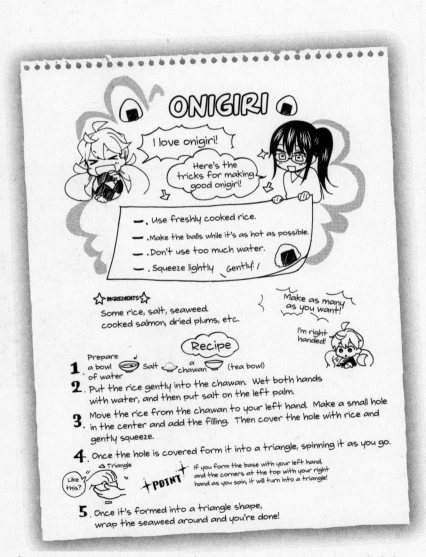

ONIGIRI

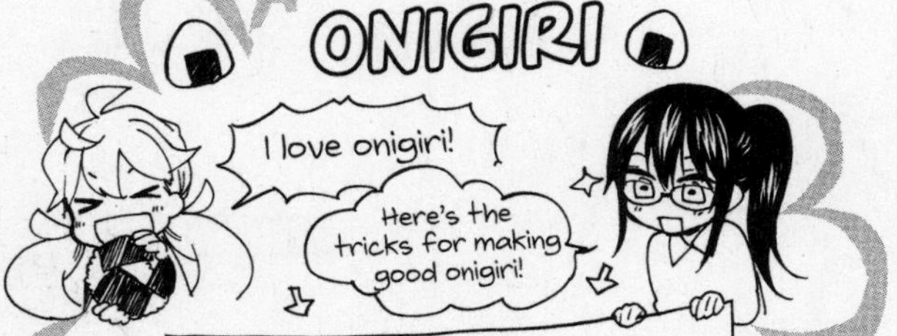
I love onigiri!
Here's the tricks for making good onigiri!

—. Use freshly cooked rice.
—. Make the balls while it's as hot as possible.
—. Don't use too much water.
—. Squeeze lightly Gently!

☆INGREDIENTS☆
Some rice, salt, seaweed.
cooked salmon, dried plums, etc.

Make as many as you want!

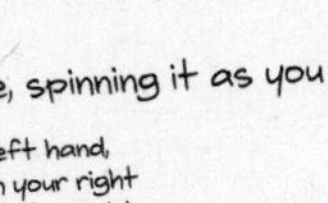
I'm right handed!

Recipe

1. Prepare a bowl of water, Salt, a chawan (tea bowl)
2. Put the rice gently into the chawan. Wet both hands with water, and then put salt on the left palm.
3. Move the rice from the chawan to your left hand. Make a small hole in the center and add the filling. Then cover the hole with rice and gently squeeze.
4. Once the hole is covered form it into a triangle, spinning it as you go.

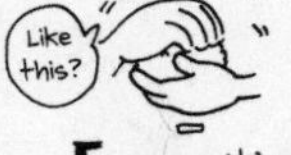
Like this?
△ Triangle

POINT: If you form the base with your left hand, and the corners at the top with your right hand as you spin, it will turn into a triangle!

5. Once it's formed into a triangle shape, wrap the seaweed around and you're done!

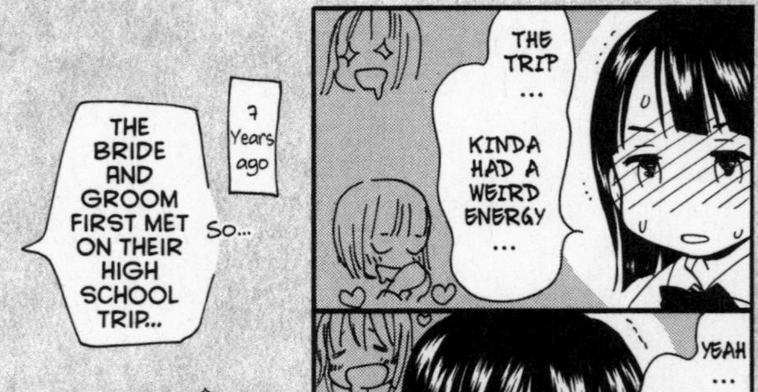
THE TRIP ... KINDA HAD A WEIRD ENERGY ...
YEAH ... LIKE SOME-THING WAS ABOUT TO BURST ...
YOU GUYS GOT *WAY* TOO CAUGHT UP IN THE MOOD.
JUST FORGET IT!!
7 Years ago
So...
THE BRIDE AND GROOM FIRST MET ON THEIR HIGH SCHOOL TRIP...
THE SCHOOL TRIP ...!!

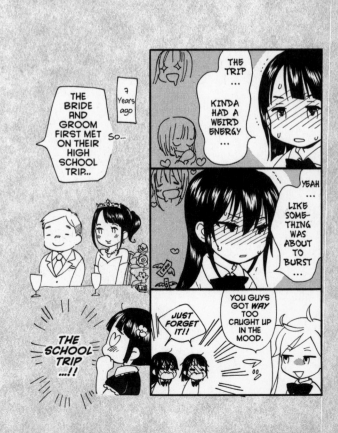

Chapter 30: Welcome Home and Chicken Cream Stew

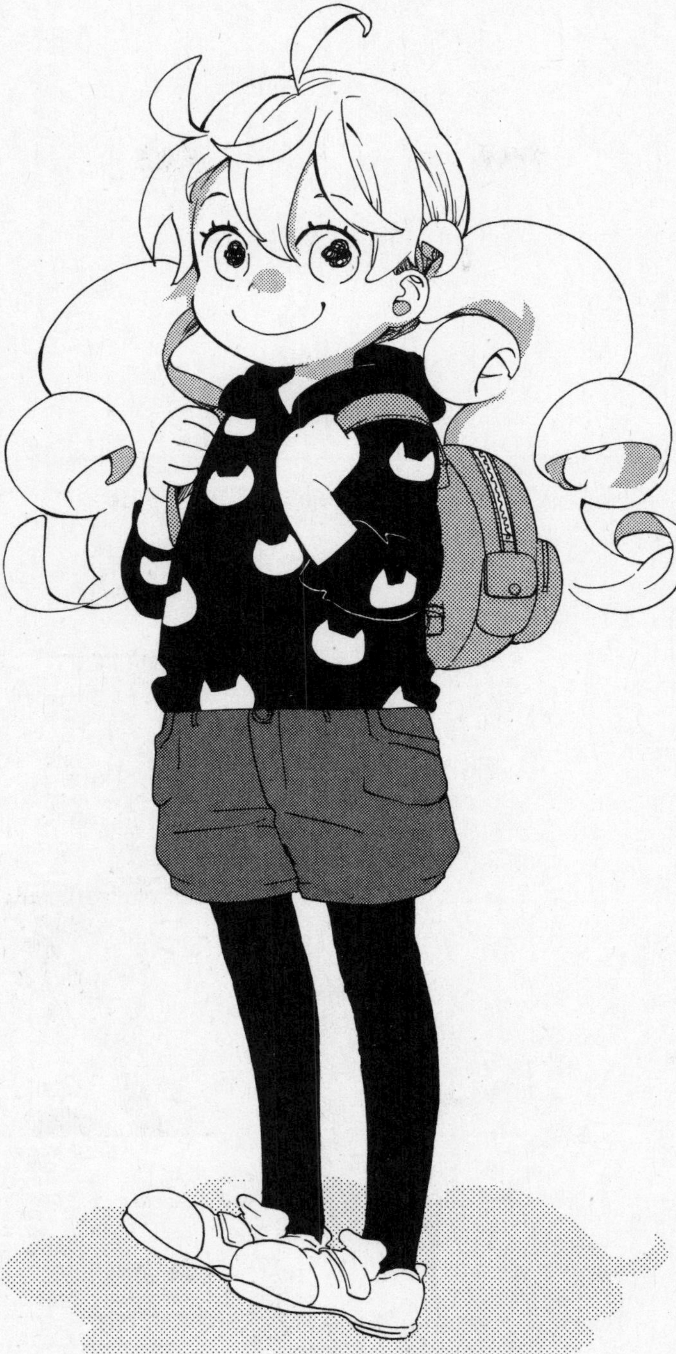

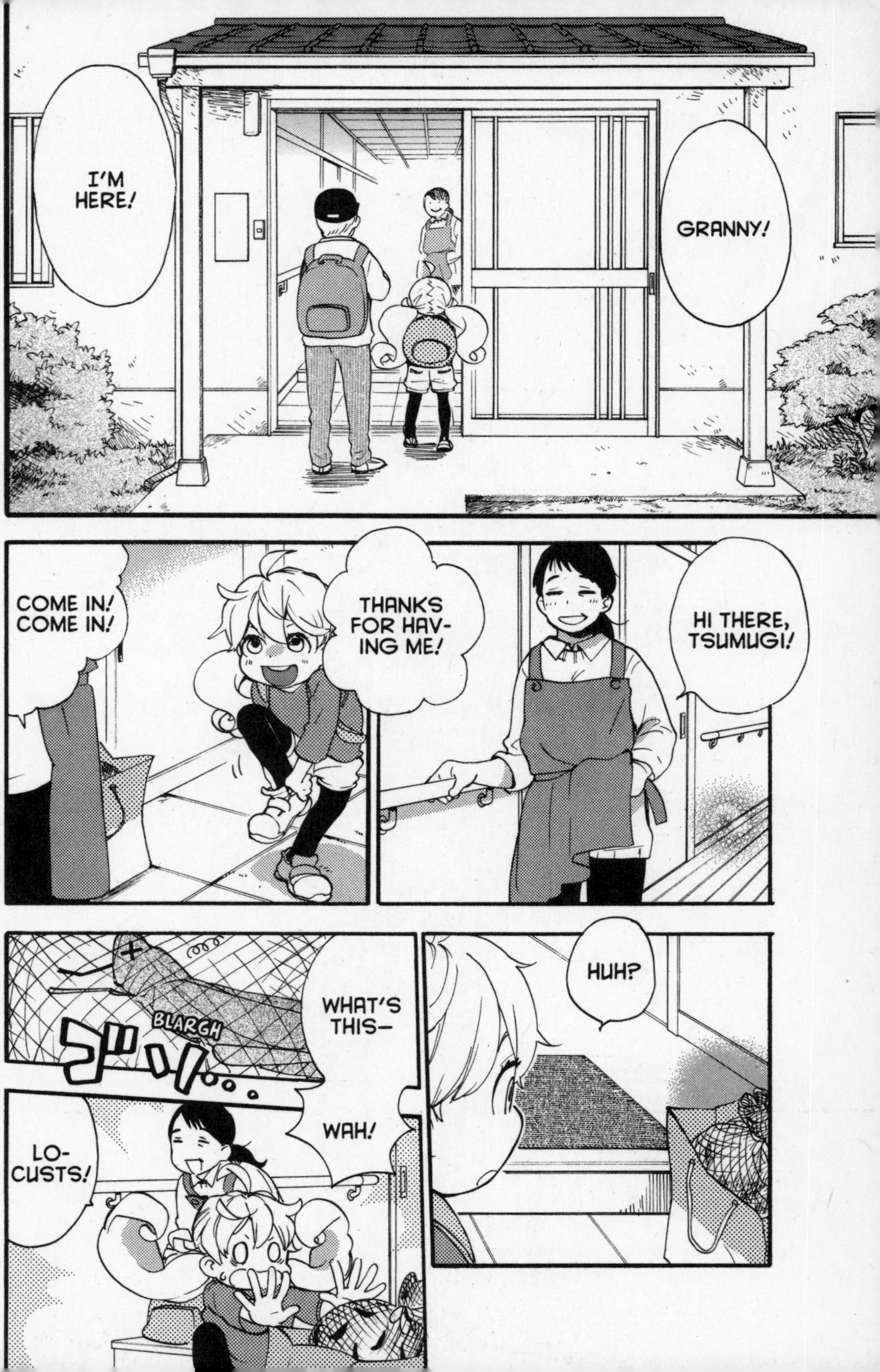
GRANNY!
I'M HERE!
HI THERE, TSUMUGI!
THANKS FOR HAV-ING ME!
COME IN! COME IN!
HUH?
WHAT'S THIS—
BLARGH
WAH!
LO-CUSTS!

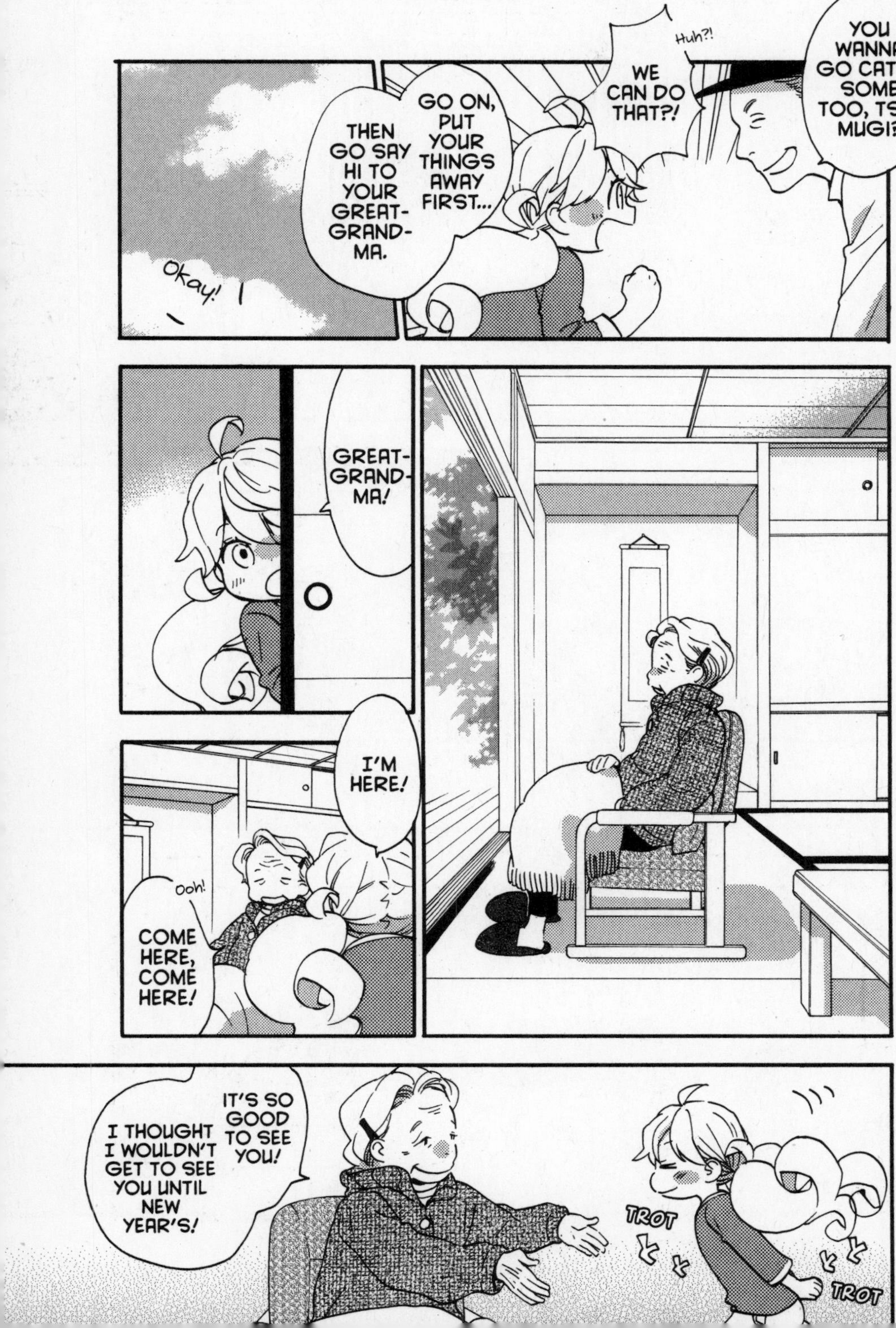
YOU WANNA GO CATCH SOME TOO, TSU-MUGI?
Huh?!
WE CAN DO THAT?!
GO ON, PUT YOUR THINGS AWAY FIRST...
THEN GO SAY HI TO YOUR GREAT-GRAND-MA.
Okay!
GREAT-GRAND-MA!
I'M HERE!
Ooh!
COME HERE, COME HERE!
TROT
TROT
IT'S SO GOOD TO SEE YOU!
I THOUGHT I WOULDN'T GET TO SEE YOU UNTIL NEW YEAR'S!

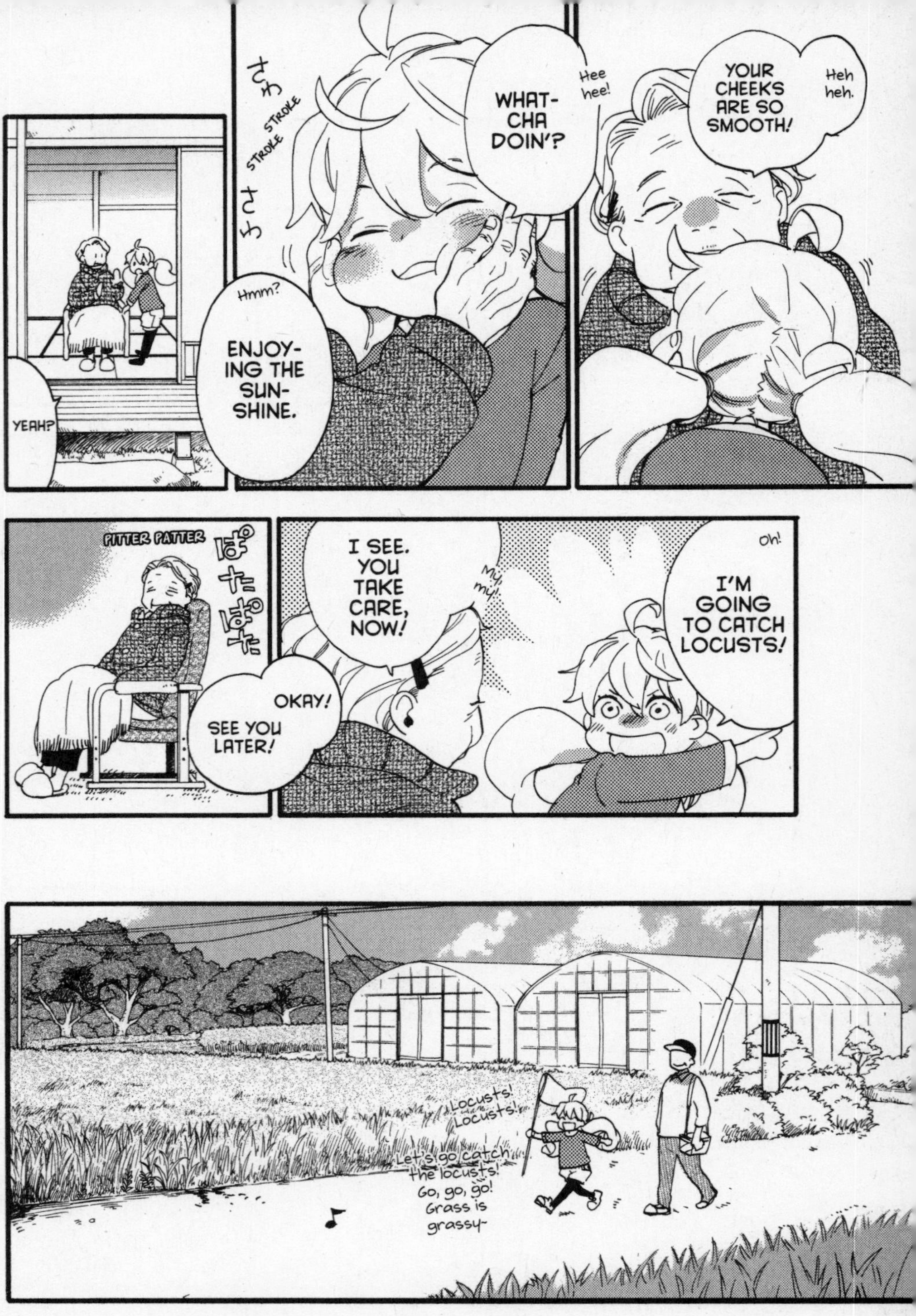
YOUR CHEEKS ARE SO SMOOTH!
Heh heh.
WHAT-CHA DOIN'?
Hee hee!
さわさわ
STROKE STROKE
Hmm?
ENJOYING THE SUN-SHINE.
YEAH?
Oh!
I'M GOING TO CATCH LOCUSTS!
My, my!
I SEE. YOU TAKE CARE, NOW!
OKAY! SEE YOU LATER!
ぱたぱた
PITTER PATTER
Locusts! Locusts!
Let's go catch the locusts! Go, go, go! Grass is grassy~

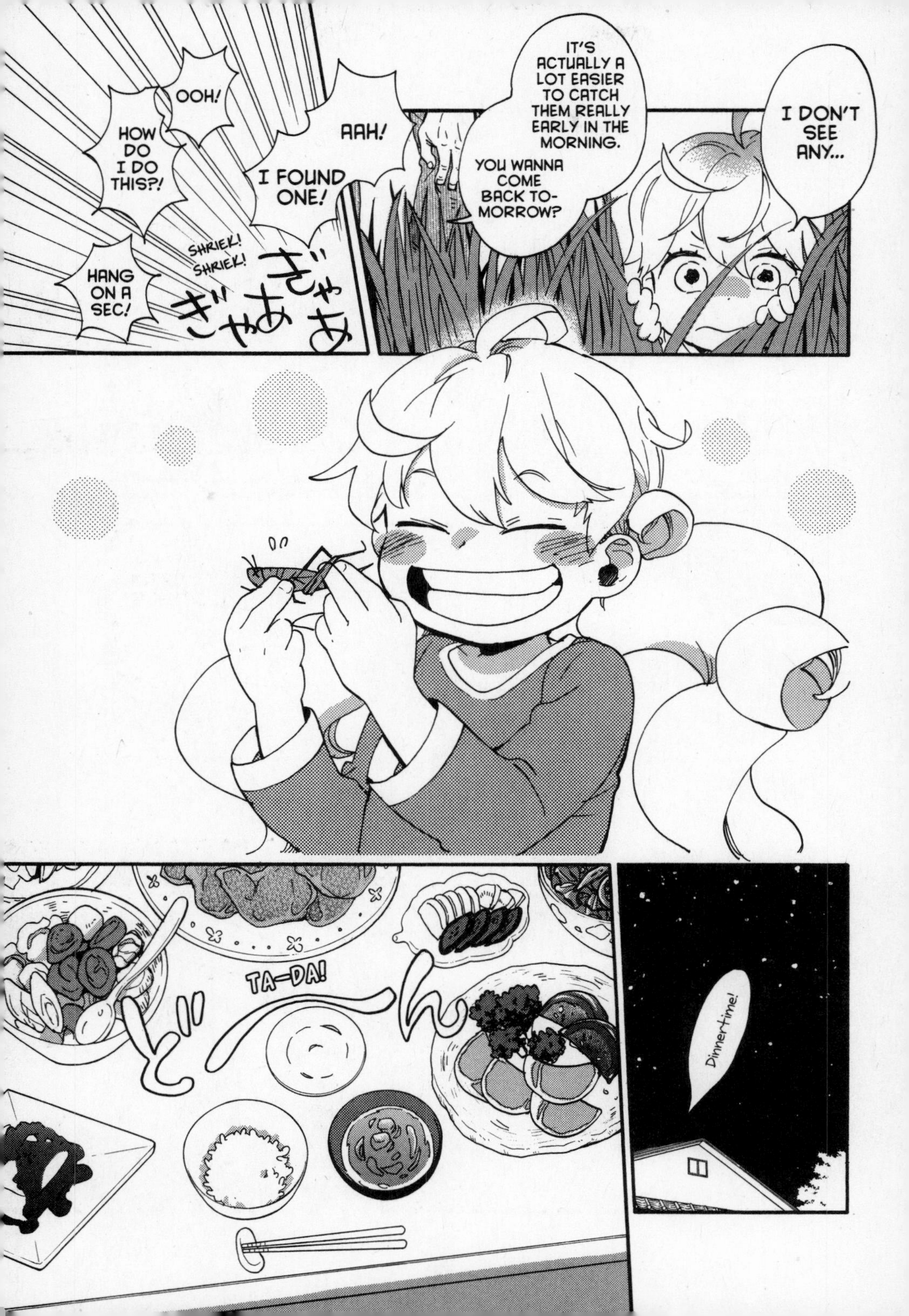
I DON'T SEE ANY...
IT'S ACTUALLY A LOT EASIER TO CATCH THEM REALLY EARLY IN THE MORNING.
YOU WANNA COME BACK TO-MORROW?
AAH!
I FOUND ONE!
OOH!
HOW DO I DO THIS?!
HANG ON A SEC!
SHRIEK! SHRIEK!
ぎゃあぎゃあ
Dinnertime!
TA-DA!
どーん

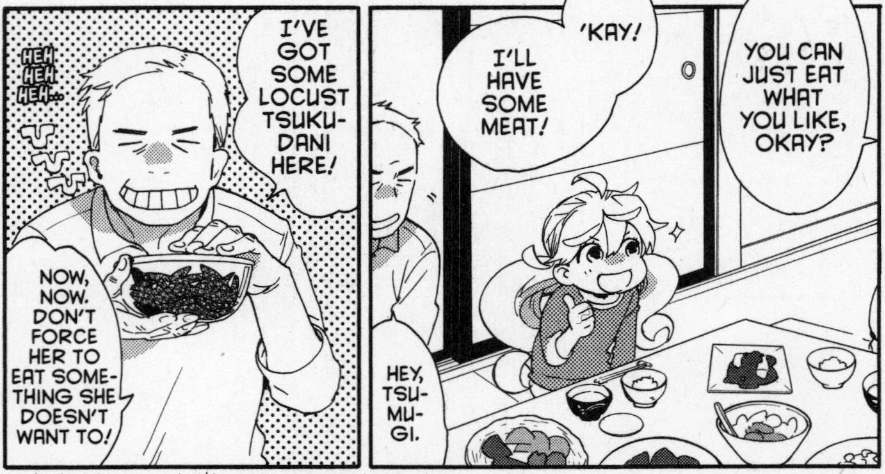
YOU CAN JUST EAT WHAT YOU LIKE, OKAY?
'KAY!
I'LL HAVE SOME MEAT!
HEY, TSU-MU-GI.
I'VE GOT SOME LOCUST TSUKU-DANI HERE!
HEH HEH HEH...
NOW, NOW. DON'T FORCE HER TO EAT SOME-THING SHE DOESN'T WANT TO!

Tsukudani: Preserved with a soy sauce and mirin glaze.

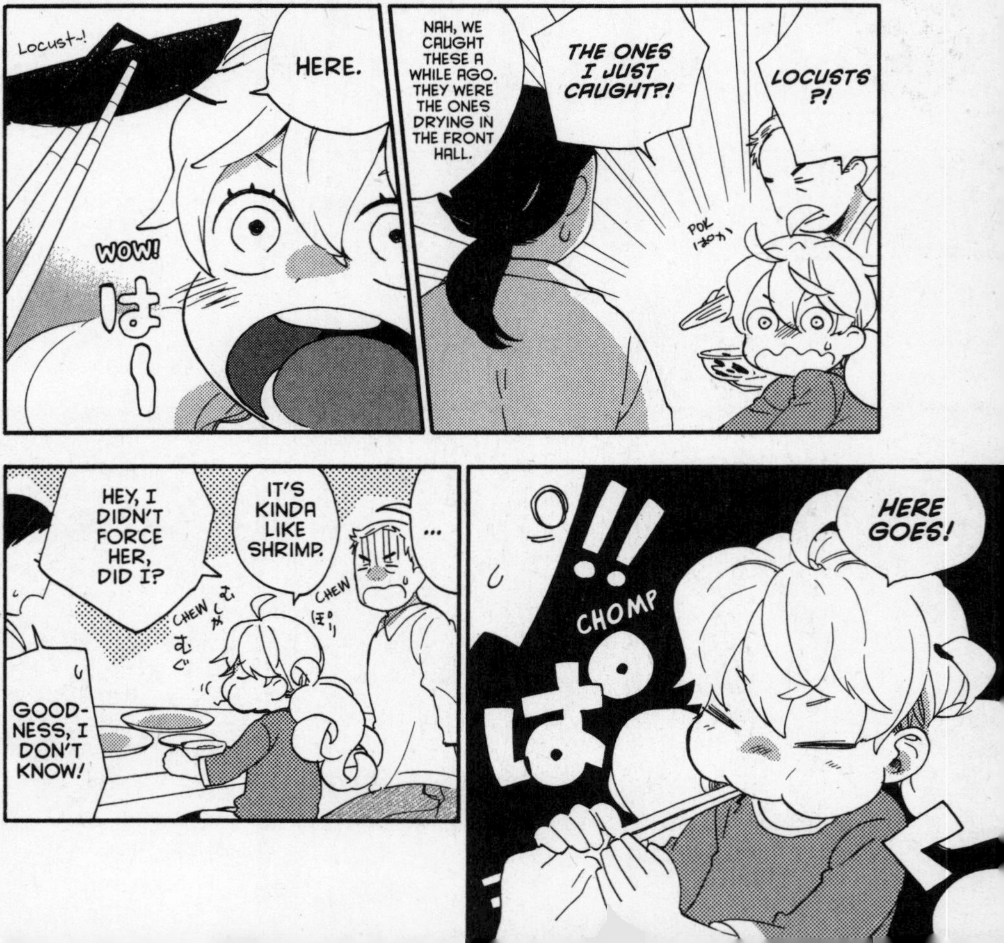
LOCUSTS ?!
THE ONES I JUST CAUGHT?!
NAH, WE CAUGHT THESE A WHILE AGO. THEY WERE THE ONES DRYING IN THE FRONT HALL.
POK
HERE.
Locust~!
WOW!
HERE GOES!
CHOMP
...
IT'S KINDA LIKE SHRIMP.
CHEW
HEY, I DIDN'T FORCE HER, DID I?
CHEW
GOOD-NESS, I DON'T KNOW!

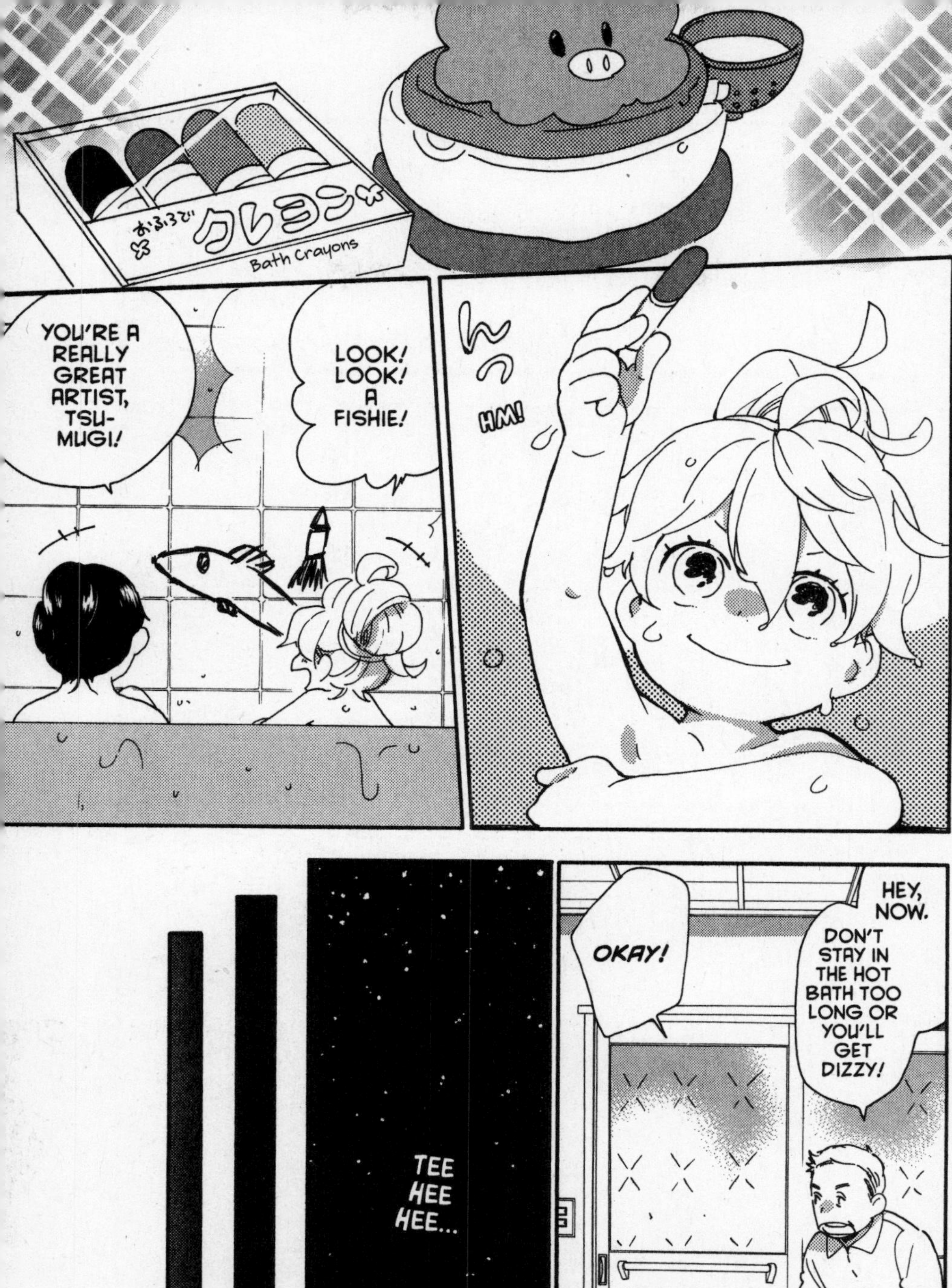
おふろで クレヨン
Bath Crayons
んっ
HM!
LOOK! LOOK! A FISHIE!
YOU'RE A REALLY GREAT ARTIST, TSU-MUGI!
HEY, NOW. DON'T STAY IN THE HOT BATH TOO LONG OR YOU'LL GET DIZZY!
OKAY!
TEE HEE HEE...

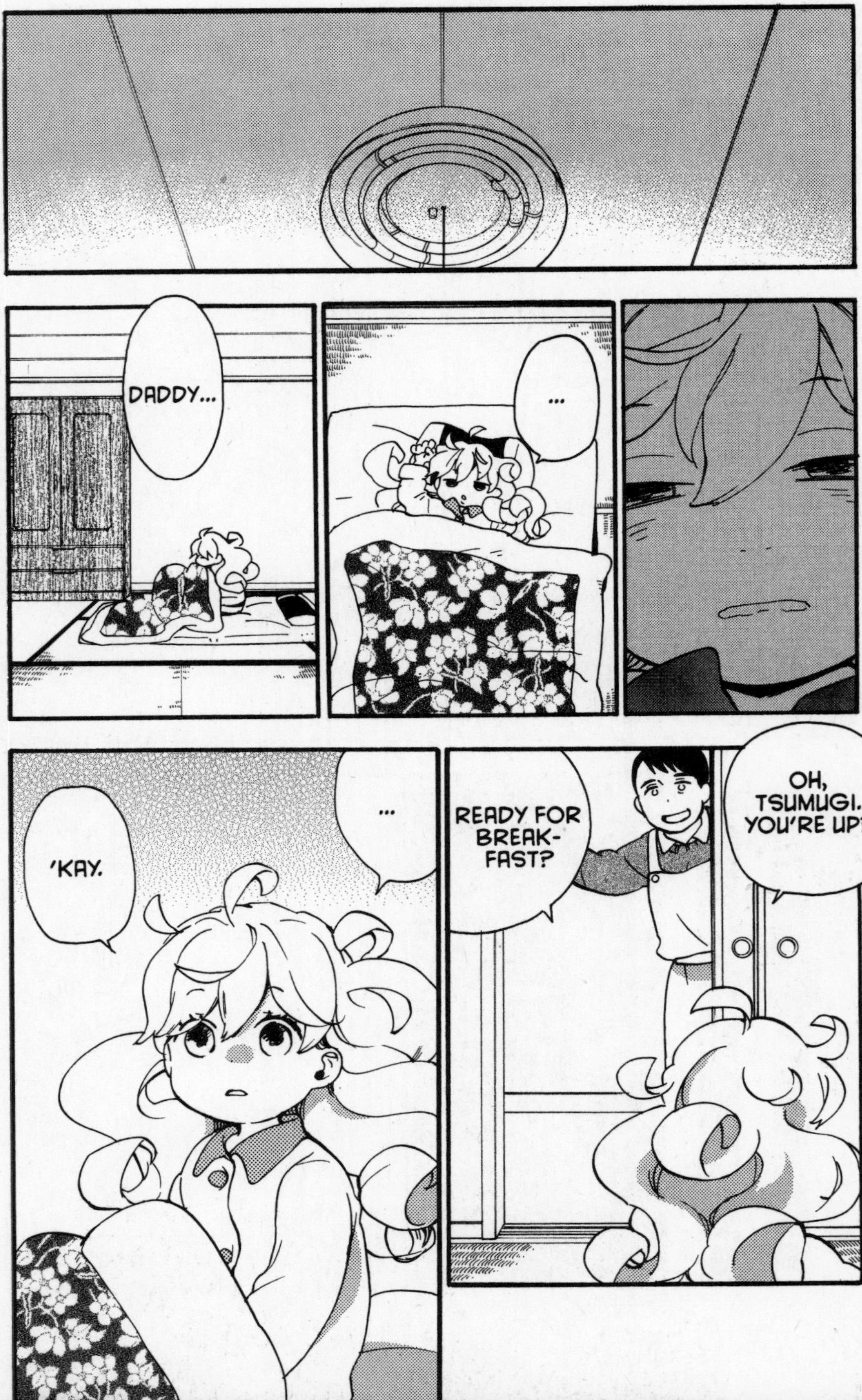
...
DADDY...
OH, TSUMUGI. YOU'RE UP?
READY FOR BREAK-FAST?
...
'KAY.

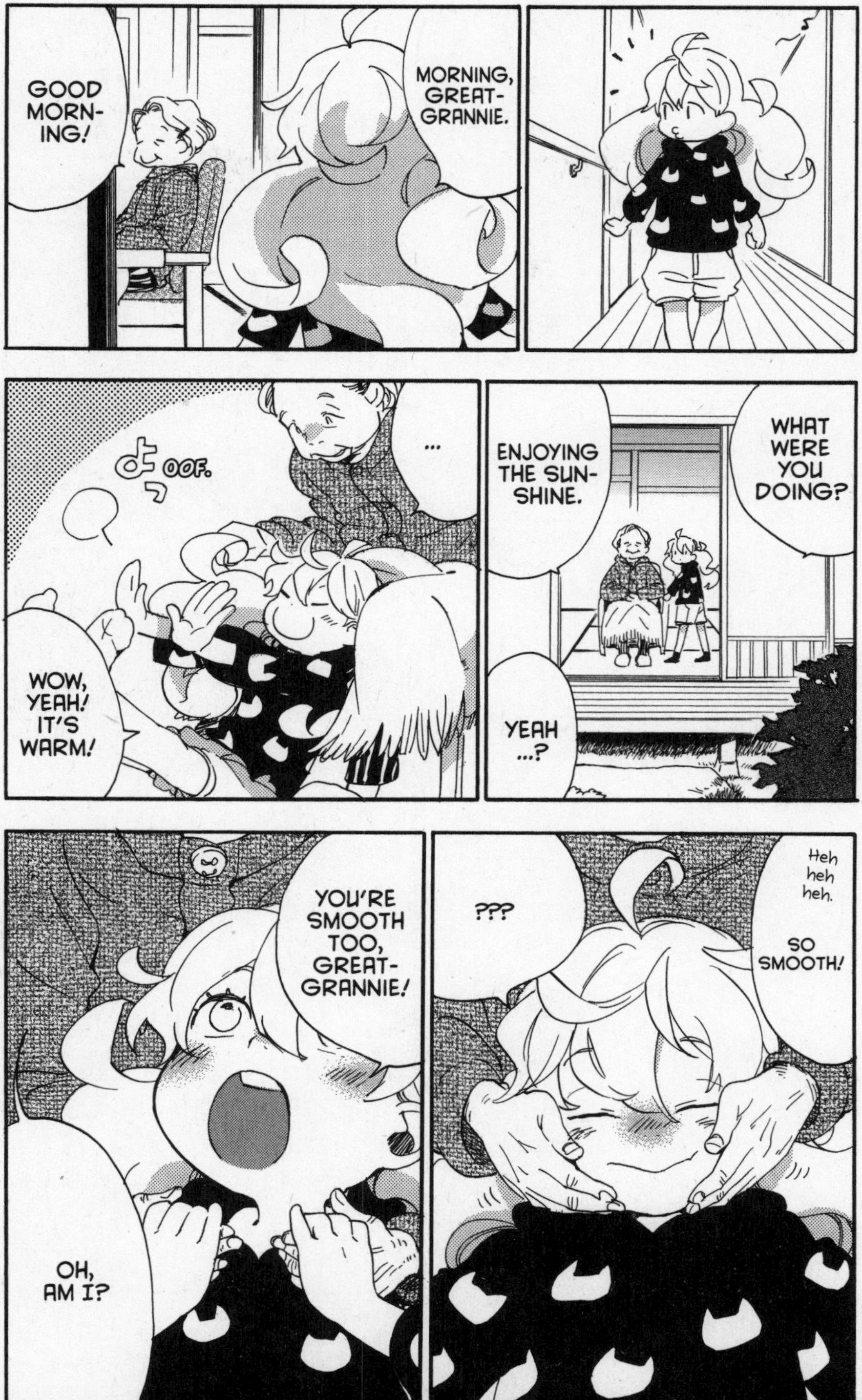
MORNING, GREAT-GRANNIE.
GOOD MORN-ING!
WHAT WERE YOU DOING?
ENJOYING THE SUN-SHINE.
YEAH ...?
...
よっ OOF.
WOW, YEAH! IT'S WARM!
Heh heh heh.
SO SMOOTH!
???
YOU'RE SMOOTH TOO, GREAT-GRANNIE!
OH, AM I?

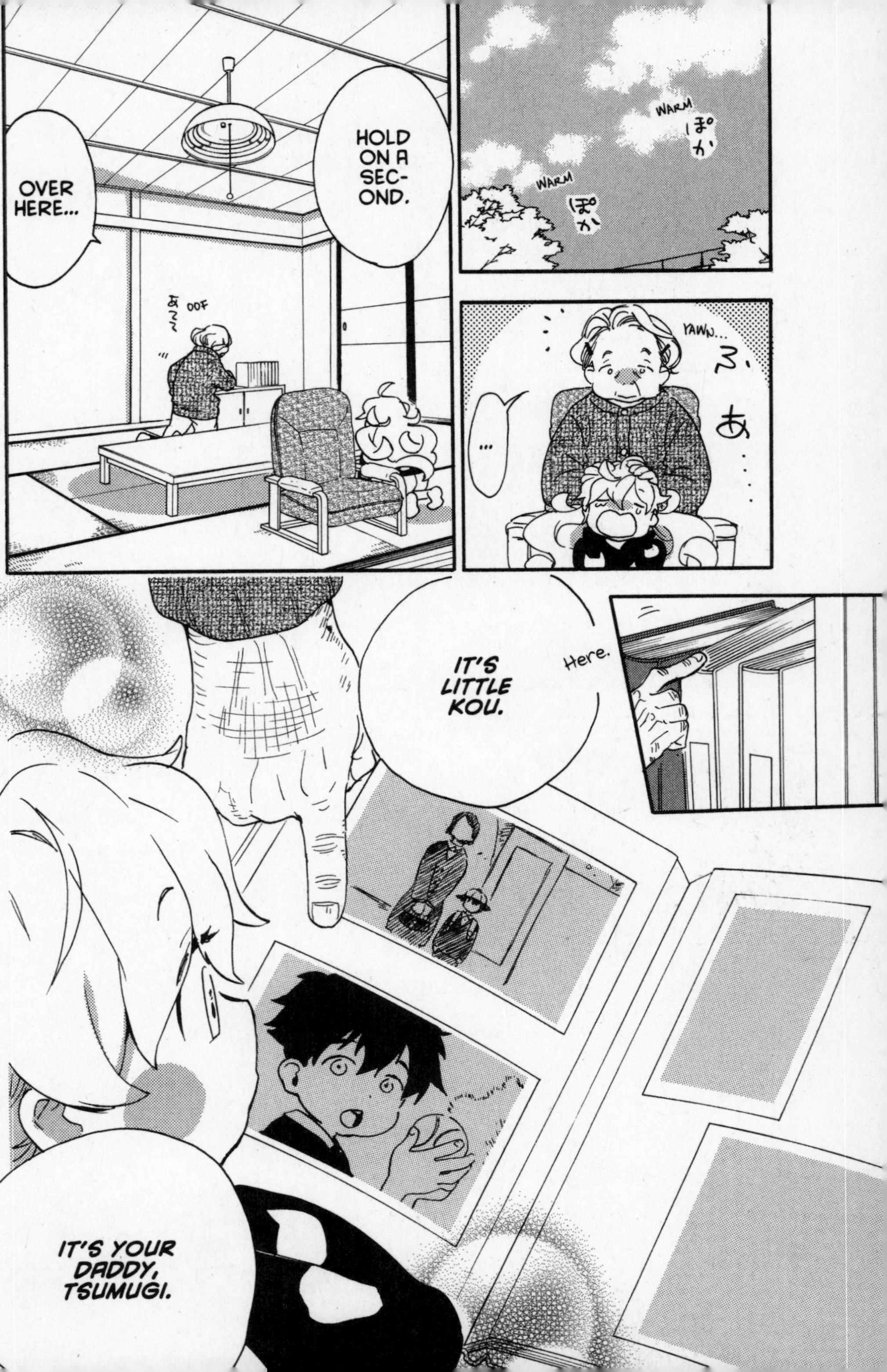
WARM
ぽか
WARM
ぽか
YAWN...
ふあ...
...
HOLD ON A SEC-OND.
OVER HERE...
OOF
Here.
IT'S LITTLE KOU.
IT'S YOUR DADDY, TSUMUGI.

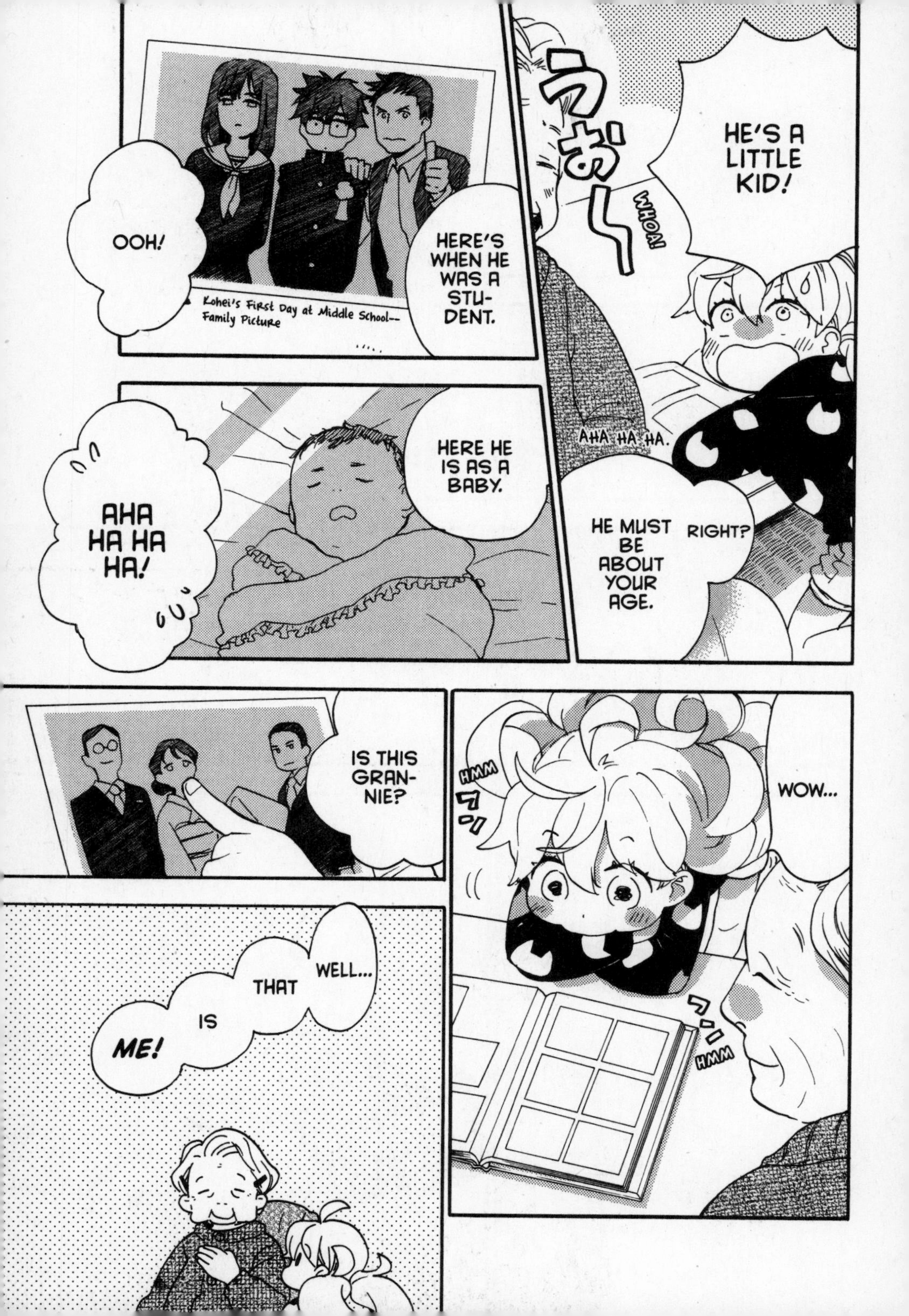
HE'S A LITTLE KID!
うぉ〜
WHOA!
AHA HA HA.
RIGHT?
HE MUST BE ABOUT YOUR AGE.
HERE'S WHEN HE WAS A STU-DENT.
OOH!
Kohei's First Day at Middle School-- Family Picture
HERE HE IS AS A BABY.
AHA HA HA HA!
WOW...
HMM
HMM
IS THIS GRAN-NIE?
WELL...
THAT
IS
ME!

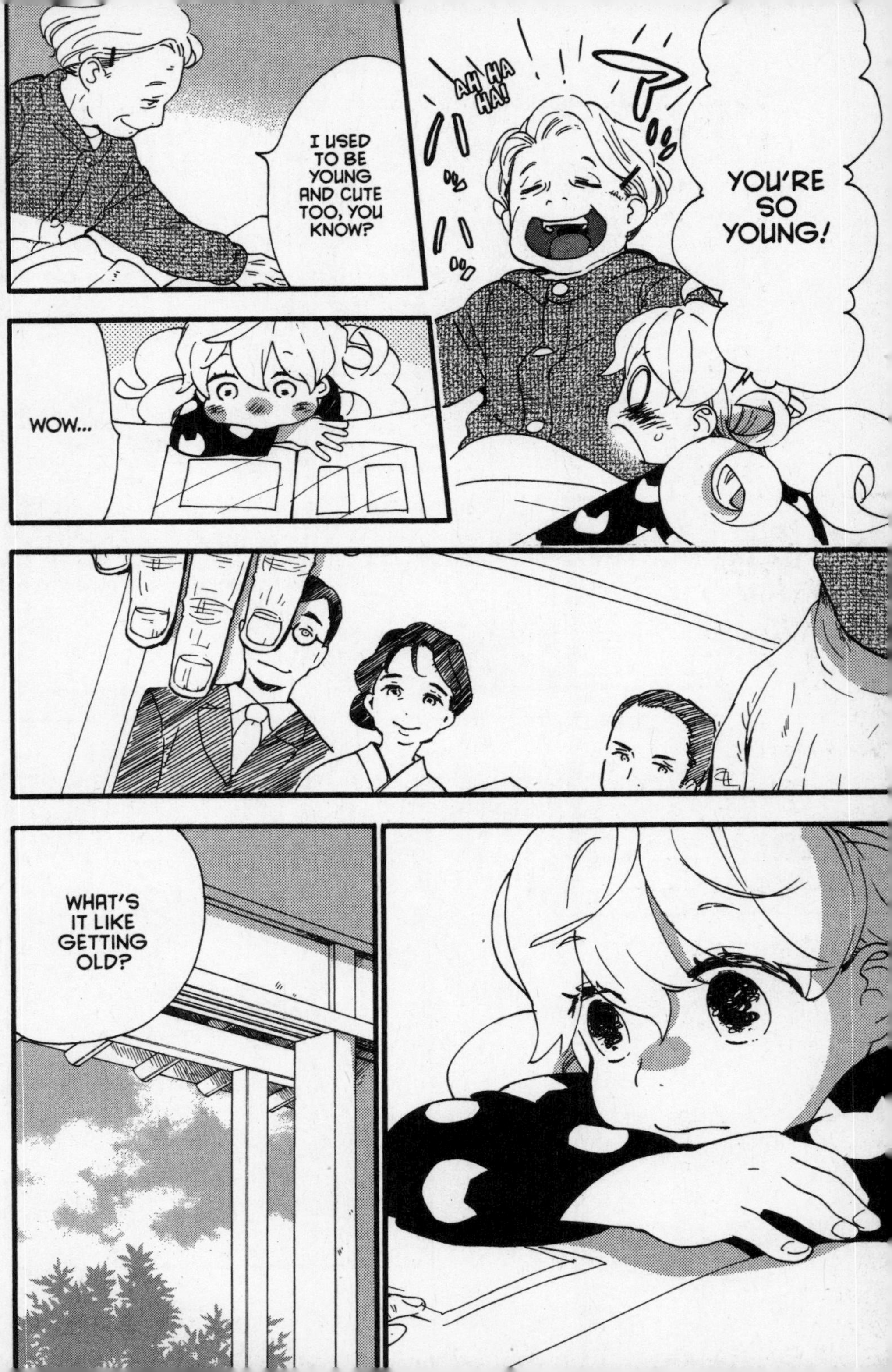
AH HA HA!
YOU'RE SO YOUNG!
I USED TO BE YOUNG AND CUTE TOO, YOU KNOW?
WOW...
WHAT'S IT LIKE GETTING OLD?

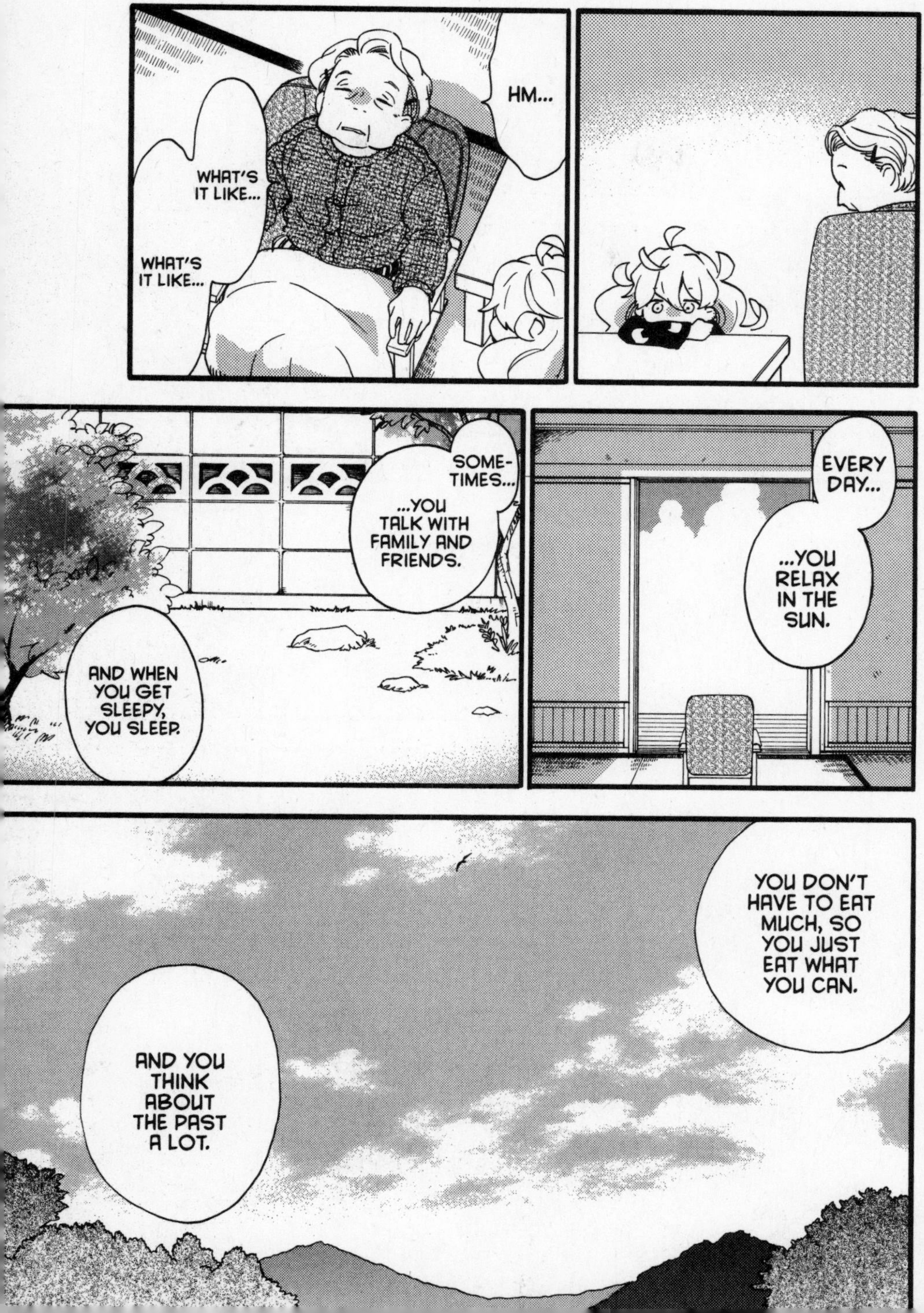
HM...
WHAT'S IT LIKE...
WHAT'S IT LIKE...
EVERY DAY...
...YOU RELAX IN THE SUN.
SOME-TIMES...
...YOU TALK WITH FAMILY AND FRIENDS.
AND WHEN YOU GET SLEEPY, YOU SLEEP.
YOU DON'T HAVE TO EAT MUCH, SO YOU JUST EAT WHAT YOU CAN.
AND YOU THINK ABOUT THE PAST A LOT.

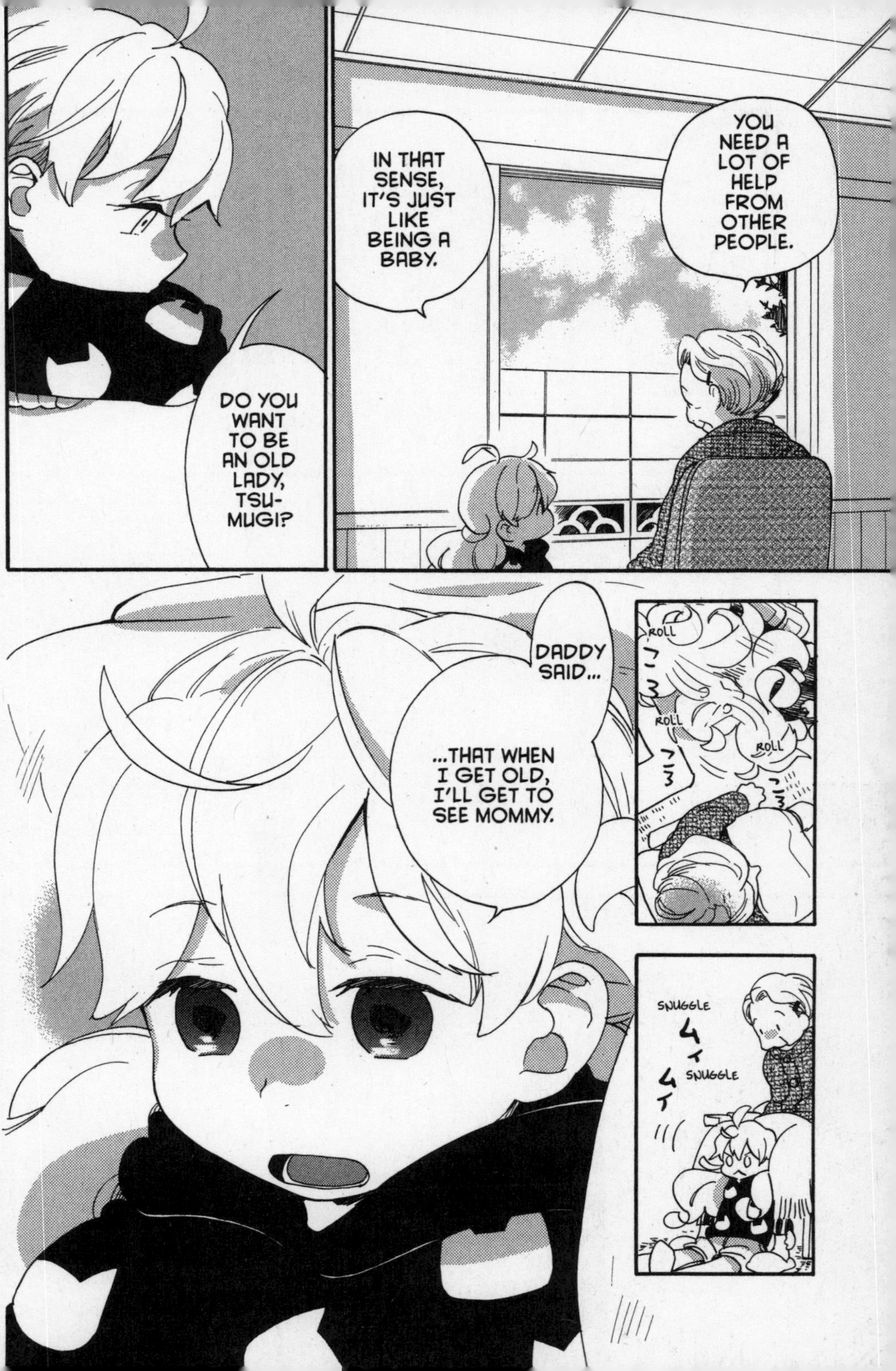
YOU NEED A LOT OF HELP FROM OTHER PEOPLE.
IN THAT SENSE, IT'S JUST LIKE BEING A BABY.
DO YOU WANT TO BE AN OLD LADY, TSU-MUGI?
ROLL
ROLL
ROLL
SNUGGLE
SNUGGLE
DADDY SAID...
...THAT WHEN I GET OLD, I'LL GET TO SEE MOMMY.

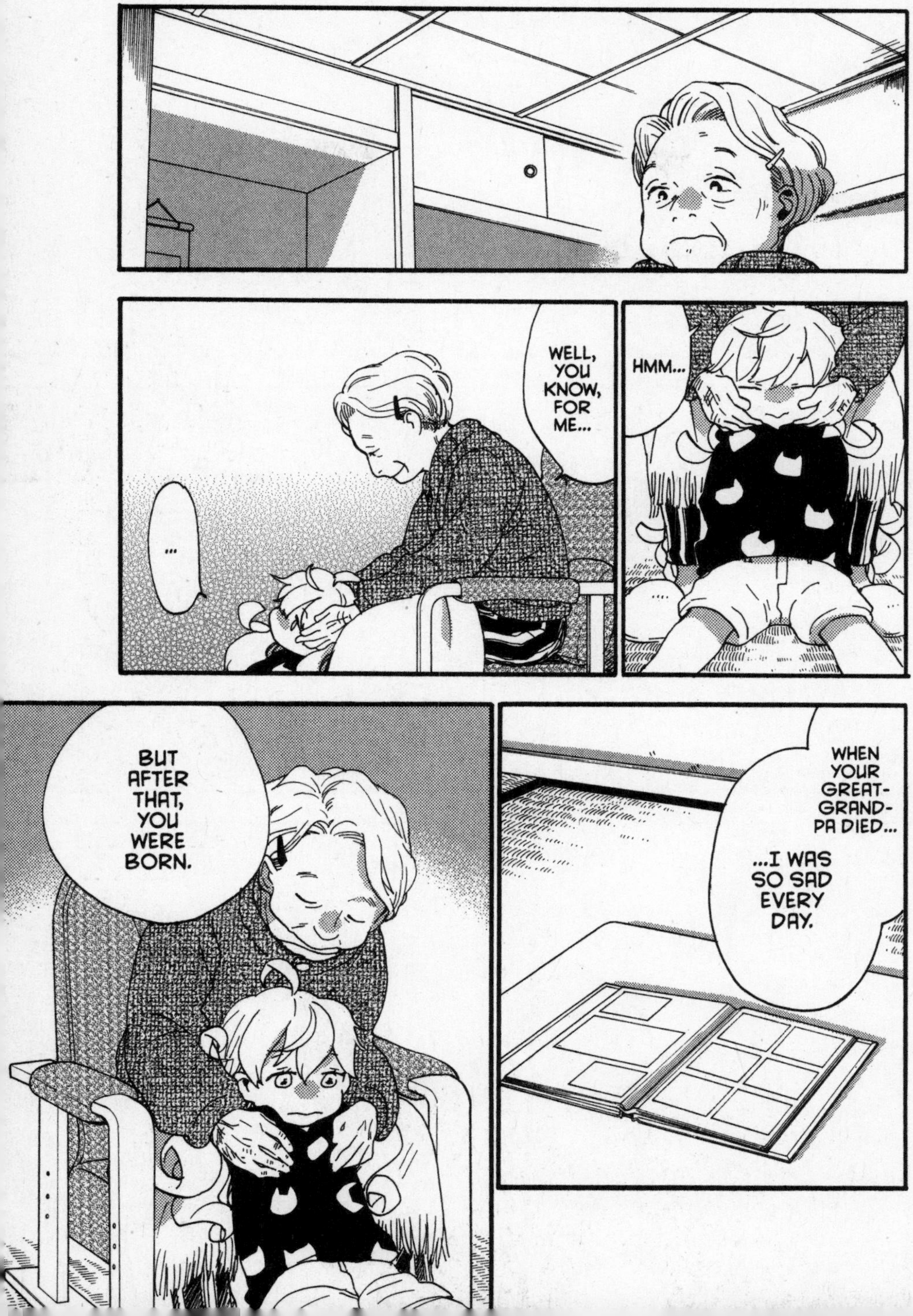
HMM...
WELL, YOU KNOW, FOR ME...
...
WHEN YOUR GREAT-GRANDPA DIED...
...I WAS SO SAD EVERY DAY.
BUT AFTER THAT, YOU WERE BORN.

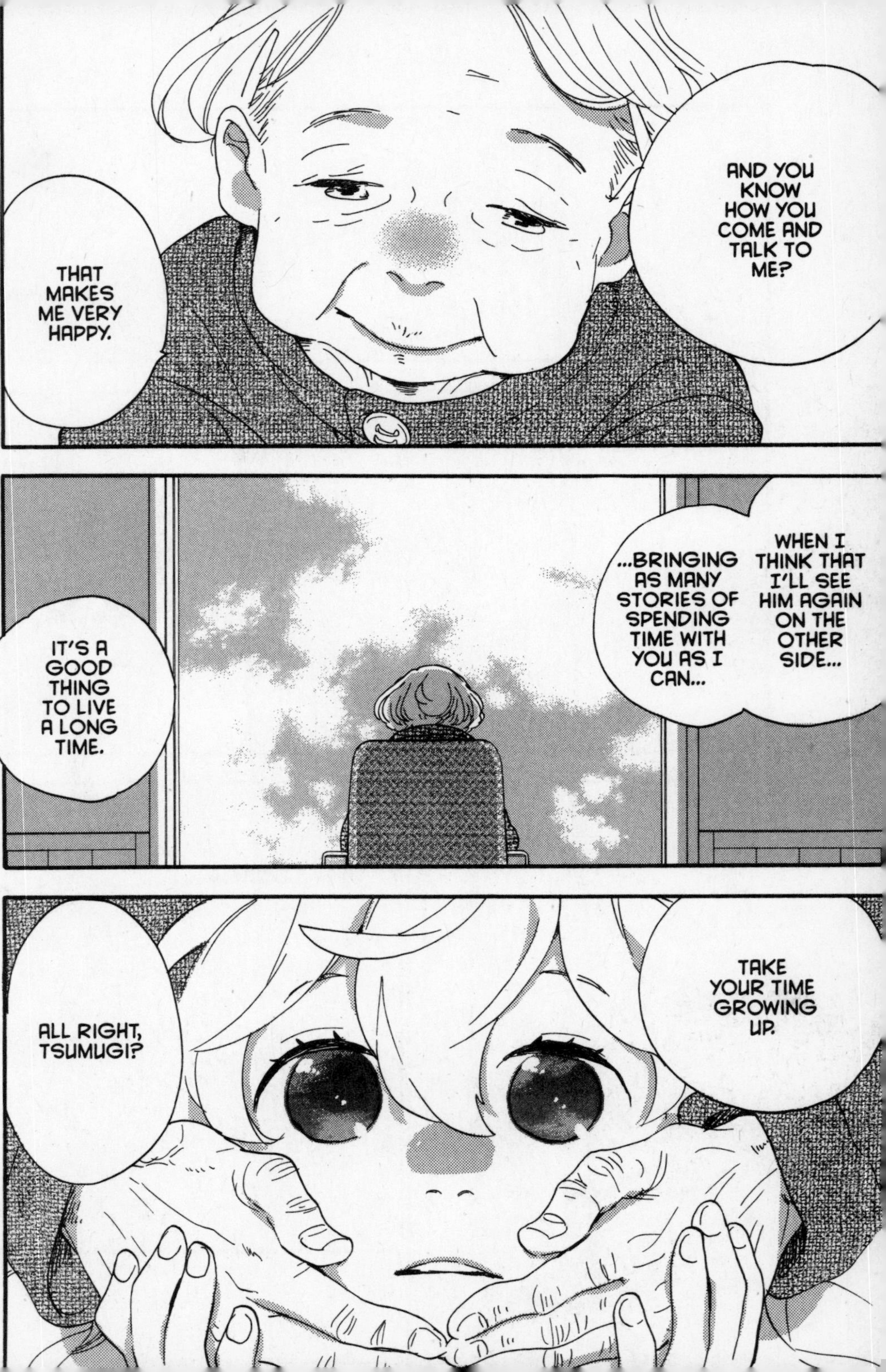
AND YOU KNOW HOW YOU COME AND TALK TO ME?
THAT MAKES ME VERY HAPPY.
WHEN I THINK THAT I'LL SEE HIM AGAIN ON THE OTHER SIDE...
...BRINGING AS MANY STORIES OF SPENDING TIME WITH YOU AS I CAN...
IT'S A GOOD THING TO LIVE A LONG TIME.
TAKE YOUR TIME GROWING UP.
ALL RIGHT, TSUMUGI?

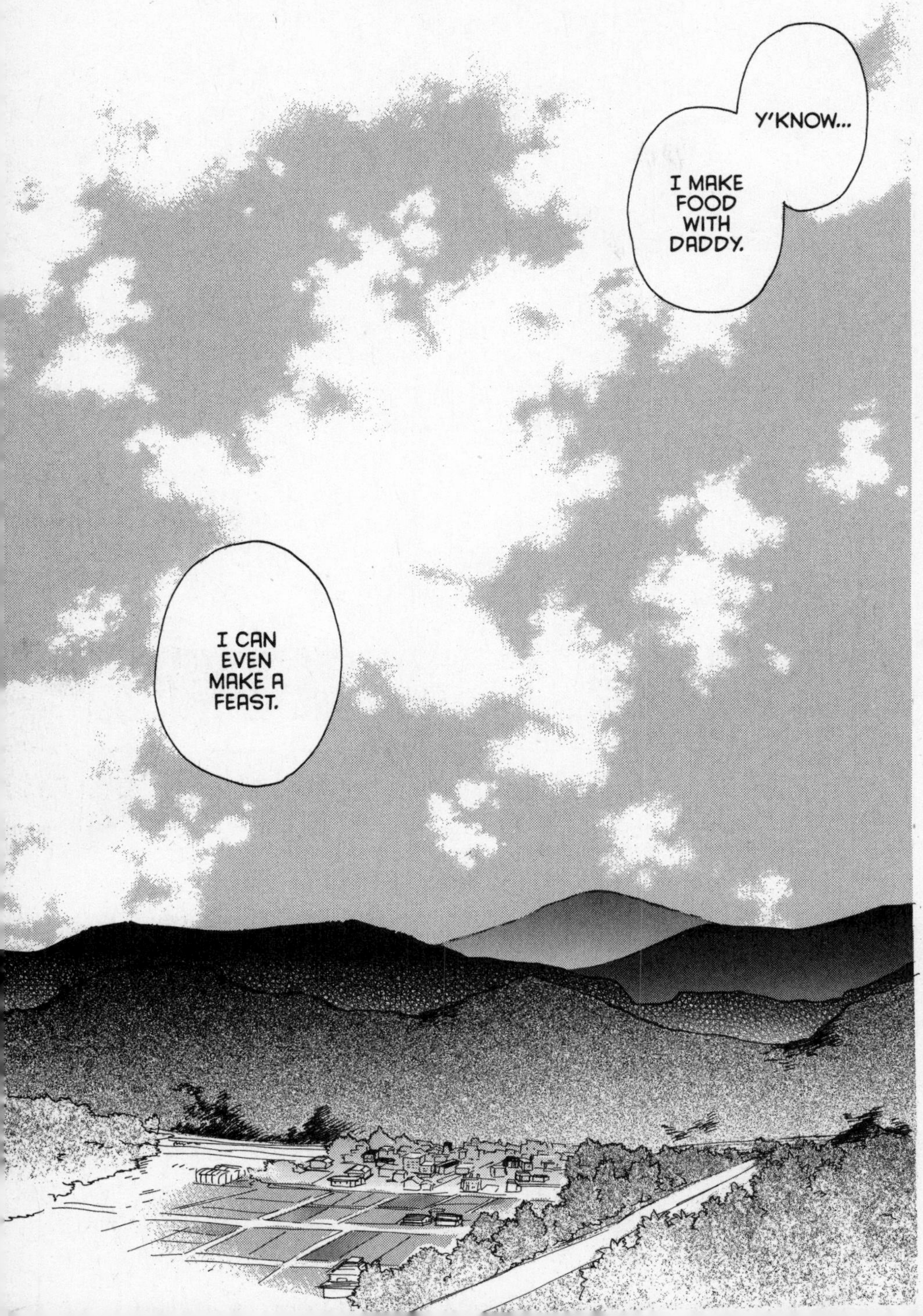
Y'KNOW...
I MAKE FOOD WITH DADDY.
I CAN EVEN MAKE A FEAST.

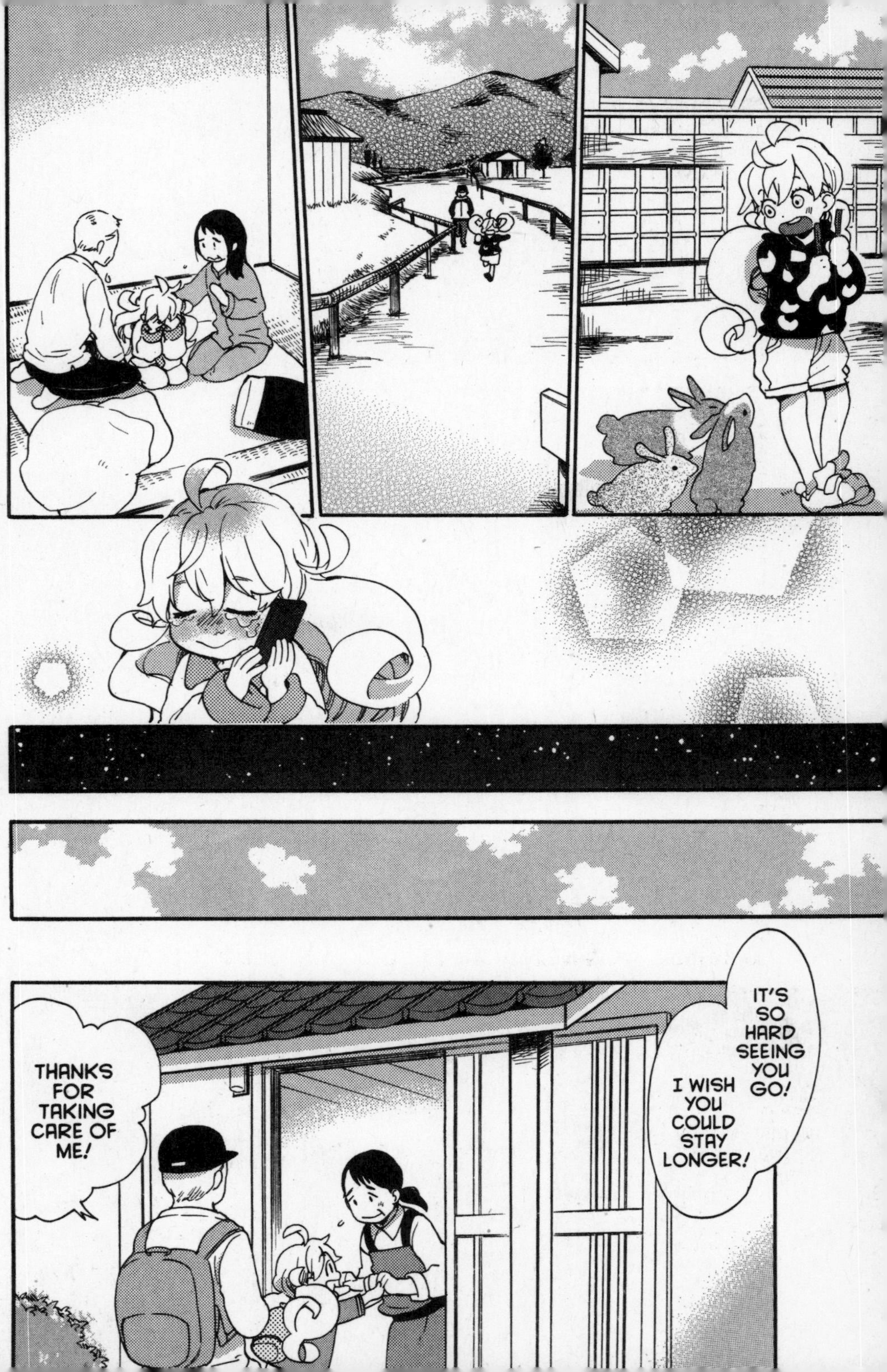
IT'S SO HARD SEEING YOU GO!
I WISH YOU COULD STAY LONGER!
THANKS FOR TAKING CARE OF ME!

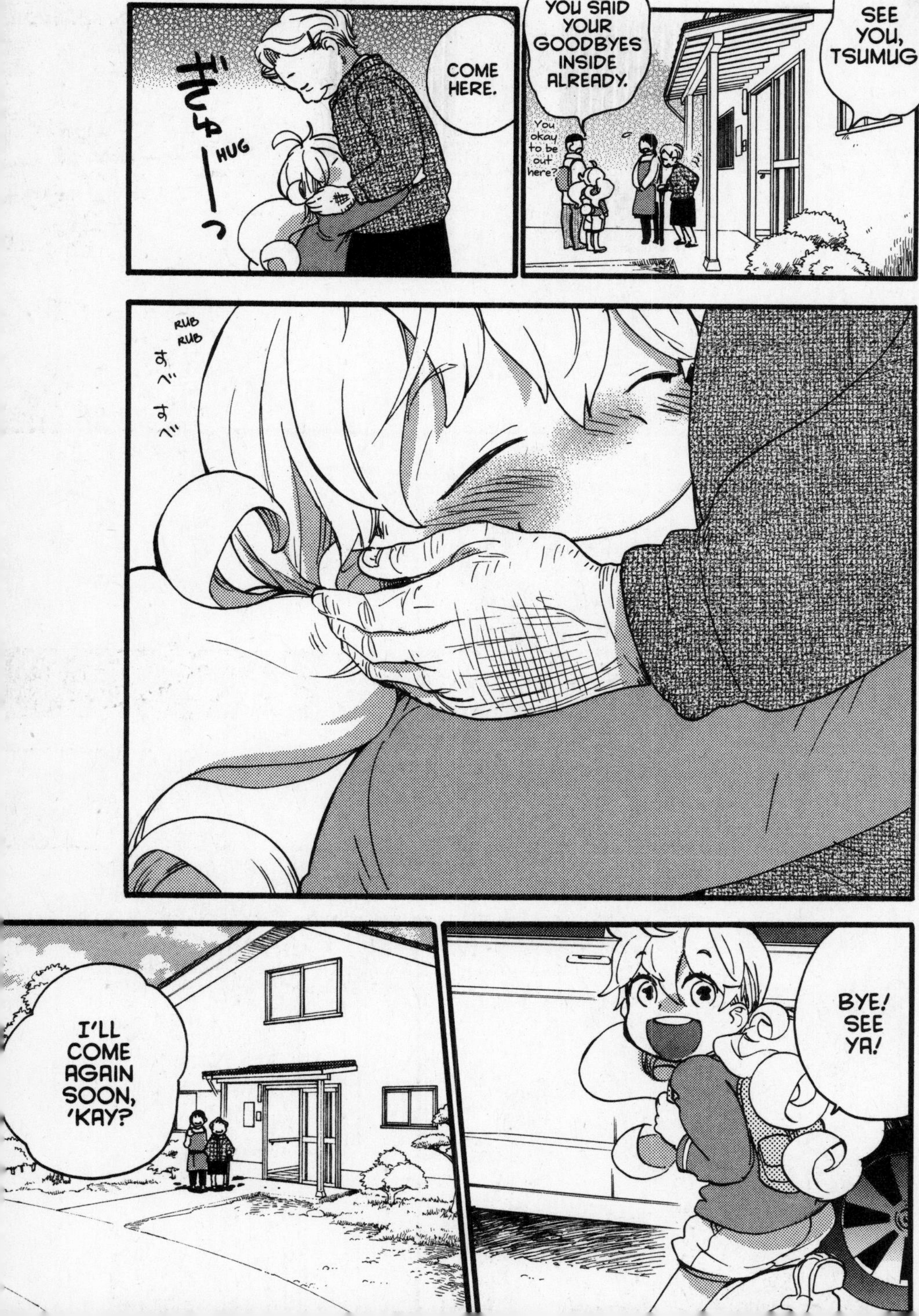
SEE YOU, TSUMUGI.
Hey... YOU SAID YOUR GOODBYES INSIDE ALREADY.
You okay to be out here?
COME HERE.
ぎゅーっ
HUG
すべすべ
RUB RUB
BYE! SEE YA!
I'LL COME AGAIN SOON, 'KAY?

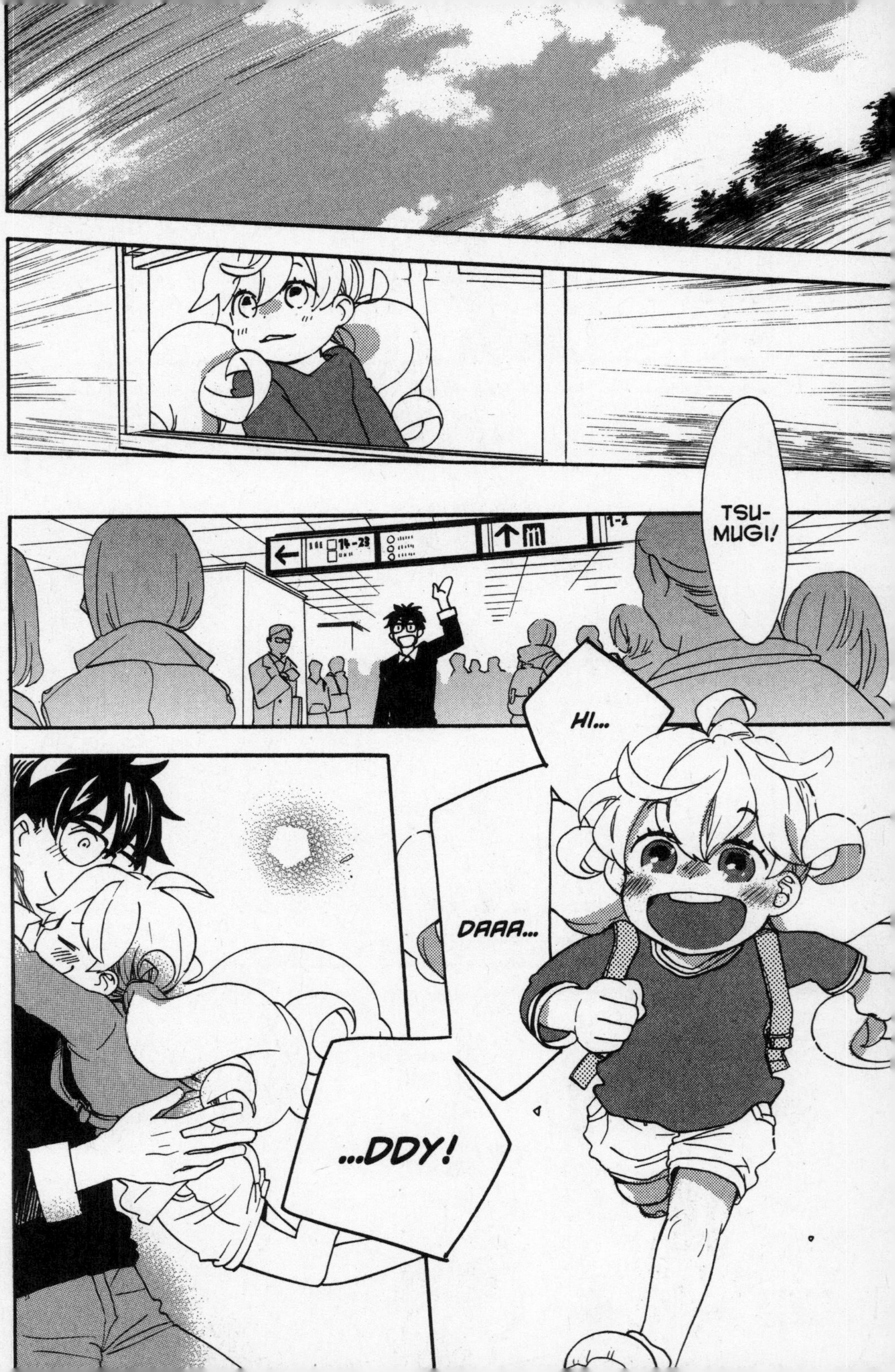
TSU-MUGI!
HI...
DAAA...
...DDY!

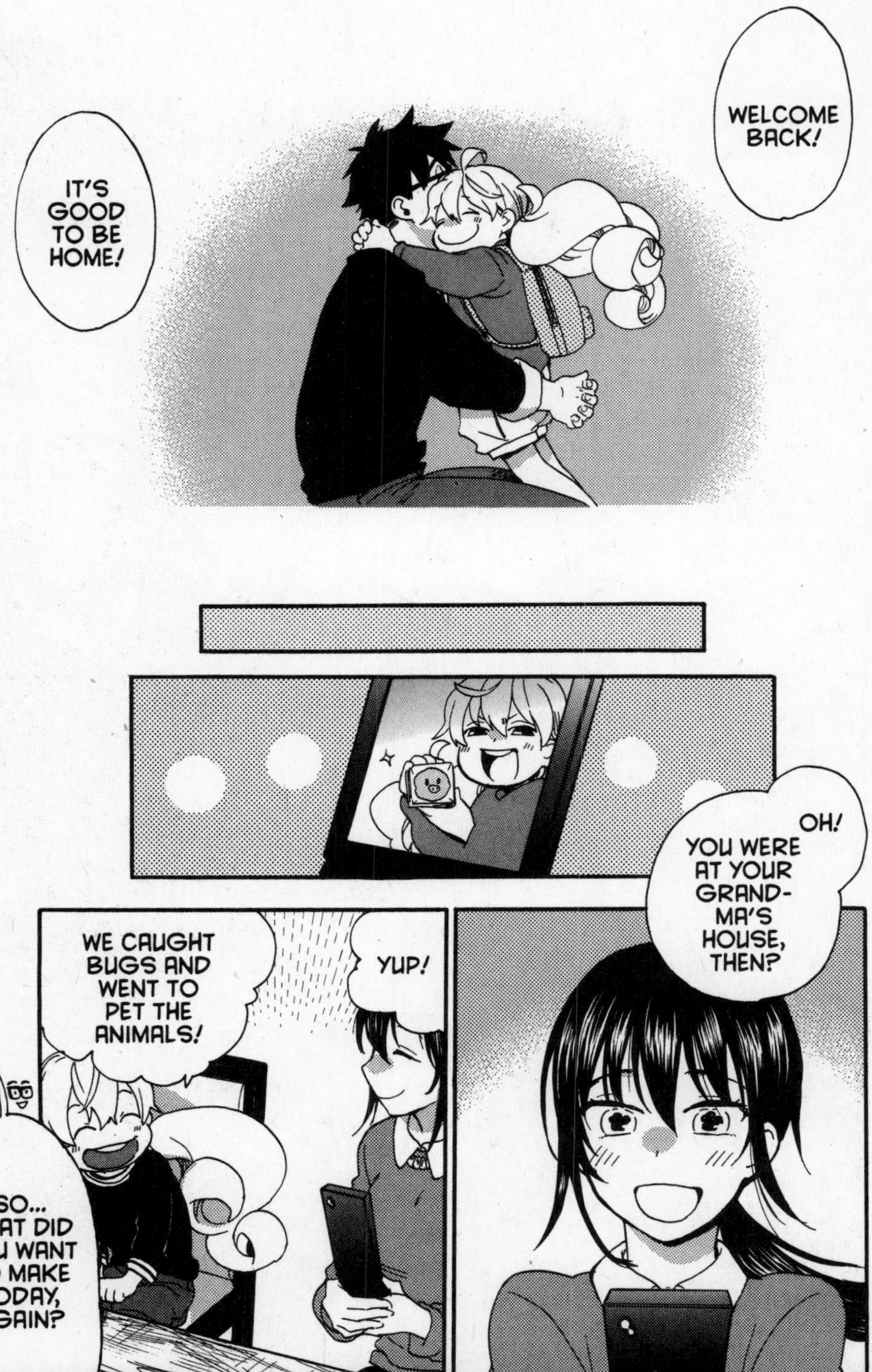
WELCOME BACK!
IT'S GOOD TO BE HOME!
OH! YOU WERE AT YOUR GRAND-MA'S HOUSE, THEN?
YUP!
WE CAUGHT BUGS AND WENT TO PET THE ANIMALS!
SO... WHAT DID YOU WANT TO MAKE TODAY, AGAIN?

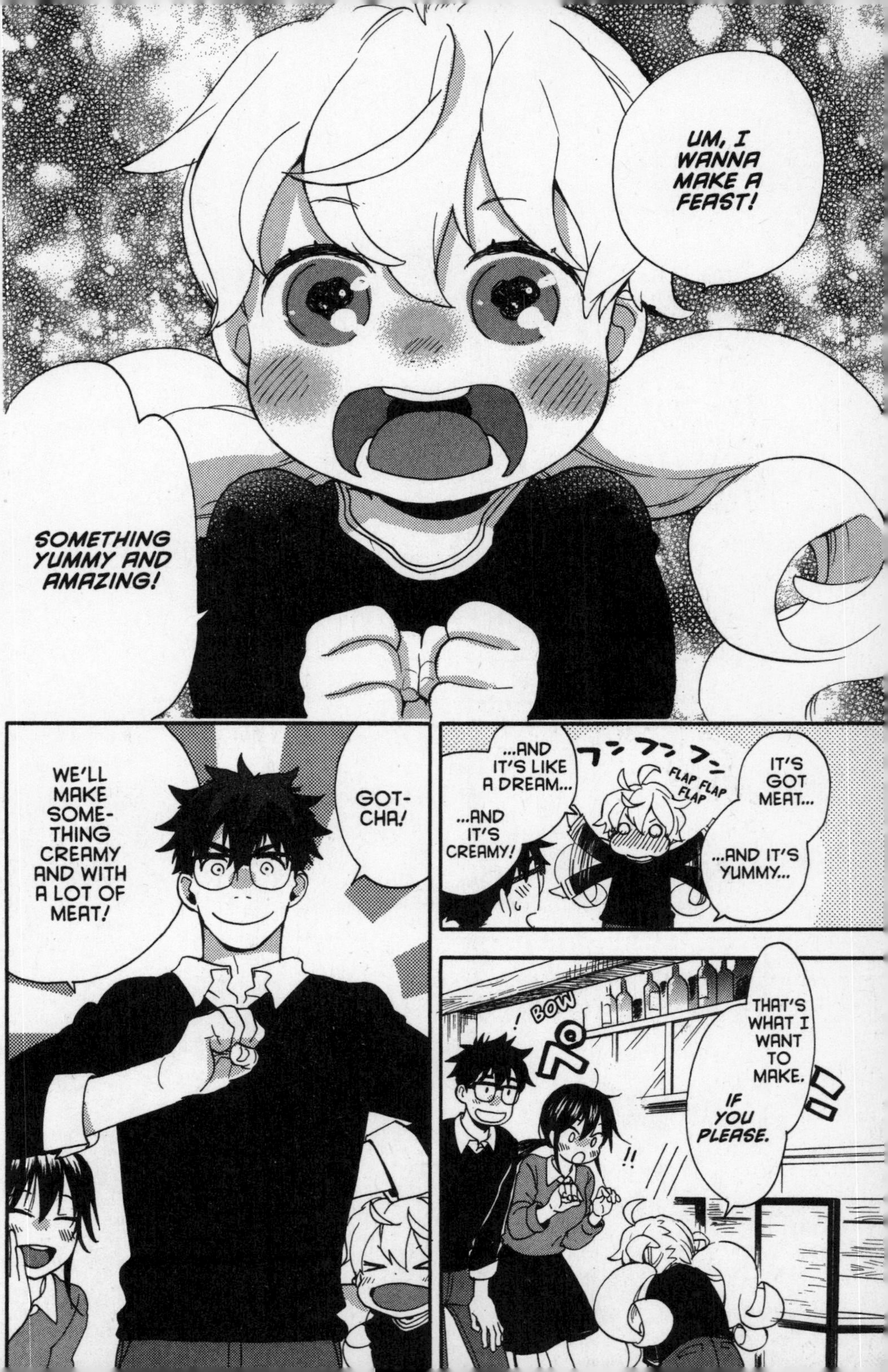
UM, I WANNA MAKE A FEAST!
SOMETHING YUMMY AND AMAZING!
IT'S GOT MEAT...
...AND IT'S YUMMY...
FLAP FLAP FLAP
...AND IT'S LIKE A DREAM...
...AND IT'S CREAMY!
BOW
THAT'S WHAT I WANT TO MAKE.
IF YOU PLEASE.
!!
GOT-CHA!
WE'LL MAKE SOME-THING CREAMY AND WITH A LOT OF MEAT!

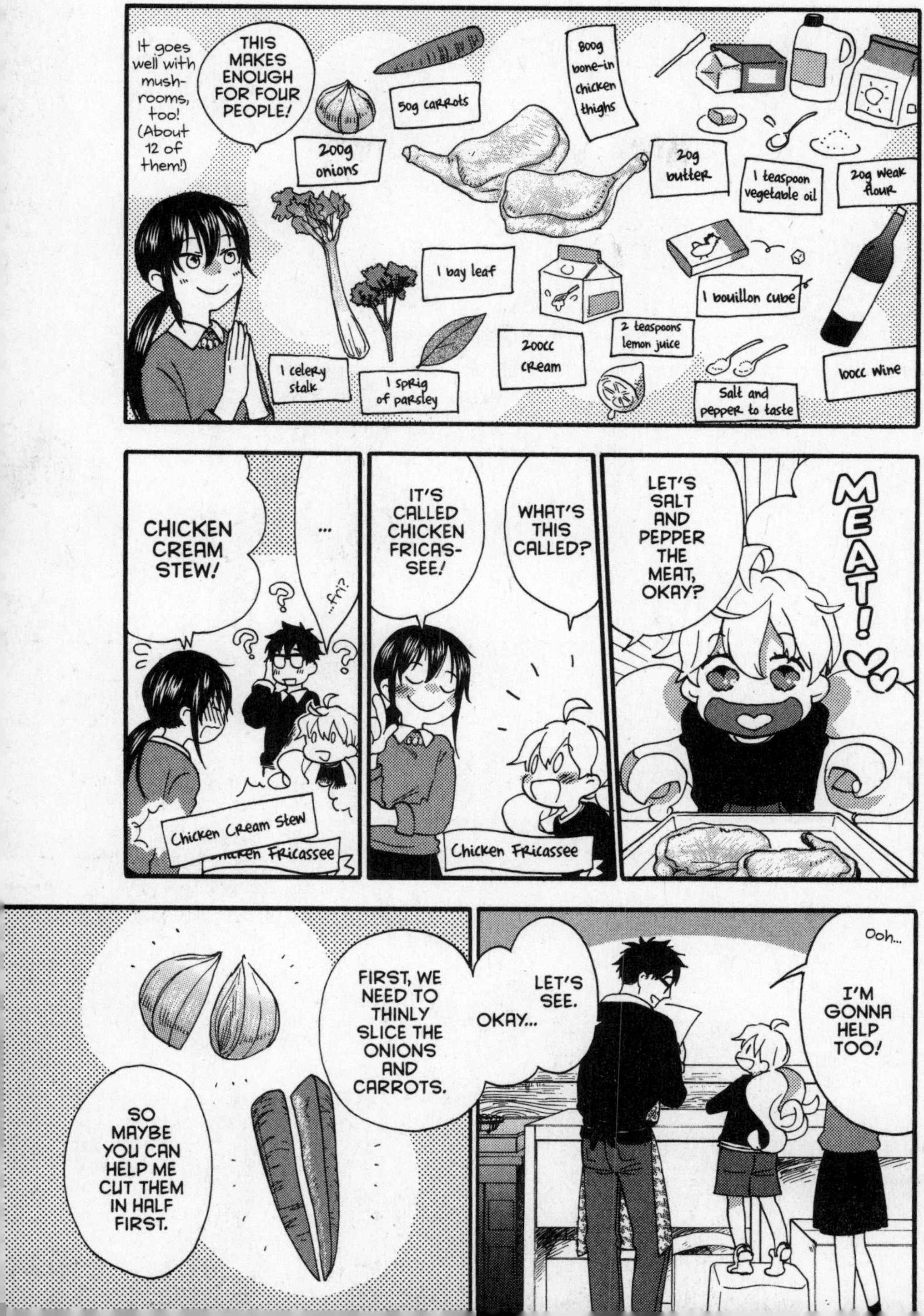
800g bone-in chicken thighs
50g carrots
THIS MAKES ENOUGH FOR FOUR PEOPLE!
It goes well with mush-rooms, too! (About 12 of them!)
20g weak flour
1 teaspoon vegetable oil
20g butter
200g onions
1 bouillon cube
1 bay leaf
100cc wine
2 teaspoons lemon juice
200cc cream
Salt and pepper to taste
1 sprig of parsley
1 celery stalk
MEAT!
LET'S SALT AND PEPPER THE MEAT, OKAY?
WHAT'S THIS CALLED?
IT'S CALLED CHICKEN FRICAS-SEE!
Chicken Fricassee
...
...fri?
CHICKEN CREAM STEW!
Chicken Cream Stew
Chicken Fricassee
Ooh...
I'M GONNA HELP TOO!
LET'S SEE.
OKAY...
FIRST, WE NEED TO THINLY SLICE THE ONIONS AND CARROTS.
SO MAYBE YOU CAN HELP ME CUT THEM IN HALF FIRST.

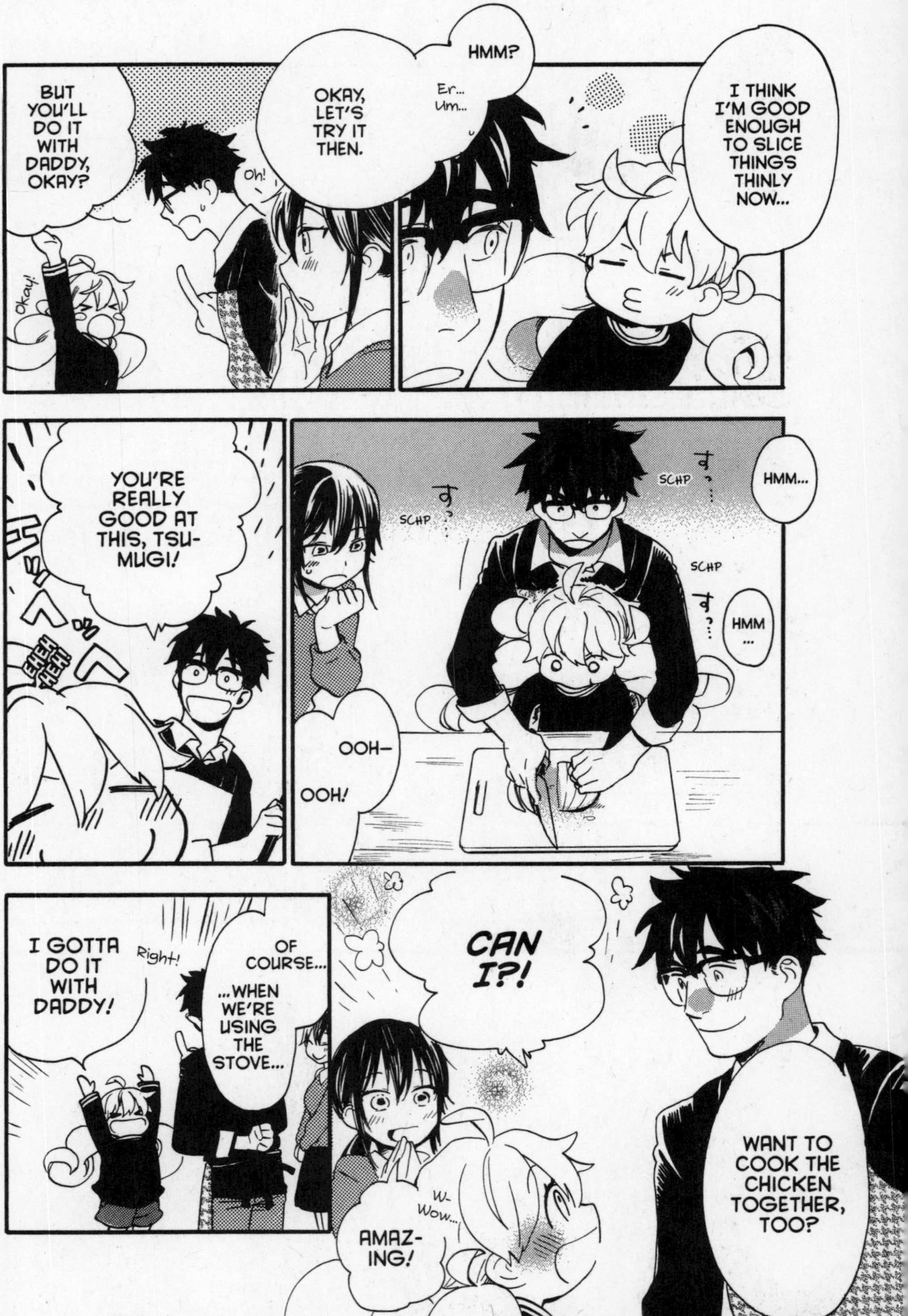
I THINK I'M GOOD ENOUGH TO SLICE THINGS THINLY NOW...
HMM?
Er... Um...
OKAY, LET'S TRY IT THEN.
Oh!
BUT YOU'LL DO IT WITH DADDY, OKAY?
Okay!
HMM...
SCHP
SCHP
SCHP
HMM...
OOH—
OOH!
YOU'RE REALLY GOOD AT THIS, TSU-MUGI!
EHEH HEH
WANT TO COOK THE CHICKEN TOGETHER, TOO?
CAN I?!
W-Wow...
AMAZ-ING!
OF COURSE...
...WHEN WE'RE USING THE STOVE...
Right!
I GOTTA DO IT WITH DADDY!

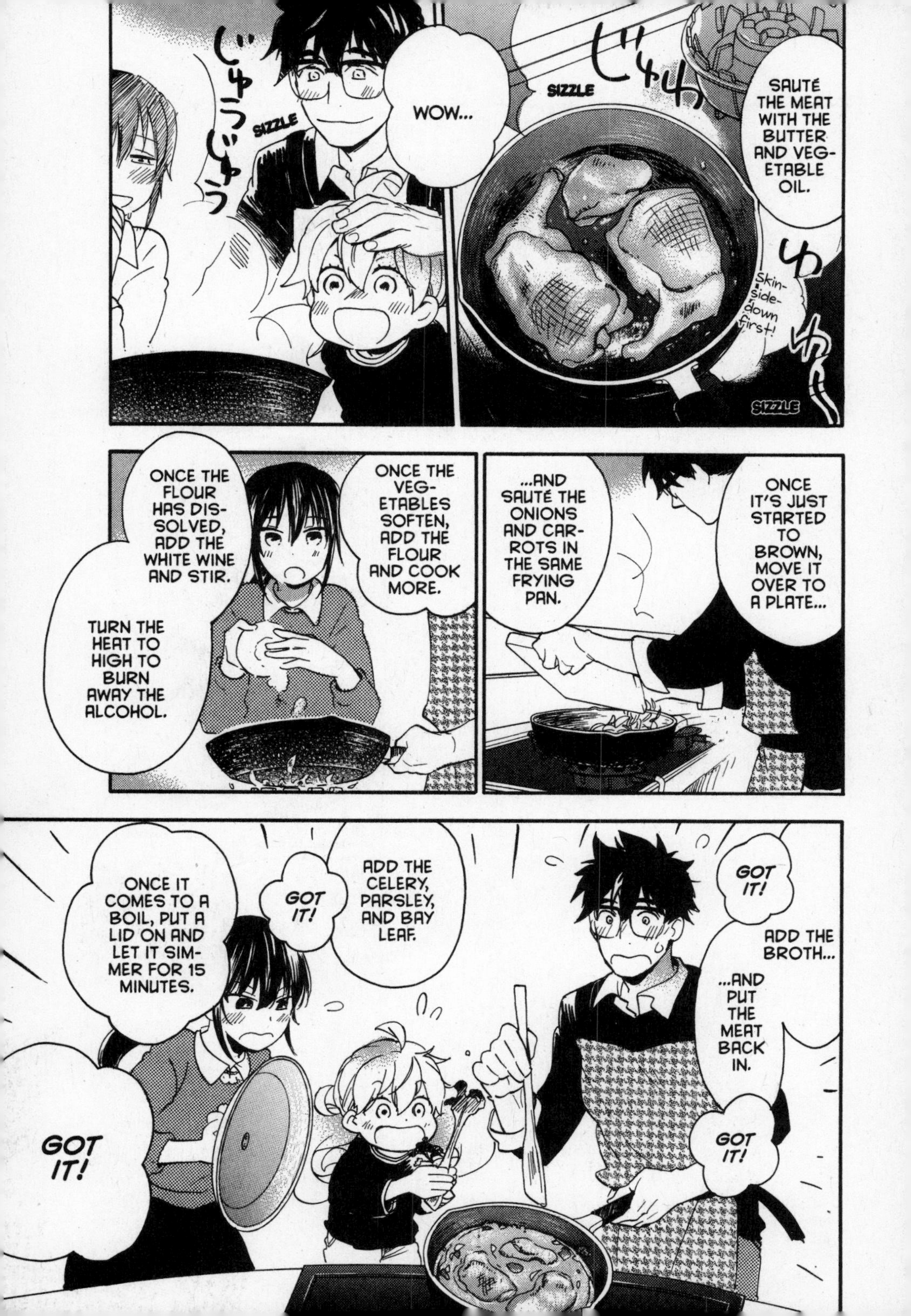
SIZZLE
SAUTÉ THE MEAT WITH THE BUTTER AND VEGETABLE OIL.
Skin-side-down first!
SIZZLE
SIZZLE
WOW...
SIZZLE
ONCE IT'S JUST STARTED TO BROWN, MOVE IT OVER TO A PLATE...
...AND SAUTÉ THE ONIONS AND CARROTS IN THE SAME FRYING PAN.
ONCE THE VEGETABLES SOFTEN, ADD THE FLOUR AND COOK MORE.
ONCE THE FLOUR HAS DISSOLVED, ADD THE WHITE WINE AND STIR.
TURN THE HEAT TO HIGH TO BURN AWAY THE ALCOHOL.
GOT IT!
ADD THE BROTH...
...AND PUT THE MEAT BACK IN.
GOT IT!
ADD THE CELERY, PARSLEY, AND BAY LEAF.
GOT IT!
ONCE IT COMES TO A BOIL, PUT A LID ON AND LET IT SIMMER FOR 15 MINUTES.
GOT IT!

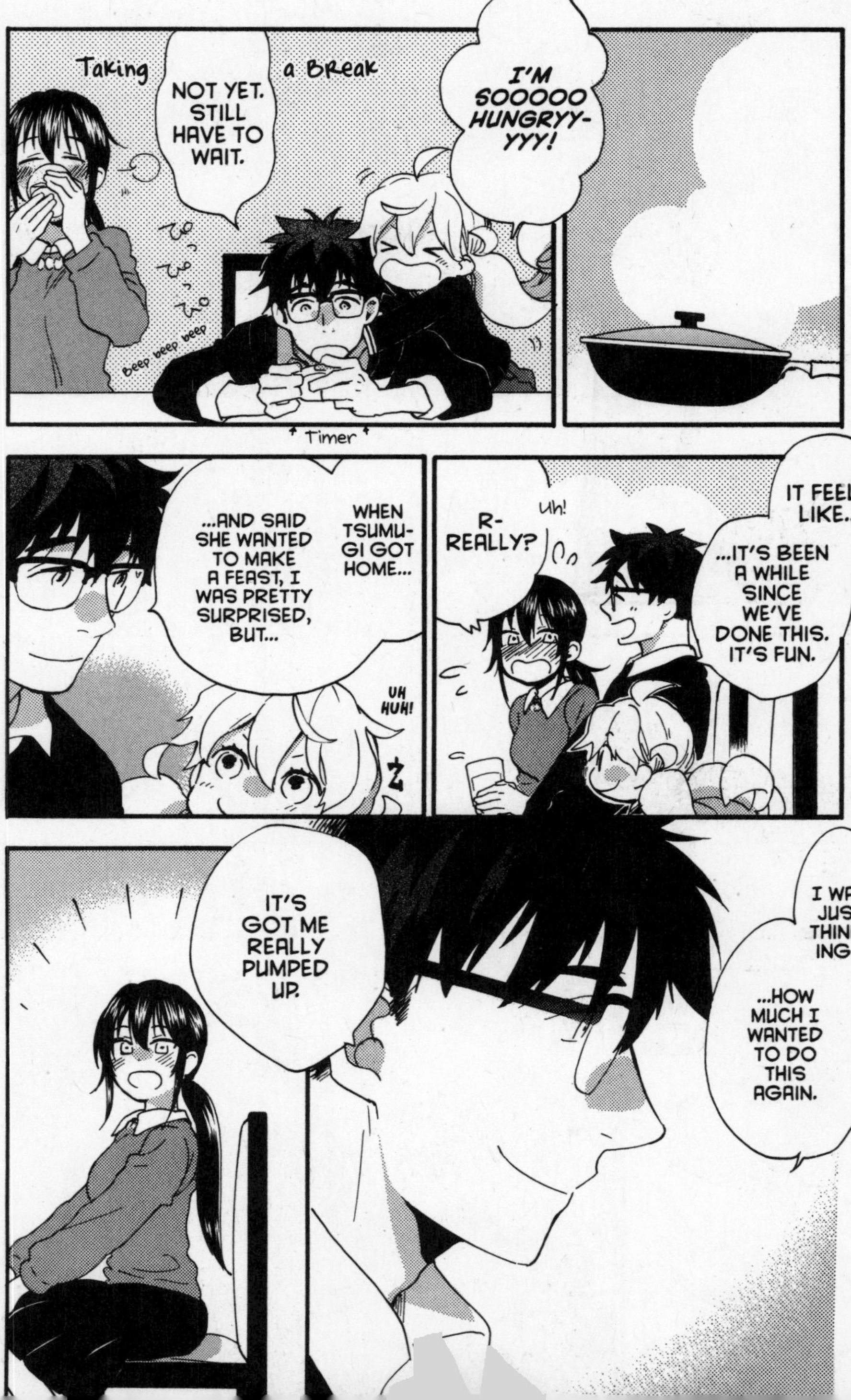
Taking a Break
I'M SOOOOO HUNGRYY-YYY!
NOT YET. STILL HAVE TO WAIT.
beep beep beep
Timer
IT FEELS LIKE...
...IT'S BEEN A WHILE SINCE WE'VE DONE THIS. IT'S FUN.
Uh!
R-REALLY?
WHEN TSUMUGI GOT HOME...
...AND SAID SHE WANTED TO MAKE A FEAST, I WAS PRETTY SURPRISED, BUT...
UH HUH!
I WAS JUST THINKING...
...HOW MUCH I WANTED TO DO THIS AGAIN.
IT'S GOT ME REALLY PUMPED UP.

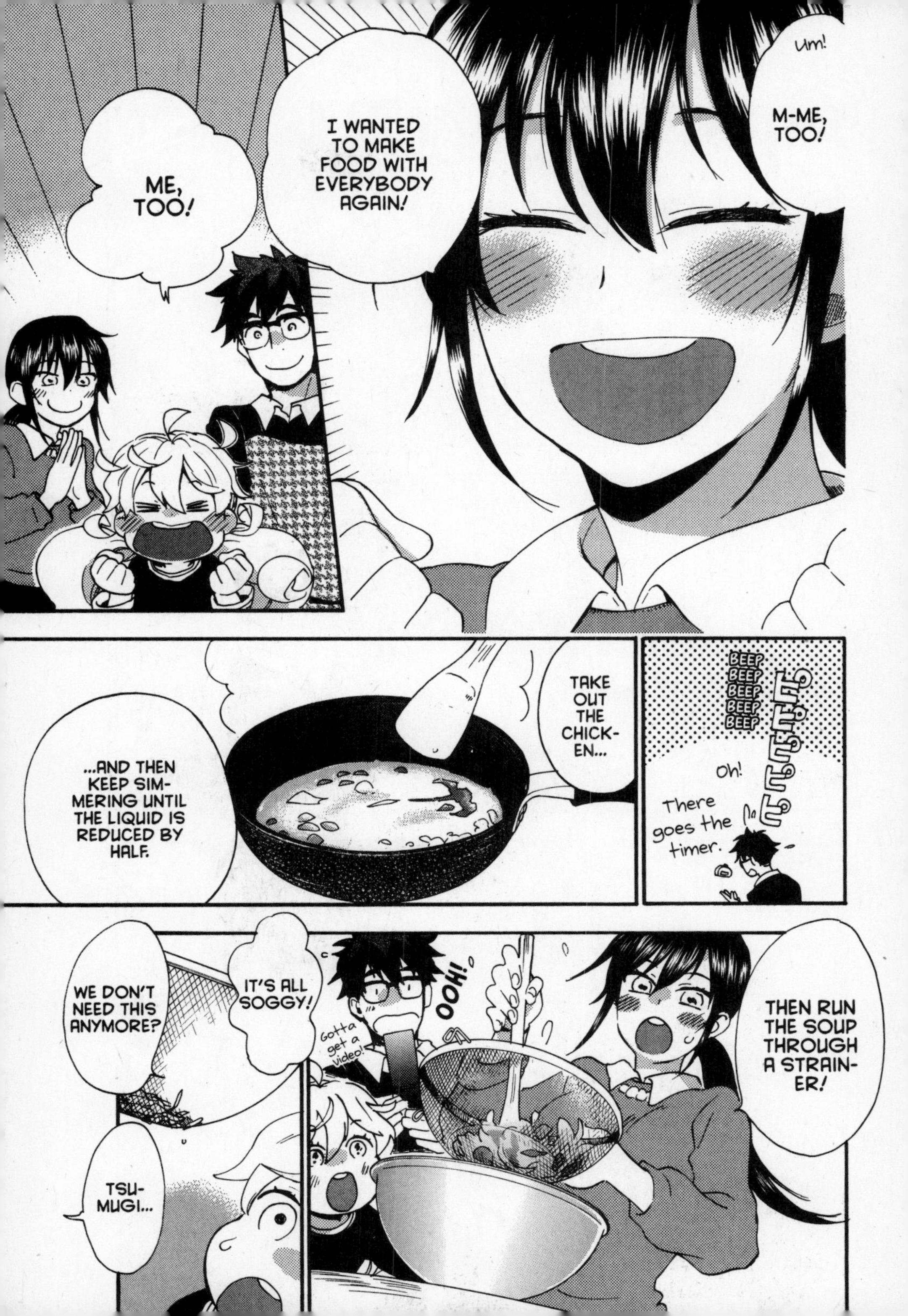
Um!
M-ME, TOO!
I WANTED TO MAKE FOOD WITH EVERYBODY AGAIN!
ME, TOO!
BEEP BEEP BEEP BEEP BEEP
Oh!
There goes the timer.
TAKE OUT THE CHICKEN...
...AND THEN KEEP SIMMERING UNTIL THE LIQUID IS REDUCED BY HALF.
THEN RUN THE SOUP THROUGH A STRAINER!
OOH!
Gotta get a video!
IT'S ALL SOGGY!
WE DON'T NEED THIS ANYMORE?
TSUMUGI...

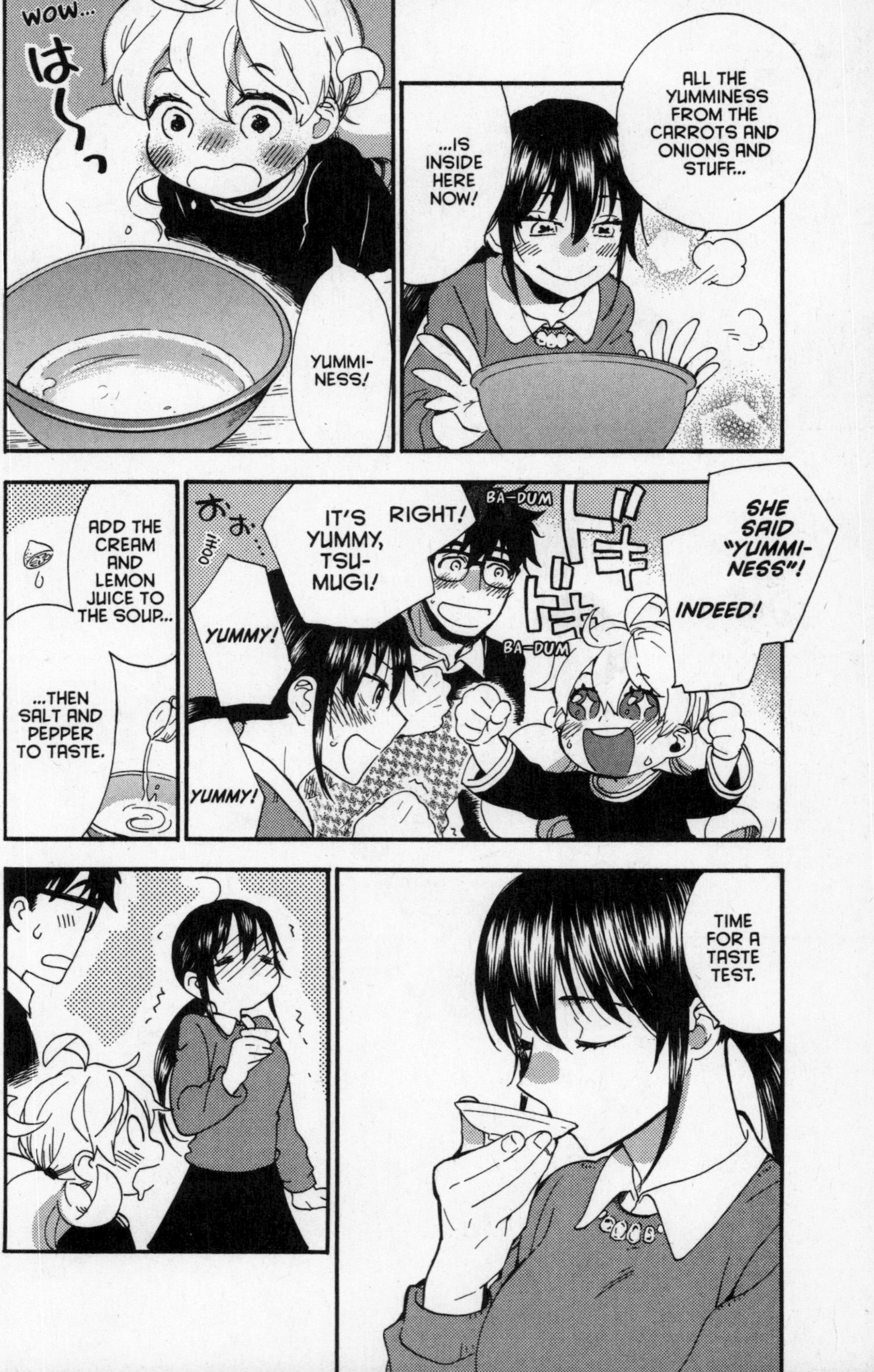
ALL THE YUMMINESS FROM THE CARROTS AND ONIONS AND STUFF...
...IS INSIDE HERE NOW!
WOW...
は～っ
YUMMI-NESS!
SHE SAID "YUMMI-NESS"!
INDEED!
BA-DUM
ドキドキ
BA-DUM
RIGHT!
IT'S YUMMY, TSU-MUGI!
おぉ
OOH...
YUMMY!
YUMMY!
ADD THE CREAM AND LEMON JUICE TO THE SOUP...
...THEN SALT AND PEPPER TO TASTE.
TIME FOR A TASTE TEST.

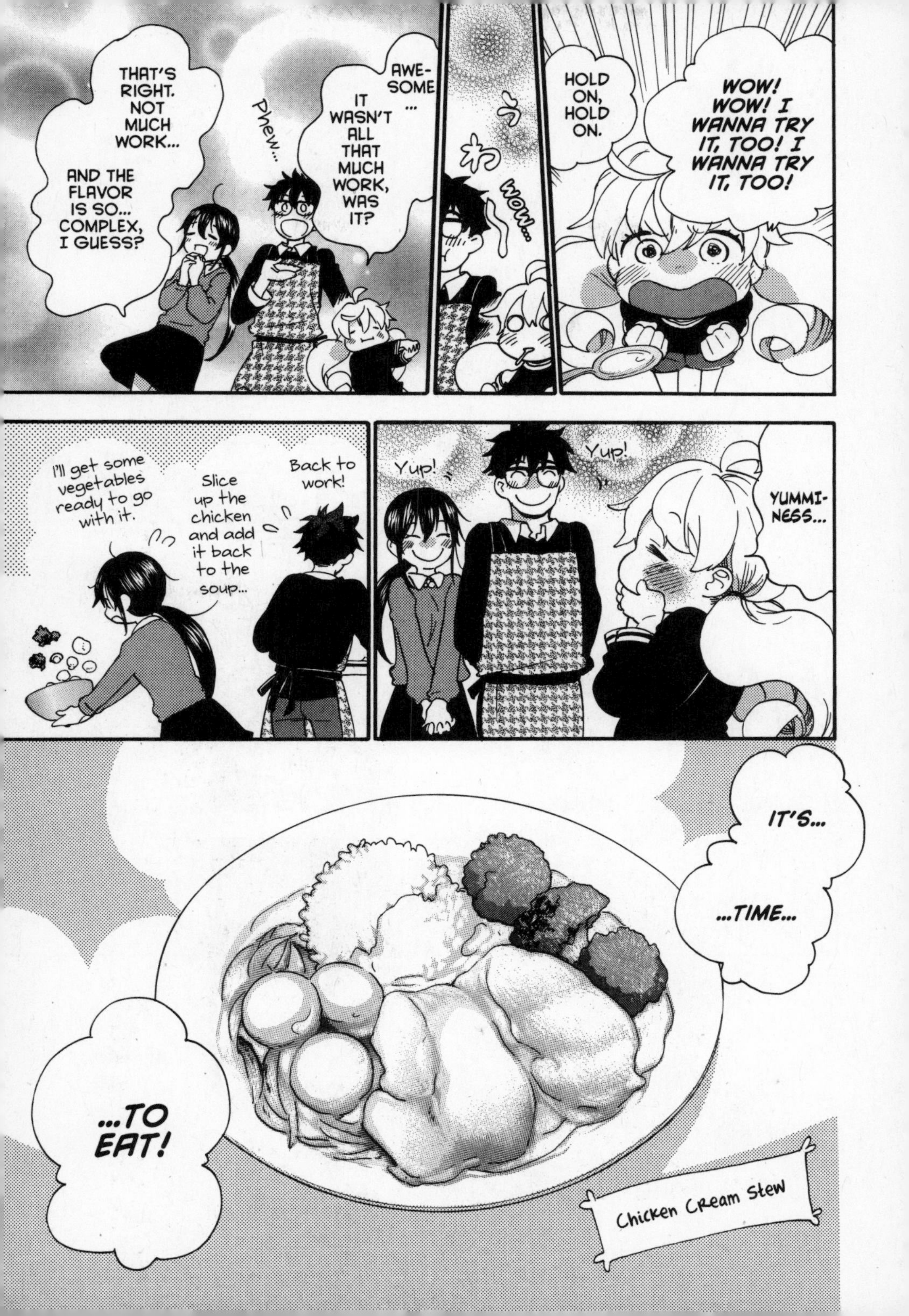
WOW! WOW! I WANNA TRY IT, TOO! I WANNA TRY IT, TOO!
HOLD ON, HOLD ON.
うわ
WOW...
AWE-SOME...
IT WASN'T ALL THAT MUCH WORK, WAS IT?
Phew...
THAT'S RIGHT. NOT MUCH WORK...
AND THE FLAVOR IS SO... COMPLEX, I GUESS?
YUMMI-NESS...
Yup!
Yup!
Back to work!
Slice up the chicken and add it back to the soup...
I'll get some vegetables ready to go with it.
IT'S...
...TIME...
...TO EAT!
Chicken Cream Stew

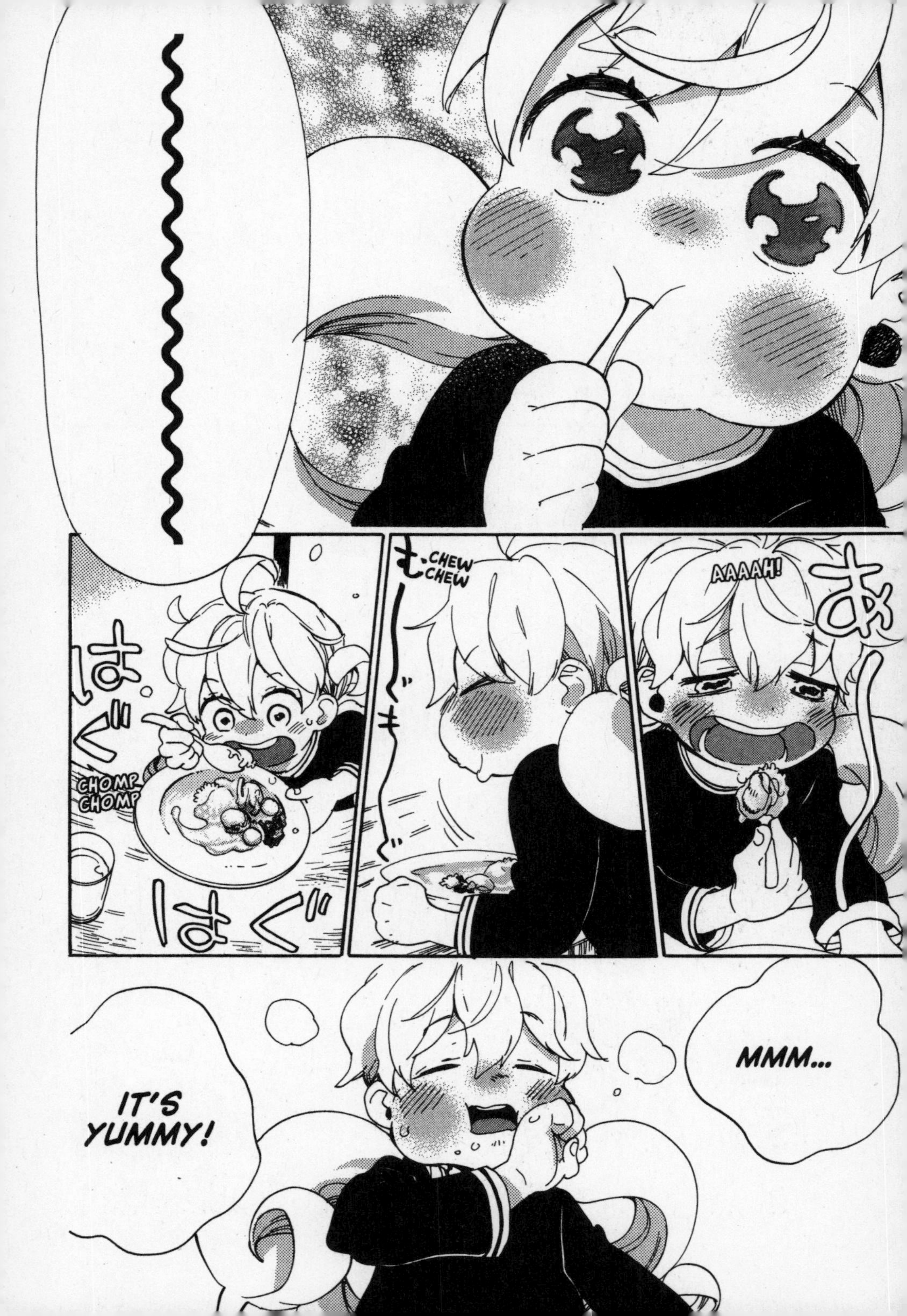
AAAAH!
あ
CHEW CHEW
CHOMP CHOMP
はぐ
はぐ
MMM...
IT'S YUMMY!

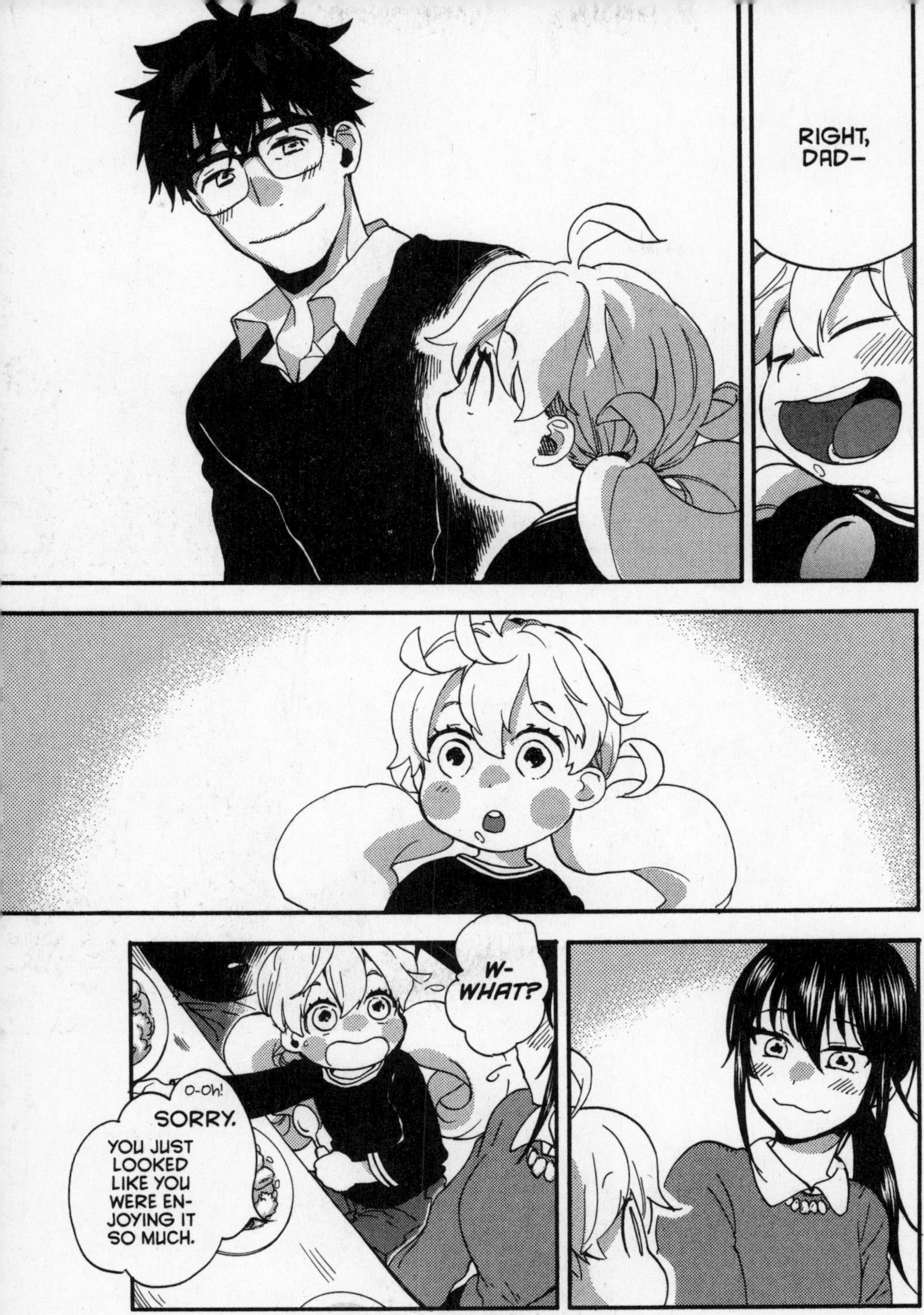
RIGHT, DAD—
W-WHAT?
O-Oh!
SORRY.
YOU JUST LOOKED LIKE YOU WERE EN-JOYING IT SO MUCH.

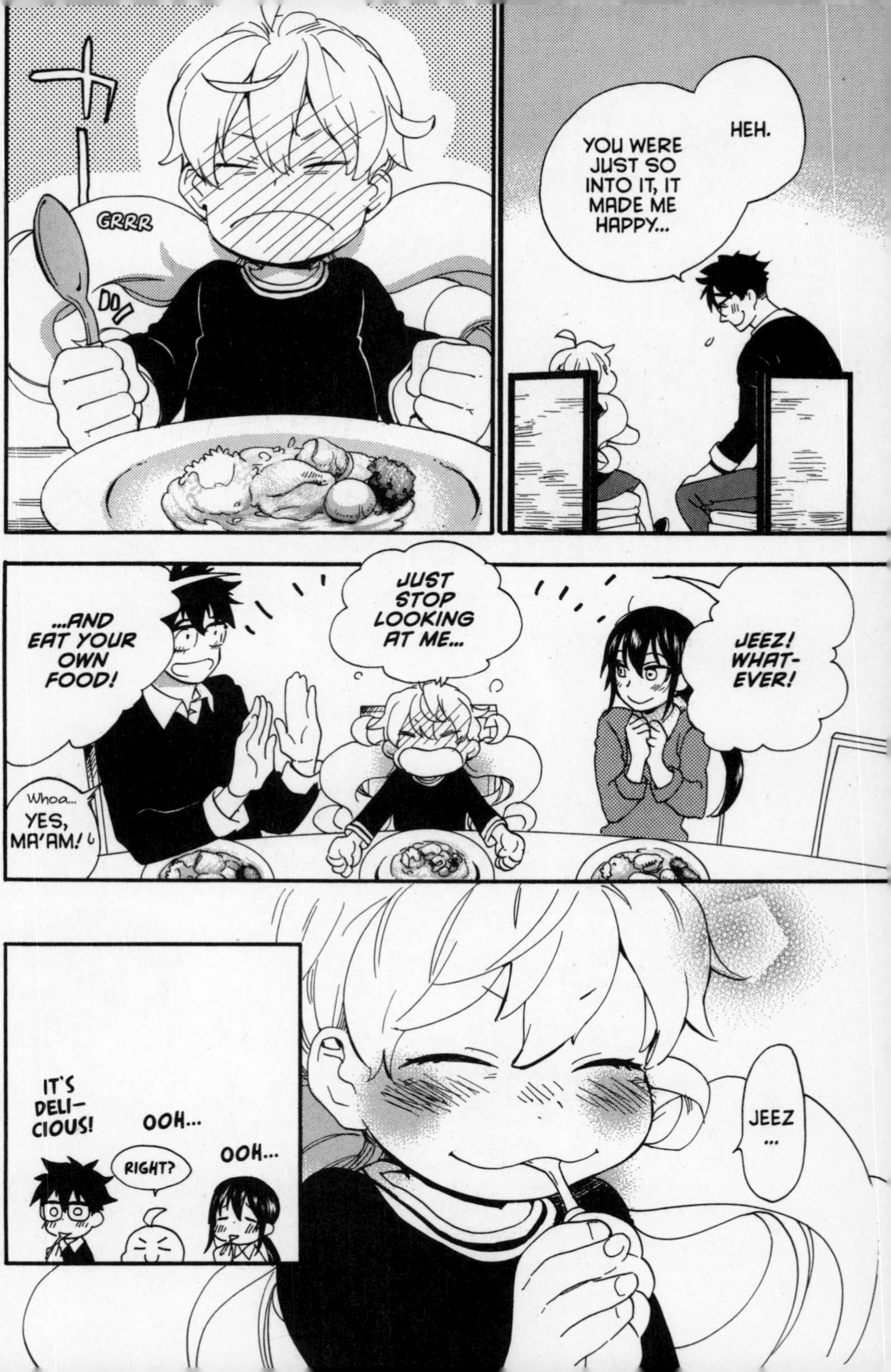
HEH.
YOU WERE JUST SO INTO IT, IT MADE ME HAPPY...
GRRR
DOI
JEEZ! WHATEVER!
JUST STOP LOOKING AT ME...
...AND EAT YOUR OWN FOOD!
Whoa... YES, MA'AM!
JEEZ ...
IT'S DELICIOUS!
OOH...
RIGHT?
OOH...

🐔 CHICKEN STEWED IN CREAM

 ☆INGREDIENTS☆ (For Four People)

Roughly 800g of Bone-In Chicken Thigh
200g Onion ..... 50g Carrots ..... 12 Mushrooms
1 Cube of Chicken-Flavor Bouillon Cube
2-3 Teaspoons Lemon Juice
20g Butter ..... 1 Teaspoon Vegetable Oil .... 20g Weak Flour
100cc White Wine ..... 200cc Cream .... Some Salt and Pepper

(A) 1 piece of celery & parsley, 1 bay leaf.

Recipe

1. Salt and pepper the chicken breasts. Cut the onions and carrots into thin slices. Clean the mushrooms and remove the bottom part of the stem.

2. Dissolve the bouillon cube in 600cc of hot water, then add in 1 teaspoon of lemon juice and a pinch of salt. Put the mushrooms in cap down. Once the water comes to a boil turn off the heat and let sit.

3. Heat butter and vegetable oil in a frying pan, then put the chicken thighs in skin-side down. Cook both sides and remove.

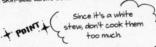

✦ POINT ✦ Since it's a white stew, don't cook them too much.

Even if they aren't fully cooked they'll be stewed later so it's okay!

4. Put onions and carrots into the frying pan from 3, and then fry until soft.

5. Add the weak flour to the ingredients in step 4 and fry. Once the powdery-ness goes away, add the white wine and stir. Turn up the heat to get rid of the alcohol.

6. Add the soup from step 2 to the results of step 5. Leave the mushrooms and a small amount of the soup in the pot. Return the chicken from step 3 to the pan and add the ingredients in A. Once it comes to a boil turn to low heat and cook for 15 minutes.

7. Take the chicken out and then cook until the remaining liquid is about half its original height.

8. Strain the results from step 7 thoroughly, then add the cream, and 1-2 teaspoons of lemon juice. Add salt, pepper to taste.

9. Remove the bones from the chicken and cut it into easy to eat pieces. Put it in the sauce from step 8 and bring to a boil.

10. Put the chicken on a plate and add the mushrooms. Then add the sauce and it's done!

For side dishes, you can use potatoes boiled in salt, or cauliflower, or fried onions.

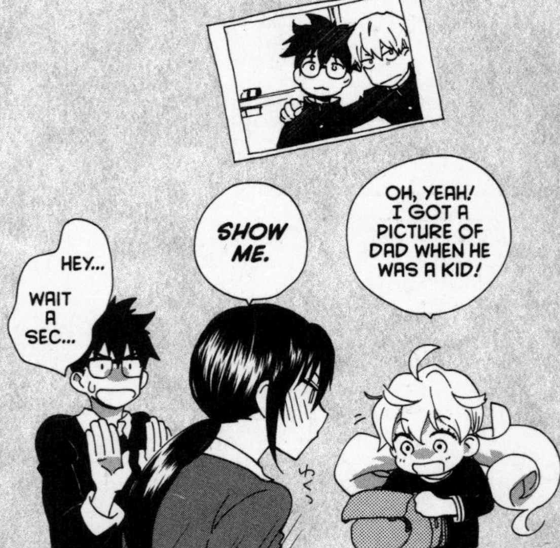
OH, YEAH! I GOT A PICTURE OF DAD WHEN HE WAS A KID!
SHOW ME.
HEY... WAIT A SEC...

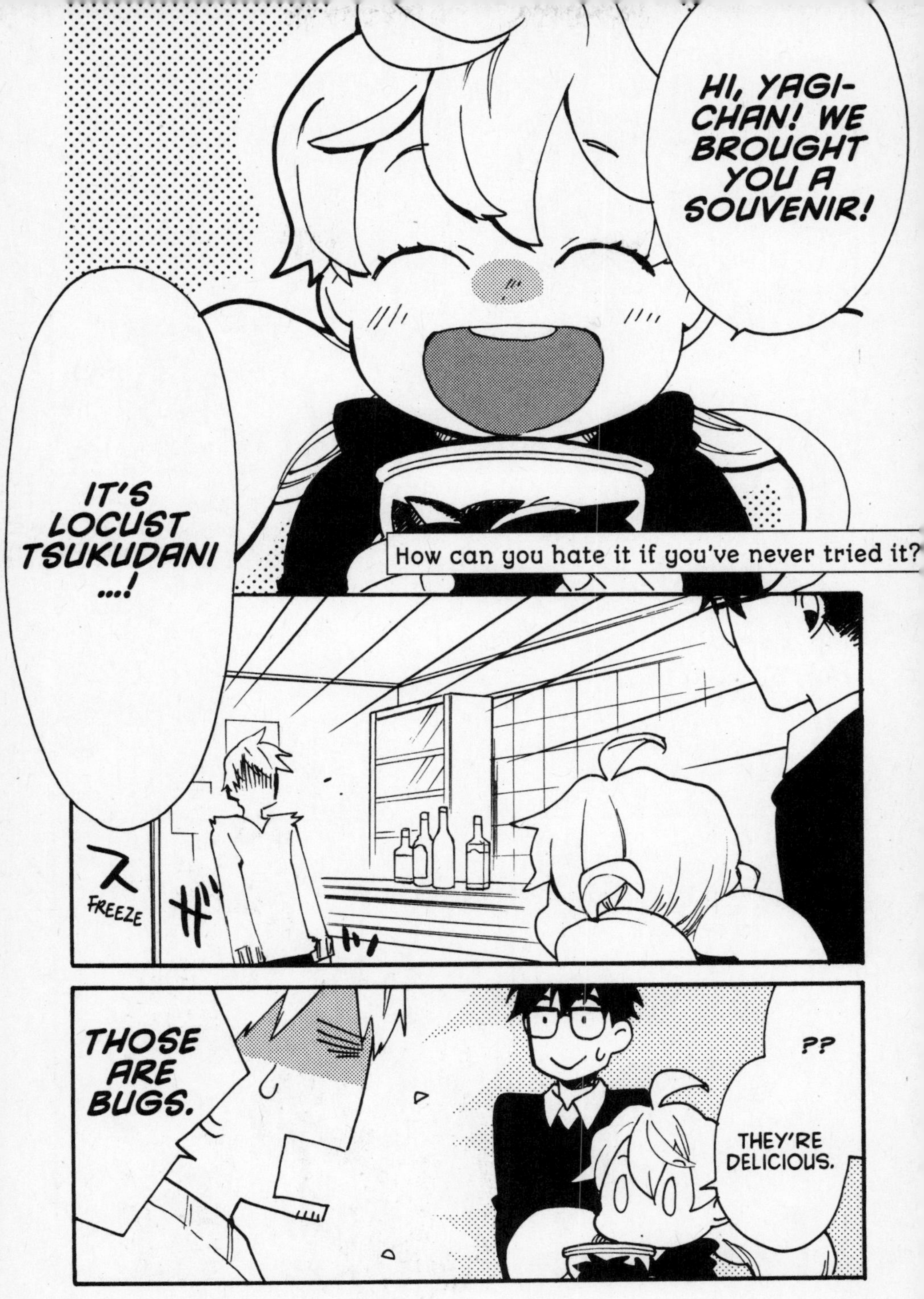
HI, YAGI-CHAN! WE BROUGHT YOU A SOUVENIR!
IT'S LOCUST TSUKUDANI ...!
How can you hate it if you've never tried it?
ス
FREEZE
??
THEY'RE DELICIOUS.
THOSE ARE BUGS.

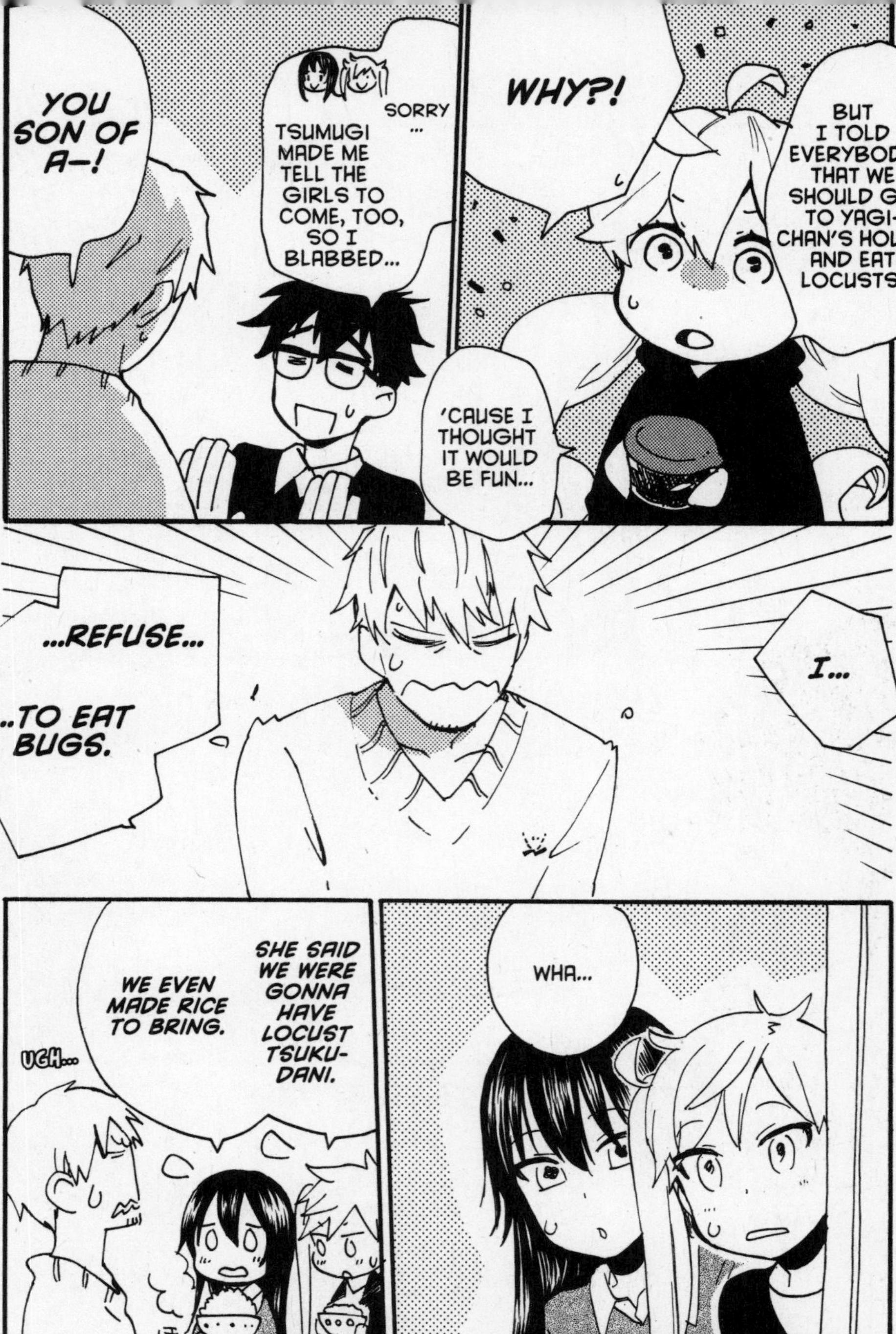
WHY?!
BUT I TOLD EVERYBODY THAT WE SHOULD GO TO YAGI-CHAN'S HOUSE AND EAT LOCUSTS.
'CAUSE I THOUGHT IT WOULD BE FUN...
SORRY ...
TSUMUGI MADE ME TELL THE GIRLS TO COME, TOO, SO I BLABBED...
YOU SON OF A—!
I...
...REFUSE...
...TO EAT BUGS.
WHA...
SHE SAID WE WERE GONNA HAVE LOCUST TSUKU-DANI.
WE EVEN MADE RICE TO BRING.
UGH...
ほか
ほか

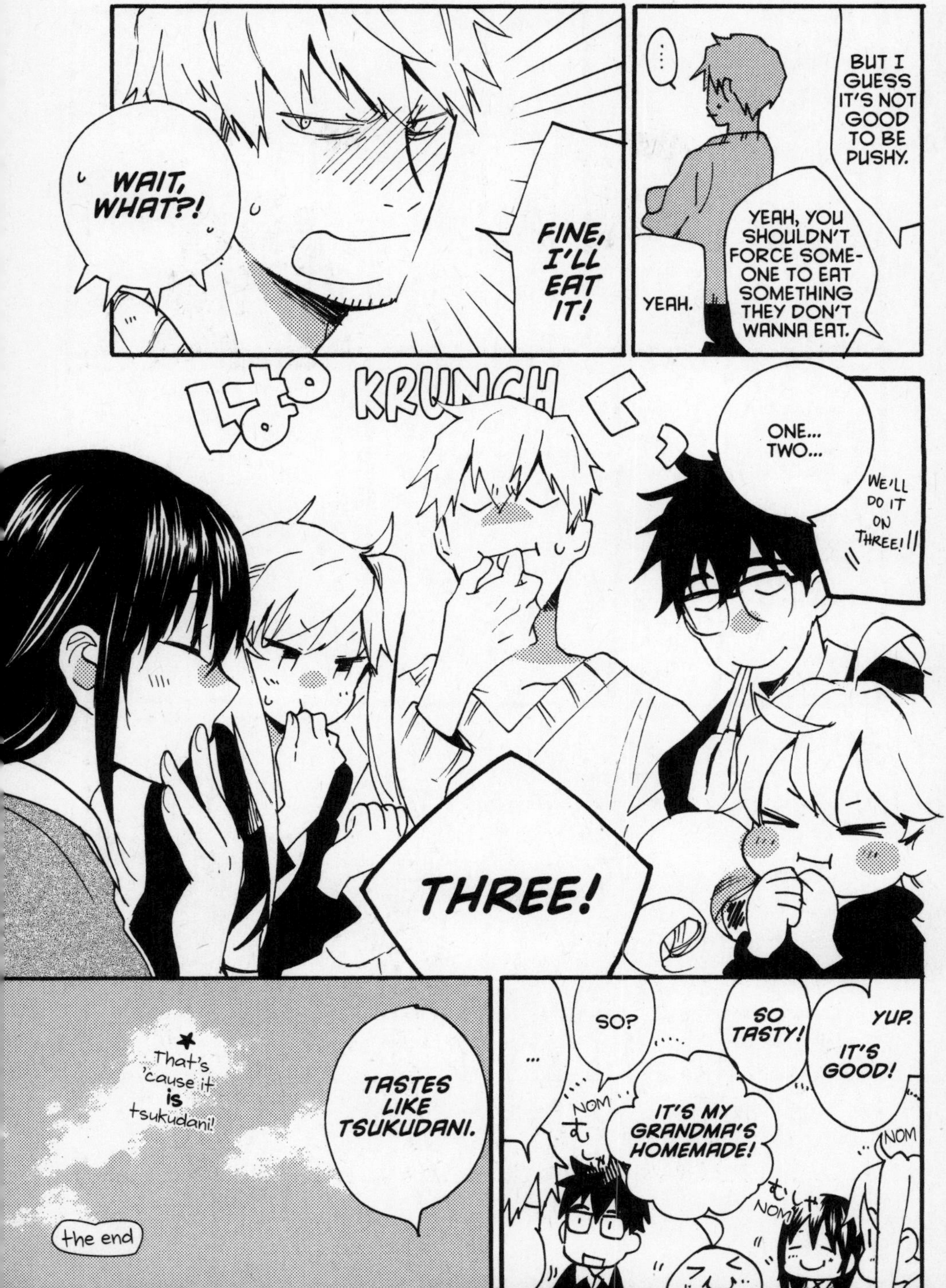
...
BUT I GUESS IT'S NOT GOOD TO BE PUSHY.
YEAH, YOU SHOULDN'T FORCE SOME-ONE TO EAT SOMETHING THEY DON'T WANNA EAT.
YEAH.
FINE, I'LL EAT IT!
WAIT, WHAT?!
KRUNCH
ONE... TWO...
WE'LL DO IT ON THREE!
THREE!
YUP.
IT'S GOOD!
SO TASTY!
SO?
...
IT'S MY GRANDMA'S HOMEMADE!
NOM
NOM
NOM
TASTES LIKE TSUKUDANI.
That's 'cause it is tsukudani!
the end

Afterword

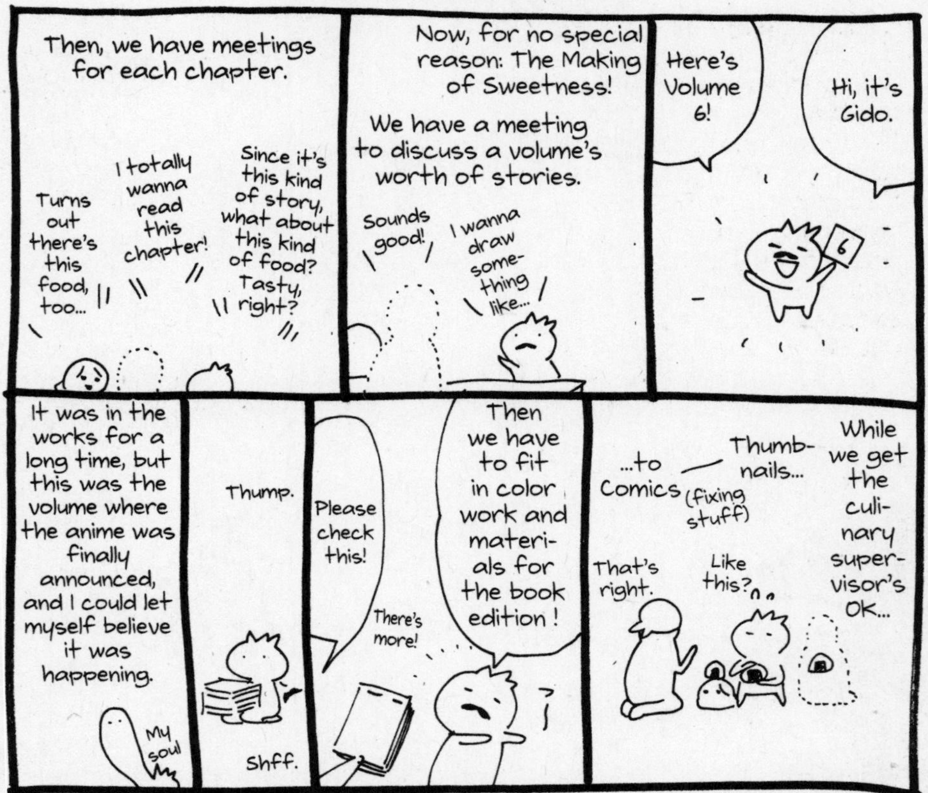
Hi, it's Gido.
Here's Volume 6!
6
Now, for no special reason: The Making of Sweetness!
We have a meeting to discuss a volume's worth of stories.
I wanna draw some-thing like...
Sounds good!
Then, we have meetings for each chapter.
Since it's this kind of story, what about this kind of food? Tasty, right?
I totally wanna read this chapter!
Turns out there's this food, too...
While we get the culi-nary super-visor's OK...
Thumb-nails...
...to Comics
(fixing stuff)
Like this?
That's right.
Then we have to fit in color work and materi-als for the book edition !
Please check this!
There's more!
Thump.
Shff.
It was in the works for a long time, but this was the volume where the anime was finally announced, and I could let myself believe it was happening.
My soul

Sweetness is an anime!

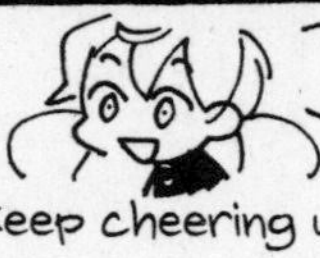
Does it move?

Hope you enjoy it! Keep cheering us on!

See you in Volume 7

Gido Amagakure

! Thank you all so much! !

W-yama-san, Tsuru-san, GON-chan, KOZ-Tan, Mom and Dad
T-shiro-sama, K-Yama-sama, Jun Abe-sama
Photo and Research Cooperation: Tabegoto-ya Norabou-sama
Cooking Advisor: Yô Tatewaki-sama

Thank you all for your help!

Translation Notes

"Achoo!", page 38: In Japan, a commonly-held notion is that when you sneeze, it means someone, somewhere is talking about you. Here, Tsumugi has just mentioned that she things "there was somebody else who said the same thing" as she just did. As Kohei thinks back, Kotori sneezes, since she is indeed the person being discussed.

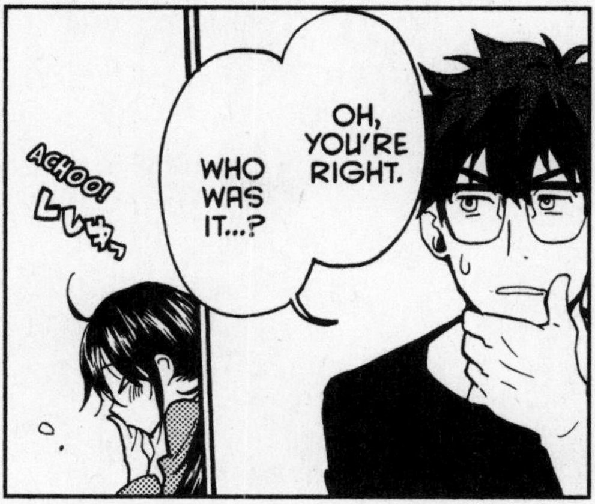
OH, YOU'RE RIGHT.
WHO WAS IT...?
ACHOO!

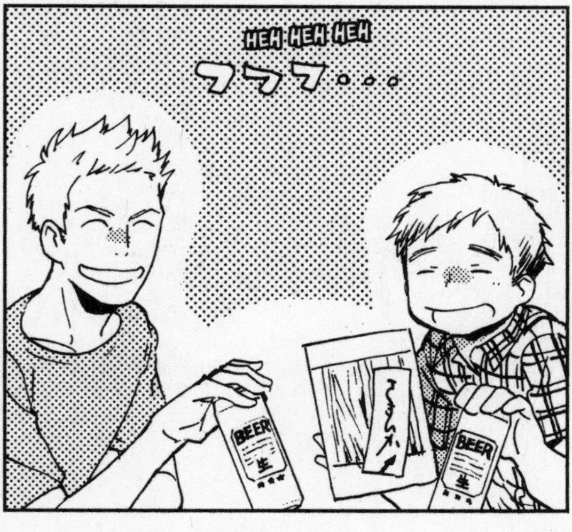
HEH HEH HEH
BEER
BEER

Yakiika, page 55: Along with the beer, the other two dads have brought along a package of *yakiika*—strips of dried, roasted squid. It's a salty, fishy, jerky-style snack that's commonly enjoyed with a frosty beer.

Umami, page 172: Although it's translated as "yumminess" here, the word Kotori originally uses is *umami*. Umami has been adopted into English to describe the basic taste of savoriness. (There are four other basic tastes: sweet, sour, bitter, and salt.) Umami is thought of as a meaty, brothy flavor. The word is the noun form of the adjective "umai," which means "tasty"—hence our translation

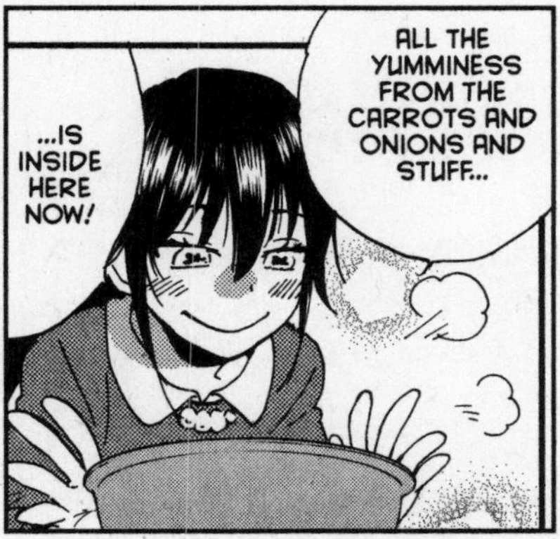
ALL THE YUMMINESS FROM THE CARROTS AND ONIONS AND STUFF...
...IS INSIDE HERE NOW!

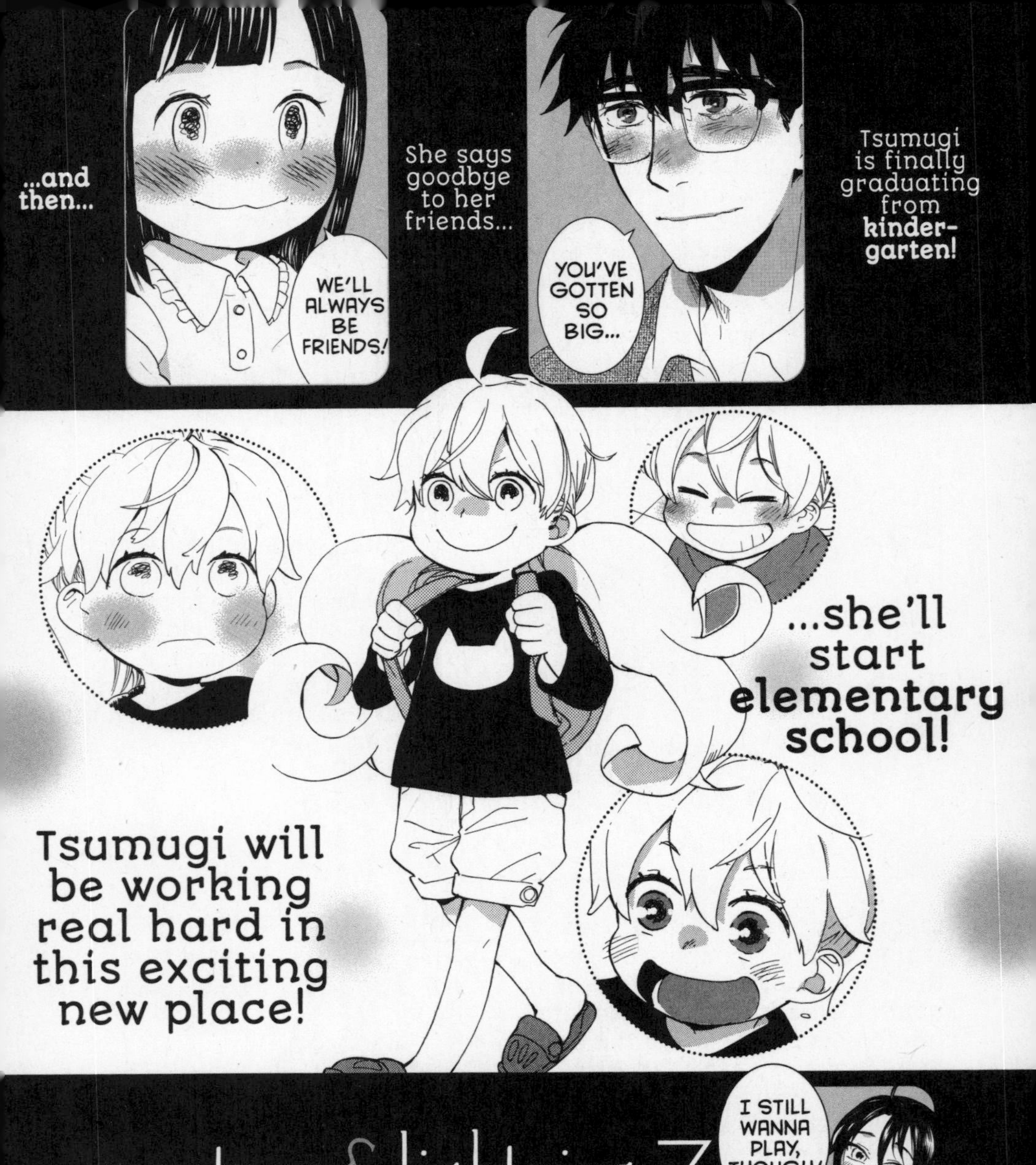
Tsumugi is finally graduating from kinder-garten!
YOU'VE GOTTEN SO BIG...
She says goodbye to her friends...
WE'LL ALWAYS BE FRIENDS!
...and then...
...she'll start elementary school!
Tsumugi will be working real hard in this exciting new place!
I STILL WANNA PLAY, THOUGH!
sweetness & lightning 7

sweetness
&lightning

Say I Love You.

KC
KODANSHA
COMICS

Mei Tachibana has no friends — and says she doesn't need them!

But everything changes when she accidentally roundhouse kicks the most popular boy in school! However, Yamato Kurosawa isn't angry in the slightest— in fact, he thinks his ordinary life could use an unusual girl like Mei. But winning Mei's trust will be a tough task. How long will she refuse to say, "I love you"?

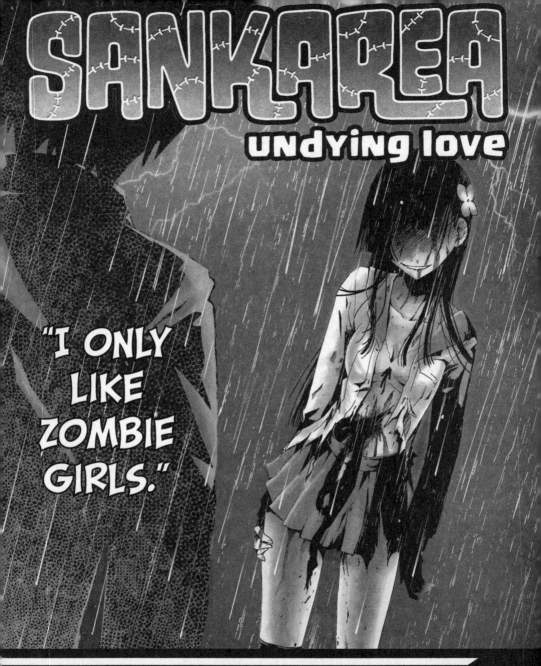

SANKAREA

undying love

"I ONLY LIKE ZOMBIE GIRLS."

Chihiro has an unusual connection to zombie movies. He doesn't feel bad for the survivors – he wants to comfort the undead girls they slaughter! When his pet passes away, he brews a resurrection potion. He's discovered by local heiress Sanka Rea, and she serves as his first test subject!

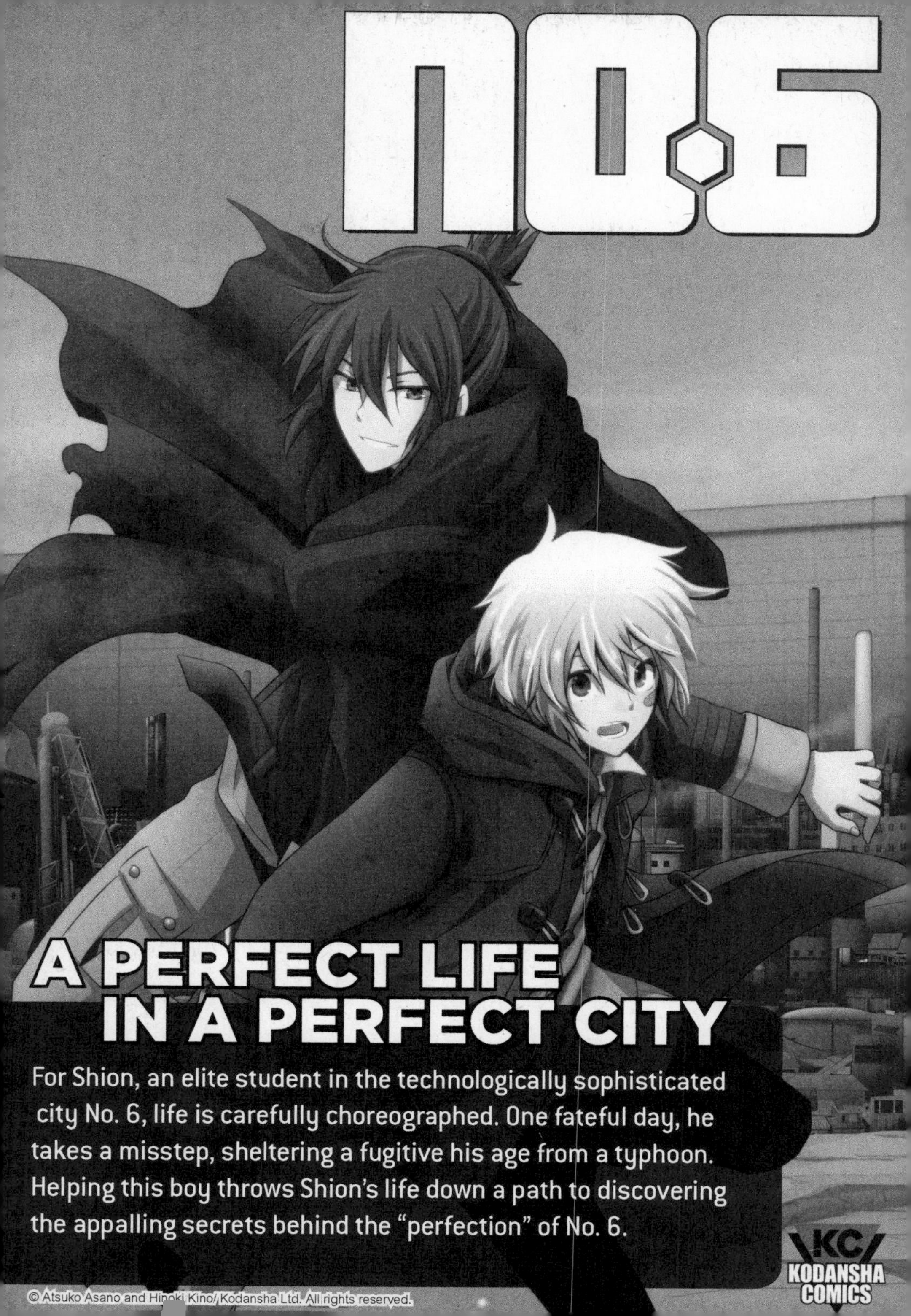
NO.6
A PERFECT LIFE
IN A PERFECT CITY
For Shion, an elite student in the technologically sophisticated city No. 6, life is carefully choreographed. One fateful day, he takes a misstep, sheltering a fugitive his age from a typhoon. Helping this boy throws Shion's life down a path to discovering the appalling secrets behind the "perfection" of No. 6.
KC
KODANSHA COMICS
© Atsuko Asano and Hinoki Kino/ Kodansha Ltd. All rights reserved.

My Little Monster

OPPOSITES ATTRACT...MAYBE?

Haru Yoshida is feared as an unstable and violent "monster." Mizutani Shizuku is a grade-obsessed student with no friends. Fate brings these two together to form the most unlikely pair. Haru firmly believes he's in love with Mizutani and she firmly believes he's insane.

KC
KODANSHA
COMICS

Maria
THE VIRGIN WITCH

PURITY AND POWER

As a war to determine the rightful ruler of medieval France ravages the land, the witch Maria decides she will not stand idly by as men kill each other in the name of God and glory. Using her powerful magic, she summons various beasts and demons —even going as far as using a succubus to seduce soldiers into submission under the veil of night— all to stop the needless slaughter. However, after the Archangel Michael puts an end to her meddling, he curses her to lose her powers if she ever gives up her virginity. Will she forgo the forbidden fruit of adulthood in order to bring an end to the merciless machine of war? Available now in print and digitally!

INUYASHIKI

A superhero like none you've ever seen, from the creator of "Gantz"!

Ichiro Inuyashiki is down on his luck. He looks much older than his 58 years, his children despise him, and his wife thinks he's a useless coward. So when he's diagnosed with stomach cancer and given three months to live, it seems the only one who'll miss him is his dog.

Then a blinding light fills the sky, and the old man is killed... only to wake up later in a body he almost recognizes as his own. Can it be that Ichiro Inuyashiki is no longer human?

Comes in extra-large editions with color pages!

FINALLY, A LOWER-COST OMNIBUS EDITION OF FAIRY TAIL! CONTAINS VOLUMES 1-5. ONLY $39.99!

- NEARLY 1,000 PAGES!
- EXTRA LARGE 7"x10.5" TRIM SIZE!
- HIGH-QUALITY PAPER!

Fairy Tail takes place in a world filled with magic. 17-year-old Lucy is a wizard-in-training who wants to join a magic guild so that she can become a full-fledged wizard. She dreams of joining the most famous guild, known as Fairy Tail. One day she meets Natsu, a boy raised by a dragon which vanished when he was young. Natsu has devoted his life to finding his dragon father. When Natsu helps Lucy out of a tricky situation, she discovers that he is a member of Fairy Tail, and our heroes' adventure together begins.

FAIRY TAIL

MASTER'S EDITION

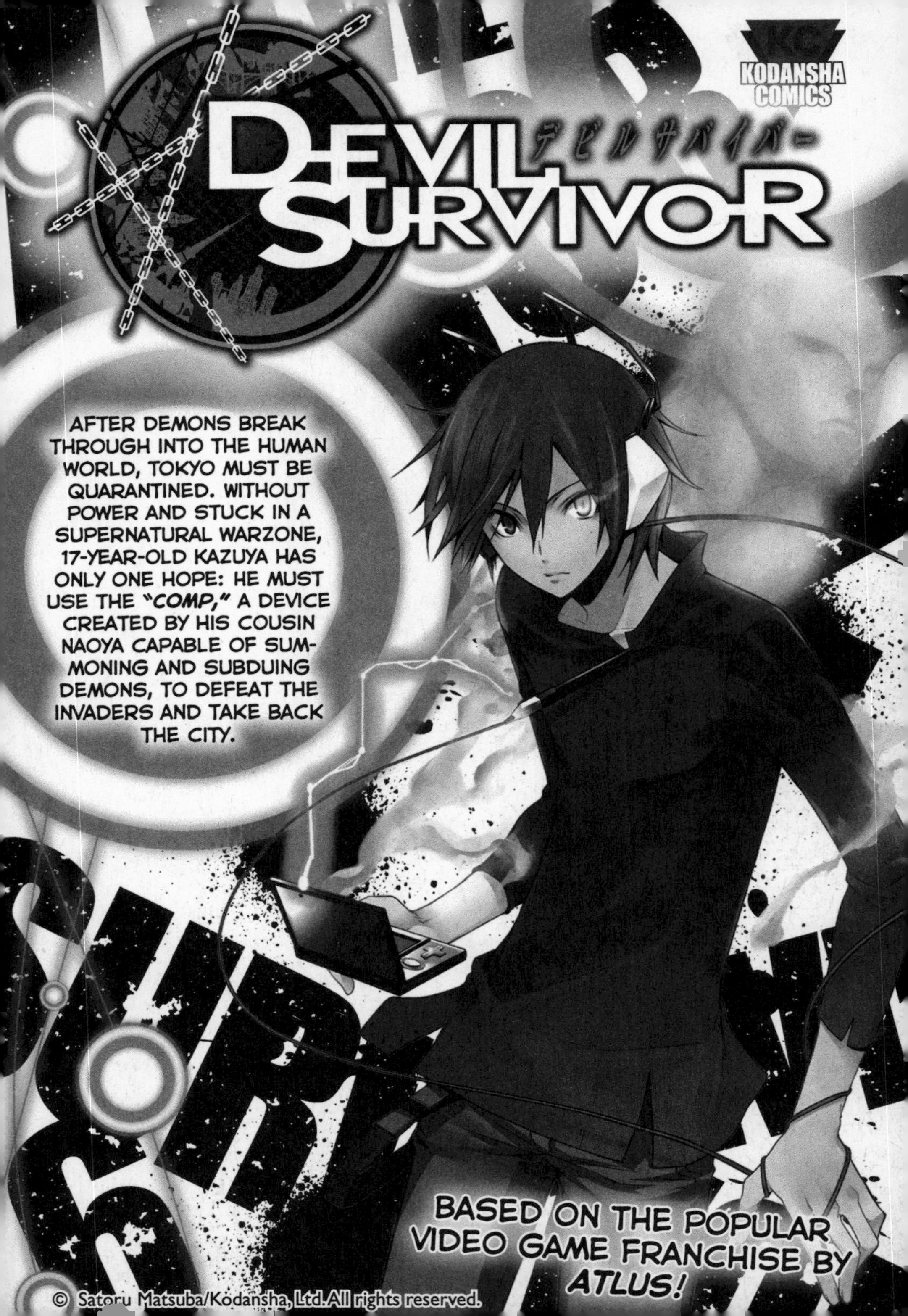
KODANSHA COMICS
DEVIL SURVIVOR
デビルサバイバー
AFTER DEMONS BREAK THROUGH INTO THE HUMAN WORLD, TOKYO MUST BE QUARANTINED. WITHOUT POWER AND STUCK IN A SUPERNATURAL WARZONE, 17-YEAR-OLD KAZUYA HAS ONLY ONE HOPE: HE MUST USE THE *"COMP,"* A DEVICE CREATED BY HIS COUSIN NAOYA CAPABLE OF SUMMONING AND SUBDUING DEMONS, TO DEFEAT THE INVADERS AND TAKE BACK THE CITY.
BASED ON THE POPULAR VIDEO GAME FRANCHISE BY *ATLUS!*
© Satoru Matsuba/Kodansha, Ltd. All rights reserved.

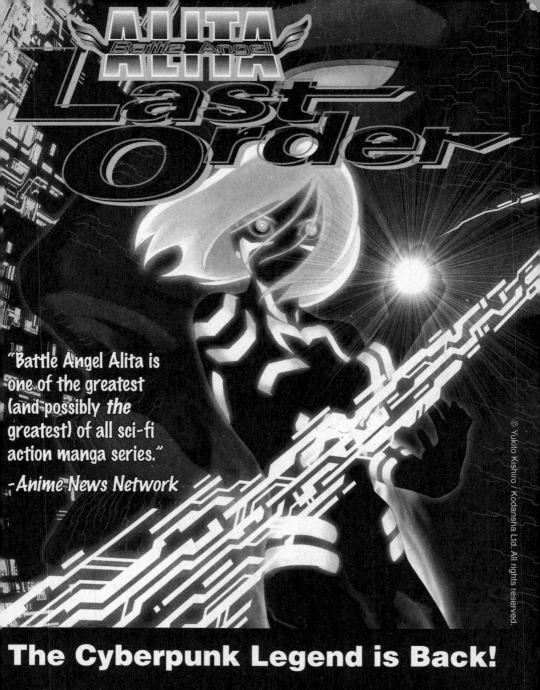

ALITA
Battle Angel
Last Order

"Battle Angel Alita is one of the greatest (and possibly *the* greatest) of all sci-fi action manga series."

-Anime News Network

The Cyberpunk Legend is Back!

In deluxe omnibus editions of 600+ pages, including ALL-NEW original stories by Alita creator Yukito Kishiro!

KC
KODANSHA
COMICS

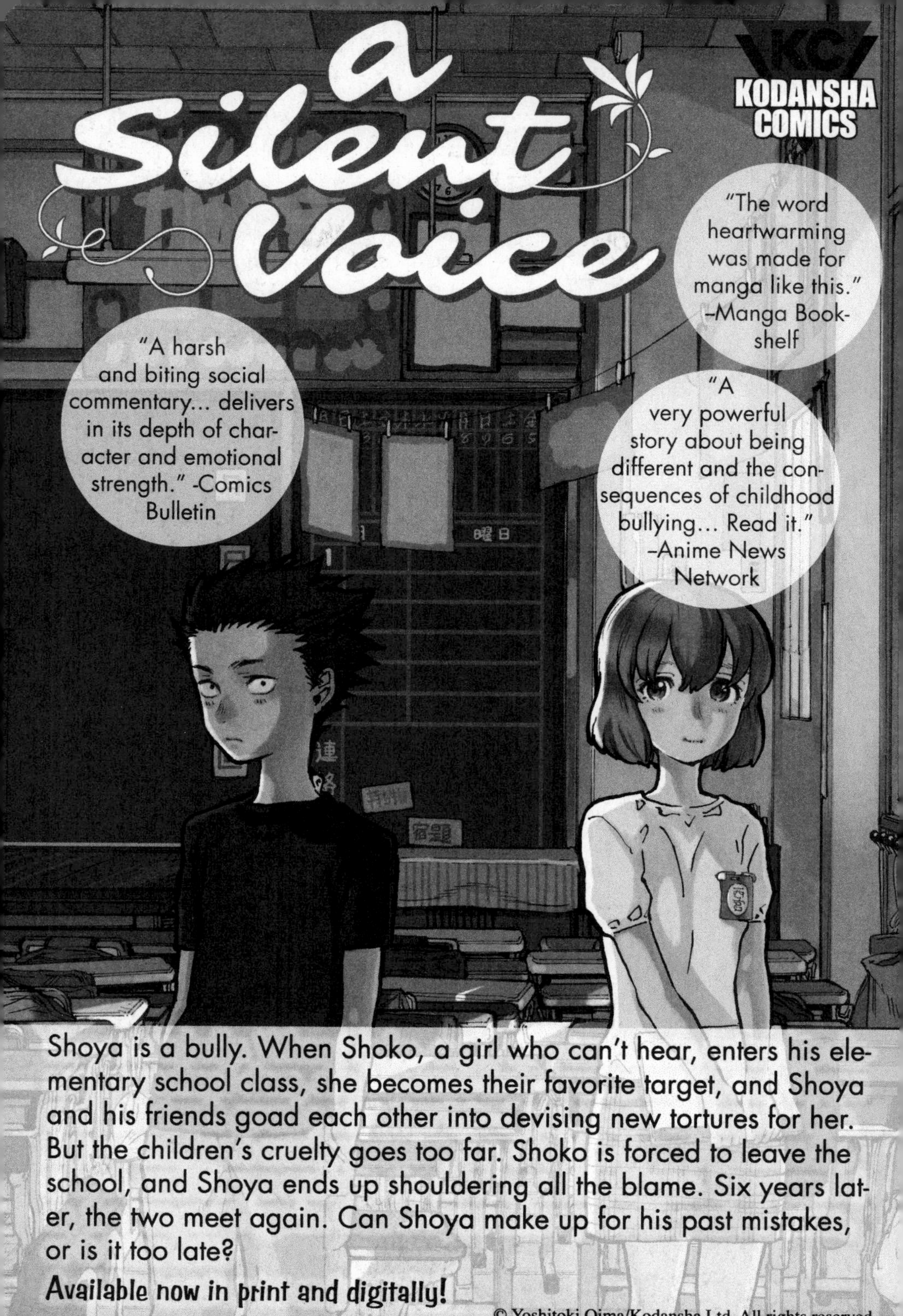
a Silent Voice
KC
KODANSHA COMICS
"The word heartwarming was made for manga like this." –Manga Bookshelf
"A harsh and biting social commentary... delivers in its depth of character and emotional strength." -Comics Bulletin
"A very powerful story about being different and the consequences of childhood bullying... Read it." –Anime News Network
Shoya is a bully. When Shoko, a girl who can't hear, enters his elementary school class, she becomes their favorite target, and Shoya and his friends goad each other into devising new tortures for her. But the children's cruelty goes too far. Shoko is forced to leave the school, and Shoya ends up shouldering all the blame. Six years later, the two meet again. Can Shoya make up for his past mistakes, or is it too late?
Available now in print and digitally!

Sweetness & Lightning volume 6 is a work of fiction. Names, characters, places, and incidents are the products of the author's imagination or are used fictitiously. Any resemblance to actual events, locales, or persons, living or dead, is entirely coincidental.

A Kodansha Comics Trade Paperback Original.

Published in the United States by Kodansha Comics,
an imprint of Kodansha USA Publishing, LLC, New York.

Publication rights for this English edition arranged through Kodansha Ltd., Tokyo.

First published in Japan in 2016 by Kodansha Ltd., Tokyo, as *Ama-ama to Inadzuma* volume 6.

ISBN 978-1-63236-402-9

Printed in the United States of America.

www.kodanshacomics.com

9 8 7 6 5 4 3 2 1

Translation: Adam Lensenmayer
Lettering: Carl Vanstiphout
Editing: Paul Starr
Editorial assistance: Tiff Ferentini
Kodansha Comics Edition Cover Design: Phil Balsman